EUROPE'S NEW STATE OF WELFARE

Unemployment, employment policies and citizenship

Edited by Jørgen Goul Andersen, Jochen Clasen, Wim van Oorschot and Knut Halvorsen

First published in Great Britain in November 2002 by

Policy Press
University of Bristol
1-9 Old Park Hill
Bristol
BS2 8BB
UK
t: +44 (0)117 954 5940
pp-info@bristol.ac.uk
www.policypress.co.uk

North America office:
Policy Press
c/o The University of Chicago Press
1427 East 60th Street
Chicago, IL 60637, USA
t: +1 773 702 7700
f: +1 773-702-9756
sales@press.uchicago.edu
www.press.uchicago.edu

Reprinted 2004

Transferred to Digital Print 2016

British Library Cataloguing in Publication Data
A catalogue record for this book is available from the British Library.

Library of Congress Cataloging-in-Publication Data
A catalog record for this book has been requested.

ISBN 978-1-86134-437-3 paperback

Jørgen Goul Andersen is Professor of Political Sociology, Centre for Comparative Welfare Studies, Aalborg University, Denmark, **Jochen Clasen** is Professor of Comparative Social Research, Centre for Comparative Research in Social Welfare, University of Stirling, **Wim van Oorschot** is Professor of Sociology, Faculty of Social and Behavioural Sciences, Tilburg University, the Netherlands and **Knut Halvorsen** is Research Director, Faculty of Economics, Public Administration and Social Work, Oslo University College, Norway.

Cover design by Qube Design Associates, Bristol.
Printed and bound in Great Britain by Marston Book Services, Oxford.

Contents

Notes on contributors

Denis Bouget is Professor of Economics at the University of Nantes, France. He specialises in social policies for social exclusion, long-term care for older people, public local assistance and the comparison of social welfare systems. He is Director of the Maison des Sciences de l'Homme (MSH) Ange Guepin, Nantes, and chairman of COST A15: 'Reforming Social Protection Systems in Europe'.

Jochen Clasen is Professor of Comparative Social Research and Director of the Centre of Comparative Research in Social Welfare (CCRSW), Department of Applied Social Science, University of Stirling, UK. His research interests include comparative social policy, social security policy, unemployment and employment policy and welfare state theory.

Heikki Ervasti is Senior Research Fellow at the Department of Social Policy, University of Turku, Finland. He is currently National Coordinator of the European Social Survey. His main research interests include comparative analyses on labour markets and unemployment, and social, political and economic attitudes.

Bengt Furåker is Professor of Sociology, Department of Sociology. University of Gothenburg, Sweden, and presently Visiting Fellow at Yale University, New Haven, USA. He is also an Expert Committee member of the European Foundation for the Improvement of Living and Working Conditions, Dublin. His research is mainly focused on labour market issues, employment and unemployment, labour market policy, the public sector, the relationship between the labour market and the welfare state, and class and social stratification.

Jørgen Goul Andersen is Professor of Political Sociology and Director of the Centre for Comparative Welfare Studies (CCWS), Aalborg University, Denmark. He is working group coordinator and Management Committee member of COST A13: 'Changing Labour Markets, Welfare Policies and Citizenship', coordinator of the Danish Election Programme and ISSP Programme, and member of the board of the Danish Democracy and Power Programme. His research fields include comparative welfare state research, political behaviour, and political power and democracy.

Knut Halvorsen is Research Director and Professor of Social Policy at the Department of Economics, Public Administration and Social Work, Oslo University College, Norway. He is a member of the Management Committee of COST A13. His main research fields are unemployment and marginalisation, and comparative social policy.

Miroljub Ignjatović is Researcher at the Organisations and Human Resource Research Centre, Faculty of Social Sciences, University of Ljubljana, Slovenia. His research topics are labour market, unemployment and employment issues, labour market flexibilisation, social policy, post-modern society and issues of vocational education and training.

Anja Kopač is Researcher at the Organisations and Human Resource Research Centre, Faculty of Social Sciences, University of Ljubljana, Slovenia. Her key fields of work are social policy, employment policy, the welfare state, EU social policy issues, education and training.

Jan Bendix Jensen is currently a PhD scholar at CCWS, Aalborg University, Denmark, working on a project of targeting social benefits.

Wolfgang Ludwig-Mayerhofer is Professor of Sociology at the University of Leipzig, Germany. He is involved in teaching and research on social inequalities, research methods, the sociology of the family, labour market and unemployment, and the sociology of law.

George Sheldon is Professor of Economics at the Forschungsstelle für Arbeitsmarkt- und Industrieökonomik (FAI), Wirtschaftwissenschaftliches Zentrum, University of Basel, Switzerland. He is a Management Committee member of COST A13.

Ivan Svetlik is Professor of Sociology and Human Resource Management at the Organisations and Human Resource Research Centre, Faculty of Social Sciences, University of Ljubljana, Slovenia. He is a member of the Management Committee of COST A13. He participates in the CANET network on human resources research, cooperates with ETF, Torino and the European Foundation for Social Quality, Amsterdam. He is involved in research on labour, employment, education, human resources and social policy.

Martina Trbanc is Researcher at the Organisations and Human Resource Research Centre, Faculty of Social Sciences, University of Ljubljana, Slovenia. Her research topics are labour market, employment and unemployment, employment policy, marginalisation and social exclusion, links between education and employment, and issues of vocational education and training.

Pascal Ughetto is Researcher at the Institut de Recherches Économiques et Sociales in Noisy-le-Grand and at the IRIS Institute of the University Paris-Dauphine, France, where he teaches economics and sociology. His main research field is the process of structural changes in work.

Wim van Oorshot is Professor of Sociology, Faculty of Social and Behavioural Sciences, Tilburg University, the Netherlands. He is also co-chair of ESPA net – *the network for European social policy analysis*. His research fields include poverty, local social policy, welfare state legitimacy, issues of solidarity and equity in social protection, the history of Dutch social security, client satisfaction in social security administration, disability benefits and reintegration measures, activation of unemployed people and occupational welfare arrangements.

Glossary

Activation	Obligatory job training or education for unemployed people.
Compressed wage structure	A wage structure with small wage differentials that do not reflect differences in productivity and thus tend to disturb the market clearing of demand and supply.
Discouraged workers	Unemployed workers who have given up looking for a job and consequently are not registered or counted as unemployed. They form part of 'hidden unemployment'.
Early retirement allowance (Dk)	Ordinary early retirement in Denmark, for those aged 60-66 (from 2004, those aged 60-64 due to lower pension age). No health requirements but conditional on 25 years' membership of unemployment insurance fund.
Flexibility	An umbrella concept to describe employment protection, wage structures, and working hours.
Flexible employment protection	Few limitations in employers' right to hire and fire people.
Flexible wage structure	Few limitations in market-determined wages. In practice, first and foremost, few formal or informal rules that ensure high minimum wages.
Flexicurity	Flexibility + security: programme that combines new flexibility demands with high social protection. For instance, liberal employment protection with few limitations in the right to hire and fire people, combined with generous protection for those who are unemployed.
Frictional unemployment	Unemployment in relation to transitions from one job to another, from education to job, from job to retirement, and so on. With high mobility on the labour market, there is bound to be quite high frictional unemployment.

Ghent model	Voluntary state-subsidised unemployment insurance based on membership of unemployment insurance funds typically controlled by unions. Denmark, Sweden, Finland and Belgium follows this model, named after the city of Ghent.
Hysteresis	Unemployment becomes self-reinforcing, first and foremost because of loss of qualifications during unemployment.
ILO	International Labour Organization (office in Geneva). Independent UN agency with the goal of promoting decent work for everybody. Labour market statistics and research.
ILO definition of unemployment	Not having, actively seeking, and being available for a job. Can be operationalised in different ways. In register-based accounts of unemployment, being registered as 'job seeking' satisfies these criteria. Both in administrative practices, and in survey measurement, more precise and stricter requirements may be applied. This leads to comparability problems, unless common operationalisations are applied, as in the European labour force surveys.
Inactive unemployed	Wanting a job, but not actively seeking one.
Long-term unemployment	Can be operationalised either as being unemployed for a certain period, typically a year, or as a certain incidence of unemployment, for example 80% during a 12-month period.
Natural Rate of Unemployment	See structural unemployment, NAIRU and NAWRU.
NAIRU	Non-Accelerating Inflation Rate of Unemployment. Estimated from time series data on the relationship between unemployment rate and inflation (the 'Philips curve'). NAIRU is the lowest possible unemployment (a 'natural' unemployment) that is compatible with stable prices (a specified inflation rate). In economics, NAIRU and NAWRU are the main indicators of the level of structural unemployment. This level is mainly determined by mismatch problems but excessively lenient controls may also increase frictional

	unemployment to relatively high levels that forms part of the natural rate of unemployment.
NAWRU	Non-Accelerating Wage Rate of Unemployment: the measure preferred by OECD and others; see NAIRU.
OECD	Organisation for Economic Co-operation and Development. Founded in 1960, it comprised 30 member countries by 2002. The Secretariat in Paris surveys economic development and increasingly analyses all sorts of public policy.
Poverty	Usually refers to relative poverty measured in relation to median disposable income. Poverty level typically operationalised as 50% or 60% of median equivalent disposable income. 'Equivalence' is established by correcting for differences in household size and composition. Competing equivalence scales are applied for this correction.
Reservation wage	The lowest wage a person is willing to accept if he/she is to accept a job.
Structural unemployment	In economics, structural unemployment means a 'natural' level of unemployment that does not disappear even if the economy improves. Instead, increased demand for labour power will lead to higher wage increases and inflation (see NAIRU and NAWRU). At the micro level, this is mainly explained by mismatch problems in segments of the labour market. Mismatch between wages and productivity for low-skilled workers is a key instance; another 'classic' is mismatch between the *types* of qualifications demanded and supplied, resulting in 'bottlenecks'.
Transitional allowance (Dk)	A Danish arrangement which enabled long-term unemployed people aged 50-59 to receive 80% of maximum unemployment benefits until the age of 60, at which age they are eligible for early retirement allowance. Entrance closed 1996; phased out by 2006.

Preface

This volume is the outcome of the research network COST Action A13, 'Changing Labour Markets, Welfare Policies and Citizenship'. COST is an intergovernmental framework for European cooperation in the field of scientific and technical research (including related social science research fields), allowing the coordination of nationally funded research on a European level (for further information about COST, see http://cost.cordis.lu).

The purpose of COST A13 is to examine the effects of social security systems and welfare institutions on processes of social marginalisation, from a citizenship perspective. This includes intended and positive effects as well as possible negative side effects, and the development of policies in relation to such challenges. Some 80 experts, appointed by 17 countries, participate in the COST A13 network, which runs for the five years 1998-2003 (for further information about COST A13, see http://www.socsci.auc.dk/cost).

The work is divided between four working groups: unemployment, ageing and work, gender issues, and youth employment/unemployment. This volume has been prepared by the working group on unemployment, which is an interdisciplinary group of sociologists, economists and political scientists. The book provides an up-to-date and comparative overview and analysis of general trends in unemployment, policy strategies and their theoretical underpinnings, and a series of country analyses focusing on the most interesting aspects from a comparative perspective.

ONE

Changing labour markets, unemployment and unemployment policies in a citizenship perspective

Jørgen Goul Andersen and Knut Halvorsen

Introduction

Ever since T.H. Marshall's groundbreaking essay *Citizenship and social class* (1950), the goal of the welfare state – in Europe at least – has been formulated as a quest for the ideal of 'full citizenship'. This is conceived as full participation for everybody (that is, as equal *citizens*) in all spheres of social and political life, and in the ways and standards of life that are predominant in society. This ideal currently faces a number of challenges. Prominent among them are the threats of increasing social inequality, marginalisation, and even social exclusion due to mass unemployment.

High and persistent unemployment, in turn, has typically been interpreted as an effect of globalisation and technological change on the labour markets. During the 1990s, it was frequently claimed that European welfare states had not only lost the ability to attain the goal of full citizenship, but that they had even become counter-productive. At worst, they were hit by a kind of 'Eurosclerosis' (Blanchard, 2000); at best, they faced a trade-off between equality and employment (Krugman, 1994), which at any rate involves a threat to the ideal of full citizenship. Such ideas strongly influenced policy recommendations to political decision makers, who acted accordingly.

In the mid-1990s, various lines of economic analyses converged into a 'dominant paradigm' or 'standard interpretation' of Europe's unemployment problems. According to this interpretation, unemployment is structural in the sense that it is mainly rooted in mismatches and other labour market rigidities. Consequently, efforts to combat unemployment have little effect, allegedly, unless they embody structural reforms of labour markets and welfare systems.

How serious are such challenges? What have been the policy responses? And what are the effects on social protection systems, in particular for their ability to maintain full citizenship?

From a citizenship perspective, these unemployment problems of course deserve attention as serious threats. But so do the suggested solutions, among which quite a few may themselves be considered threats to citizenship if they do not work as intended.

The main purpose of this book is to provide an updated overview of unemployment and unemployment policies in a number of European countries, and to give a detailed description of the structure of unemployment, as well as trends and paths of policy responses. It also critically examines some of the premises behind current changes of labour market policies and systems of social protection. In both respects, however, the book highlights elements that are particularly relevant to a discussion about citizenship, or, more precisely, to a discussion about the prospects for maintaining the ideal of full citizenship in European welfare states, and indeed improving its fulfilment. As such, the book is a point of departure for further research on the social and political effects of unemployment and on the role of the welfare state in modifying (or unintentionally reinforcing) such consequences.

The book is concerned not only with a *theoretical* context of citizenship, but also with an *empirical* context of significant labour market improvements that took place in several European countries around 2000. In both respects, it appears that many of the assumptions that have guided policy formulation rest on rather uncertain empirical foundations. During the 1990s, two almost hegemonic assumptions emerged:

- that labour market inclusion was an indispensable condition of full citizenship;
- that 'inflexible' European welfare states, under new conditions of globalisation and technological change, obstructed an improvement of the employment situation (in contrast to the job-generating capacity of the American economy).

True, European political leaders have been reluctant to adopt such radical measures as lowering minimum wages. At the 1997 summit in Luxembourg, and in particular at the 2000 summit in Lisbon, the EU formulated an alternative employment strategy which emphasised active labour market policies and the maintenance of social protection standards much more than the mainstream economic Jobs Strategy of the OECD (1994b), for example. Normally, EU documents refer more cautiously to 'reviewing social protection systems'. However, 'making work pay', and 'allowing evolution of wages according to productivity developments and skills differentials', in the words of the Presidency Conclusions of the Barcelona European Council (2002), are also ingredients of the European strategy. Furthermore, its underlying economic *diagnoses* are not wholly dissimilar.

There has been widespread agreement that European welfare states are under pressure and might have to give in on equality and social protection in order to avoid social exclusion as well as economic overload. Both assumptions, however, are open to criticism.

As to the assumption that there is no citizenship without labour market inclusion (Pixley, 1993, p 199), empirical analyses based on the European Household Panel Survey (Gallie and Paugam, 2000a) fail to confirm many of the premises, and so does a comparative Nordic survey of the relationship between labour market marginalisation and social and political citizenship (Halvorsen and Johannessen, 2001; Goul Andersen, 2002a; Goul Andersen et al, forthcoming), just to mention a few. Even more so, one may question the implicit assumption that labour market inclusion is tantamount to full citizenship. These concepts and arguments are elaborated later in this chapter.

This book focuses, rather, on the other set of assumptions. The pessimistic view of the future of European welfare arrangements was stimulated by the situation in the early and mid-1990s when mass unemployment was almost universal in Europe. Although simultaneously warning against simple diagnoses, Jackman (1998, p 60) feared a Europe "condemned to high unemployment". Likewise, Ljungkvist and Sargent (1998, p 546) referred to European welfare states in the 1960s and 1970s as "virtual 'time bomb[s]' waiting to explode".

In the second half of the 1990s, however, many European countries experienced a decisive decline in unemployment, and in 2002 Western European countries with a low to moderate level of unemployment actually outnumber the countries with high and persistent unemployment problems (see Chapter Two of this volume).

It is remarkable that the countries with a positive unemployment record have pursued quite different strategies. Even though most of these countries are rather small and economically less important, it nevertheless changes the premises of the discussion. First, it seems that there are several possible routes to improving employment rather than a single, market-oriented path inspired by the US. Second, it seems that the pessimistic interpretations of the 1990s were coloured by the tightening of economic policies taking place throughout Europe to meet the convergence criteria of the Eurozone. This may have beneficial effects in the long run, but in the short run it undoubtedly aggravated the crisis. In summary, too many long-term conclusions were probably drawn from short-term phenomena.

This points to the need to scrutinise variations among European countries, highlight alternative routes to improved employment, critically evaluate 'success stories' as well as 'policy failures', and discuss, more generally, the compatibility between preserving generous social protection and improving employment. We evaluate this from a citizenship perspective. That is, we break with the implicit inclination to see employment as a goal in itself. Basically, employment should be seen as a means – maybe indispensable, but still as a means – to ensure full citizenship, on the one hand, and economic sustainability on the other.

The next section discusses the changing employment policies in Europe and their underlying 'economic philosophies' to put the dominant interpretation and the policy changes of the 1990s in perspective. It then discusses the citizenship perspective, various welfare regimes and the guiding questions of the book in more detail.

Chapter Two provides a very brief summary of some main empirical findings in the economic literature and an overview of the changing unemployment situation as an overture to an up-to-date survey of short and long-term changes in employment and unemployment in Europe up until 2001. As well as serving as a point of reference and as a method of shortening the following chapters, Chapter Two sums up some of the lessons that can be drawn in relation to the European unemployment problems. One conclusion is that we find it difficult to make judgements on isolated aspects of welfare policies without considering the context. This is done in the following ten chapters (Chapters Three to Twelve), which present in-depth studies of the situation on the labour market, policy changes, and the workings of these policies in particular countries. These chapters cover the three major welfare models in northern Europe as well as welfare states with highly different unemployment records, including the welfare states of Norway, Switzerland and Slovenia, along with seven EU member countries. In addition, Chapter Two briefly surveys those EU countries and central European countries that are not covered by these particular chapters.

Chapter Thirteen summarises the evidence and discusses the prospects for the future of social protection and labour market regulation in Europe.

Changing unemployment policies and underlying philosophies

Even though strategies are different, most policy recommendations about labour market policy since the early 1990s were guided by ideas that add up to a sort of paradigm or 'standard interpretation' of unemployment problems in Europe. This interpretation rests on a legacy of policies and policy failures, which constituted a learning process that paved the way for new ideas.

Our point of departure is a simple classification of possible and actual policies. Figure 1.1 shows a list of such policy options, rooted in different philosophies of (un)employment. It also represents a historical development from traditional macroeconomic steering rooted in variants of Keynesian demand strategies to structural (supply-side) strategies aimed at modifying market distortions and restoring incentives.

From Keynesianism to competitiveness

When the first oil crisis hit Western economies in the mid-1970s, the routine reaction of most governments was to stimulate aggregate demand. In Scandinavia especially, this was combined with rapid growth in public sector employment. In most cases, however, this strategy came to be seen as inefficient, leading to stagflation, unless it was combined with a very tight incomes policy (as happened, for example, in Austria; see Scharpf, 1987; Hemerijck et al, 2000). Another negative side effect was increasing state debt, which became a structural problem in many countries as the expected improvement in economic activity failed to materialise. In the early 1980s, Denmark and Belgium were prototypical of

Figure 1.1: A typology of (un)employment policies (with examples)

	Strategies and substrategies
Stimulate domestic demand	1. Demand strategy • Stimulate aggregate demand • Increasing public sector employment
Competitiveness	2. Competitiveness/export strategy • Currency devaluation • Wage moderation (corporatism, incomes policy) • Lower corporate taxes/social contributions/higher subsidies
Redistribution of labour	3. Reduction/redistribution of labour supply • Early exit programmes • Leave programmes • Increasing inflow into education • Shorter working hours/longer holidays
Structural strategies	4. Activation/qualification strategy • Education, job training
	5. Market/incentive strategy • Lower *de facto* minimum wages – can be compensated by in-work benefits/tax credit • Stronger work incentives: less generous social protection – lower benefits, shorter duration, tighter eligibility • Stronger work incentives: lower income taxes • More flexible employment protection • More flexible working hours
	6. Subsidy/service strategy • Subsidies to household services, lower VAT
	7. Stricter controls/higher requirements • Stricter works test and mobility requirements • 'Workfare': duty to work in return for benefits

the problem of accumulating deficits and increasing interest payments on state debts (Goul Andersen, 1997b). In addition, a strategy of devaluations, which was widely used in small European economies in the 1970s, was typically given up in the early 1980s. In a globalised economy, these strategies proved counterproductive. True, the effects of globalisation are often exaggerated: for small, open economies that are used to acting within a balance of payment constraint, the imperative of competitiveness is nothing new, and the devaluation strategy was one of the classical Keynesian instruments to improve competitiveness. But conditions had changed. Free capital movements and rational expectations jointly limited the applicability of such traditional macroeconomic steering instruments. Basically, in a system with free capital movements, rational expectations of investors mean that the negative effects of (fear of) inflation or devaluations, especially increasing interest rates, come before the positive effects. Therefore, at least for small countries, there was no alternative to fixed currency policy, anti-inflationary policies, and more or less balanced state budgets. Providing an opportunity for 'blame avoidance'

(Pierson, 1994), the convergence criteria of the Eurozone often seemed to be welcomed by governments as a means to carry such policies through.

Strategies of competitiveness in old and new surroundings

An alternative to stimulating domestic demand was to stimulate demand from abroad by improving competitiveness. Whereas the traditional competitiveness strategy of devaluations had to be given up as counter-productive, a large number of other instruments has remained (for example general industrial policy, research and technology policy, educational policy, as well as more targeted instruments such as lower corporate taxes and a rich variety of direct or indirect subsidies to firms). Even though gross labour costs must be assumed, in the long run, to be independent of the form of financing, reducing employers' social insurance contributions (as in France; see Palier, 2000) may also be a means to enhance competitiveness in the short run. All such strategies of competitiveness have survived into the 21st century.

Wage moderation – another classical strategy of competitiveness – is slightly more contested. Negotiated wage moderation is beneficial in the short run, but it often requires something in return such as improved social protection or wage solidarity. As both contribute to higher de facto minimum wages, this may, according to mainstream economics, further reduce the employment chances of the least skilled and least productive workers. Besides, due to wage drift, wage moderation may be difficult to control in practice. Unless such side effects can be avoided, wage moderation may even have negative long-term effects. Finally, corporatist interest intermediation may contribute to successful implementation of changes; but the need to obtain consent from the social partners may also function as a 'veto point' against necessary changes and adaptations. In short, from a market-oriented point of view, corporatism may appear quite problematic.

Reduction/redistribution of labour supply

If unemployment cannot be effectively combated by increasing demand for labour power, the logical alternative is to reduce the supply of labour power, or remove some groups (such as elderly workers) from the labour force in order to improve the employment chances for others (in particular, the young). This strategy became one of the most important in the efforts of European welfare states to reduce unemployment, and outlived the demand strategy by over a decade. It was seldom rooted in a belief that globalisation or technological development would create 'jobless growth' or permanently reduce the need for labour power (as some assumed it would; Offe, 1996; Gorz, 1999, for example), but was rather dictated by urgent political needs and often practically irreversible once in action.

First and foremost, reducing the labour supply includes a large variety of early-exit arrangements (or lower pension age) and leave arrangements. Job sharing – or enhanced capacity of the educational system – also serves the same purpose. And finally, shorter working hours and longer holidays may, to some extent, be counted among such measures[1].

Such measures tend to improve quality of life, and they were widely used until the mid-1990s. However, they became increasingly criticised, partly due to the debate about increasing dependency ratios caused by ageing populations. Together, the measures added up to what critics dubbed 'politics of inactivity', which was perhaps most visible in the 'Dutch disease' of the mid-1980s (Van Kersbergen, 1995; Esping-Andersen, 1996b, 1999). In the short run, replacement of retired workers tends to be low (unless negotiated at the company level). And in the long run, net replacement may be even lower due to negative dynamic effects (higher-wage increases and less investment in human capital on behalf of both employers and employees in anticipation of early retirement). Therefore, the net effect on unemployment tends to be negligible or even negative (Røed, 2000). The only certain effect is declining employment rates and increasing dependency ratios.

The 'standard interpretation' of the 1990s

It is against this backdrop that the structural strategies should be seen. Apart from the strategies of competitiveness, the policies we have described were intended to counteract market imperfections – 'politics against markets' – and nearly all measures appeared inefficient. This paved the way for more market-oriented interpretations – according to which the market is the solution – whereas regulations that impede market forces are part of the problem. Most importantly, if wages are allowed to reflect differences in productivity, far more people will be employed. And if wages are above that level, low-productive workers will be unemployable[2].

Each of the interpretations outlined earlier were based on the premise that, if only economic growth is sufficiently high, and demand for labour power increases accordingly, will unemployment gradually be eliminated. According to the dominant interpretation of the 1990s, however, this will *not* happen, because unemployment is *structural* rather than cyclical, that is, a product of inflexible labour markets and welfare states. Even high economic growth will only reduce unemployment down to the threshold of structural unemployment[3]. Beyond that point, employers will not hire low-productive unemployed workers; rather, they start competing for the more highly skilled and bid up the wages of those already employed. Therefore, in economics, structural unemployment is defined as the lowest level of unemployment that is compatible with a stable development of prices or wages. The typical measures are:

- Non-Accelerating Inflation Rate of Unemployment (NAIRU);
- Non-Accelerating Wage Rate of Unemployment (NAWRU).

These are estimated on the basis of econometric analyses of the relationship between unemployment and inflation (Layard et al, 1991; Elmeskov and MacFarland, 1993).

Structural unemployment has other sources than the discrepancy between productivity and minimum wage costs. For example, there may be a mismatch between supply and demand of specific *types* of qualifications. So-called 'frictional' unemployment, related to job changes or to transitions from education to employment, also generates a 'natural' minimum level of unemployment, the size of which depends on the search intensity (and 'moral hazard') of people who become unemployed. However, the combination of low productivity and high 'reservation wages' (the lowest wages unemployed people are willing to accept if they are to take a job) is one of the most important sources.

Furthermore, since long-term unemployment means a progressive loss of qualifications, social security – which keeps the unemployed from taking the low-wage jobs they can get – may create an 'unemployment trap'. Therefore, each recession may lead to sedimentation of new groups that have become unemployable, so that long-term unemployment becomes self-reinforcing. This phenomenon is referred to as 'hysteresis' (Blanchard and Summers, 1986).

In the 1990s, this paradigm of structural unemployment became the 'standard interpretation' of unemployment in Europe. It was in particular put forward in the OECD Jobs Study (1994b) and in the proposed OECD Jobs Strategy (OECD, 1994c, pp 43-9), as well as in country recommendations. Furthermore, as structural unemployment was estimated to be very close to the actual level of unemployment (OECD, 1997a, pp 10-11), whereas the (residual) cyclical component appeared negligible, the message was that there was little these countries could do other than strengthen competitiveness in general and labour market flexibility in particular.

According to this standard interpretation, European welfare states face a basic dilemma in a new world of globalisation and technological change: These processes do not lead to unemployment per se, but they do reinforce the problems of the low-skilled while at the same time constraining the coping capacity of (nation-)states. Previously, it might be possible to counteract such problems, at worst at the cost of a somewhat reduced economic growth. But nowadays, European welfare states face a trade-off, or at least a dilemma, between equality and employment (OECD, 1994b; 1997a; see also Esping-Andersen, 1999, pp 180-4). Others have spoken of a *tri*lemma between equality, employment and balanced state budgets (Iversen and Wren, 1998).

According to this standard interpretation, then, unemployment in Europe is basically a structural problem, mainly rooted in inflexibility and disincentives of regulated labour markets, compressed wage structures (in particular high minimum wages), and generous welfare states. Even though the package of solutions suggested by OECD and others comprises a wide array of measures to enhance competitiveness, as well as education and activation in order to enhance productivity (to justify high labour costs), deregulation, improved incentives, and wage flexibility have been imperative elements. Wage flexibility

Figure 1.2: The 'standard interpretation' of structural unemployment: problem definitions and possible solutions

Problem	Solution
1. Gap between wages and productivity for low-skilled workers	1.1. More wage flexibility and less compressed wage structures/lower reservation wages • Presuppose less generous social protection • Inequality may be alleviated by tax compensation 1.2. Higher productivity • Activation of unemployed • Education/qualification 1.3. Subsidise low-productive services
2. Inflexibility and distortions to smooth functioning of markets	2.1. More flexible employment protection 2.2. More flexible working hours 2.3. Avoid disincentives/distortions of tax/welfare system 2.4. Stricter works test/workfare

means lower de facto minimum wages (not least with the aim of creating more service jobs for low-skilled workers). Lower minimum wages, in turn, presuppose less generous social protection.

Even within this paradigm or framework of interpretation, however, there are a number of available options (Figure 1.2). The core problem is the gap between wages and productivity for low-skilled workers. Logically, there are three solutions:

- *Wage flexibility:* lower minimum wages and less compressed wage structures that reflect differences in productivity. This presupposes less generous social protection in order to secure lower 'reservation wages' among the unemployed. should distributional consequences for the working poor become unacceptable, it might be alleviated through a tax credit like the American Earned Income Tax Credit (EITC) or the British Working Families' Tax Credit (WFTC).
- *Higher qualifications:* in the labour force in general, as well as among the unemployed in particular. Not surprisingly, the labour movement prefers to bridge the gap using this solution. This measure is also given high priority in the employment strategy of the EU.
- *A reduction in the costs of low-productive service labour:* through a variety of direct or indirect subsidies (for example subsidies, tax deductions, or lower VAT for particular services), wage costs of service jobs may be reduced.

However, there are also other disturbances to the smooth functioning of markets which could lead to higher structural unemployment or lower competitiveness (Figure 1.2, solutions 2.1-4):

- too rigid employment protection;
- inflexible working hours;
- disincentives in the tax/welfare system;
- too easy access to unemployment benefits.

Again, the main solution is deregulation and improved work incentives. Structural unemployment is seen, basically, as an effect of disturbances of market forces, and most solutions – for example 'wage flexibility' (larger wage dispersion and lower de facto minimum wages), flexible employment protection, and flexible working hours – are concerned with restoring market flexibility. Together with general measures to stimulate growth and productivity, the solutions sketched in Figure 1.2 reflect proposals such as OECD's Jobs Strategy (1994c, 1997a), which recommended a mix of systemic changes towards more flexibility, less generous social protection, activation, and stricter works tests. Although increasingly active labour market policy is also part of that package, it is given lower priority, and it is worth noting that OECD has had few country-specific recommendations for the US (OECD, 1999g).

To some extent, elements of this diagnosis were accepted even by sworn supporters of the welfare state (Esping-Andersen, 1996a; 1999; but see Esping-Andersen and Regini, 2000; Esping-Andersen et al, 2001) whereas prominent sociologists (such as Giddens, 1998, pp 114-15) have endorsed arguments about 'moral hazard' effects of social protection systems. According to Gilbert (1995, p 77), Murray's idea that social protection disincentives lead to a 'dependency culture' among welfare recipients that passes on from one generation to another (Murray, 1984) nearly became conventional wisdom in American public debates (for a critique, see Dean and Taylor-Gooby, 1992; Halvorsen, 1999a).

Above all else, however, the economic diagnosis of structural unemployment achieved credibility from a comparison between Europe and the US (OECD, 1994b). In the 1960s and 1970s, the unemployment rates in the US were twice as high as the European average (Figure 1.3a-b). However, from the mid-1980s until the turn of the century, it was the other way around. From an economic perspective, employment rates were even more alarming: in the US, employment rates showed a nearly constant increase, whereas in Europe, they declined or stagnated as a result of attempts to fight unemployment by reducing the labour supply, especially through early retirement. This led to the image of European welfare states as caught in structures of inflexibility where the welfare state's attempts to combat unemployment had little effect in the short run and made the situation even less sustainable in the long run.

The 'job miracle' of the US is further discussed in Chapter Two. The important point being made here is that the apparent failure in Europe contributed to the path-breaking reorientation of economic philosophies among policy makers in many European countries. The new economic philosophies prescribed adjustments in eligibility, levels and duration of unemployment benefits, expanded duties or even 'workfare' (Lødemel and Trickey, 2001), less employment protection, and/or activation efforts[4].

Figure 1.3(a): Employment rates in Europe (EU15) and US (1960-2000) (as a percentage of population from 15 to 64 years)

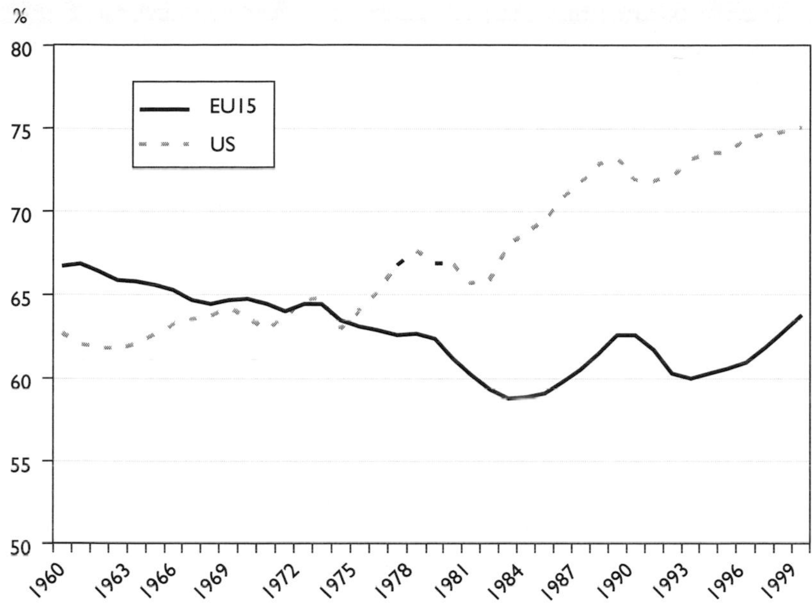

Figure 1.3(b): Unemployment rates in Europe (EU15) and US (1960-2000) (as a percentage of total labour force)

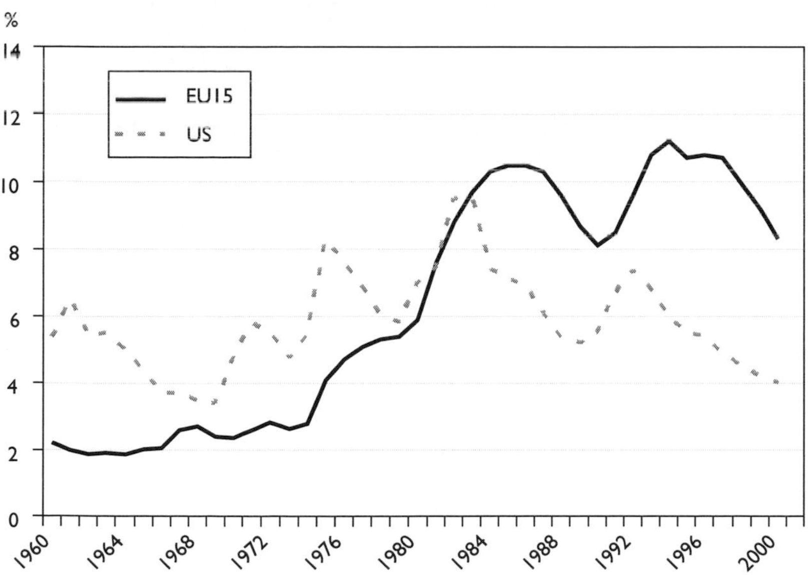

Moreover, it facilitated a new conception of social rights and citizenship. Rather than seeing social rights as a means to alleviate the social consequences of labour market problems and as a way to keep people integrated in society (and allegedly easier to reintegrate in the labour market), the new conception sees social rights as a necessary evil and emphasises active employment and self-reliance as the only path to maintaining full citizenship. Such communitarian ideas of a balance between rights and obligations, sometimes referred to as the 'Clinton–Blair orthodoxy' (Jordan, 1998), have mainly been put forward in Anglo-Saxon countries. However, the changing economic philosophies have come to influence policies in nearly all European countries, including continental Europe (Palier, 2002).

In practice, though, policy change has not gone as far as recommended. As OECD notes (1999g), recommendations about minimum wages have almost not been followed at all (net implementation is negative), and with the exception of the UK and the Netherlands (OECD, 2000c; Blundell, 2000; Blundell and Hoynes, 2001; Evans, 2001), European countries have so far been reluctant to introduce tax credits or 'in-work' benefits (such as EITC) that have become a major element in the American welfare system (Quadagno, 1999).

Most, if not all, European countries, however, have been influenced by these changing ideas, and most of them have cut benefit levels, adjusted tax systems or tightened duration and conditionality for unemployment benefits and social assistance (Kalisch et al, 1998; Evans, 2001). Typically, though, these cuts have taken place at the margins. Such changes and their impact on citizenship are described in Chapters Three to Twelve.

Citizenship

This volume's perspective does not – in principle, at least – regard employment as an end in itself, but rather as one means among others to ensure citizenship, with the addition that in an economically unsustainable welfare state it makes little sense to discuss citizenship at all. Elaborating a little bit on the ideas of T.H. Marshall (1950), we define citizenship – in the sociological sense – as *full and equal membership of society* (that is, regardless of differences in social position or other characteristics). We suggest that, as a sociological concept, citizenship is comprised of these three dimensions:

- rights
- participation
- identity[5].

Non-stigmatising[6], generous social rights enable full citizenship. But being a full and equal citizen is, basically, a question of practices: living a decent life in accordance with the prevailing standards in society, being able to act autonomously (Rothstein, 1998)[7], being able to participate in social and political life in the broadest sense, and having 'civic' orientations to the political community and to one's fellow-citizens. Loss of citizenship, by contrast, means division of society into first and second-class citizens, poverty (exclusion from participating in the prevailing standard of living), social isolation (marginalisation from social networks and feeling of loneliness), passivity (in relation to social and political life), dependency, powerlessness, 'un-civicness', or constrained participation.

To what extent unemployment entails a loss of citizenship is basically an empirical question. However, the concept of citizenship links to the notion of *active* actors who have the potential to cope with their problems (Fryer and Payne, 1984; Halvorsen, 1994), and it seems reasonable to assume that the ability of the unemployed to cope with unemployment depends on generous, non-stigmatising social rights.

Correspondingly, it is an empirical question whether or not social security contributes more or less to citizenship than activation, or in comparison with earning your own income by being gainfully employed in a very precarious job. The latter may certainly be necessary for economic purposes, but ultimately, there are no logically compelling grounds that it necessarily involves a gain in terms of citizenship.

Although it is outside of the scope of this volume to engage in any description or testing of these questions (the subject of forthcoming publications in this series), they should be kept in mind as the ultimate dependent variables. In this book we restrict ourselves to dealing with participation on the labour market, and especially with particular aspects of *social citizenship rights* that have been affected by policy changes. Such changes include:

- adequacy of social protection (such as compensation rates, duration, and so on);
- access to benefits (are some groups excluded?);
- balance between unconditional rights and means-tested benefits;
- conditionality of entitlements;
- redefinition of rights and duties, including stronger rhetorical emphasis on obligations;
- equal treatment of employed and unemployed in relation to other social rights;
- stigmatisation;
- the situation of those who are difficult to place within a stricter activation context (for instance, loss of individual freedom and autonomy for vulnerable groups such as lone mothers, older workers, slightly disabled, immigrants, and so on)[8];
- even though it is not the prime target of analysis, some chapters also briefly address the link between unemployment and social exclusion.

Finally, this volume will also describe the changing conceptions of citizenship that guide social and labour market policy reforms (even if they are rarely phrased in the language of citizenship).

Citizenship, poverty and social exclusion

Thus, although the focus of this volume is almost exclusively on social rights, it is written in a broader perspective. It might be useful, therefore, to elaborate very briefly on the relationship between citizenship and related concepts.

Many of the questions that can be raised from a citizenship perspective are frequently addressed under umbrella concepts such as 'poverty', 'new poverty', 'social integration', or 'social exclusion'. To some extent, this is a matter of terminology, and few studies would discuss (new) poverty or social exclusion without reference to T.H. Marshall (1950). Still, some differences in connotations and underlying concerns linger.

The concept of poverty, for example, frequently has rather narrow economic and distributional connotations, or else it may become all-embracing and fluid. The concept of citizenship, on the other hand, is concise: it embodies the notion of different, specified arenas or fields of marginality (Roche, 1992; Goul Andersen, 1996)[9].

The concept of social exclusion comes closer (Room, 1995; Littlewood and Herkommer, 1999; Vleminckx and Berghman, 2001), but it usually entails a notion of cumulative deprivation, of spatial segregation, and sometimes of group formation, or even the formation of an 'underclass'. Certainly, such aspects are interesting, but they are not implied by the notion of citizenship. In one respect, the concept of social exclusion is too narrow, as it tends to cover an extreme where citizens are 'non-citizens' rather than 'just' second-class citizens (Roche, 1992, p 57; Johannessen, 1997; Halvorsen, 2000b). Just as important, some of the most important component variables of citizenship are not included in most conceptions of social exclusion. Neither concepts of poverty nor social exclusion embody the notion of *social rights*, which is a core component of the concept of citizenship. To this comes the fact that in official uses (Levitas, 1996) and in economic analyses, concepts such as social exclusion or marginalisation frequently become one-dimensional concepts, which are simply equated with degree of *labour market inclusion* and sometimes connote systemic (and occasionally moral) adaptation (Born and Jensen, 2001).

Finally, the concept of social integration may simply be used as the opposite of social exclusion. However, it is typically rooted in a more narrow, functionalist perspective that fails to include any notion of 'empowerment/disempowerment', which is usually connoted by the concept of poverty, and in particular by the concept of citizenship.

On a practical level, the citizenship perspective of this volume is not a radical departure from other perspectives on unemployment and employment policies. However, it *is* a different perspective. And most importantly, the analysis differs from those studies of unemployment in which employment is automatically considered a goal in itself and not a means towards an end; where labour market marginalisation or exclusion is implicitly considered tantamount to social marginalisation or exclusion; where social integration is equated with employment; and where contribution to employment is the only success criterion of social policy. From a citizenship perspective, the most fundamental 'success criterion' of a policy is whether it integrates people in society as citizens[10].

Institutional variations

As far as institutionally determined variations between nations are concerned, our point of departure is Esping-Andersen's classical distinction (1990, 1996a) between three welfare regimes: liberal, corporatist, and universal[11]. His concept of welfare (state) *regime* goes beyond institutions in the narrow sense as it refers to the mutually reinforcing interplay between welfare arrangements, the economy/labour market (and therefore the social structure), and the family[12]. This volume, however, focuses more narrowly on the aspects relating to the labour market. To avoid the somewhat broader connotations of 'welfare regimes', we prefer the term 'employment regimes' (Gallie and Paugam, 2000b).

Ideal-typically, a liberal employment regime designates one with little state regulation and flexible labour markets[13]. This means relatively low coverage of benefits and low replacement rates, to a high extent means-tested at the family level, and labour markets with low employment protection, low minimum wages and high wage differentials. According to most economic theories, the liberal regime, acting more in conformity with the market, should be most adapted to new requirements of globalisation and a knowledge-intensive society. Hypothetically, it should generate more jobs for the low skilled, but also a danger of considerable numbers of working poor. In terms of citizenship, it should, according to economic theory, prevent poverty traps and long-term unemployment. Also, this model should enhance labour force participation, including female labour force participation.

From a sociological perspective, on the other hand, one would also expect it to be associated with stigmatisation and poor living conditions for those who do not manage to find a job. Critics allege that in the real world, this regime produces poverty rather than inclusion, and, occasionally, counterproductive results due to perverse incentives. For example, means-tested social security easily produces perverse incentives that encourage unemployment among couples (Halvorsen, 2000a).

The beneficial effects on female labour-force participation are expected to be even stronger in the universal employment regime, which is characterised by high minimum wages, generous social protection, and encompassing provision of public care services. Employment protection may differ, but economic protection of the unemployed (in particular minimum levels) is high and unrelated to principles of seniority, except eligibility. Rights are individualised (rather than family-oriented), and unemployment benefits prevail instead of means-tested social assistance.

Ideally, duration of benefits is long or even infinite, but may be conditional on participation in active labour market programmes and on fulfilment of strict mobility requirements. Hypothetically, this model should provide many low-skilled service jobs in the public sector (Esping-Andersen, 1996a, 1999). Whether this is sufficient – and economically sustainable – remains an open question. Obviously, the universal model may face difficulties in providing low-skilled, high-paid service jobs in the private sector. If this is the case, unemployment should be higher in low-skilled jobs than in the liberal model. In terms of citizenship, universalism is the ideal model as far as protection is concerned. However, from an economic perspective, it has often been accused of involving dangers of poverty traps, clientelism and welfare dependency. Weak economic incentives may also produce long-term unemployment according to economic search theory. This question will be explained below.

The corporatist (contribution-based) regime is defined by the strong association between employment and social rights. Ideally, this is the male breadwinner model, which provides generous income replacement, often with long duration, for people with a long job record on a full-time basis. Unfortunately, it tends to discriminate against all others, as it is based on a strong link between contributions and rights. Furthermore, it is usually coupled with strong job protection and quite high minimum wages. Therefore, this welfare model, according to standard explanations, would have low labour-market flexibility and tend to produce strong insider/outsider divisions (Lindbeck and Snower, 1988).

In terms of citizenship, this model is family oriented, discriminatory against women and the young, and against all people with less than full-time employment and a long contribution record. In terms of equality, it is usually claimed to build on maintaining a status difference (Esping-Andersen, 1990). However, as it is also a system of extensive and sometimes quite solidaristic risk sharing (Baldwin, 1990; Overbye, 1998; Esping-Andersen, 1999), it may promote equality to a larger extent than usually acknowledged.

As far as economic consequences are concerned, the outcome of a corporatist regime is usually described as low labour force participation, high reliance on early exit (in short an 'inactivity' bias), and a low development of both private and public services that could produce new workplaces. Furthermore, there may be vicious circles (Manow and Seils, 2000a, 2000b), as increasing unemployment led immediately to higher social contributions and therefore higher wage costs for firms at the worst possible moment (as this system is usually real wage resistant as far as social contributions are concerned). Therefore, from an economic point of view, we should expect this welfare regime to be pressured under present economic conditions (even though this is rarely emphasised in mainstream economics).

The southern European welfare systems differ on family responsibility, absence of social assistance and on other dimensions that could warrant the label 'model' (Ferrera, 1996a), even though the reforms of the 1990s (Moreno, 2000; Ferrera and Gualmini, 2000) have blurred distinctions somewhat (Ferrera, 2000). Still, these systems differ due to their extremely strong emphasis on the family as provider of social protection. This means that pensions are often overdeveloped, whereas social minimum protection tends to be absent or seriously underdeveloped. The result is a dramatic insider/outsider division that should provide unusually strong divisions between a core labour force (prime age men), and all others, in particular the young.

These models are ideal types, of course. It is common, however, to regard the Scandinavian welfare states as close to the universal model, the continental European welfare states as close to the corporatist model (with Mediterranean or southern European welfare states forming a subgroup), and the Anglo-Saxon and Swiss welfare states as the European welfare states that come closest to the liberal model. Ireland is usually regarded as a hybrid between the corporatist and liberal model (here it is counted among the liberal), and Netherlands has traditionally been seen as a hybrid between the social democratic and corporatist model (but, as far as the labour market is concerned, mainly the latter).

We do not intend to engage in a 'welfare modelling' discussion here. Rather, this serves as a practical classification and as tool to point out what is remarkable in descriptions. Chapter Two, however, explores somewhat more systematically how much the employment/unemployment patterns continue to conform with this typology, and whether there are significant differences in success in fighting unemployment. From a citizenship perspective, however, an equally important question is whether or not unemployment strategies, as judged from a citizenship perspective, follow similar lines.

Basically, we can distinguish between three strategies of citizenship (or 'inclusion'):

- a strategy of protecting citizenship by maintaining generous social security for the unemployed;
- a market-oriented strategy of flexibility and stronger incentives aimed at integration through work;
- an activation/qualification strategy that also regards work as the key to integration, but applies other means, more in accordance with a European social policy tradition.

But do differences between countries follow the same lines as welfare regimes? What (combination of) strategies are followed in various countries, and which strategies appear most efficient in terms of both employment and citizenship?

Public policy formation and the plan of this volume

Comparative economic analyses of welfare state institutions are often based on a variable-by-variable approach, trying to find systematic associations between institutions and policies on the one hand, and level or structure of unemployment on the other. The in-depth studies of this volume, rather, focus on context.

However, Chapter Two describes the overall pattern of employment and unemployment in Europe on the basis of easily accessible comparative data. This allows the country-specific chapters (Chapters Three to Twelve) to concentrate on more detailed analyses of aspects that are particularly interesting from a comparative perspective. In addition, Chapter Two assesses to what extent current information about the level and structure of unemployment in Europe conforms to the 'standard interpretation' discussed earlier in this chapter.

This also allows the country-specific chapters to focus mainly on policy changes and their effects on unemployment and citizenship rights, rather than on detailed descriptions of the level and structure of unemployment. Such data are dealt with, however, where the more detailed national statistics provide new or even contradictory information (as compared to accessible comparable data sources). Relying on Chapter Two for comparable information, the country-specific chapters also focus on the aspects that appear most significant from a comparative perspective, rather than on systematical, but not very deep-reaching, comparative accounts of policy changes which can be found elsewhere (for example, Kalish et al, 1998). In Chapter Thirteen, however, we also consider whether or not the policies of the individual countries converge, and if so, what are the sources of policy change – similar economic pressures, or policy recommendations from OECD, the EU, and others?

Notes

[1] It should be added that other long-term trends, such as earlier retirement, longer holidays and shorter working hours, are also part of the workers' share of increased wealth of society.

[2] Due to flexibility needs it also appears that the protection of weak, especially old, workers on 'the internal labour markets' within the [big] companies (a sort of 'postponed wage') evaporates (Gautié, 2002).

[3] The theory of the natural rate of unemployment was originally developed by Phelps (1967) and Friedman (1968), but did not really enter mainstream economics until the 1990s.

[4] Although activation may also serve as a works test, it should not be conflated with 'workfare', which is sometimes part of a neoliberal strategy. In principle, activation is an alternative to neoliberal strategies (for a discussion, see Barbier, 2002).

[5] The latter are sometimes referred to as 'practices'. (See Goul Andersen et al, 2000, 2001c; Siim, 2000; Lister, 2002.)

[6] Stigmatisation may take many forms. Language can be important, even if it does not directly address the unemployed. Therefore, dubbing social benefits 'passive support' may create a division between active citizens who are employed, and passive, dependent citizens on public support, who are often regarded as second-class citizens (Sinfield, 1997; Faulks, 2000).

[7] This was exactly the classical criterion that was discussed for granting full political citizenship including voting rights to citizens: people who were 'dependent' were not able to make autonomous (political) choices. Originally, only a small group was considered competent for political citizenship, but gradually it came to include people who were not proprietors, people who were not self-employed, women, and people who had received social assistance from the state.

[8] Citizenship of immigrants is one of the greatest current challenges in European countries. Unfortunately the scope of this volume does not allow us to comment on this problem.

[9] Strictly speaking, 'marginalisation' refers to a process, 'marginality' to a situation, but in this volume the two terms are used interchangeably. Unlike competing concepts, the concepts of marginalisation or marginality are not rooted in any particular theoretical frame of reference, but derive meaning from the framework within which they are used (for example, the notion of citizenship in this volume).

[10] It is important to re-emphasise that this does not ignore economic concerns. In an economically unsustainable welfare state, there is no point in discussing citizenship. This also means, for instance, that there may be a case for activation even when it is not rational in a narrow economic sense (economic costs exceed economic benefits) if it contributes positively to maintaining full citizenship.

[11] Gallie and Paugam (2000b, p 5) speak of a 'sub-protective' regime as a fourth type largely corresponding with southern European welfare states. They differ from the liberal type where the underdevelopment of social protection reflects a deliberate ideological choice.

[12] We follow Esping-Andersen's (1990) distinctions without necessarily endorsing the theory about underlying social and political forces (see also Baldwin, 1990). That is why the terms 'corporatist' and 'universal' are preferred, rather than Esping-Andersen's political labels, conservative and social democratic. In the case of liberal welfare states, Esping-Andersen's term is less problematical. (For equivalent distinctions that are more narrowly oriented towards the institutions of social protection, see, for example, Ferrera, 1996; Kuhnle and Alestalo, 2000.)

[13] Gallie and Paugam (2000b, p 6) distinguish this model from a 'sub-protective' type by the criterion that the liberal model "reflects an explicit political will not to intervene" rather than sheer absence of social protection.

TWO

Employment and unemployment in Europe: overview and new trends

Jørgen Goul Andersen and Jan Bendix Jensen

Introduction

This chapter provides a broad comparative overview of trends and patterns in employment and unemployment in European countries as a reference point for the country-specific analyses of Chapters Three to Twelve. It is largely descriptive, but also examines to what degree unemployment levels and patterns in Europe still fit the expectations from the economic 'standard interpretation' of structural unemployment described in Chapter One.

The first section contains a brief overview of main findings in the comparative economic literature, and the following section assesses the new picture of unemployment in Europe in the early 2000s, as compared to the mid-1990s. The remaining sections examine the changes in labour-force participation, the structure of unemployment, and discuss employment precariousness, living conditions and citizenship.

The chapter is based almost exclusively on international comparative statistics (that is, on the ILO definition of unemployment, mainly on survey-based measurement, and on OECD corrections and modifications[1]). Although other international statistics may in some respects be superior (see Sorrentino, 2000; Threlfall, 2000), the differences are increasingly small, and OECD provides the most comprehensive, easily accessible and updated data set, especially when we also want to compare Europe and US. As international statistical comparability is sometimes obtained at the cost of data validity, country-specific chapters (Chapters Three to Twelve) will, when necessary, comment on differences between international and national statistics.

Empirical findings from the comparative economic literature

The 'standard interpretation' discussed in Chapter One represents a logically coherent paradigm for interpretation of unemployment problems and for formulation of policy solutions. Although policy recommendations rooted in this paradigm are often not followed, a comprehensive alternative paradigm currently does not exist. Even the employment strategy of the EU, at the level of *diagnosis*, represents a variation of that paradigm rather than a genuine alternative. As a paradigm – exclusively emphasising the supply side (Ljungqvist and Sargent, 1996) – it does not easily lend itself to empirical testing. And even though the sub-field of labour economics is highly empirical, for instance, it should come as no great surprise that many theoretical propositions rest more on strong theoretical grounds than on strong empirical evidence (Holmlund, 1998; Calmfors and Holmlund, 2000). As Blanchard and Katz have indicated, there has been "great theoretical progress", but "empirical knowledge sadly lags behind" (1996, p 52). This section briefly summarises some of the main empirical findings.

A number of propositions derived from the 'standard interpretation' have been critically tested – along with other hypotheses about the impact of institutional variables, not least by the OECD itself – partly by time series analyses, and partly by cross-country regressions using OECD member countries as units, or both.

From such a cross-country regression, OECD (1999g) finds a strong correlation between implementation of the OECD Jobs Strategy and reduction of structural unemployment, according to the Non-Accelerating Wage Rate of Unemployment (NAWRU) criterion, that is, the estimated lowest possible rate of unemployment with stable wage increases. However, the independent variable in that analysis is a composite index, including recommendations that are by no means specific to the standard interpretation of structural unemployment. When it comes to the specific aspects, the evidence seems rather thin.

High (de facto or de jure) *minimum wages* and compressed (inflexible) wage structures should have negative employment effects and should affect in particular the employment chances of young people and unskilled workers (OECD, 1994b, p 53). However, several US studies challenge the mainstream idea there that American minimum wages have adverse effects (Card and Krueger, 1995). And in Europe, it has always been difficult to find cross-national evidence to confirm a trade-off between equality and employment (Freeman, 1995; Galbraith et al, 1999). As we shall see below, recent data on country variations appear even less convincing.

When it comes to *work incentives*, there is also a discrepancy between the strong concern for incentive structures and the uncertain empirical evidence about incentive *effects*. As far as *unemployment benefits* are concerned, most studies seem to point in the same direction: the *level* of unemployment benefits has little, if any, effect on unemployment (Goul Andersen, 1995; Nickell, 1997; Holmlund 1998; Halvorsen 2000a; Sjoberg, 2000)[2], but *duration* of benefits does seem to affect both job search and duration of unemployment (Nickell, 1997)[3].

In the 1980s, *taxation* was usually believed to play a major role (Layard et al, 1991; Blanchard and Katz, 1996, pp 66-7). However, even though tax incentives have continued to play an important role in policy discussions, the evidence since the mid-1980s is very mixed (Jackman et al, 1996; Nickell, 1997).

When it comes to *flexibility*, employment protection legislation is generally found to have little effect on the level of unemployment (see, however Blanchard, 2000; Gautié, 2002, for qualitative counter-arguments). However, rigid employment protection is found to have a clear impact on the *structure* of unemployment, for example on insider/outsider divisions as reflected in the proportion of long-term unemployment and on precarious jobs for the outsiders (Bertola et al, 1999; OECD, 1999b, p 88; Calmfors and Holmlund, 2000; Esping-Andersen and Regini 2000). Low-employment protection obviously means that employers are less reluctant to hire new workers, but data seem to indicate that, on average, much of what may be gained across countries in 'external flexibility' is lost in 'internal flexibility', if employers have fewer incentives to provide training or alternative tasks for example older workers.

Corporatism is another key factor (at least outside the economic literature) in recent attempts to explain for example the 'Dutch miracle' (Visser and Hemerijck, 1997; Auer, 2000), or the differences between the Netherlands and Austria on the one hand, and Belgium and Germany on the other (Hemerijck and Visser 2000; Hemerijck, Manow and Van Kersbergen, 2000; Hemerijck, Unger and Visser, 2000; see also Bonoli et al, 2000, pp 148-50). In fact, such arguments tend to rest, implicitly, on an alternative economic diagnosis, namely that competitiveness and wage moderation are key problems in a global economy. Wage moderation is exactly the policy goal that corporatism is 'designed' to obtain. This is explicitly acknowledged by Hemerijck et al (2000, p 228), who endorse the interpretation of the Dutch Central Planning Bureau that, "wage moderation has been the single most important weapon in the Dutch adjustment strategy ... *two-thirds of job growth between 1983 to 1996 should be attributed to wage moderation*". They also conclude that:

> ... looking back on twenty-five years of policy adjustment, one is struck by the ongoing importance of wage restraint for maintaining competitiveness.... Apparently there were no alternative policy options in economies exposed to international competition. (Hemerijck, Unger and Visser, 2000, p 252)

From the point of view of the standard interpretation, however, corporatism could be as much part of the problem as part of the solution (van Oorschot, 2000), as it may well involve concessions to the unions (high minimum wages or generous social protection), which make labour markets even less flexible[4]. However, at this point, empirical economic analyses seem in agreement with the policy literature. There seems to be evidence that both strong centralisation of wage formation and strong decentralisation may have positive effects on competitiveness and employment (Nickell, 1997; Calmfors and Holmlund, 2000). In other words, the curve seems to be U-shaped curve. It seems therefore that both the market and sufficiently broad-wage negotiations can lead to wages that are compatible with competitiveness (see also Scharpf, 2000). Still, the hypothetical intervening variable (competitiveness) does not conform too well to the standard interpretation.

As to *activation*, which, along with 'flexicurity' (a more flexible regulation that does not give in on social security), is an attractive alternative to market-oriented reforms among European labour movements, results have not been too convincing. Most, but certainly not all, activation programmes do seem to have measurable effects, but it is highly uncertain whether they would pass a test in terms of cost/effectiveness (Martin, 2000; Larsen, 2002a).

A similar conclusion pertains to *service strategies*, which emphasise the necessity to strengthen the service sector: Employment growth normally takes place in the service sector, but the direction of causality is uncertain (OECD, 2000a, pp 79-128). Growth in service employment could seem to be an 'essential side effect'; that is, it cannot be obtained by goal-directed efforts, but only as a side effect of policies that strengthen the economy more generally.

We will not survey the empirical findings in more detail here. Considering the significant, but seemingly enduring changes in unemployment levels in many countries since the mid-1990s, it is uncertain to what extent the results above, mainly based on evidence from the mid-1980s to the mid-1990s, could even be reproduced. In any case, it is not our aim here to put forward new theories, but rather to point out the considerable uncertainty and the increasing number of anomalies that cast doubt on the standard interpretation. In particular, we question the arguments that are most relevant from a citizenship perspective, namely that social rights – which ensure a high degree of social protection and equality (preconditions of full citizenship) – are becoming counter-productive in a modern, internationally competitive economy[5].

The changing unemployment situation

The discussion about the sustainability takes place in a quite different economic context than it did just a few years ago. In fact. very significant changes have taken place in the level of unemployment in European countries in recent years. By 1994, when OECD published its comprehensive Jobs Study, the contrast between Europe and the US was very sharp. Nearly every European country suffered from high and persistent unemployment, which furthermore appeared to be almost completely structural rather than cyclical. As Table 2.1 shows, Norway, Switzerland and Luxembourg were exceptions, but that could be explained by their special economies (Norway's oil economy, Luxembourg's status as centre of financial capital, Switzerland's use of foreign workers as a buffer, and so on). Even Sweden's much-heralded 'third way' labour market policy had failed: its main effect was to conceal an unemployment that was considerably higher (Sorrentino, 1995, pp 45-6) than the official rates of nearly 10%. Among the EU countries, only Austria and Luxembourg maintained an unemployment rate below that of the US.

By 2002, the aggregate difference between the US and the EU countries persists, but the difference in unemployment rates is down to about two percentage points, and the division is blurred by the success of many small European economies. Europe has become very heterogeneous. In the

Table 2.1: Standardised unemployment rates in Western Europe (1980-2002) (% of labour force)

	1980	1985	1990	1991	1992	1993	1994	1995	1996	1997	1998	1999	2000	2001	May/ June 2002
Portugal	7.7[a]	8.7	4.8	4.2	4.3	5.6	6.9	7.3	7.3	6.8	5.2	4.5	4.1	4.1	4.3
Greece	2.8[a]	7.8[a]	6.4	7.0	7.9	10.5	10.9	10.5	10.6	10.4	9.8	9.0	8.1	7.6	–
Spain	10.5	21.7	16.1	16.2	18.3	22.5	23.9	22.7	22.0	20.6	18.6	15.8	14.0	13.0	(11.4)
Italy	5.6	8.3	8.9	8.5	8.7	10.1	11.0	11.5	11.5	11.6	11.7	11.2	10.4	9.5	9.0
France	5.8	10.1	8.6	9.1	10.0	11.3	11.8	11.4	11.9	11.8	11.4	10.7	9.3	8.6	9.2
Belgium	9.3	10.4	6.6	6.4	7.1	8.6	9.8	9.7	9.5	9.2	9.3	8.6	6.9	6.6	6.8
NL	6.1	8.3	5.9	5.5	5.3	6.2	6.8	6.6	6.0	4.9	3.8	3.2	2.8	2.4	2.6
Luxembourg	0.7[a]	2.9	1.7	1.7	2.1	2.6	3.2	2.9	3.0	2.7	2.7	2.4	2.4	2.4	2.3
Germany	2.6	7.2	4.8	4.2	6.6	7.9	8.4	8.2	8.9	9.9	9.3	8.6	7.9	7.9	8.1
Austria	1.9[a]	3.6[a]	–	–	–	4.0	3.8	3.9	4.4	4.4	4.5	4.0	3.7	3.6	4.1
Denmark	6.9[a]	7.3[a]	7.2	7.9	8.6	9.6	7.7	6.8	6.3	5.3	4.9	4.8	4.4	4.3	4.2
Sweden	2.0	2.9	1.7	3.1	5.6	9.1	9.4	8.8	9.6	9.9	8.3	7.2	5.9	5.1	5.1
Norway	1.7	2.7	5.3	5.6	6.0	6.1	5.5	5.0	4.9	4.1	3.3	3.2	3.5	3.6	3.9
Finland	5.3	6.0	3.2	6.6	11.6	16.4	16.7	15.2	14.5	12.6	11.4	10.2	9.7	9.1	9.3
Ireland	7.3[a]	16.9	13.4	14.7	15.4	15.6	14.3	12.3	11.7	9.9	7.5	5.6	4.2	3.8	4.4
UK	6.2	11.5	6.9	8.6	9.8	10.2	9.4	8.5	8.0	6.9	6.2	5.9	5.4	5.0	5.1
Switzerland	0.2[a]	0.9[a]	–	2.0	3.1	4.0	3.8	3.5	3.9	4.2	3.5	3.0	2.6	–	–
Czech Republic	–	–	–	–	–	4.4	4.4	4.1	3.9	4.8	6.5	8.8	8.9	8.2	–
Slovenia	–	2.2	4.9	7.3	8.0	9.1	9.0	7.4	7.3	7.1	7.7	7.4		–	–
EU15	–	–	–	8.1	9.0	10.5	10.9	10.5	10.6	10.4	9.8	9.0	8.1	7.6	(7.6)
US	7.2	7.2	5.6	6.8	7.5	6.9	6.1	5.6	5.4	4.9	4.5	4.2	4.0	4.8	5.9

[a] Not standardised rates; based on national definitions.

Sources: 1980-89: OECD (1999c); 1990-2001: OECD (2002a); 1999-2002: OECD homepage (www.oecd.org/statistics/news-releases #Standardised Unemployment Rates August 2002). Standardised unemployment rates are based on labour force surveys. They are frequently slightly lower than official figures, due to delineation between employed and unemployed, and between unemployed and inactives (requirement about active job seeking and availability). Today, these figures are largely comparable with the US. For details about comparability, see Sorrentino (2000). For Germany, figures until and including 1991 refer to Western Germany only. For Spain, the OECD homepage figures are substantially lower than those reported in Employment Outlook (for 2001, 13.0 and 10.7 %, respectively). For the EU, deviance is 0.2% in 2001. Otherwise, deviance is negligible, or figures are identical.

Netherlands, Ireland, the UK and Denmark, unemployment rates declined significantly in the second half of the 1990s, and in 2001 even Sweden joined the group with low unemployment rates. To this come the 'special economies' (Norway, Switzerland and Luxembourg) as well as Austria and Portugal, who maintained rather low unemployment rates throughout the 1980s and 1990s, but were more or less forgotten in the overall picture.

This also means that the 'special economies' are not so special anymore. By 2002, Western European countries with unemployment rates around or below 5% in fact outnumber those with high unemployment. Among the small, open economies, only Finland, Greece and, to a lesser extent, Belgium, maintained high unemployment rates by 2002. Some have speculated whether this should be attributed to the fact that these economies are small and open (Ormerud, 1998; Halvorsen, 2000a). It also raises the question about what should be explained – the successes or the failures?

Even though the small countries do not count much in aggregates compared to France, Italy and Germany, the new experience *does* seem to indicate that there are solutions other than those suggested by the 'standard interpretation'. Furthermore, the sudden improvements could seem to question the standard diagnosis of structural unemployment: how could unemployment decline so rapidly in so many countries if it was mainly structural? Have economic, labour market and welfare reforms really had *that* big an impact?

One could of course argue that the apparent successes may only be short-term or cyclical. But first of all, we should not even expect short-term, cyclical improvements to be possible, since increasing inflation would soon reverse them. Second, most of the countries that have recovered seem to have escaped from what for many years looked like impenetrable minimum levels of unemployment.

As an illustration, we have summarised the different pictures of unemployment in Europe by 1996, 1998 and 2001 in Table 2.2. Using the US as our benchmark, we could start by asking which countries have lower unemployment levels than US? By 1996, apart from Luxembourg, this was the case for only three countries: Norway, Switzerland and Austria. Furthermore, according to NAWRU calculations, structural unemployment in nearly all the countries was very close to the actual unemployment figures, leaving little hope of improvement of the unemployment situation, except in the case of major structural reforms. Moreover, in ten of the 16 European countries, the trend in structural unemployment was rising (OECD, 1997a, p 11). However, by March of 2002, six more EU countries had lower unemployment rates than the US (where unemployment had meanwhile increased a little).

To check for unexpected improvements in unemployment among the remaining countries, we have somewhat arbitrarily chosen as criterion for 'unexpected improvement' that unemployment in 2002 should be at least one-third below the calculated structural unemployment (NAWRU) in 1996. Three more countries – Belgium, Finland and Spain – fulfilled that criterion, leaving only four countries that conformed fully to what we would expect from the

1996 NAWRU calculations – Germany, France, Italy and Greece[6]. Here we find persistent high unemployment in accordance with expectations based on the calculations of the structural unemployment rate. In short, 13 countries fully conformed to the expectations from the 'standard interpretation' in 1996; 11 countries in 1998; but only four countries in 2002.

Now, it is possible that, in accordance with the theory of the natural rate of unemployment, improvements are not sustainable. This would be indicated by a high inflation rate in those countries that have seemingly managed to cross the threshold of the structural unemployment rate. As an arbitrary criterion, we have chosen an unemployment rate of 3%. It does turn out that three out of 12 countries with low or unexpected decline in unemployment rates have inflation problems: the Netherlands, Portugal and Ireland. However, this holds true also for one out of four countries that conform to the expectations – Greece.

Of course, these simple calculations only serve as an illustration, but they do demonstrate that the idea that European welfare states were caught in insurmountable problems is far less plausible in 2002 than it was in 1996. In other words, 'unemployability' does not seem as serious a problem as it was previously portrayed.

However, there is still considerable disagreement about the causes – and frequently even about the extent – of successes and failures of many of the individual countries. Some of the improvements may also reflect that structural reform of labour markets and welfare systems has in fact been adopted. In-depth country-specific studies of unemployment and unemployment policies are necessary to provide a more reliable picture of the 'true' unemployment situation and its causes, including intended and unintended effects of welfare systems and of welfare and labour market reforms. Such in-depth studies are also needed to assess the citizenship effects of the employment situation and of welfare reforms.

Employment and labour force participation

Table 2.3 shows the well-known long-term trends of low and stagnating labour force participation in Europe compared to high and increasing rates in the US. In the 1960s, labour force participation was the same across the Atlantic, but from 1970 to 1990, the participation rate increased from 67% to 77% in the US, whereas it remained constant in the EU15. This reflected low participation among women and increasing use of early retirement. However, during the 1990s, the gap between Europe and the US narrowed. This reflects both higher participation among women and a stagnation, or reversal, of early retirement.

Europe has become very heterogeneous, however. In Scandinavia, participation rates had already reached a high in the 1980s and have remained well above the American level. Since the mid-1990s, Denmark, Sweden and Norway have hovered around 80%, whereas Finland has fallen significantly behind. At the peak, Sweden was close to 85%, which may be the maximum obtainable

Table 2.2: Unemployment in European countries, 1996, 1998 and 2002, compared to unemployment in the US and to estimated structural unemployment by 1996 (%)

	Country	Structural unemployment NAWRU estimate 1996	Actual (standardised) unemployment 1996	1998	March 2002	Unemployment March 2002 more than 1/3 below NAWRU 1996	Inflation March 2002 >3%
	US	5.6	5.4	4.7	5.7		
	EU15	–	10.6	9.8	7.5		
Unemployment always below US	Norway	5.1	4.9	3.3	3.9		
	Switzerland	3.1	3.9	3.5	(2.4)[a]		
	Austria	5.4	4.4	4.5	4.0		
US	US	5.6	5.4	4.7	5.7		
Unemployment fallen below US by 2002	Netherlands	6.3	6.0	3.8	2.6	+	+
	Denmark	9.0	6.3	4.9	4.2	+	
	Portugal	5.8	7.3	5.2	4.3		+
	UK	7.0	8.0	6.2	5.1		
	Ireland	12.8	11.7	7.5	4.4	+	+
	Sweden	6.7	9.6	8.3	5.2		
'Unexpected' decline in unemployment	Belgium	10.6	9.5	9.3	6.8	+	
	Finland	15.4	14.5	11.4	9.0	+	
	Spain	20.9	22.0	18.6	(11.3)[b]	+	
Conform fully to expectations	Germany	9.6	8.9	9.3	8.0		
	France	9.7	11.9	11.4	8.0		
	Italy	10.6	11.5	11.7	9.0		
	Greece	8.0	10.6	9.8	(7.6)[b]		+
Predictions confirmed (N)			13	11	4		
Predictions disconfirmed (N)			3	5	12		
Trend in structural unemployment 1996 (N)							
increasing		10					
stable		3					
declining		3					

[a] Figures refer to 2000.

[b] Apparently data break in statistics.

Source: OECD (1997a) *Implementing the OECD jobs strategy*, p 11, Table 2.1 above, and OECD homepage. Calculated structural unemployment rates refer to national statistics whereas the figures for 1996, 1998 and 2002 are standardised unemployment rates. This gives a minor 'optimistic' bias

participation rate in an advanced industrial society. In addition, the liberal welfare systems of the UK and Switzerland had high participation rates – 82% in Switzerland and 76% in the UK. In Continental Europe and in Ireland, by contrast, participation rates declined until the mid-1980s, especially in southern Europe. Interestingly, the transition economies also vary significantly from a 'Mediterranean' level in Hungary to an above-European average in the Czech Republic.

Also, Continental European patterns have been quite uneven since 1985. The Netherlands used to be the 'country of inactivity' par excellence (Van Kersbergen, 1995) but by 2001 it had obtained a participation rate (75.7%) close to the US. In neighbouring Belgium, the figure was only 63.6%. In most other countries (except Ireland), aggregate figures changed slowly. By 2001, Italy still marked the extreme with only 60.7% – 15 percentage points less than the Netherlands. The Netherlands and Finland are examples of increasing divergence *within* welfare/employment regimes. At the same time, we observe some convergence *between* such regimes.

As indicated, trends in aggregate labour force participation reflect different forces:

- higher labour force participation by women;
- lower participation among the young due to higher education;
- lower participation among the elderly due to early retirement;
- lower participation among core age groups due to disability or 'unemployability' (and, to a lesser extent, life-long learning).

Gender and labour force participation

Labour force participation among women took a new direction in the 1960s when Scandinavian figures began to increase[7]. By 1985, Scandinavian women had become almost fully integrated on the labour market (Table 2.4). The liberal welfare regimes of Switzerland, the US, and the UK have followed a nearly similar path, only a little slower, with participation rates between 67.6 and 73.0 % in 2001. For long, the Continental European welfare states were more resistant to change, but since the mid-1980s, when regime differences peaked, there has been an almost uniform increase in female labour force participation, leading to significant convergence. There remains a difference between the Scandinavian level of some 75% and a Continental European level of some 60-65% (but around 50% or less in Italy, Greece and Spain). The Dutch and British figures are a little inflated, as many women work very short hours (inclusion level in the statistic is one hour per week). However, increasing labour force participation among women today looks like a universal and irreversible trend.

This is accompanied by increasing part-time employment, most significantly in the Netherlands where more than 55% of all employed women worked

Table 2.3. Labour force participation rates among population aged 15-64 years (%)

	Total labour force/ population 15-64			Labour force participation rate among 15-64-year-olds							
	1960	1970	1980	1980	1985	1990	1995	1998	1999	2000	2001[d]
Portugal	59.4	67.0	70.5	69.3	70.0	70.9 |	71.6	70.1	70.6	71.1	71.8
Greece	65.8	57.8	55.9	–	60.0	59.1 |	60.1	62.5	62.9	63.0	62.1
Spain[b]	61.6	61.7	57.1	58.9	58.0	60.9 |	61.4 |	64.5	65.3	66.7	65.8
Italy	66.6	59.5	60.8	58.3	58.0	59.5 |	57.3	59.2	59.8	60.3	60.7
France	70.4	67.8	68.5	68.3	66.4	66.0	66.8	67.4	67.8	68.0	68.0
Belgium	60.7	62.0	63.0	–	59.6	58.7 |	62.1	63.2	64.6	65.2	63.6
Luxembourg	61.8	63.2	64.4	–	60.2	60.1 |	60.3	61.9	63.1	64.2	64.2
Netherlands	61.7	59.3	57.7	57.1 |	58.3	66.2 |	69.2	72.6	73.6	74.9	75.7
Germany[a]	70.3	69.5	68.5	67.4 |	65.8	68.4 |	70.5	71.4	71.6	72.2	71.6
Austria	70.7	67.3	64.6	–	–	– |	71.5	71.3	71.6	71.3	70.7
Denmark	71.2	74.9	81.0	–	80.3	82.4 |	79.5	79.3	80.6	80.0	79.2
Sweden[b]	74.3	74.3	81.0	81.7	82.8	84.6 |	79.5	78.1	78.5	78.9	79.3
Norway[b]	64.3	64.1	75.3	73.5	77.1	77.1 |	77.4 |	80.9	80.6	80.7	80.3
Finland	78.0	72.0	76.4	74.2	76.2	76.5	72.3 |	72.4 |	73.6	74.3 |	74.6
Ireland	67.3	65.7	62.3	–	60.5	60.2	61.5 |	64.8	66.3	67.4	67.5
UK[b]	72.0	72.4	74.4	–	75.1	77.8	75.3	75.9	76.3	76.6	74.9
Switzerland	75.5	76.8	74.4	–	–	79.7	80.8	81.0	80.9	80.5	81.2
Czech Republic	–	–	–	–	–	–	72.3	72.2	72.2	71.6	71.1
Slovenia[c]	–	59.7	68.3	–	–	68.0 |	67.9	69.6	68.4		
Hungary	–	–	–	–	–	–	58.9	58.4	59.9	60.2	60.0
Poland	–	–	–	–	–	–	67.4	66.1 |	65.9	65.8	65.7
EU15	68.3	66.3	66.5	64.3 |	67.5	67.4 |	67.4 |	68.6	69.1	69.6 |	69.2
US[b]	66.2	66.8	72.0	72.5	74.4	76.5	76.9	77.4	77.2	77.2	76.8
US-EU difference	–2.1	0.5	5.5	8.2	6.9	9.1	9.5	9.2	8.1	7.6	7.6

| indicates break in series

The figures for EU15 do not include estimates for countries with missing data

[a] Prior to 1992 data refer to Western Germany only.

[b] Refers to persons aged 16 to 64.

[c] Information about 1970 refers to 1971, 1980 refers to 1981, and 1990 to 1991.

[d] The 2001 figures reveal an unexpected drop in several EU countries which may not be reliable.

Sources: 1960-80: OECD (1999c): Historical Statistics 1960-97. 1980 and 1985: OECD (2000c) Labour Force Statistics 1979-99. (1990 same source but updated and quoted from OECD, 2000a, 2002a. For Austria, Belgium, Denmark, Greece, Luxembourg and the Netherlands the figures are derived from European Labour Force Survey . The Slovenian figures for this chapter are based on national labour force statistics and were provided by Professor Ivan Svetlik, University of Ljubljana.

Table 2.4: Female labour force as a percentage of female population aged 15-64 (%)

	Labour force/population 15-64			Labour force participation rate among 15-64-year-olds								Part-time (%)	
	1960	1970	1980	1980	1985	1990	1995	1998	1999	2000	2001	1990	2001
Portugal	19.9	32.0	54.3	52.4	56.4	59.6	59.9	62.0	62.8	63.7	64.6	11.8	14.3
Greece	41.6	31.9	33.0	–	41.0	42.6	44.3	48.5	49.7	49.7	48.8	11.5	8.5
Spain[b]	26.0	28.4	32.2	32.8	34.2	41.8	46.2	49.9	50.9	52.9	51.6	11.5	16.8
Italy	38.7	32.9	39.1	38.4	39.9	44.0	42.5	44.6	45.5	46.3	47.3	18.2	23.7
France	46.6	48.5	54.4	55.1	55.5	57.2	59.8	60.8	61.4	61.7	61.8	21.7	23.8
Belgium	36.4	39.8	47.0	–	45.1	46.1	51.7	53.8	56.0	56.6	54.5	29.8	33.4
Luxembourg	32.6	33.8	39.9	–	41.4	42.4	44.1	47.6	50.2	51.7	52.0	19.1	29.9
Netherlands	26.2	28.0	35.5	36.1	40.9	52.4	58.3	62.5	64.4	65.7	66.9	52.5	58.1
Germany[a]	49.2	48.0	52.8	51.9	51.3	55.5	61.1	62.5	62.6	63.2	63.8	29.8	33.9
Austria	52.1	49.9	48.7	–	–	–	62.3	62.5	62.7	62.5	62.3	–	24.8
Denmark	43.5	58.0	71.4	–	74.6	77.6	73.3	75.1	76.1	75.9	75.0	29.6	20.8
Sweden[b]	50.1	59.4	74.1	75.3	79.4	82.5	77.2	75.5	76.0	76.4	77.1	24.5	21.4[c]
Norway[b]	36.3	38.8	62.3	62.2	67.8	70.7	72.1	76.1	76.1	76.5	76.4	39.8	32.6
Finland	65.6	61.3	70.1	69.4	73.2	73.5	69.5	69.7	71.2	72.1	72.5	10.6	14.0
Ireland	34.8	34.3	36.3	–	39.7	42.6	47.0	52.1	54.3	55.7	56.0	20.5	33.0
UK	46.1	50.7	58.3	–	62.2	67.3	67.1	67.9	68.4	68.9	67.6	39.5	40.8
Switzerland	51.0	52.3	54.1	–	–	68.2	71.1	71.8	72.2	71.6	73.0	42.6	44.7
Czech Republic	–	–	–	–	–	–	64.1	64.0	64.1	63.7	63.2	–	5.4
Slovenia	–	50.5	60.9	–	–	65.3	62.5	65.4	63.8			–	7.8
Hungary	–	–	–	–	–	–	50.3	50.8	52.3	52.7	52.4	–	4.0
Poland	–	–	–	–	–	–	61.0	59.7	59.8	59.9	59.9	–	16.6
Total EU15	42.0	42.5	48.7	47.9	50.4	54.8	56.9	58.7	59.4	60.1	60.1	27.0	30.0[c]
US[b]	42.6	48.9	59.7	59.9	64.1	67.8	69.7	70.7	70.7	70.8	70.5	20.0	18.2
US-EU difference	0.6	6.4	11.0	12.0	13.7	13.0	12.8	12.0	11.3	10.7	10.4	7.0	11.8

Notes and sources: as Table 2.3.

[c] Refers to 2000 because of sudden changes in figures 2000-01 which are either wrong or reflect major changes in measurement (the figure for Sweden jumped from 21.4 % to 29.3 % from 2000 to 2001. For the EU, data indicate a sudden decline from 30.0 to 25.2 % part time workers. Obviously, these figures are misleading).

Part-time employment is defined as *normally* working less than 30 hours per week in *main* job (as declared by interview person), calculated as percentage of all persons who answer the question about normal working hours. For Finland and Poland, data are based on actual hours. For Switzerland it is based on hours worked in all jobs.

part-time by 2001. In the Mediterranean countries and in France, part-time employment remains below 25%, compared to 40% or more in the UK and in Switzerland. However, higher part-time employment among women is *not* a universal phenomenon. In Denmark, Norway and Sweden (where part-time employment on a massive scale was first introduced), it has declined significantly – in Denmark from 29.6% in 1990 to 20.8 % in 2001[8]. Even the US shows a decline, from 20% to 18.2 %. This indicates that part-time employment could only be a first step towards full labour market integration, but it remains to be seen whether the new one-and-a-half breadwinner families in Europe will eventually become two-breadwinner families.

Among men, we observe a universal long-term decline in labour force participation, due to longer education and earlier retirement (Table 2.5). Still, there is a significant difference – in 1960, American figures were below Europe, but since 1975, participation rates in US have remained almost constant (some 84%) whereas the EU average dropped from 86.8% to only 78.4%. However, trends in Europe are diverging and have become less regime-specific, and all liberal welfare states have maintained high participation rates.

Among the Continental European countries, however, the Netherlands is an exception. From 1985 to 2001, male participation rates went up by nearly nine percentage points to 84.2%; that is, a little above even the Scandinavian and the American level. Austria and Germany maintained participation rates around 80% whereas France, Belgium and Italy fell below 75%. Towards the end of the 1990s, however, the declining participation trend culminated or reversed in almost all countries; it is uncertain whether the 'deviant' 2001 figures reflect yet another reversal or (more likely) changes in measurement.

How much work is involved?

From an economic perspective, a high incidence of part-time employment modifies the picture of some European 'job miracles'. With great caution (the OECD explicitly warns against comparisons, but differences are very significant), we compare the total amount of work per capita across European countries by multiplying employment rates with average working hours per employed (for measurement and comparability problems, see OECD, 2002a, p 321). Not surprisingly, Italy comes out as the country with the lowest level of paid labour – an estimate of some 882 hours per capita (15-64 years) in 2001 (Table 2.6). Belgium follows closely, and in France the estimate is 950 hours. Due to longer working hours, Spain and Greece are above this level, whereas the Netherlands, in spite of high labour force participation rates, remains close to Germany. Therefore, increasing participation rates only mean that the Netherlands has caught up with Germany, from a very low position.

As expected, the work effort is higher in Scandinavia than in the Continental European welfare states. The Swedish estimate in 2001 is about 1,200 hours, slightly higher than Denmark and Finland, and significantly higher than Norway (which is catching up but still remains the lowest in Scandinavia, despite high

Table 2.5: Male labour force as a percentage of male population aged 15-64 years

	Total labour force/ population 15-64			Labour force participation among 15-64-year-olds							
	1960	1970	1980	1980	1985	1990	1995	1998	1999	2000	2001
Portugal	104.4	106.9	87.7	87.1	84.2	82.8	77.3	78.6	78.7	78.9	79.4
Greece	91.8	85.1	79.6	–	80.5	76.8	77.2	77.1	76.9	77.1	76.2
Spain[b]	99.5	96.4	82.3	85.5	81.3	80.4	76.8	79.1	79.6	80.4	79.8
Italy	93.0	85.3	81.7	79.0	76.3	75.1	72.4	73.9	74.1	74.3	74.2
France	94.6	86.9	81.7	81.5	77.3	75.0	73.9	74.1	74.4	74.4	74.3
Belgium	85.5	84.4	78.9	–	74.2	71.3	72.3	72.5	73.0	73.8	72.7
Luxembourg	91.3	92.9	83.7	–	79.2	77.4	75.9	76.0	75.7	76.4	76.1
Netherlands	97.8	90.2	79.4	77.6	75.3	79.7	79.9	82.4	82.6	83.9	84.2
Germany[a]	94.4	92.6	84.3	83.2	80.4	79.0	79.5	79.9	80.3	81.1	79.3
Austria	92.0	86.5	81.3	–	–	–	80.8	80.2	80.5	80.1	79.0
Denmark	99.5	91.8	89.0	–	86.0	87.1	85.6	83.5	85.0	84.0	83.3
Sweden[b]	98.5	88.8	87.8	87.9	86.[illegible]	86.7	81.7	80.7	80.9	81.2	81.4
Norway[b]	92.2	89.0	88.0	84.3	86.[illegible]	83.4	82.4	85.6	85.0	84.8	84.0
Finland	91.4	83.2	82.8	79.3	79.[illegible]	79.6	75.0	75.1	75.9	76.4	76.7
Ireland	99.0	96.4	87.6	–	80.[illegible]	77.5	75.8	77.4	78.3	79.1	79.0
UK[b]	99.1	94.4	90.5	–	88.[illegible]	88.3	84.7	83.9	84.1	84.3	82.2
Switzerland	100.4	101.2	94.5	–	–	91.1	90.1	90.1	89.6	89.4	89.2
Czech Republic	–	–	–	–	–	–	80.6	80.3	80.2	79.4	79.0
Slovenia	–	69.5	75.9	–	–	70.2	73.5	73.7	72.9		
EU15	95.7	90.6	84.0	83.5	80.[illegible]	79.9	77.8	78.4	78.7	79.1	78.3
US[b]	90.5	85.4	84.7	85.8	85.[illegible]	85.6	84.3	84.2	84.0	83.9	83.4

Sources and notes as Table 2.3

Table 2.6: Employment rates, annual hours per employed, and estimated annual hours per capita in15-64 age group (2001)

	Employment ratio 15-64 (2001)	Working hours per employed (2001)	Estimated average working hours per capita 15-64		% of US (2001)
			1990	2001	
Greece	55.6	1,921	1,048	1,068	80
Spain	58.8	1,816	–	1,068	80
Italy	54.9	1,606	881	882	66
France	62.0	1,532	993	950	71
Belgium	59.7	1,528	913	912	69
Netherlands	74.1	1,346	888	997	75
Germany	65.9	1,467	1,062	967	73
Denmark	75.9	1,482	1,125	1,125	85
Sweden	75.3	1,603	1,287	1,207	91
Norway	77.5	1,364	1,047	1,057	79
Finland[a]	67.7	1,694	1,306	1,147	86
Ireland	65.0	1,674	–	1,088	82
Switzerland[a]	79.1	1,568	–	1,240	93
UK	71.3	1,711	1,281	1,220	92
US	73.1	1,821	1,317	1,331	100

[a] Finland: Labour Force Survey; Switzerland: 2000.

Source: Calculated on the basis of OECD (2002) figures on annual hours and employment rates among 15-64 year-olds. Note that the information in this table should be read with great precaution as measurement differs much from country to country. However, the country differences are so significant that the main trends are reliable, and comparability over time is fairly good.

Norwegian participation rates). Scandinavia is close to the high workload in the liberal welfare states of the UK and Switzerland. Not surprisingly, the US tops the chart with an estimate of 1,331 hours. Despite large problems of comparability, these figures do summarise a major difference between Europe and the US, demonstrating that the work-generating capacity of the American economy is more than an illusion. Whether this should be considered an advantage, however, is more questionable. From a social perspective, one becomes concerned about what is left for civil society, and from an economic perspective, the waste of labour in low-productive jobs deserves attention.

Age and labour force participation

The other sources of changing aggregate participation rates are shorter working-age due to education (including 'life-long learning') and early retirement, alongside higher rates of 'unemployability'. Among women, such changes are blurred by generational changes in labour force participation[9]. To decipher the underlying trends, our focus henceforth shall be men.

As Table 2.7 illustrates, it is labour force participation among the young and the elderly that distinguishes Europe from the US. Among prime-age men (25-54), European figures are about the same as in the US, if not slightly higher. Among the 60-64 year-olds, on the other hand, American participation rates are much higher than in the EU15. Early retirement is especially pronounced in Continental Europe. Among the 60- to 64-year-olds, figures are lowest in France, Austria, Belgium and the Netherlands (from 13% to 23%). Despite great and partly successful efforts to prevent early retirement, the Dutch figure (26%) remains below the German figure (30%). In Norway, by contrast, the corresponding figure was as high as 59%, above even the US (57%). In the UK and Denmark, figures were 51% and 44%, respectively.

However, regime divisions are somewhat blurred southern European participation rates among elderly workers are typically above the EU average, whereas Finland has approached the Continental European pattern with only 30% of the 60-64 year-olds in the labour force. Finnish figures are also low (but rapidly increasing) among the 55-59 year-olds (70%), although far above Belgium (53%). Germany and the Netherlands have converged, and both countries are now close to the EU average of 72%. In Denmark and Norway, by contrast, figures for this age range remain above 80%.

Participation rates among the young are equally different. First and foremost, this reflects differences in propensity among students to have a second job[10]. In some of the countries with high aggregate participation rates (especially Denmark, the Netherlands, Norway, the UK and the US), these figures are very high. Consequently, aggregate participation rates may be quite misleading. For instance, Denmark has the highest aggregate participation rate in the EU for men, but among prime-age men, Denmark is below the EU average[11].

To conclude, labour force participation among prime-age men is roughly the same in Europe and the US, female participation rates and second jobs

Table 2.7: Labour force participation among men (1983 and 2001) (by age group)

	15-19[a]		20-24		25-34		35-44		45-54		55-59		60-64	
	1983	2001	1983	2001	1983	2001	1983	2001	1983	2001	1983	2001	1983	2001
Portugal	66.2	30.6	88.8	71.9	96.5	92.5	96.0	95.0	90.4	90.8	76.9	72.1	62.7	54.9
Greece	31.8	14.1	76.7	63.0	96.5	94.0	97.3	96.9	91.8	91.2	78.7	73.3	59.8	43.1
Spain	51.5	32.1	82.9	66.1	95.4	91.1	96.4	93.8	91.8	89.8	81.7	74.2	58.9	46.1
Italy[b]	30.6	19.8	73.8	62.1	91.6	81.0	98.2	94.4	97.1	95.2	82.0	70.2	36.8	31.0
France	22.5	11.0	79.7	56.1	96.5	93.8	97.8	95.8	93.7	92.5	71.0	66.8	33.7	15.6
Belgium	19.8	11.3	72.8	62.3	96.0	92.1	96.5	93.6	90.3	86.7	65.0	52.5	28.6	19.9
Netherlands	28.4	61.5	76.3	81.8	94.6	94.2	93.5	94.7	86.9	91.0	69.2	73.3	37.4	26.4
Germany	44.3	36.0	78.2	78.5	89.4	92.6	98.3	96.5	95.5	93.4	81.4	72.9	40.3	29.7
Austria[c]	–	48.0	–	74.9	–	91.7	–	96.2	–	90.9	–	62.8	–	17.3
Denmark	52.2	52.4	86.9	85.6	94.4	91.3	95.6	92.9	91.9	90.0	83.8	82.1	50.1	43.8
Sweden[d]	47.7	33.3	84.4	70.6	94.4	89.7	96.3	91.6	94.4	90.4	–		–	
Norway	49.3	49.5	82.1	76.8	91.6	91.7	98.2	92.3	96.4	90.0	84.0	83.5	76.8	59.4
Finland	39.7	29.4	81.9	71.1	95.0	92.2	95.8	93.5	88.2	87.7	64.2	69.5	41.1	29.8
Ireland[e]	43.1	32.3	89.4	78.0	97.1	93.3	96.4	93.9	92.2	87.5	–		–	
UK[f]	71.6	62.3	90.2	80.1	95.8	93.2	96.5	92.5	93.5	87.9	82.8	75.5	57.5	51.2
Slovenia[g]	–	10.3	–	63.5	–	94.0	–	93.5	–	87.4	–	47.3	–	23.8
EU15[h]	42.8	33.5	80.8	70.8	93.9	91.7	97.1	95.5	93.7	92.2	78.5	71.9	44.8	33.8
US	56.2	50.7	84.8	81.5	94.2	92.7	95.3	92.5	91.2	88.5	81.9	77.3	57.0	56.5
US-EU difference	13.4	17.2	4.0	10.7	0.3	1.0	-1.8	-3.0	-2.5	-3.7	3.4	5.4	12.2	22.7

[a] For Spain, Sweden, Norway, UK and US this age category is 16 to 19.

[b] Age categories are: 15-19; 20-24; 25-29; 30-39; 40-49; 50-59; 60-64.

[c] Figures for 2001 refer to 2000.

[d] Age categories 55-59 and 60-64 collapsed. In 1983, participation rate for 55-64 year old was 77.0, in 2001 it was 73.5.

[e] Same as Sweden for 55-64 years old. Figures for 1983 and 2001 are 78.0 and 66.1, respectively.

[f] Figures for 1983 refers to 1984.

[g] Figures for 2001 refer to 1999.

[h] Own calculation of weighted EU average (1998 age distribution of population as weight). Not including countries with missing data.

Source: OECD (2002b)

among students are much higher in the US, whereas early retirement is much rarer. As annual working hours are also higher in the US, the amount of work is substantially greater than any European country. However, Europe is heterogeneous – in the liberal welfare states of the UK and Switzerland, and in Scandinavia (with the exception of Finland), participation rates are at least as high as in the US. Only average annual working hours are much lower.

As female participation rates are rapidly increasing in the Continental European welfare states, and as the rising trend in early retirement in most countries is coming to an end, we may envisage a regime convergence in Europe, and to some extent between Europe and the US. Still, the total workload in the US is markedly higher than in Europe.

Level and structure of unemployment

Although low participation rates may undermine the sustainability of the welfare state, it is high and persistent unemployment that has been Europe's main problem.

According to the 'standard interpretation', we should expect less long-term unemployment, less youth unemployment, and less unemployment among the unskilled in the US, as compared to Europe. Among European welfare states, we should expect similar differences between the liberal welfare states on the one hand and the universalist and corporatist welfare states on the other.

Prime-age men

For reasons that once seemed obvious, prime-age men were traditionally the main target of social protection in Continental Europe, since unemployment for this group had the most far-reaching social consequences. Furthermore, this is the group that most easily lends itself to international comparison (Buchele and Christiansen, 1999).

'Prime age' is usually defined as age 25-54, but due to postponed and higher education, age 30-54 or even 35-54 seems more appropriate today. It turns out that European unemployment figures for this group are relatively low (Table 2.8). Still, this represents a significant increase for some of the Mediterranean countries. In Italy, unemployment among the 30- to 49-year-olds[12] was only some 3% in 1991 due to employment office priorities (Ferrera and Gualmini, 2000), and even in Spain, figures were quite moderate, due to unusually high job protection (Moreno, 2000). By 1991, unemployment among 35- to 54-year-old men was higher in the US than in Europe, with the exception of a few countries with very liberal employment protection legislation such as the UK and Denmark. Job protection of prime age men deteriorated in Europe in the 1990s, but by 2001, unemployment in countries like Spain and Italy were again below European average for the 35- to 54-year-olds.

It is well known that there are problems in comparing unemployment rates across countries. For instance, 'discouraged workers', or people in activation

Table 2.8: Unemployment rates by age, men only (1991 and 2001) (percentages of labour force)

	20-24		25-34		35-44		45-54		55-59	
	1991	2001	1991	2001	1991	2001	1991	2001	1991	2001
Portugal	5.6	6.3	3.1	3.0	1.7	2.3	1.2	2.5	2.7	3.9
Greece	16.6	19.9	6.1	9.1	2.6	3.8	2.1	3.5	1.8	4.8
Spain	22.7	14.3	13.3	8.4	7.5	5.2	7.5	4.8	9.6	5.9
Italy[b]	24.4	21.7	11.5	12.9	4.0	5.9	2.0	3.4	2.3	3.5
France	15.6	15.8	7.7	8.2	5.0	5.6	5.2	5.2	6.3	6.1
Belgium	9.7	14.5	5.1	6.6	3.2	4.4	3.2	3.5	2.5	4.3
Netherlands[a]	10.1	3.8	4.7	1.6	3.7	1.5	4.1	1.7	4.9	1.5
Germany	5.1	10.1	4.5	7.0	3.9	6.9	4.0	8.0	6.7	11.3
Austria[c]	4.5	4.5	3.4	2.7	2.5	2.4	3.2	3.3	6.0	4.6
Denmark	14.2	6.9	9.4	2.8	7.2	2.9	7.1	3.0	9.9	4.8
Sweden[d]	7.6	10.8	4.5	4.8	2.3	4.5	1.7	3.8	2.2	
Norway	11.7	7.5	6.6	3.9	3.7	2.6	3.1	1.4	2.9	1.7
Finland	16.0	15.3	7.5	7.5	6.2	6.1	5.6	7.1	6.7	10.3
Ireland[e]	21.1	5.3	15.1	3.9	13.1	2.9	11.2	3.4	8.2	
UK	15.0	9.5	9.2	4.7	6.7	4.0	6.3	3.5	8.4	3.9
Czech Republic[g]	–	12.8	–	6.4	–	5.5	–	5.6	–	4.7
Slovenia[g]	–	17.8	–	6.8	–	5.6	–	6.2	–	7.3
EU15[i]	14.3	13.0	8.0	7.4	4.9	5.2	4.5	4.8	6.0	6.1
US	11.6	8.9	7.0	4.3	5.5	3.6	4.8	3.2	5.0	3.2
EU-US difference	2.7	4.1	1.0	3.1	-0.6	1.6	-0.3	1.6	1.0	2.9

[a] Age categories are 15-24, 25-29, 30-39, 40- 49, 50-59, 60-64.

[b-g] See footnotes to Table 2.7. For the 55-64-year-olds in Sweden in 1991 and 2001, unemployment was 2.2% and 5.4 %, respectively. For Ireland, corresponding figures are 8.2 and 2.7%.

Source: OECD (2002b)

who fail to look actively for a job, are not counted as members of the labour force; the same goes for prison inmates, who constitute a significant proportion of prime-age men in the US (Buchele and Christiansen, 1999) report an incarceration ratio of 1.7%). To handle such problems, the US Bureau of Labour has developed a series of more or less inclusive definitions of unemployment (Sorrentino, 1993, 1995). Even though it will be undermined in the long run by life-long learning, the best method when it comes to prime-age men is often to use the most comprehensive definition of unemployment simply as non-employment, especially in comparisons between the US and Europe[13]. As a consequence of high labour force participation and protection against unemployment, employment rates among prime-age men used to be higher in Europe than in the US (Table 2.9). In other words, the one-breadwinner and family-oriented Continental European welfare states in fact were superior in fulfilling what was once their main rationale: to secure employment for prime-age men. This deteriorated in the 1990s (data not presented), but most recently, Europe has again taken the lead among the 35- to 54-year-olds.

Table 2.9: Employment rates by age, men only (1991 and 2001) (percentages of population)

	20-24		25-34		35-44		45-54	
	1991	2001	1991	2001	1991	2001	1991	2001
Portugal	76.7	67.4	92.2	89.7	95.2	92.8	89.3	88.5
Greece	57.0	50.5	88.6	85.4	94.0	93.2	88.1	88.0
Spain	58.2	56.6	81.7	83.4	89.1	88.9	84.5	85.5
Italy	52.5	48.6	79.2	70.6	93.2	88.8	94.3	92.0
France	52.4	47.2	88.1	86.1	92.2	90.4	88.0	87.7
Belgium	57.3	53.3	90.0	86.0	92.0	89.5	83.7	83.7
Netherlands	69.2	79.8	90.8	93.0	91.7	93.0	85.2	88.7
Germany	74.9	70.6	87.5	86.1	93.4	89.8	90.7	85.9
Austria	–	71.5	–	89.2	–	93.9	–	87.9
Denmark	72.5	79.7	85.0	88.7	88.2	90.2	87.3	87.3
Sweden	75.9	63.0	88.4	85.4	93.4	87.5	92.6	87.0
Norway	65.7	71.0	84.0	88.1	90.5	89.9	87.6	88.7
Finland	58.1	60.2	86.0	85.3	88.2	87.8	82.5	81.5
Ireland	62.6	73.9	79.6	89.7	80.7	91.2	78.4	84.5
UK	75.1	72.5	87.0	88.8	89.2	88.8	85.7	84.8
Czech Republic	–	68.8	–	90.4	–	91.2	–	87.2
Slovenia	–	52.2	–	87.6	–	88.2	–	82.0
EU15	64.4	61.6	85.8	84.9	91.7	90.5	88.6	87.8
US	73.8	74.2	87.0	88.7	88.9	89.2	86.2	85.7
US-EU difference	9.4	12.6	1.2	3.8	–2.8	–1.3	–2.4	–2.1

Source: Calculated from Table 2.7 and 2.8 above and OECD (2002b) Labour Force Statistics 1981-2001

Gender variations

What is gained in employment protection for prime age men is usually lost for women and for the young. Unemployment figures for Europe reveal a strong gender bias, especially in southern Europe and in France and Belgium, where unemployment among women has frequently been twice as high as among men (Table 2.10). However, these biases are declining, and in Germany, Austria and the Netherlands, gender differences are more moderate. In Scandinavia, a systematic gender bias is only found in Denmark. In the UK, women's unemployment is systematically lower than that of men. Most of these cross-country differences were already visible in the 1960s. On average, the ratio between female and male unemployment in the EU declined from 1.7 to 1.3 from 1990 to 2001.

Long-term unemployment

From a citizenship perspective, the most interesting aspect of unemployment is long-term rather than aggregate unemployment. Also, from an economic perspective on structural unemployment, the incidence of long-term unemployment is a core parameter, and the low incidence of long-term unemployment in the US has been a key argument in favour of market-oriented

Table 2.10: Standardised unemployment rates for men and women (%)

	1982		1990		2001		ratio w/m		
	men	women	men	women	men	women	1982	1990	2001
Portugal	2.9[a]	12.2[a]	3.3	6.2	3.4	5.4	4.2[a]	1.9	1.6
Greece	–	–	4.4[a]	12.0[a]	6.9	15.6	2.7[a]	2.2[a]	2.3
Spain	13.5	18.2	11.9	24.2	7.5	15.3	1.4	2.0	2.0
Italy	4.5	10.2	6.4	13.7	7.4	13.1	2.3	2.1	1.8
France	5.8	10.3	6.8	11.9	7.1	10.8	1.8	1.8	1.5
Belgium	6.6	16.0	4.1	10.7	5.7	6.9	2.4	2.6	1.2
Netherlands	6.9	10.3	4.3	9.1	1.8	2.5	1.5	2.1	1.4
Germany	5.9[a]	7.4[a]	4.0[a]	5.9[a]	7.9	8.2	1.3[a]	1.5[a]	1.0
Austria	–	–	–	–	4.0	4.1	–	–	1.0
Denmark	8.0	8.8	7.0	8.4	3.7	4.8	1.1	1.2	1.3
Sweden	3.2	3.4	1.7	1.7	5.4	4.7	1.1	1.0	0.9
Norway	2.4	3.0	5.8	4.8	3.6	3.4	1.3	0.8	0.9
Finland	5.6[a]	5.3[a]	3.6	2.7	8.7	9.7	0.9[a]	0.8	1.1
Ireland	11.0	12.4	12.9	14.6	3.9	3.5	1.1	1.1	0.9
UK	11.3	8.9	7.4	6.6	5.3	4.2	0.8	0.9	0.8
Switzerland	–	–	–	–	1.8	3.5	–	–	1.9
Czech Republic	–	–	–	–	6.8	9.9	–	–	1.5
Slovenia[b]	2.0	2.4	5.0	4.7	7.2	7.6	1.2	0.9	1.1
EU15	7.4	10.4	6.4	10.8	6.5	8.7	1.4	1.7	1.3
US	9.9	9.4	5.7	5.5	4.9	4.7	1.0	1.0	1.0

[a] Unstandardised figures.

[b] For Slovenia, 2001 figures refer to 1999.

Source: OECD (1999, 2000, pp vi, 3, 142, 147, 2002a). Supplemented by unstandardised figures from OECD (2000c)

reforms. Measuring long-term unemployment in activation-oriented countries is an increasingly difficult task, as people in active labour market programmes may disappear from the unemployment statistics. With this reservation in mind, let us look at the figures in Table 2.11.

It is a conventional finding that employment protection legislation (EPL) does not affect aggregate unemployment, but tends to create more insider/outsider division and, hence, higher proportions of long-term unemployed (see, for example, Bertola et al, 1999; OECD 1999b, pp 47-132; Calmfors and Holmlund 2000)[14]. Basically, that is confirmed by the simple cross-country comparison here.

There is a striking difference between Europe and the US, as nearly one-half of the unemployed in Europe have been unemployed for at least one year, and nearly two-thirds for more than six months. In the US, corresponding figures are very small, and as aggregate unemployment is also lower, the figures for long-term unemployed as a proportion of the labour force really exhibit large differences – 0.2% in the US versus 3.9% in the EU by 2000 (if we take 12 months of unemployment as our basis of comparison).

Table 2.11: Long-term unemployment (LTU) as percentage of total unemployment, and as percentage of the labour force[a, b]

	1990		1996		2000		2000
	6 months and over	12 months and over	6 months and over	12 months and over	6 months and over	12 months and over	LTU (12 months) as % of labour force
Portugal	62.4	44.8 |	66.7	53.1 |	60.0	42.9	1.7
Greece	71.9	49.8 |	74.7	56.7	73.6	56.5	6.3
Spain	70.2	54.0	72.2	55.7	64.8	47.6	6.6
Italy	85.2	69.8 |	80.8	65.6	75.3	60.8	6.4
France	55.5	38.0	61.5	39.5	61.9	42.5	4.1
Belgium	81.4	68.7 |	77.3	61.3	71.8	56.3	5.7
Netherlands	63.6	49.3 |	81.8	50.0	46.5	32.7	1.0
Germany	64.7	46.8 |	65.3	47.8	67.6	51.5	4.2
Austria	–	–	42.5	25.6	43.8	28.4	1.0
Denmark	53.2	29.9 |	44.4	26.5	38.1	20.0	0.9
Sweden	22.2	12.1 |	48.4	30.1	41.5	26.4	1.5
Norway	40.8	20.4 |	31.1	6.0	16.3	5.0	0.2
Finland	32.6	9.2	55.5	34.5 |	46.5	29.0	2.8
Ireland	81.0	66.0 |	75.7	59.5	76.1	55.3	2.4
UK	50.3	34.4 |	58.1	39.8	43.2	28.0	1.5
Switzerland	26.2	16.4	52.1	25.0	46.6	29.1	0.8
Czech Republic	–	–	52.3	31.3	61.9	37.1	3.2
Slovenia	–	37.4	71.5	52.4	73.6	56.7	4.2
EU15	65.3	48.6 |	67.4	49.3 |	63.1	46.6	3.9
US	10.0	5.5	17.5	9.5	11.4	6.0	0.2

| Indicates break in series.

Notes:

[a] Questionnaire wording and design, survey timing, differences across countries in the age groups covered, and other reasons mean that care is required in interpreting cross-country differences in levels. Persons for whom no duration of employment was specified are excluded. See OECD (2000, Table G, p 220).

[b] Data refers to persons aged 15 and over; for Spain, UK and the US 16 and over; Finland 15-64; Sweden 16-64; Norway 16-74. For Ireland, 1990 refers to 1991; for Czech Republic and Slovenia, 2000 refers to 1999.

Source: OECD (2000a, 2001a) and own calculations on the basis of unstandardised unemployment rates

However, long-term unemployment mainly characterises the Continental European – especially the Mediterranean – welfare states, where the proportion by 2000 varied between 6% and 7% of the labour force. In France, Belgium, and Germany, the proportion was 4-5%. In Scandinavia and in the UK, on the other hand, figures are low. Even in Finland, only 2.8% of the labour force was long-term unemployed by 2000, and Norway matches the extremely low American figures.

As was already mentioned earlier, the lower incidence of long-term unemployment in the US is nearly always quoted in favour of the standard interpretation of Europe's unemployment problems. However, even though our data do not contradict this, and even though they also confirm that high employment protection generates insider/outsider problems and long-term unemployment, we also find some reservations to such interpretations.

- Several European countries, even though they cannot match the US figures, do not suffer from really serious long-term unemployment problems.
- Among the Scandinavian countries, only Denmark has a very liberal employment protection (as liberal as the UK). Nevertheless, the (absolute or relative) incidence of long-term unemployment in the other Nordic countries is pretty low – in Norway even slightly lower than in the US.
- Even though long-term unemployment is a problem especially in the Continental European welfare states, the figures for Austria and the Netherlands demonstrate that even these welfare states are able to obtain (or maintain) low long-term unemployment rates.

In short, even though the data on long-term unemployment still lend support to the standard interpretation, they are also open to other interpretations. This holds true even more for the other implications of the standard interpretation which are rarely tested.

Age structure of unemployment

From the perspective of the standard interpretation, one would expect that both employment protection legislation and compressed wage structures should have highly adverse effects on youth unemployment. And, as Table 2.12 illustrates, youth unemployment is certainly a problem in the EU: average unemployment among young people under 25 years-of-age is more than twice as high as prime-age unemployment. Among men, the ratio was 2.4 by 2001. In absolute terms, youth unemployment is highest in Continental Europe. In Italy, the figures were between 26% and 34% in the 1990s – three to four times prime-age unemployment. In Spain, youth unemployment reached 45% by 1994 and remained above 30% until 1998. France and Belgium also experienced very high youth unemployment, which varied between 25% and 28% in France, and between 20% and 23% in Belgium in the second half of the 1990s.

However, in 2001, even though these figures remain high, they have been

Table 2.12: Unemployment rates among population under 25 (%), and ratio between youth and prime age (25-54-years-old) unemployment

	1990	1995	1996	1997	1998	1999	2001	Youth/ prime age 1990	Youth/ prime age 2001	Men only 2001
Portugal	9.6	16.0	16.3	14.6	10.2	8.7	9.2	2.5	2.6	2.8
Greece	23.3	27.9	31.2	31.0	29.7	–	28.0	4.6	3.2	3.8
Spain	30.1	40.3	39.8	37.1	34.1	28.5	20.8	2.3	2.2	2.6
Italy	28.9	32.8	34.1	33.6	33.8	32.9	27.0	4.4	3.6	4.1
France	19.1	25.9	26.3	28.1	25.4	26.6	18.7	2.4	2.3	2.6
Belgium	14.5	21.5	20.5	21.3	20.4	22.6	15.3	2.2	2.8	3.0
Netherlands	11.1	12.8	11.4	9.7	8.8	7.4	4.4	1.5	2.6	3.0
Germany	5.6	8.5	9.3	10.2	9.1	8.5	8.4	1.0	1.1	1.2
Austria	–	5.9	6.9	7.6	7.5	5.9	6.0	–	1.7	1.8
Denmark	11.5	9.9	10.6	8.1	7.2	10.0	8.3	1.5	2.4	2.5
Sweden	4.5	20.6	22.5	22.5	16.8	14.2	11.8	3.5	2.9	2.9
Norway	11.8	11.9	12.4	10.6	9.1	9.6	10.5	2.8	4.0	3.9
Finland	9.4	26.9	27.9	25.3	23.8	21.5	19.9	4.5	2.7	2.8
Ireland	17.6	19.9	18.2	16.1	11.5	8.5	6.2	1.4	1.9	1.9
UK	10.1	15.3	14.7	13.5	12.3	12.3	10.5	1.7	2.7	2.9
Switzerland	3.2	5.5	4.7	6.0	5.8	5.6	5.6	2.0	2.7	5.8
Czech Republic	–	7.9	7.2	8.6	12.4	17.0	16.6	–	2.3	1.9
Slovenia	16.0	18.8	18.8	18.5	19.2	19.7	–	3.3	3.2	3.2
EU15	15.8	20.8	21.0	20.5	18.7	17.2	13.9	2.3	2.1	2.4
US	11.2	12.1	12.0	11.3	10.4	9.9	10.6	2.4	2.8	3.1

Source: OECD (1999, 2000)

reduced quite significantly – 15% in Belgium, 27% in Italy. More surprisingly, high levels were encountered also in Sweden and Finland during the crisis in the 1990s, when youth unemployment peaked at 22% and 28% respectively. Even by 2001, the figures remain pretty high, and in all Scandinavian countries, at least relative figures are high[15]. Only in Germany and Austria, youth unemployment has remained comparatively low, both in absolute and relative terms.

However, relative figures are pretty high also in the UK and the US. In spite of market-oriented, youth-targeted reforms in the UK and optimal flexibility in the US, the ratio between youth and prime age unemployment for both countries is close to the European average, such as in Scandinavia. As youth is a state of transition to the labour market where 'frictional' unemployment is unavoidable, the British and US figures do not necessarily indicate a youth unemployment problem. However, the record is no better than in Scandinavia, and the figures do not match the low figures in Germany and Austria. Only France, Belgium, and the Mediterranean welfare states are outperformed on this indicator.

Education

According to the 'standard interpretation', compressed wage structures should produce large differences in unemployment between the higher and lower educated, whereas more 'flexible' wages should improve the employment chances among the lower educated. The major obstacle to this expectation could be the use of the education system as a means to fight (or conceal) youth unemployment. Again, we do not enter into any strict testing here; suffice to say that it is highly remarkable that the ratio between unemployment among lower educated and higher educated both in the US and the UK (around 4.0) is among the highest, and far above the EU average ratio of 1.8 (Table 2.13).

In the Mediterranean countries, the favourable ratios for the lower educated reflect to some extent very high unemployment rates among the better educated. This is not typical, however, and it is noteworthy, for instance, that even the absolute level of unemployment among lower educated is lower in a country like Denmark than in the US. It seems that on this crucial point, the 'standard interpretation' is clearly not confirmed.

Table 2.13: Unemployment by educational attainment for persons aged 25-64 (1996, 1998 and 2000)

	2000			low/high ratio		
	Less than upper secondary education	Upper secondary education	Tertiary level education	1996	1998	2000
Portugal	3.6	3.3	2.8	2.0	1.7	1.3
Greece	7.9	10.9	7.2	0.8	0.9	1.1
Spain	13.7	11.0	9.5	1.4	1.3	1.4
Italy	10.0	7.4	5.9	1.3	1.5	1.7
France	13.9	7.9	5.1	2.2	2.3	2.7
Belgium	9.8	5.3	2.7	3.7	4.1	3.6
Netherlands	3.5	2.1	1.8	2.0	2.7	1.9
Germany	13.7	7.8	4.0	2.7	3.0	3.4
Austria	6.3	3.0	1.6	2.6	2.7	3.9
Denmark	6.3	3.9	2.6	3.0	2.1	2.4
Sweden	8.0	5.3	3.0	2.3	2.9	2.7
Norway	2.2	2.6	1.9	1.9	2.4	1.2
Finland	12.1	8.9	4.7	3.0	2.4	2.6
Ireland	6.8	2.5	1.9	4.0	3.9	3.6
UK	8.9	4.5	2.1	3.1	4.0	4.2
Switzerland	5.0	2.0	1.3	2.4	2.0	3.8
Czech Republic	19.3	6.7	2.5	11.1	7.6	7.7
Slovenia	–	–	–	3.3	3.4	–
EU15	10.6	6.5	4.3	2.1	1.8	2.5
US	7.9	3.6	1.8	4.5	4.0	4.4

Sources: 'Education at a glance' quoted from OECD (1998a, 2000a, 2002a)

Conclusion

With the exception of long-term unemployment, levels and structure of unemployment do not seem to follow the pattern expected from the standard interpretation of structural unemployment. Market-oriented welfare systems did have a positive employment record around 2000, but so too did most Scandinavian and some Continental European countries. Even the overall difference between the US and EU is less convincing than it had previously appeared, and the apparent trend towards what was interpreted as increasing structural or natural levels of unemployment seems to have been reversed.

Flexible, market-oriented welfare systems may be successful in avoiding long-term unemployment, but they are not the only ones, and they do not seem to provide the improved employment opportunities for the low skilled that should be expected in return for high wage differentials and less generous social security. From a citizenship perspective, this kind of market-oriented reform does not seem to have much to offer.

Delineation problems and precarious jobs

With few exceptions, the information presented throughout this chapter is based on the International Labour Organisation's (ILO) definitions of employment and unemployment, mainly operationalised through surveys. According to these criteria, 'the employed' usually include everybody who works at least one hour per week. 'The unemployed' are those who do not have a job, are (more or less) actively seeking employment, and are in a position to take a job. Everybody else is outside the labour force.

Operationalisations differ slightly from country to country, but the deviance is small, and comparability across countries has improved, at least as far as unemployment figures are concerned (Sorrentino, 1993, 1995, 2000). However, the fact that data are equivalent does not ensure that they also have high validity, which, of course, depends on the purpose. Economic and sociological perspectives on employment and unemployment differ in many respects, for instance in the perspective on students having or seeking a second job. Likewise, people who want a job, but are not actively looking for one, or are unavailable, do not count as unemployed according to ILO criteria. This may be reasonable from an economic perspective, but it is questionable from a sociological perspective.

Furthermore, people who interrupt their job search due to participation in an activation programme are not counted as unemployed. From both an economic and a sociological perspective, this may be misleading. There is no point in suggesting alternatives but it is important to be aware of the implications (for example, inflated figures of part-time employed or the highly different contribution of students to the labour force from country to country). Also, there may be a strong deviance compared to national figures based on administrative categories, and depending on the problem, such accounts may

Figure 2.1: The blurred delineation of the labour force, and between employment and unemployment, with indications of typical coding according to ILO definitions

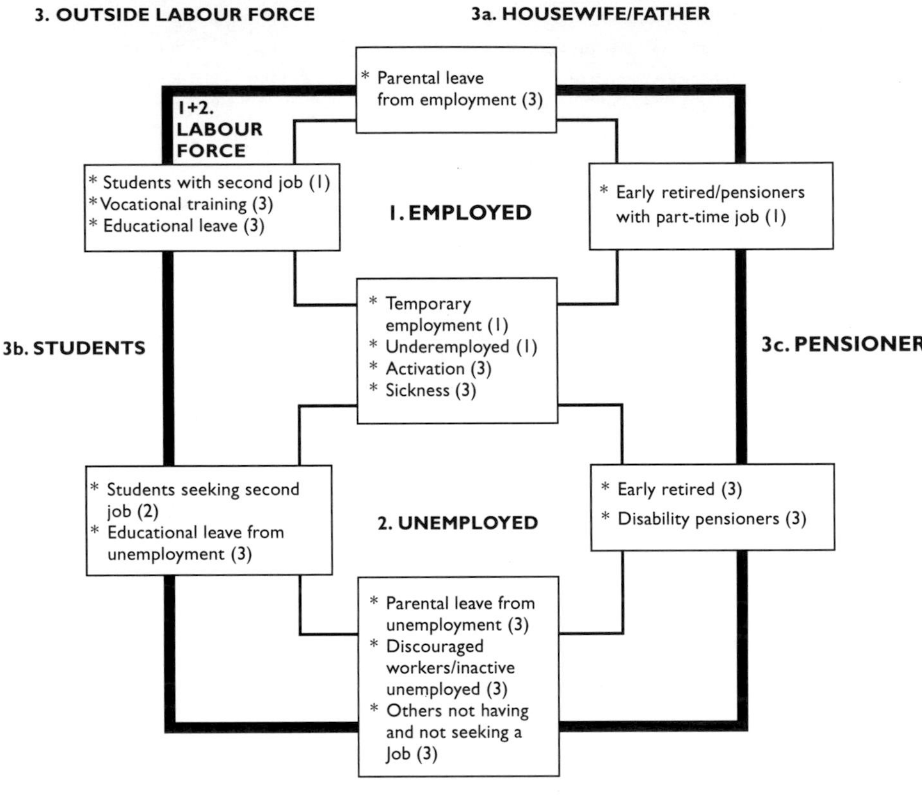

Source: Elaborated on the basis of personal communications with Leif Søllinge (Consultant), Statistics Denmark

sometimes be more valid. Figure 2.1 provides an overview of intermediate groups with ambiguous positions. To begin with the delineation of the employed vis-à-vis people outside the labour force, there are several intermediate groups:

- pensioners or early retirees with a part-time job;
- students with a second job;
- those on leave from employment (maternity, parental, educational leave, and so on); vocational training.

The size of these groups, in particular the first two, can strongly affect the impression of the size and composition of the labour force, as well as its flexibility and precariousness (for example, part-time labour, fixed-term contract, and so on) unless data are specified to sort these groups out.

At the fringe of the unemployed are even more groups. Only one of these – job-seeking students – is sometimes considered among 'the unemployed' by the ILO definition. As we pointed out earlier, this can mislead accounts of unemployment in general and youth unemployment in particular. This holds also for the groups that are typically *not* considered unemployed by ILO criteria:

- discouraged workers/inactive unemployed;
- early retirees and disability pensioners;
- leave from unemployment (maternity, parental, educational leave, and so on);
- unemployed taking part in an activation programme;
- others of working age without and not seeking a job;
- under-employed and people in unstable jobs.

Leave arrangements, early retirement and disability pension are important measures of social welfare, but sometimes they also conceal unemployment, in particular among older people. More restricted access to early retirement does not automatically lead to an equivalent increase in unemployment, but, in the short run, the two are connected. Likewise, people in activation are often not considered unemployed by national statistics, nor do they appear as unemployed in statistics based on ILO definitions should they fail to meet the criteria of job seeking and availability. Inactive unemployed also fail to meet the criterion of job seeking, but may well appear as unemployed in national statistics, and from a sociological perspective, they should probably most often be considered unemployed. The same goes for discouraged workers who are not registered or actively job seeking, but nonetheless want a job[16]. Therefore, unemployment figures are easily biased – and each bias may differ from one country to another.

Part-time and temporary employment: precarious jobs?

A particular problem is the apparent growth in part-time and temporary employment. To what extent does this represent under-employment and precariousness? And is this just as much a threat to citizenship as increasing unemployment? A few years ago, such 'atypical employment' was frequently seen as more or less precarious employment. However, as the conventional life course – (full-time) education, (full-time) work, (full-time) retirement – becomes blurred and is replaced by more flexible organisation of education, work, care, and retirement (CRG, 2002), it becomes increasingly difficult to delineate what counts as 'precarious' jobs, and operational measures must probably be more narrow than previously.

Inter alia, do such jobs represent:

- involuntary under-employment?
- dead-end jobs without transition to permanent jobs or education?

- bad work and wage conditions?
- insufficient social protection?

Statistical information is rather scanty, even on national level, and we can only present a few indicators of the incidence of involuntary part-time employment (for an overview of research on temporary employment, see OECD, 2002a, pp 127-85).

The data in Table 2.14 shows that the Netherlands, followed by Switzerland, the UK and Norway are the countries with most widespread part-time employment. In the Netherlands, it represents one-third of all employment, and in the others countries between 20% and 25%. However, part-time employment among men remains rare – the EU average increased from 4.2% to 6.0% during the 1990s (compared to around 8% in the US).

Considering that these figures include students with a second job, part-time employment remains a marginal phenomenon among men, and we may also notice that countries with high male part-time employment are the countries where most students have a second job: Denmark, the Netherlands, the US, UK and Norway. These are also the countries where part-time employment for men most frequently means short-term employment (less than 20 hours per week).

As indicated earlier, part-time work for women quite often means short-term work. This is especially the case in the Netherlands and Switzerland (above 30% of the female labour force), Norway and the UK (above 20%). In Belgium, Germany and Ireland, the proportion is well above 10%. This holds also for Denmark but the fact that there is little gender difference in short-time employment indicates that this is typically students' second job. Among men, part-time work is more often temporary than among women – and in Italy, France, Sweden, Finland and Ireland high figures for both men and women indicate that part-time is often a surrogate for full-time employment. This is also confirmed by data on preference for full-time employment, which seem particularly high in these countries. Therefore, in France, 53% of male and 39% of female part-time workers indicated that they would rather have full-time employment. A high preference for full-time employment is also indicated in other Mediterranean countries, but here, part-time work is negligible.

In the countries where part-time employment among women is most widespread – the Netherlands, Switzerland, the UK, Belgium, Norway and Germany – we find few indications of dissatisfaction (see also OECD, 1999b, p 32). Therefore, most typically, female part-time employment seems to be a flexible adaptation to new needs and possibilities (Blossfeld and Hakim, 1997; Bielenski et al, 2001; Lilja and Hämälainen, 2001), not a marginalisation effect of firms' increasing need for flexibility. For a minority of both men and women, however, we do find signs of marginalisation – involuntary part-time employment and/or temporary jobs of some significance, first and foremost (by 1997) in Sweden, Finland, France, to a lesser extent in Italy (few part-

Table 2.14: Proportion in part-time jobs, proportion of part-timers in temporary jobs, proportion that prefer full-time or are involuntarily on a part-time job (%)

	% of labour force in part-time[a] Men		Women		Part-time as % of total employment	% less than 20 hours per week[b] Men	Women	% of part-time workers in temporary jobs[c] Men	Women	% prefer full-time (1994)[d] Women	% involuntary part-time[e] Men	Women
	1990	2001	1990	2001	2000	1997	1997	Men	Women	Women	Men	Women
Portugal	3.1	5.1	11.8	14.3	3.2	2.1	7.3	–	–	40	16.1	24.1
Greece	4.0	2.6	11.5	8.5	4.8	1.3	3.8	–	–	25	50.2	36.0
Spain	1.4	2.7	11.5	16.8	7.9	1.1	7.1	–	–	37	–	–
Italy	3.9	5.4	18.2	23.7	12.2	2.9	8.3	56(6)	27(7)	42	–	–
France	4.4	5.1	21.7	23.8	13.8	2.0	8.9	48(10)	22(11)	35	52.9	38.8
Belgium	4.6	5.6	29.8	33.4	17.6	1.4	13.5	25(4)	10(8)	25	–	–
Netherlands	13.4	13.8	52.5	58.1	33.0	7.8	31.4	28(5)	17(10)	7	8.2	4.6
Germany	2.3	4.8	29.8	33.9	17.6	2.2	14.2	24(11)	7(15)	12	17.8	12.6
Austria	–	2.7	–	24.8	12.4	1.1	5.6	11(7)	5(10)	–	–	–
Denmark	10.2	9.1	29.6	20.8	14.5	8.9	12.2	16(10)	8(13)	8	13.1	13.9
Sweden	5.3	7.1	24.5	21.4	17.8	3.9	7.6	43(7)	21(9)	–	34.7	31.3
Norway	6.9	9.0	39.8	32.6	20.1	5.7	21.0	30(8)	17(12)	–	17.2	15.2
Finland	4.7	7.3	10.6	14.0	10.5	3.3	5.0	45(13)	35(16)	–	32.8	40.2
Ireland	4.2	7.1	20.5	33.0	18.4	2.4	11.4	61(4)	33(6)	30	–	–
UK	5.3	8.4	39.5	40.8	23.0	5.1	23.9	25(5)	11(6)	22	23.8	9.5
Switzerland	6.8	8.9	42.6	44.7	24.8	4.9	33.2	–	–	–	8.4	5.8
Czech Republic	–	1.6	–	5.4	3.2	0.7	1.5	–	–	–	1.8	3.7
Slovenia	–	5.6	–	7.8	–	34.8	33.4	16(10)	13(12)	–	22.1	19.2
EU15	4.2	6.0	27.0	30.0	13.8			–	–	–		
US	8.3	8.1	20.0	18.2	13.0	3.4	8.0	–	–	–	7.4	8.0

Note:

For Slovenia, all figures, except for 1990, refer to 1999.

[a] *Source:* OECD (2002a). Due to very odd 2001 figures, 2000 figures are presented for Sweden and the EU.

[b] *Source:* OECD (1999b, p 39) (entries are % of labour force)

[c] *Source:* OECD (1999b, p 28) Based on European Labour Force Survey 1997. Proportion of temporary jobs among full-timers in parantheses

[d] *Source:* OECD (1999b, p 33) Based on European Commission (1995b, Tables 26a-c). Based on ad 1994 ad hoc labour market survey, fieldwork done by market research organisations (because of unusually small sample sizes, figures for men are not reliable and are omitted here). Question: 'Would you rather have full-time employment?'

[e] *Source:* OECD (1999b, p 33) Based on OECD data base and Eurostat (1997)

timers/high dissatisfaction) and in the UK and Ireland (many part-timers/ some dissatisfaction).

Looking at temporary employment, both for full-time and part-time employed, we do find an increase across the EU countries from less than 9% in 1985 and less than 11% in 1990 to almost 13% by 1998 (European Commission, 2000, pp 39-40) – 12% among men and 13.5% among women. Among Mediterranean countries, this seems to some extent to be the flip side of strong employment protection, while in other countries it seems to be a response to high unemployment. In other countries still, it is mainly a mechanism of transition from education to work and, finally, in some countries, it mainly reflects a large proportion of students in the workforce. Only to a limited degree, and only in some countries can it be seen as a sort of 'new marginalisation' on the labour market (Hoffmann and Walwei, 2000; OECD 2002a, pp 132-41; Sarfati, 2002). According to the 1997 European Community Household Panel Survey, temporary workers are usually somewhat lower paid, especially in the Netherlands, Spain and France, and least so in Denmark, Belgium and Austria (OECD 2002a, p 144).

In most countries, satisfaction with job security is rather low among temporary employed but overall job satisfaction and satisfaction with pay is only a little lower than among permanent workers (in the Netherlands even high). Satisfaction with working conditions is nearly as among permanent workers (OECD 2002a, p 151). Upward mobility varies much from country to country: in Austria, Denmark, UK and the Netherlands, less than 30 % remain in temporary jobs or unemployment after two years; in France and Spain, it is nearly two-thirds, and in Belgium, Italy and Greece, it is close to 50 % (OECD 2002a, p 163). Also, social rights of temporary workers vary considerably from one country to another.

The rise in atypical jobs is not tantamount to increasing precariousness as such, and it does not undermine European welfare arrangements either. The major trend is probably increasing social protection coverage where it is relevant.

Temporary jobs are frequently seen as an effect of excessively strict employment protection legislation (EPL), and strict EPL, in turn, is seen as a cause of strong insider/outsider divisions, including reduced chances of re-employment among the unemployed. Statistically speaking, the first proposition is confirmed, with the UK and US having low EPL and low share of temporary employment, whereas Spain comes close to the top of both dimensions (Table 2.15). However, as high frequency of temporary employment in Finland and the low frequency in Italy indicates, the association is not so straightforward.

The association between re-employment chances and EPL is even more blurred. Denmark fits the expected pattern with low EPL and very high re-employment; but Portugal is next, in spite of the (formally) strongest EPL. The UK follows next, in accordance with theory, but Ireland (at least until 1997) fared extremely poor in terms of re-employment chances, despite low EPL, and so on. There *is* an association even here, but in this case, it is certainly not a very convincing one.

Table 2.15: Employment protection strictness, re-employment, and regional disparities in unemployment

	EPL strictness late 1990s[a]		Share of temporary employment 2000%[b]	Current status of those unemployed a year earlier: proportion employed[c]			Regional disparities: coefficient of variation[d]
	Index	Rank[a]		1983-89	1990-97	Average	
Portugal	3.7	18	21	33.6	35.4	34.5	27.4
Greece	3.5	17	13	33.6	26.6	30.1	24.7
Spain	3.1	15	32	28.2	28.7	28.4	26.5
Italy	3.4	16	10	25.9	21.3	23.6	61.0
France	2.8	14	14	31.5	31.9	31.7	20.5
Belgium	2.5	10	9	20.3	23.5	21.9	40.4
Netherlands	2.2	8	13	–	–		15.5
Germany	2.6	11	12	16.7	25.3	21.0	43.8
Austria	2.3	9	8	–	33.1		26.1
Denmark	1.5	4	10	43.8	35.1	39.5	–
Sweden	2.6	11	15	–	29.4		18.2
Norway	2.6	11	10	–	–		16.9
Finland	2.1	6	18	–	26.8		18.7
Ireland	1.1	3	4	18.2	19.1	8.7	4.1
UK	0.9	2	7	31.9	33.0	32.5	31.0
Switzerland	1.5	4	12	–	–		–
Czech Republic	2.1	6	8	–	–		41.1
EU15	–						55.0
US	0.7	1	4	–	–		28.7

[a] *Source:* OECD (1999, p 66), based on weighted measure for regular contracts, temporary contracts and collective dismissals (1999, pp 115-18). For an overview of alternative indicators, see OECD (1999, p 67). See also Finansministeriet (1998)

[b] *Source:* OECD (2000a, p 133)

[c] *Source:* OECD (2000a, p 167). Based on OECD calculations on basis of Eurostat European Labour Force Survey

[d] *Source:* OECD (2000a, p 39)

Finally, regional disparities should be noted not only as interesting phenomena by themselves, but also as a precaution against generalisations. In relation to unemployment, some countries constitute two or more regions with similar formal institutions and rules, but highly different realities. This holds in particular for Italy, Germany, the UK, Belgium and the Czech Republic (the latter countries illustrating that such heterogeneity is not only a matter of country size). Were Italy to be split into two countries, there would be two very different stories to tell. The problems of southern Italy and Wallonia, for example, cannot simply be considered effects of national welfare institutions and policies. Evaluating such aggregates from the perspective of institutional effects, we can hardly ignore the figures for northern Italy and Flanders (in other instances, for example the UK, regional disparities may perhaps to a larger extent be considered an *effect* of past policies). This is yet another reason why detailed country studies are necessary.

Social citizenship of the unemployed

Judging the social citizenship of the unemployed requires detailed national studies; here we will just point at a few distinct characteristics related to the discussion about overall interpretations and strategies. One of the most important questions for the future of welfare is whether European countries face a trade-off between equality and employment. The evidence given throughout this chapter does not point in that direction, and this argument may be substantiated a little further by measures of poverty and income distribution. Although different data sources (and occasionally different measures) produce very different results, some trends are undisputed. Table 2.16 shows that two of the most significant successes in the second half of the 1990s – Denmark and the Netherlands – were the two countries in the EU12 with the lowest incidence of poverty among the unemployed in 1988. Table 2.17 shows that these are also two of the countries with the lowest wage dispersion. Furthermore, Denmark is one of the very few countries that experienced *increasing* equality among the working-age population during the recession up until 1995. Therefore, equality and generous social protection indeed do not seem to be obstacles to significantly improved employment. Nor are they preconditions – at the opposite extreme we find the UK and US with high and increasing inequality, widespread poverty among the unemployed, but positive employment records. Still other EU countries have roughly as unequal an income distribution as the UK, yet they have high and persistent unemployment. In short, then, there does not seem to be much association between equality and generous social protection, on the one hand, and unemployment, on the other.

Table 2.16: Relative poverty rates in households where head of household is unemployed (%[a])

	LIS data, 1988[b]	European Community Household Panel Survey 1994[c]	EPUSE data[d] 1980s	1990s	Proportion lifted out of poverty by transfer
Denmark	3	8	7.6	7.6	88.6
Netherlands	23	25	11.3[e]	25.2[e]	
Greece	25	26			
Belgium	29	23			
Spain	30	33			
France	35	28	23.1	23.3	52.4
Italy	36	37	37.1	45.7	
EU12	**38**				
Ireland	43	31	38.7[f]	33.4[f]	58.0
Germany	43	27	25.5	37.8	32.0
Luxembourg	44				
Portugal	47	30			
UK	48	49	32.9[f]	49.4[f]	19.0
Sweden			27.3	30.4	51.2

[a] Relative poverty: below 50% of average equivalent disposable income (adjusted for household composition).

[b] *Source:* European Commission (1995)

[c] Gallie, Jacobs and Paugam (2000, p 51)

[d] Hauser and Nolan (2000); Nolan, Hauser and Zoyem (2000, pp 92-3). Administrative registers

[e] Income refers to last year, tends to underestimate poverty.

[f] Income refers to last week, tends to overestimate poverty.

Table 2.17: Earnings dispersion in selected OECD countries

	9th decile/5th decile ("how rich are the rich?")			5th decile/1st decile ("how poor are the poor?")			gini working age population (x 100)	
	1979	1986	1995	1979	1986	1995	mid-1990s	change mid-1980s to mid-1990s
Italy	150	143	160	196	175	175	34.2	+3.7
France	194	196	199	167	162	165	27.7	+1.0
Germany	–	164	161	–	158	144	28.2	+2.4
Netherlands	–	162	166	–	155	156	25.4	+2.1
Austria	178	180	182	194	193	201	23.3	+0.8
Denmark	152	155	–	141	142	–	20.5	–0.8
Sweden							24.7	+2.3
Norway							24.9	+2.7
Finland							23.4	+3.0
UK	165	178	187	169	174	181	30.4	+4.1
US	–	–	210	–	–	209	33.3	+0.6

Source: OECD (1996) quoted in Bertola et al (1999). Ginis from Förster (2000, p 76)

Conclusion

We have encountered a large number of anomalies in relation to the 'standard interpretation' of Europe's unemployment problems. First and foremost, the positive unemployment records of quite a large number of European countries by 2000 change the premises of the discussion about 'inflexible' European labour markets and welfare states. European welfare states do not appear to be so poorly adapted to the challenges of globalisation after all, and many of them have been able to obtain unemployment rates far below previously estimated limits of structural unemployment. Conversely, the US system does not appear as flexible as expected, and it does not appear superior in terms of avoiding concentration of unemployment among the lower educated, despite huge wage dispersion. It certainly pushes people towards work, but it is not clear whether this should be considered an advantage. The diagnoses from the 1990s of the problems of European labour markets and welfare states seem much too pessimistic, and the 'standard interpretation' seems less plausible than it did just a few years ago. There is not much comparative evidence to substantiate the claim that high minimum wages and generous social protection are impediments to improved employment.

It is more difficult, however, to formulate positive visions of what could or should be done. The countries with the most positive unemployment record by 2000 – the UK, Ireland, Norway, Sweden, Denmark, the Netherlands, Luxembourg, Switzerland, Austria, and Portugal – do not have much in common, nor are there many common denominators in their strategies. The immediate conclusion is that there are many routes to improving the employment situation. The UK has advanced quite far along a liberal path, while the Netherlands has adopted some reforms in this direction. However, a big part of the 'Dutch miracle' seems to rest on wage moderation, and this argument also seems to apply to Austria where there has been less change. The Nordic countries have recovered, with considerable cutbacks in the public sector in Sweden, and with active labour market policies in Denmark, but without breaking significantly with the Scandinavian model in any of the fields that could have effect on unemployment. Most countries have been reluctant to follow the core recommendations of the 'standard interpretation' and have preferred marginal adjustments – but often out of simple budgetary constraints. To what extent policy experiences are transferable from one country to another remains an open question. 'Context-stripped' systematic analyses have not found many convincing associations[17].

There are lessons to be learned, however. Although econometric analyses have found no significant association between welfare financing form and (un)employment performance, it does seem that, by 2000, high and persistent unemployment was found mainly among the corporatist welfare states (even though the Netherlands and Austria came out as this group's success stories). Rather clearer associations were found between flexibility and *structure* (rather than level) of unemployment. It also seems that tight economic policies may cost in the short run, but are beneficial in the long run, and that competitiveness (for example, via wage moderation, improved qualifications, technological innovation, and so on) is more important than ever. This belongs, however, to the traditional policy tool kit, and 'sound' economic policies are not at odds with generous social protection, equality or labour market regulation. For small, open economies, competitiveness has always been mandatory, and this *could* be one of the reasons why the success rate is highest among these countries. Apart from this, however, it seems that countries should look for moderate measures of activation, flexibility and enhanced competitiveness that fit into the individual countries' institutional set-up.

We do not claim that there is a causal association between the employment recovery of some countries and their social protection systems or initiatives against unemployment. The tacit assumption in much current literature and in the debates over the welfare state that welfare and labour market policies are the key to economic recovery was until recently quite a controversial idea. Even if one accepts the idea that inflexible labour markets may have adverse economic effects, and even if one abstains from resorting to any variant of Keynesianism, there are many other places to look for explanations of employment failure and success. Maybe most of the explanation of macroeconomic success should be found in factors such as innovative capacity, industrial structure, and so on, factors that have very little to do with the welfare state. We only suggest that generous social protection does not appear to be an *obstacle* to employment recovery, and that such recovery is compatible with quite different institutional set-ups of social protection systems. There is little comparative evidence to indicate that it is necessary or even economically beneficial to sacrifice generous social protection systems. When it comes to lower minimum wages and less generous social rights, the risk of creating an underclass is substantial if such policies fail to achieve the goal of labour market integration; if they succeed, there is the risk of creating a group of working poor.

It is questionable how much further a context-stripped research strategy can take us. At any rate, more detailed information is needed about unemployment problems, policy responses and consequences for citizenship in the individual countries. This is the subject of the country-specific chapters of this volume (Chapters Three to Twelve).

Notes

[1] More specifically, we use standardised unemployment rates for the general population and for gender divisions. Otherwise, the main source is OECD Labour Force Statistics/ Employment Outlook, supplemented by OECD Historical Statistics and Eurostat Labour Force Statistics. Series breaks are marked in the tables. Additional information is provided when comparability is problematic.

[2] Carling et al (2001) find that it had an effect on unemployment when the compensation level of unemployment benefits in Sweden was lowered from 90% to 80% (temporarily 75%) during the crisis of the 1990s. However, critics have replicated the study and argue that the finding is unreliable as the effect came 'too early', that is, mainly before the retrenchment was implemented (Johansson and Selén, 2000, 2001).

[3] In microeconomic search theory (Mortensen, 1977; Devine and Kiefer, 1991), some of the hypothetical links are spelled out in terms of the unemployed's incentives to seek a job. Surprisingly, however, a Danish panel study indicates that neither job-search intensity nor wage flexibility (in terms of so-called 'reservation wages') affect *actual* employment chances (Bach 1999; Larsen 2002b). Besides, the debate about whether or not the unemployed should desperately seek any job as soon as possible or take more time to find an appropriate job is a long-standing one (Gallie and Alm, 2000).

[4] In Austria, and to some extent even in the Netherlands, corporatism has not prevented high wage dispersion (see Table 2.17, and Hartog, 1999). However, centralised and coordinated wage negotiations have given Norway the most compressed wage structure among all OECD countries (Barth, 2000). Nevertheless, Norway has been able to reduce structural unemployment to a minimum.

[5] We do not even imply that particular welfare arrangements are the solution to unemployment problems. Implicitly, most current theories build on the assumption that welfare and labour market policies and institutions are the decisive determinants of unemployment. It may well be the case that the most important factors are to be found elsewhere. As is well known, Keynesians would tell quite a different story, and even if one rejects this approach and look exclusively for supply-side explanations, there would be innumerable alternatives (such as innovative capacity).

[6] In Portugal, UK and Sweden, the improvements were not entirely unexpected from the NAWRU calculations. The figures are not entirely commensurable, since NAWRU was calculated on the basis of official national unemployment figures, which are usually a little higher (but in the Swedish case lower) than the standardised figures. Since it is of little practical importance to the argument, however, we simply use the standardised figures here.

[7] This increase, however, was not synchronous throughout Scandinavia: it began in Sweden and soon after in Denmark, and a decade later in Norway. Finland is the deviation, as women had high participation rates throughout the postwar period.

[8] The Danish figures for 1999 are inflated by students' second jobs. Reliable national figures based on actual hours worked in all jobs (register-based labour force statistics) reveal a decline in part-time employment among 25-39 year old women, from 30-35% in 1982 to 5-7% in 1998 (Goul Andersen, 2000a). Many women work slightly reduced hours, and declining part-time frequency is not an indication of less flexibility. Women

want full- or nearly full-time jobs, although sometimes for purely economic reasons. Thirty hours work or more per week are counted as full-time in these statistics.

[9] In the Scandinavian countries, for example, where women have long been fully integrated on the labour market, the underlying trends are observable for both men and women.

[10] There are also differences in the inclusion of conscripts, but they do not contribute much to explaining country differences.

[11] Danish register-based data show that aggregate participation rates (for both sexes, among 15-64 year olds) drop from 82.5% to 73.4% when students are excluded (Goul Andersen, 2000a). The effect on the statistics presented here is a little less dramatic, however, because of a slightly narrower definition of employment.

[12] In Italy, age brackets were slightly different compared to the other countries (see notes to Table 2.6).

[13] Since 'employment' is also sometimes difficult to define, it does not solve all problems. For 'prime age men', however, the number of borderline cases is small. In the future, life-long learning may make even this measure more difficult to apply (Goul Andersen, 2002b).

[14] Even OECD (1999b, p 88) finds no (controlled) association between EPL and share of workers in temporary jobs, which is often believed to be the response to strict EPL.

[15] In Scandinavia, 'youth unemployment' depends heavily on definitions. Job-seeking students constitute a large proportion both in Denmark and Sweden. In Sweden, the contribution of students to the figures on aggregate unemployment in the 1990s was close to two percentage points (Sorrentino, 2000, p 19). This is partly a reflection of people in activation seeking job, partly a reflection of students seeking a second job. In Denmark, official figures on youth unemployment are significantly below general unemployment. And whereas the latter figures may be too optimistic, survey-based figures like the OECD figures are clearly too pessimistic in the Scandinavian case.

[16] Occasionally, even students may be an intermediary category were young people strongly encouraged to enter education in order to avoid youth unemployment.

[17] An example is OECD's (2000a, pp 129-54) survey of the impact of eligibility criteria and their implementation. Although it finds definite conclusions hard to come by, it identifies vicious circles of sustained falls in unemployment and tighter implementation of eligibility criteria (p 143). Similarly, Manow and Seils (2000a) describe vicious circles in the contribution-financed German social security system. Such findings do not presuppose any systematic, context-stripped association, but are basically contingent.

THREE

Unemployment and unemployment policy in the UK: increasing employability and redefining citizenship

Jochen Clasen[1]

Introduction

For most of the past three decades the UK has ranked among the countries with one of the worst labour market records in Western Europe. Unemployment rates hovered around the 12% mark for most of the 1980s. For a very long time, the prospect for a return to anything approximating full employment seemed very bleak indeed. Any improvements turned out to be temporary and the persistence of high levels of unemployment became an all but accepted characteristic of late 20th century Britain.

Then, in 1993, unemployment started to fall gradually but steadily. At the same time employment levels started to climb. This time the improvement was long-lasting and non-inflationary, so that at the start of the 21st century, the UK can be considered as one of the labour market 'success' countries in Europe next to Denmark, the Netherlands and Ireland (see Chapter Two of this volume). While other countries (Austria and Luxembourg in particular) have lower unemployment, it is these four countries which have witnessed significant reductions of unemployment during the last decade. What is more, among the large economies in Europe, the UK is the only one that can boast a sustained labour market improvement, while Italy, Germany and France are now faced with the highest unemployment rates in Western Europe.

On the face of it, the turnaround in the British labour market is remarkable indeed. By the end of the 1990s, the labour force participation rate of those aged 16-64 reached 76% – a higher figure than that for the mid 1970s. This was largely due to women entering the labour market to an extent which is now close to levels found in Scandinavia. By contrast, as in many other countries, the labour force participation among men dropped over the past three decades. However, this trend seems to have slowed down in the mid-1990s and the current rate of 84% is one of the highest in Europe and certainly higher than in any other large European economy.

Equally, unemployment levels dropped to the lowest levels since the early 1980s, with 1.47 million people out of work in spring 2001, which represented just below 5.0% of the workforce according to the ILO definition, which is now the government's preferred measure. Previously the preferred unemployment count was the so-called 'claimant count' (that is, registered job seekers who are in receipt of benefits or credits for contributory benefits). The latter rate has declined even further than survey based unemployment, to 3.3% in spring 2001, which was the lowest rate since 1975.

The purpose of the first section of this chapter is to reflect on these aggregate figures and to demonstrate that the labour market improvement is somewhat overstated. It has not benefited all groups in society, either. De-industrialisation is a major cause for the unequal spatial distribution of unemployment and employment which, in some respect, has become even more pronounced in the 1990s. The spatial dimension of labour market chances is also one of the factors which exacerbate problems of tackling poverty, inequality and social exclusion which, as Gallie et al (2000) have demonstrated, are more closely linked with unemployment in Britain than in other advanced European welfare states.

Against this background, this chapter concludes with a reflection on the New Deal, which is at the heart of current unemployment and labour market policies. Primarily geared towards increasing employability, the New Deal has contributed significantly to an ongoing redefinition of citizenship. Whether it is sufficient, as a largely supply-side oriented policy, to bring about lasting labour market success remains questionable.

Unemployment and employment: some British characteristics

In Chapter Two, Jørgen Goul Andersen and Jan Bendix Jensen provide a considerable amount of background data that points out some of the peculiarities of the British labour market performance over the past 20 years or so. Below this aggregate level, some features are worth highlighting. These include the pronounced growth in female employment and the decline of male employment, the high level of part-time work particularly among women, the persistence of youth unemployment relative to prime-age unemployment, and the high level of unemployment among those with low educational attainment.

As in many other countries, the most striking change in the labour market in the UK has been the increased participation of women in paid employment since the early 1970s. In 1971 just over half of women in the 25-44 age group were in work or were seeking work. This had risen to about three-quarters by 1997. At the same time, economic activity among men has fallen. This is a trend with parallels in other European countries and includes a shift towards part-time work which rose steadily from the early 1980s and accelerated during the 1990s, while the number of full-time jobs declined. Therefore, although the economic recovery in many countries led to more people finding jobs from the early 1990s, this was marked with a shift from full-time to part-time employment. Between 1994 and 1997, for example, the number of part-time jobs increased across the EU by over 10%. This shift affected both men and women. Nevertheless, the extent of part-time work varies greatly across countries, and is less pronounced for men than for women (see Chapter Two).

After the Netherlands, the UK has the second highest female part-time employment rate in the EU, with over 40% of all women working on a part-time basis. Unlike elsewhere however, this share has not changed significantly since the mid-1970s. It is also noticeable that for many British women, part-time work often means half-time work, or even fewer hours, and part-time earnings that keep them out of the contributory National Insurance scheme. In 1971 there were about 500,000 women in work but outside National Insurance. Twenty years later, the number had increased to 2.3 million (Land, 1994). In short, the much improved British employment rates are, to some extent, attributable to the prevalence of part-time work – and to the fact that international measures such as the EU Labour Force Survey recognise any form of employment (anything greater than one hour per week) as employment. It should be pointed out however that the share of involuntary part-time work is lower in the UK than in most other European countries (see Chapter Two, Table 2.14 of this volume).

The UK has also one of the highest male part-time rates in the EU. While the latter is still relatively low with around 9%, the share of previously unemployed men entering part-time employment has been growing steadily over the 1990s, reaching 20% in 1997 (European Commission, 1998, p 25). There has also been an increase in fixed-term working during the 1990s. However, in contrast to what is often assumed as one characteristic of a flexible labour market, temporary contracts for both British men and women were well below the EU average in 1997 (about 6% and 8% respectively). For previously unemployed men and women fixed-term contracts are becoming increasingly important. The share of previously unemployed men entering temporary types of work is slightly higher than the equivalent share for women (European Commission, 1998). But, once again, the rates for both men and women are lower in the UK than in most other EU countries. Finally, about 13% of those employed in industry and services in the EU are self-employed, with about 40% of those employing other people. Here, the UK's profile is fairly close to the EU average, but it is noticeable that self-employment is more pronounced than in other large economies of Germany, France or labour market success countries Denmark and the Netherlands.

Overall, the focus on non-standard forms of employment can be somewhat misleading. Throughout 1998 for example, the increase in the number of full-time employees in the UK was still two and a half times the number of the increase in part-time employees. What is more, while almost half of all women work part-time, three quarters of the increase in full-time jobs went to women

– and the growth in female full-time jobs was twice as high as the increase in female part-time jobs (*Labour Market Trends*, May 1999).

As to those seeking employment, male unemployment has been consistently higher than female unemployment for at least 20 years. Reasons for this have to do with the particularly sharp decline in predominantly male types of employment, such as in manufacturing, and the growth of, predominantly, female types of employment in services. While this is a common trend across countries, de-industrialisation has been particularly marked in the UK (Rowthorn, 2000). Other factors include cross-national differences in labour law (for example, with regard to employment protection and early retirement options), but also social security arrangements. This applies to the dominance of means-tested over social insurance-based benefits generally, and for unemployed people in particular. By the late 1990s, a little more than 10% of all unemployed were entitled to contributory-based benefits, and many of the latter had to resort to additional means-tested transfers (for example, housing benefit). Often however, means-tested benefits are claimed by men – rather than women – on behalf of the household.

Recently, the rate of youth unemployment has declined. Reasons include improved labour market conditions generally, and a stronger focus on labour market policies on younger people, particularly the New Deal for Young People (discussed later in this chapter). It should be noted, however, that young people on training programmes and such like, are not counted among the unemployed. What is more, the participation of younger people in education has increased, and has therefore lowered the rate of participation in employment and affected the age composition of unemployment. This is a common trend across EU countries, where there are now considerably fewer under-25-year-olds and more 25- to 49-year-olds in unemployment than in the mid 1980s (European Commission, 1998, p 18). In the UK, the 16-24 age group represented 38% of all unemployed in 1984. This figure dropped to 30% in 1993 (*Labour Market Trends*, May, 1998). By contrast, the proportion of 25- to 39-year-olds rose from 32% to 37%.

However, young people remain disproportionately affected by unemployment. The ratio of youth to standard unemployment had been fairly stable, at about 2:1 throughout the previous decade, but had risen to 2.5:1 against prime age unemployment by 1999 (see Chapter Two, Table 2.12 of this volume). Compared with the EU average, this represents an unfavourable position and indicates that, despite a relatively low level of labour market regulation, the transition into first-time work remains a problem for many youngsters, and males in particular. This seems a surprising feature for a flexible labour market and the removal of, in the eyes of the government at the time, potential employment barriers.

In the 1980s, successive conservative administrations adjusted wages downwards for young employees through measures such as the abolition of 'wages councils' (which secured minimum wage levels in certain industries) and changes to social security regulations (such as the removal of benefit eligibility for almost all 16- to 18-year-olds and the lowering of benefit rates for those under 25 years of age). Nevertheless, unemployment rates for younger age groups remained high. One reason for this might be the reluctance to intervene more strongly and systematically in what has traditionally been a rather patchy framework of vocational training in the UK, and a refusal to engage in active labour market policies more generally.

The outcome of the above has affected British young men more than women. In most EU countries, young women are more affected by unemployment than young men. The exceptions are Germany, Ireland and Sweden – where men have a marginally higher risk of unemployment than women – and the UK where young men are significantly more affected than young women. In fact, the unemployment rate of young men is two-and-a-half times higher than the average unemployment rate – young men without qualifications are the most affected.

Table 2.13 (see Chapter Two of this volume) illustrated the fact that a lack of educational qualifications is strongly related to unemployment in most countries. This applies to the UK in particular. As with the salience of youth unemployment this feature seems surprising given the assumption that the low skilled should have a relatively easier chance of labour market integration in countries with flexible labour markets and liberal employment regulation. Apart from possible explanations for the high levels of unemployment among the young outlined earlier, the rate of worklessness among those with few qualifications must also be linked to the salience of regional concentration of job chances.

Finally, unemployment is not equally distributed across ethnic groups. In fact, there has been little progress and relative inequalities persist. Throughout the 1980s and 1990s, men from ethnic minority groups are twice as likely to be unemployed than white men (*Labour Market Trends*, December 1999). For women from ethnic minorities, the situation has worsened since the early 1990s, with unemployment registered at 13% at the end of the decade compared to 4.6% for white women. However, there are significant differences between ethnic minorities. Unemployment rates for those with an Indian background, for example, are much lower than for other ethnic groups.

Hidden aspects and the impact of geographical disparities

Despite a significant overall improvement in British employment and unemployment figures, there are still considerable problems of labour market integration. Furthermore, as this section shows, aggregate statistics obscure the impact of the geographical concentration of unemployment and are therefore insufficient for an understanding of the scope and distribution labour market disadvantage (Webster, 2000a, 2002). Crucially, the debate has so far concentrated on unemployment and employment, but ignored the considerable level of inactivity among British men which, more than elsewhere in Europe, has considerably increased rather than decreased in the 1990s (Webster, 2002). Since the early 1980s there has been a substantial increase in sickness rates in the UK, reaching the highest rate of working age sickness in the EU (7% compared with 2.1% in Germany and 0.3% in France). In some areas which also have high levels of open unemployment (such as Glasgow, Liverpool and Manchester) sickness rates even higher, with between 15% and 20% of the working age population registered as sick (Webster, 2001).

Broad national labour market data figures depict an imbalance between near full-employment in the South of England and stubbornly high levels of joblessness in the North. In 1998, rates in Scotland, Northern Ireland, Wales, the North, North West and North Midlands were about twice the rates of the area around London and the South East of the country. While the rate of unemployment had declined to 3% in the South East by mid-2000, it remained above 9% in the North East and even higher elsewhere. Glasgow, for example, has hardly participated in the national increase in employment, with ILO unemployment figures consistently hovering above 13% in the second half of the 1990s. A growth in some sectors (banking, financial services) has largely been in part-time employment and was insufficient to compensate for the decline of jobs in construction, manufacturing, construction and transport.

Geographical disparities in unemployment have declined since the early 1970s. Nevertheless, there is still very strong spatial variation not only along regional but also along an urban–rural dimension (Webster, 2000a). Cities in the North of England – such as former industrial areas of Liverpool, Hull and Sunderland – all had unemployment rates above 10% at the end of the 1990s. More generally, a recent study (Turok and Edge, 1999) found that particularly big cities in Scotland and the North of England have not benefited from the increase in employment. While overall employment grew by 1.7 million jobs between 1981 and 1996, Britain's 20 major cities have lost 500,000 jobs. This is largely attributable to the contracting manufacturing base, which has affected the situation of men in particular. The same study found that commuting to work elsewhere has not been a viable option for many people and that both registered and hidden unemployment is very high in those urban areas.

What is more, unemployment rates reflect the problem of lack of job opportunities only partially. Normally, when employment increases the number of those out of work but not unemployed, that is the economically inactive, falls. However, as Gregg and Wadsworth (1999) pointed out, the number of men out of work but not actively seeking employment has sharply increased since the early 1990s (see also Beatty et al, 2000; Bacon, 2002). Taking students out of the equation, the number of economically inactive men was 1.5 million in 1990; by 1998 this figure had risen to 2.3 million. This dramatic increase was obscured by a sharp decline of female inactivity resulting in little overall change (Gregg and Wadsworth, 1999). As with unemployment, educational attainment is strongly correlated with inactivity. More than 30% of men with no formal qualification were inactive by the end of the 1990s compared with 8% of those with university degrees (Gregg and Wadsworth, 1999). As regards self-confessed reasons for inactivity, early retirement is a surprisingly relatively minor factor compared with sickness (across all ages for men), and home and family responsibilities for women.

Webster (2000b) points out that the UK's relative performance in terms of employment rates and ILO unemployment is much less impressive than general national and international labour market data indicate. For example, the UK has no less than 23 out of the 30 most economically inactive regions in the EU where people actually want to work (that is, involuntarily inactive persons). Inner London is ranked the worst of all regions in the entire EU. Once again the spatial dimension of employment prospects is important here. Male inactivity occurs predominantly in areas of high male unemployment. The reverse also holds true. Areas with the best employment performance have also witnessed the best improvements in inactivity rates. However, it requires a strong upsurge in employment for any effect on inactivity to register, which suggests that many inactive people have become somewhat detached from the labour market. As Gregg and Wadsworth (1999, p 57) conclude,

> Britain's inactive are a serious and growing problem. Reconnecting these people with the labour market or preventing disconnection needs to be a serious target for government policy in order to reduce poverty and social exclusion.

Another aspect which puts the British labour market performance in a less-than-rosy light is the disproportionately high rate of working-age households where nobody is in paid work. This is not an exclusively British phenomenon, of course. In many European countries a polarisation has developed since the early 1980s between work-rich two-earner and workless (no earner) households. In most EU countries the number of both types of households has increased while the share of mixed households has been declining (Gregg et al, 1999). However, as with spatial disparities and levels of inactivity, the incidence of workless households is particularly high in the UK. By contrast, by the mid-1990s almost 20% of all households did not contain a single person in paid employment. Since then the rate has dropped to about 16% (DWP, 2002). Nevertheless, recent employment gains have not benefited households equally. Instead, "jobs have been disproportionately taken by households where a working adult was already present" (Gregg and Wadsworth, 1998, p 34). While long-term unemployment declined in the 1990s (see Chapter Two), the average period for workless households since any adult had been in paid work increased, irrespective of family type. In the early 1990s almost half of all workless households had not received any earnings for three years or more. By the end of the 1990s the rate was close to 60%.

The workless household rate in the UK has continued to increase in recent decades, even at times when employment picked up. Despite some recent improvements, its extent is conspicuous given the above-average employment performance of the UK compared with many other European countries. It is also a cause of concern given the increase in inequality and poverty over the 1980s and 1990s. In the UK, the correlation between poverty and (particularly long-term) unemployment is extremely strong, as Gallie et al (2000) have demonstrated. Not surprisingly therefore, the rate of income poverty (that is below half average household equivalent income) among workless households is very high (over 70%, after housing costs). From a different perspective, over half of those in poverty live in workless households (Gregg et al, 1999).

It should be noted here that child poverty is a major problem in the UK. By the mid 1990s couples with children represented 40% of all those living on less than half average income, while, applying the same definition, a third of all children in 1992/3 were born into poverty (George and Wilding, 1999). Indeed, compared with other OECD countries, the UK has by far the greatest proportion of children growing up in workless households (Gregg et al, 1999). More than half of those households are headed by a single parent – and more than half of all lone parents did not have work in 2000, which is a much higher rate than in most other European welfare states. This is one of the major concerns in British labour market policy. Married or cohabiting women with dependent children are much more likely to be economically active than single women. In spring 1998, 60% of married women with pre-school children were economically active compared with 36% of lone parents. Several surveys have shown that the majority of non-working mothers would work were suitable childcare available. This has been reflected in welfare to work policies (discussed later in this chapter).

To conclude, there are several related labour market imbalances which are not – or at least insufficiently – indicated by general labour market data. Irrespective of the ways in which employment and unemployment is measured, the British labour market has picked up considerably since the early 1990s. However, the employment gains have not benefited the country evenly or equally. On the contrary, some indicators (such as male inactivity) seem to have become more pronounced despite increasing levels of employment. Regional disparities in unemployment may have softened but there continue to be intransigent spatial disadvantages along a north–south and rural–urban dimension. The fall in overall unemployment seems to have done little in terms of having created opportunities particularly for young male people in northern cities. Equally, the high level of workless households points to an accumulation of serious disadvantage in terms of labour market integration and, because of a high correlation, the threat of social exclusion and deprivation.

Improving employability – the major route towards securing full citizenship

The UK has never been a leader in active labour market policy. However, back in the 1970s Labour administrations made use of both job creation and job subsidy measures as a response to unemployment. This approach was largely abandoned under the Conservative governments of the 1980s when two major labour market problems were identified: rigidities in pay, working time and employment patterns on the one hand, and chronic skill shortages on the other. The response was the adoption of a supply-side approach which emphasised labour market deregulation, the relaxation of laws regulating employment and wages, weakening of the influence of trade unions, cut backs in benefits for unemployed people and greater pressure on unemployed people to move into paid work. Strike votes became subject to a secret ballot, pickets were restricted and no longer immune from civil actions, the closed shop abolished, and strikers' benefit entitlements reduced. Trade union membership declined from 52% to 27% of the labour force between 1979 and 1995 and has since recovered slightly to 30% (ONS, Labour Force Survey, various years).

Reluctant to increase spending on training or job creation measures, the preferred Conservative strategy to reduce unemployment in the 1980s was to drive down the reservation wage of a group of workers who, it was felt, had priced themselves out of a job, and to intensify job search activities. Wage regulating elements, which had applied particularly to younger employees in certain industries, were abolished and unemployed people became increasingly subject to more intensive counselling, job-search seminars, and compulsory attendance at job clubs. By 1994, the UK had no regulation of working time or wage levels, no legal protection for those hired under fixed-term contracts and no right to representation at the workplace. The UK scored zero in a composite index of labour market standards, covering regulation of working time, minimum wages, employment protection, employee representation and fixed-term contracts – lowest among EU and EFTA countries and alongside the US (OECD, 1994a, p 154; see also Chapter Two). The UK negotiated an opt-out clause from the Social Chapter of the Maastricht Treaty extended majority voting to issues of health and safety at work, equal opportunities, protection for pensioners and the unemployed, consultation and other matters.

A large number of generally incremental, but cumulatively substantial, benefit changes introduced in the 1980s and the first half of the 1990s reduced the value of benefits in relation to average earnings. Policies made it harder for jobless people to qualify for contributory benefits, excluded certain groups from benefit eligibility, introduced reduced rates for younger claimants and lowered the number of unemployed claiming benefits (see Alcock, 1991; Clasen, 1992; Bradshaw, 1993; Hill, 1994). Since the end of the 1980s, the main thrust of labour market policies has been to make conditionality of benefits more explicit, to tighten controls, to prescribe job-seeking behaviour and to stiffen sanctions for non-compliance (Finn, 1997). Unemployment benefits have been made subject to increasingly stringent tests of availability to work, culminating in the replacement of National Insurance benefit by the Jobseeker's Allowance in 1996, which reduced entitlement to contributory benefit from 12 to six months.

The introduction of the Jobseeker's Allowance, and the cut in benefit eligibility, was criticised by Labour in opposition. However, having returned to power in 1997, the Labour government did not revoke the change. Unlike previous

Labour Party policy, the Blair administration accepted that the provision of social security could have detrimental effects on individual behaviour. Benefit fraud and unemployment traps, for example, became problems perceived as attributable to the impact of welfare systems on job seekers, and the effect of long-term unemployment as detrimental on job search and employability. In addition, the government acknowledged labour market research, which had shown that the rise in employment levels since 1993 has benefited jobless people unevenly, bypassing younger people and many households (discussed earlier in this chapter). The response was a shift within the Labour Party towards a more active and paternalistic approach to social security. This would make unemployed benefit claimants more 'employable' and thereby increase the effective competition for jobs, reducing upward wage pressure (Hyde et al, 1999; Peck and Theodore, 2000).

Therefore, while the current Labour government has accepted certain frameworks (such as the Maastricht Treaty conditions, the introduction of works' councils and other measures), it has maintained the Conservative's emphasis on supply-side measures and the need for a deregulated and flexible labour market. In fact, as far as unemployment policy in concerned, the Labour government intensified the emphasis on behavioural aspects, which reflects a more general attempt to redefine citizenship by balancing rights and responsibilities within the British welfare state (Plant, 1998). In essence, this involves the propagation of a new contract between citizens and the state, with the state offering different types of assistance for labour market integration and citizens being obliged to accept this assistance (Cm 3805, 1998).

The most prominent programme in terms of mandatory welfare-to-work has been the New Deal for young unemployed people (Warton et al, 1998; Finn, 1999)[2]. Introduced in April 1998, all of its programmes are geared towards working-age benefit claimants (and, more recently, their non-employed partners). Arranged on an individual basis, a programme typically starts with an induction course and an assessment of work skills. For claimants under the age of 25, individual 'activity plans' are drawn up with the Employment Service, which requires the transition from benefit receipt to a subsidised job in the private or public sector or full-time education. Private-sector employers receive a job subsidy and a fixed sum towards the cost of training. Alternatively, claimants might work with the Environmental Task Force, offering manual support on community projects, with some opportunities for training. Participants receive an allowance that is slightly higher than benefit. A new feature of the regime for unemployed people is the emphasis on individual counselling, designed to improve motivation by making clear that benefits will not be available indefinitely, to build self-esteem, and also to attempt to ensure that placements and training are appropriate to individual needs.

Other main New Deal programmes are targeted at long-term unemployed people, lone parents, unemployed partners of benefit claimants, disabled people and people over the age of 50. Apart from the compulsory programme for young unemployed, for the long-term unemployed the advisory aspects (that is interviews with personal advisors) and participation in 'activity periods' is mandatory. The transition towards training or work experience, on the other hand, is not (Millar, 2000), even though a mandatory 'work-focused' interview with a personal advisor has now been introduced for all groups.

Within a framework of a primarily supply-side approach of increasing employability and redressing inadequate skill bases, the New Labour government has to some extent returned to the job subsidies first propagated in the 1970s. However, the introduction of welfare-to-work policies, and the New Deal in particular, marks a watershed in British labour market policy. Previous Conservative governments were reluctant to increase expenditure on labour market policies for fiscal and ideological reasons. By contrast, the Labour administration has channelled earmarked public funds into new programmes that are significantly more coherent than the patchwork of earlier schemes. Most importantly from a citizenship perspective, New Labour has introduced an element of obligation as an explicit quid-pro-quo for this investment in better labour market integration programmes, with a focus on young and long-term unemployed people.

The New Deal programmes are part of a wider welfare-to-work package which aims to move people from benefits into employment by a mixture of incentives, opportunities and encouragement/compulsion. Incentives are improved by measures that contain the benefits paid to those out of work (a new feature here is the restriction on benefits for lone parents and the greater strictness in the tests for disability benefits), while the incomes of those in work are enhanced. This was to be achieved by a minimum wage and a range of tax credit (wage subsidy) schemes initially targeted at families with children, lone parents and disabled groups. The Working Families' Tax Credit (WFTC), for example, paid via the wage packet, guaranteed a minimum income of £200 per week (for the year 2000) for families with one earner in full-time work. Since this benefit is understood as a tax reduction rather than a cash payment it does not count as public spending in national accounts and its introduction therefore does not conflict with the government's objective of reducing public spending. Currently several tax credit schemes apply to other claimant groups, but a major overhaul of the system will be introduced in 2003 which will be more comprehensive, covering all major parts of financial support for children within the same programme (child tax credit). In addition, an in-work tax credit will be introduced for people on low income without children.

Opportunities to participate in employment are also to be enhanced through an expansion of childcare provision. The government is encouraging schools to provide pre-school classes for three and four-year-olds (the compulsory entry age is five). In 1970 roughly 20% of three and four-year-olds were in nursery school. By 1998 the figure had risen to 60% and is continuing to rise. A National Child Care Strategy combines guaranteed nursery places for all four-year-olds. There are also subsidies to childcare at the beginning and end of the school day and in holidays. Approved childcare expenses are now tax deductible for working parents who are in receipt of WFTC. This strategy takes place in the context of an expansion of education and training.

Welfare-to-work policies have been in place for only a relatively short period of time, a situation that precludes anything more than a sporadic assessment. Nevertheless there are indications that the New Deal has improved the job entry levels of young unemployed people in particular, and these have not occurred at the expense of job entry rates for older long-term or shorter-term unemployed people (Bivand, 1999a). On the other hand, the introduction of the New Deal has not reduced the share of those who leave the claimant count for unknown destinations. Also, only about 34% of all participants found employment that lasted for more than 13 weeks. Overall, after about two years in operation it was estimated that the programme (for young people) reduced unemployment by 30,000 (with an estimated deadweight loss of 50%). As for the New Deal for older long-term unemployed people, about 38,000 of them found jobs. However, only 13% of all 238,000 participants' employment lasted for more than 13 weeks (Millar, 2000). Well over half returned to benefit receipt (Bivand, 1999b). In short, the New Deal has improved the labour market integration of young unemployed people in particular, but to a much lesser degree for older groups.

Millar (2000) reviewed several evaluations of the impact on individual participants and providers. Most pivotal seems to be the role of the personal advisor, who can have a crucial impact on the perception, and therefore the effect, of programmes. Overall, the personal advisor approach was regarded as a positive development. As far as particular groups were concerned, the long-term unemployed were the most cynical about the programme; on the other hand, lone parents were the most positive about the individual attention and support. Compulsion to attend an initial interview was generally regarded as more positive than mandatory participation in one of the options (of which jobs were more valued than education). Compulsion for young people (and long-term unemployed) was generally seen as more acceptable than for other groups. The requirement to move into options was sometimes seen as too rigid in the mandatory programmes, and "the gap between the individualised assessment and the fixed options that follow was felt to be too large" (Millar, 2000, p vii).

The New Deal brought about a real increase in resources allocated to labour market policies. Essentially, however, it is an instrument aimed at raising the employability of registered job seekers and therefore remains first and foremost, in line with previous policies, a supply-side instrument. Programmes such as work placements or the creation of temporary intermediary jobs – which are fairly common in other European countries – are not part of the repertoire of British labour market policies. This is perhaps due to a perception that these instruments are not only expensive but in contradiction with maintaining flexible and deregulated labour markets and avoiding possible conflict with private sector jobs creation (displacement effects). In other words, the 'employment element' (Evans, 2001) in British welfare to work policy remains underdeveloped at the expense of raising employability among target groups. Whether such an approach will be sufficient to provide effective labour market integration, particularly with respect to those who are 'hard to place', seems questionable. Furthermore, there is a strong spatial element of labour market disadvantage in terms of a correlation between areas of high unemployment and inactivity and youth unemployment, long-term unemployment, lone parenthood, and long-term sickness (that is the target groups for the New Deal). Highlighting one basic problem here, Webster (2000a, p 118) points out that "an attempt is being made to place the largest number of people into jobs in exactly the places where jobs are scarcest".

Within a broader citizenship perspective, there remains a very open question: is labour market integration via welfare to work policies an adequate solution to problems of poverty, spatial concentration of disadvantage and inequality? More so than in other European countries, income inequality in the UK rose sharply during the 1980s and the first half of the 1990s, with the lowest income groups losing out both in comparison with medium and higher income earners and in absolute terms (Goodman et al, 1997). Recent studies have underlined that the relative income position of the unemployed in the UK deteriorated during the 1980s. As Gallie et al (2000) show, unemployed people in the UK, having occupied a middle position in the mid 1980s, had become more affected by poverty by the mid 1990s than their counterparts in any of the other seven European countries of their study (Denmark, Germany, France, Italy, Ireland, the Netherlands, and Sweden). A recent empirical study confirmed the persistence of poverty. The number of people in households with less than half the average income (after housing costs) has even increased slightly between 1996/7 and 1998/9, and is still very high with over 14 million people (Rahman et al, 2000). Being strongly correlated with poverty risk, unemployment has become increasingly unevenly distributed, with a disproportionately high level of households with nobody in paid work. Between 1979 and 1996, their proportion more than doubled to about one in five working-age households, or 3.4 million. This increase can at least partly be attributed to the massive growth in means-testing which (in real expenditure terms) increased by over 600% between 1974 and 1996 (Evans, 1998). Relying exclusively on family-based, means-tested benefits makes it particularly hard for couples to move from benefit into what is often insecure, part-time and low waged work.

These problems seem to have been acknowledged by the current Labour administration. At the same time, however, there is a reluctance to openly use tax and social security policies in order to achieve a more equitable income distribution (even though some vertical redistribution has been achieved). Instead, it is the New Deal, that is labour market integration, which is at the heart of New Labour's solution to poverty, social exclusion and to achieving full citizenship. The mechanisms for this are a deregulated and flexible labour market, coupled with a more conditional approach of citizenship by requesting more individual responsibility on the part of the unemployed for increasing their employability. In addition, a range of policies are geared towards 'making work pay'; that is, towards increasing the financial reward of accepting (low) paid work by way of a combination of minimum wages, reduced National Insurance contributions and tax credits particularly for families with children.

Conclusion

The current government clearly rejects redistributive social security policies in favour of providing opportunities for entering the labour market. 'Work for those who can, security for those who cannot' and 'making work pay' are much trumpeted slogans, but also succinctly underline the government's approach towards the problems of social exclusion and unemployment in its first term of office between 1997 and 2001. A reorganisation of ministries, and the abolition of the Department of Social Security and its replacement with the Department for Work and Pensions in particular, indicates that labour market integration has become, if anything, an even more dominant aspect of welfare state policy in Labour's second term in office. Income transfers should be reserved for those who are unable to participate in the labour market, while for others the source of income, social inclusion and participation is waged work. The role for the government in this is to be interventionist, but first and foremost on the supply side of the economy and to ensure that the rights of citizens reflect their observance of duties and obligations to the community (Dean, 1999). The emphasis is on training, education and employment (rather than redistribution), and paid work is the principal mechanism for social inclusion and conferring citizenship.

As this chapter has illustrated, labour market programmes introduced since 1998 have had a positive impact on the degree of participation in waged work, particularly of young people. However, there are intransigent problems regarding the high spatial determination of job chances and accumulation of labour market disadvantage along geographical, household and gender lines. It remains to be seen whether, under different labour market conditions, supply-side oriented New Deal policies will have lasting success in terms of their impact on employment – and social integration – of young and long-term unemployed people. The notion of mutual responsibility, community involvement, the emphasis on duties and obligations and the drawing up of contracts between the state and citizens indicate a significant shift in the thinking on citizenship rights in the UK and in the policy orientation of the Labour government (Dean, 1999). A self-proclaimed aim of the government is not only to change policies but also 'the culture among benefit claimants, employers and public servants' (Cm 3805, 1998). Indeed, the success of New Labour's reinterpretation of social citizenship will depend not only on new policies but on the ability to transform social values. The interpretation of new obligations as either little more than a rhetorical justification for workfare and compulsion, or as a genuine pathway out of poverty and unemployment, will depend on both the quality of the offers and the attitude particularly of those who are not in a position to refuse them.

Will people accept their ascribed obligation towards a more active acquisition of citizenship rights? More importantly, will the emphasis on raising levels of employability be sufficient to deal with problems of concentrated unemployment and inactivity and its associated problem of partial citizenship?

Notes

[1] I would like to thank Peter Taylor-Gooby whose original review of the distribution and development of employment and unemployment in Britain provided the starting point for this chapter. I also owe thanks to Gary Slater, who read an earlier draft and provided valuable comments and suggestions, and to Heike Boeltzig for her research assistance.

[2] For a more comprehensive account of the introduction of New Deal, as well as welfare-to-work, programmes see Millar (2000) and Trickey and Walker (2001).

FOUR

To be or not to be employed? Unemployment in a 'work society'

Wolfgang Ludwig-Mayerhofer[1]

Despite all the problems it has faced during the past decades, Germany still has one of the most affluent and powerful economies of the world. Its high wages, while often accused of being a major cause of the country's unemployment problem, are in fact a sign of an economy based on quality goods produced by a well-trained labour force (Lindlar and Scheremet, 1998). When measured against (average) productivity, they are not so high after all (Kaufmann, 1997; Heise et al, 1998). Consequently, Germany always has defined itself as a 'work society', a society whose affluence, and the distribution thereof, is based on skilled, diligent work.

This image of a 'work society' has been undermined by the persistently high unemployment rate during the past two decades (see Chapter Two, Table 2.1 of this volume). To be sure, the unemployment problems Germany has been facing since the early 1980s are not as poignant as in a number of other countries. However, on account of their perception of the work society, it took Germans quite some time to get accustomed to unemployment rates of 7 to 9%. Frequent warnings that high unemployment had paved the way for the Nazi regime were especially common during the late 1970s and the early 1980s, thereby providing additional arguments for a resolute strategy to create new employment. The public continually rates unemployment among the major social problems, and the fight against it is considered one of the foremost tasks of politics (see, for instance, Fridberg and Ploug, 2000).

This chapter examines unemployment policies in Germany during the past 15 years from a citizenship perspective. The term citizenship here denotes a social and political status that entails two things:

- the terms on which social *recognition* as a member of society is based;
- the circumstances on which *social rights* are granted.

The citizenship framework is helpful in a conceptual way. The encompassing social security provisions by the German welfare system have led some sociologists (Lepsius, 1979; Krätke, 1985; see also Offe, 1991) to conceive of one or several *Versorgungsklassen*, meaning a class (or several classes) whose income and status is based on welfare state provisions, such as the tenured civil servants or the recipients of retirement pensions. However, it is not meaningful to talk about class when it comes to unemployment, or receipt of basic welfare assistance, at least as long as we can assume that there is considerable, and often rapid, flux between unemployment (or basic welfare assistance) and employment. Therefore, it seems more helpful to think about these as statuses connected with certain entitlements to citizenship, rather than classes per se.

For decades, citizenship in Germany was, at its core, work-based and the protection or maintenance of citizenship in the case of unemployment (or other risks) was derived from this work-based citizenship. It is precisely this citizenship derived from (paid) work which, despite being rooted in both public perceptions as well as in the welfare system, has come under attack in the past decades, so much so that a new kind of citizenship has emerged that represents almost a complete reversal. Earlier, unemployment benefits and so-called active labour market policies *were supposed to help* the unemployed get back to work (that is, a secure, full-time and well-paid job according to the German notion of a 'standard employment relationship'). In this new model, the unemployed either are forced to enter 'labour market measure careers' or are put on early retirement, or they even have to work (or to demonstrate a willingness to work) to 'earn' their benefits – not in jobs that provide social security but rather in publicly provided or subsidised community service measures. While this development affects at the moment only a minority of the unemployed, most specifically some of the long-term unemployed, its occurrence is severe enough to warrant closer scrutiny.

The first two sections of this chapter describe German capitalism as a 'work society', and the concomitant notions of citizenship. The third section gives an overview of the German unemployment problem and analyses the changes in citizenship that have developed in its wake. The final section gives a (necessarily preliminary) assessment of the developments since the 1998 change of the German government.

German capitalism

The German political economy is based on what Soskice (1999) calls a 'Coordinated Market Economy', or CME. Such economies are characterised by coordination between companies (for instance, through interlocking directorships), cooperative industrial relations, both concerning wage-setting and in-company industrial relations (such as co-determination), and by a strong system of vocational training. This system is important especially for the type of products on which these economies' success largely depends, sometimes termed 'diversified quality products' (Streeck, 1991). These products, such as those of the heavy industry or the machinery industry that are at the core of the German economy's success in the world market, depend on skilled employees, which are provided by the training system, and on cooperative industrial relations, leading to mutual trust between employers and employees. Furthermore, job periods – periods workers stay with one company – are considerably longer in CMEs than in their liberal market economy counterparts, such as the US or the UK (Streeck, 1997, p 38), as employers wish to deploy the skill and experience of their employees. There is more wage equality, not least because workers are more equal concerning their qualification level.

This system, especially in the German case, was (and to some extent still is) decisively male-centered. Well-trained, skilled male bread-winners devote their life to their companies (and, during leisure time, to their family), while their wives devote their life to their children and their husband's wellbeing. Wives engage only occasionally in paid work, either before marriage or childbirth, or, to a lesser degree, during the 'empty nest' stage of their lives. Certainly, women in past decades have made considerable progress concerning their schooling (surpassing young men in the 1990s as far as secondary level certificates are concerned) and increasingly try to develop skills and careers prior to, and also during, the times of child-rearing (see Chapter Two, Table 2.4 of this volume). Yet, female work is still, to a much greater extent, subordinate or middle-level work, with far fewer women entering the top ranks of management. Many mothers are still forced either to quit working or to engage in part-time work, not least because of the lack of public (or, for that matter, private) childcare facilities.

While the macroeconomic performance of such economies, according to Soskice (1999), is much better than one might expect from a neoliberal point of view (and indeed better than that of their liberal counterparts), they also have distinctive drawbacks. One of these is the lack of flexibility required in developing radically new products. Another is a concomitant lack of flexible services. More precisely, observers point out a number of features that may also have impeded an adaptation of the German economy in the times of high unemployment.

- *The service gap*: One of the drawbacks of the German economy is seen to be the (comparative) predominance of production-related jobs and the concomitant lack of service jobs (Esping-Andersen, 1996b; Freeman and Schettkat, 1999; Jochem and Siegel, 2000). While the majority of the German workforce has been working in services since the mid-1970s, the share of service jobs is considerably lower than in many other advanced countries. In addition many of these service jobs are related to the distribution and administration of goods produced in the industrial sector. Some observers have expressed doubts whether the assumed service gap is more than a statistical artifact (Wagner, 1999; Cornetz and Schäfer, 1999). However, while the service gap may indeed be overestimated, there is some truth to it (Freeman and Schettkat, 1999). Most notably, what seems to be lacking is demand for services by private households.
- *Wage equality, high wages and the tax wedge*: The service gap points to another source of possible trouble. First, Germany is one of the countries with a high wage equality. The spread between high, medium, and low income is lower than in many other countries, and salaries of top executives do not

reach the tremendous amounts that they do in the US (Streeck, 1997, p 35-6; see also Chapter Two, Table 2.17 of this volume). This comparatively high equality is not only a result of the high qualification of most of the workforce, but also reflects the 'family wage' tradition, with higher wages specifically in the male-dominated core industries. Second, and allegedly even more detrimental to a proliferation of private services and more generally of low-paid jobs, there is the 'tax wedge ', with 'tax' also including social security contributions. These make wage costs higher for employers while at the same time employees receive considerably less then they earn 'on paper'. Needless to say, this causes discontent on both sides. Therefore, in the final analysis, the 'basic culprit' resulting from most analyses is the (continental) welfare state. Its problems are aggravated even more, as social security is used – and not infrequently abused – to 'free' the labour market from workers with redundant skills, either through lay-offs or with the help of rules for early retirement (Manow and Seils, 2000a).

It is not my concern, in what follows, whether the shifts deemed necessary from this point of view towards more wage inequality and lower social contributions would indeed result in a sizeable reduction of unemployment, as presently such tendencies can be observed on a very small-scale level at best. Nor am I concerned with devising an alternative route of a more egalitarian distribution of work, which would also include a different distribution of both paid and unpaid work between the genders (Gottschall and Dingeldey, 2000). Rather, my goal is to sketch how the underpinnings of German capitalism continue to shape notions of citizenship (in the sense described earlier), and how these notions are being transformed in the light of persistent labour market problems.

Labour market policies and citizenship for a 'work society'

The difficulties referred to in the previous section did not make themselves felt during a long period of German post-Second World War history. Rather, during the 1960s and the 1970s Germany was proud of its strong welfare state, not least concerning unemployment and labour market policies. These policies, as in most other countries, consist of two types of assistance for the unemployed:

- they offer social protection against the loss of income associated with unemployment (also called 'passive labour market policies');
- they are supposed to help the unemployed getting back into employment (so-called 'active labour market policies')[2].

The basic and foremost type of *protection* – unemployment benefit (*Arbeitslosengeld*) – is based on a system of public insurance which is built on the characteristic principles of 'conservative' welfare states (Esping-Andersen, 1990); that is, conservation of social status and traditional family models with breadwinning husbands and housekeeping wives. Contributions are paid – in equal shares – by employers and employees (with state civil servants and self-employed persons not contributing to the system); they are proportional to the wages or salaries, and so are the benefits paid in case of unemployment[3]. The position of the (usually male) worker as a breadwinner is taken into account through higher benefit payments for unemployed persons with a family. When unemployment benefit is exhausted (usually after one year, for those aged 45 or older by up to three years), unemployment assistance (*Arbeitslosenhilfe*) is available, with the sums paid to the beneficiaries – still tied to previous income – being lower than those of unemployment benefit. The duration of receiving unemployment assistance generally is unlimited. However, it is means-tested; in practice this means that unemployed women especially (whose male partners usually have higher incomes) receive little unemployment assistance, or none at all. A prerequisite for receiving both types of payment is that the unemployed person is able and willing to engage in paid work. Furthermore, since both payments are based on the insurance principle, they are available only after a period of employment with the concomitant contributions (some exceptions concerning unemployment assistance notwithstanding).

Finally, basic welfare assistance (*Sozialhilfe*) is available for those who receive no unemployment benefits or assistance – because they have not contributed enough to the system, for instance – or for those who receive only low payments (or, for that matter, whose income from whatever source is not sufficient). It is entirely means-tested (taking into account the parents' or the offspring's income as well), but it is not tied to previous earnings as the money paid is supposed to reflect the 'needs' of the household.

Yet, the hallmark of the German labour market policies, as they developed during the second half of the 1960s, was not the system of social protection, but rather *'active' labour market policies*. This orientation towards such policies was brought about mainly by the economic upswing, or miracle (*Wirtschaftswunder*) during the second half of the 1950s and the early 1960s. Labour force was becoming increasingly scarce, and fears that the German export-oriented quality production firms would soon lack the well-trained workers they urgently were in need of were on the rise. It was further underlined by the short recession of 1966/67 and its successful management by the federal government, consisting at that time of a grand coalition of Christian Democrats and Social Democrats. Instead of paying benefits, the task of labour market policies was to prevent unemployment and help people to get (adequate) jobs by granting them a right to vocational training (*Fortbildung und Umschulung* [FuU]). In addition to the possibility of training in the case of unemployment, training measures were also supported for those who wanted to be upwardly mobile. Beyond these measures directed at individuals, the political climate at that time also fostered ideas of Keynesian intervention that had been the central means of overcoming the 1966/67 crisis, or so it was believed.

This constellation can be seen as a point of culmination of the development of the (West) German postwar 'work society', a society in which not only income, but also prestige and self-esteem derived from paid work (both on an individual and a collective level). Postwar German society defined itself as one that was rooted in the virtues of hard work and skilled craftsmanship. This perception of a 'work society' derives its specific colouring from features that are heavily institutionalised not only in passive and active labour market policies, but also in the entire political economy of the German system.

Seen from a citizenship perspective, this implies that, for a long time, citizenship was strongly tied to paid work. Those who enjoy most citizenship rights – in the broad sense of participation in work, consumption, public life, and finally social security – are the full-time workers with a 'standard employment relationship' (*Normalarbeitsverhältnis*); that is, a full-time, unlimited work contract with relatively clear career prospects, providing a family wage. This *work-based citizenship* is supplemented by two kinds of 'derived citizenship' (derived, that is, from the work-based type):

- *Social security citizenship:* that is, a citizenship provided by the social insurance system on the basis of continuity in work history, ideally as old-age pension, but, if necessary, also by unemployment benefits and active labour market policy measures.
- *Family security citizenship:* provided for those who are conceived as dependent on the breadwinner, both through the provision of family wages and through those regulations in the social insurance system that take care of the dependent family members through widows' or widowers' (and orphans') pensions, higher unemployment benefit payments for unemployed persons with children and the inclusion of dependent family members in health insurance. While the term 'family security citizenship' is chosen primarily because of the family-oriented social security regulations mentioned earlier, it also reflects the idea of secure, long-lasting family relationships, since much less protection is available for divorced persons or single parents, for instance.

At any rate, both types of derived citizenship were seen as part of the same system of a work society, providing esteem and similar (or, related) material rewards, as the typically male adult work-based citizenship. It is clear that, at the culmination of this trinitarian conception of citizenship in the early 1970s, foundations already had been laid, both in social practice and in (legal and other) institutions, for women not being content anymore with their derived citizenship. Yet, it was only during the second half of the 1970s that family law abandoned the rule that the husband could decide whether or not 'his' wife might enter the labour market. The number of 'economically active' women, and especially married women or those with young children, was still comparatively low.

Adapting to the crisis: the devaluation and reversal of social security citizenship

When a work society runs out of work

As in many other countries, unemployment began to rise in (West) Germany as a result of the 'oil crisis' of 1973/74. Since that, unemployment figures rose in two further large steps (1981-85 and 1992-98), with only very slow declines after 1985 and 1998. The situation was much more drastic in East Germany (the former German Democratic Republic), where unemployment levels of 17% to 18% (and even higher in several regions), corresponding to about 1 to 1.2 million persons, were frozen 'politically' by regulations that put people 55 years and older on early retirement schemes and many others in special training programmes or state-sponsored employment (discussed later in this chapter).

Flows into and out of unemployment are higher than stock, a situation that is by no means unique to Germany. This indicates some degree of labour market turnover. Yet, the German labour market exhibits a considerable amount of long-term unemployment (LTU; see Chapter Two, Table 2.11 of this volume). It is argued, that the high unemployment level results in part from a sorting process where some of the unemployed find a new job rather quickly, whereas others, the 'less employable', build up a hard core of LTU for which it becomes increasingly difficult to find a job. Indeed, the percentage of LTU in the past few years has risen considerably to a figure that is surpassed only by the southern European countries, where extreme labour market problems prevail, and by Belgium (and perhaps also the Netherlands) (Ganßmann, 2000). Even though national statistics show a somewhat lower degree of LTU than the OECD figures, the rise of LTU is evident also from these sources, indicating an increasingly closed labour market where the chances to return to work from unemployment are decreasing over time.

Labour market problems may be even more severe than the figures indicate. Several modifications of labour market statistics during the period 1983-98 seem to have had the effect of pushing down the official number of unemployed persons. However, much more important (and greater) are the numbers of those people who do not show up as 'unemployed' either because of early retirement regulations or because of labour market oriented measures, such as (re-)training or *Arbeitsbeschaffungsmaßnahmen* (make-work schemes). These measures have been especially important in East Germany, where they helped to keep unemployment figures at 'acceptable' levels (see later). Finally, it is assumed that there is a substantial number of 'discouraged workers'. The *Institut für Arbeitsmarkt- und Berufsforschung der Bundesanstalt für Arbeit* (IAB) – or, the Institute for Labour Market and Occupational Research of the Federal Labour Office – estimates that the overall figure is between 2.5 and 2.8 million for 1990-97. Numbers have been declining ever since, and reached two million in 2000. Among these, about 1.3 million were 'discouraged workers', and about

700,000 participated in labour market programs (West Germany: 420,000; East Germany: 280,000; Autorengemeinschaft, 2001, p 6).

The initial reaction to the first major rise of unemployment figures, after the 1974/5 oil crisis, had been to provide more training programmes as well as higher benefits through raising the replacement ratio. In the years that followed, however, it became clear that the continuous welfare expansion envisioned in the first half of the 1970s had come to a halt, and the government waved goodbye to the idea of economic steering via Keynesian spending. As far as unemployment was concerned, this meant that, despite official denials, the fight against unemployment was subordinated to the goals of cutting back public deficits and of pushing economic growth. Shifts towards a reduced public deficit, decreased state expenditure, fewer taxes, and fewer regulations were first brought about by the growing influence of the F.D.P. (the Liberal Party) in coalition with the Social Democrats, as well as by the change in the office of the chancellor (Helmut Schmidt, a self-proclaimed expert economist replaced Willy Brandt). Furthermore, they were reinforced by the 'conservative turn' in 1982 when Helmut Kohl came to power.

Still, these shifts were far from radical (Gottschall and Dingeldey, 2000). Such ideas not only met with opposition within the labour wing of the Christian Democrats and the Federal Labour Office (FLO). In fact, the persisting unemployment also posed serious threats to the legitimation of the government. Therefore, a double strategy of continuities and discontinuities was applied:

- Continuities in the field of *active* labour market policies, such as training programmes, re-insertion subsidies, or make-work schemes, gave the impression that unemployment was being taken seriously. At the same time, however, these measures were also used to embellish unemployment figures. Likewise, *passive* labour market policies were continued, yet with a quite different emphasis. In order to reduce the unemployment figures, early retirement measures of various kinds were deployed that swept considerable numbers of elderly unemployed (or would-be unemployed) from the labour market, such as the *Frühverrentung*, or '59er rule', and *Altersübergangsgeld* (see Manow and Seils, 2000a).
- Discontinuities, such as cuts in benefits and the introduction of deregulation measures, were to demonstrate that the goal of restructuring economy was taken seriously. However, not only were these measures not carried out rigidly enough, they did not take into account the characteristics of the German Coordinated Market Economy.

Therefore, the Conservative–Liberal government was not very successful in reducing unemployment or in providing social security for the unemployed, nor did it succeed in promoting and bringing about the more liberal 'new economic order', a few exceptions (such as privatisation of state enterprises) notwithstanding.

Continuities: the changing face of social security citizenship

Measures of active labour market policy by no means came to a halt even under Chancellor Helmut Kohl. They were considered an effective means by the FLO, which never spent much more than half of its budget for *Arbeitslosengeld*, and often considerably less than that (see Table 4.1). Yet, given that unemployment figures between 1982 and 1990 fluctuated around two million, the sums spent were much too low to have any decisive effect. Whether higher expenditures, which were claimed mainly by unions' representatives (see Arbeitskreis AFG-Reform, 1995), indeed would have had such an effect is far from certain. On the one hand, there are rather clear signs that such training programmes, mostly available for LTU, often 'cream the best'; that is, they select those cases with the best prospects for a return into the labour market[4]. On the other hand, despite this positive selection, the re-insertion effects of these measures are doubtful to say the least (see Wingens et al, 2000a, 2000b; see also the studies surveyed in Fitzenecker and Speckesser, 2000). The same probably applies to the wage subsidies available that were granted in 2001 for instance to the employers of nearly 300,000 previously unemployed persons (Bundesanstalt

Table 4.1: Expenses of the Federal Labour Office (FLO) for active (training measures, make-work schemes [ABM]) and passive (*Arbeitslosengeld*) labour market policies (in millions of DM)[a]

Year[b]	Total expenses[c]	Training[d]	Make-work[e]	*Arbeitslosengeld*
1980	21,668	4,580	1,749	8,109
1982	33,359	5,691	1,259	18,029
1984	29,640	5,562	2,106	14,139
1986	31,860	7,720	3,319	14,049
1988	40,842	10,711	4,372	18,050
1990	43,880	14,550	3,031	17,921
1992	93,523	20,251	11,330	31,557
1994	99,865	15,529	11,949	45,870
1996	105,588	18,145	13,738	55,655
1998	98,852	15,523	10,344	52,827
2000	98,716	16,858	9,865	46,179

[a] *Before 1990:* West Germany. *After 1990:* Germany.

[b] Data before 1994 have been re-calculated from Arbeitskreis AFG-Reform (1995, p 217), and are subject to rounding errors. Data for 1994 and afterwards from Statistisches Jahrbuch, various issues.

[c] Total expenses are minus *Arbeitslosenhilfe*, which after 1991 was paid directly from the federal government budget and therefore no longer appears on the FLO budget.

[d] Data for 'training' from 1992 onwards are from Online Times Series Service of the Federal Statistical Office and are not comparable to previous figures.

[e] Make-work in 1998 and 2000 comprises *Strukturanpassungsmaßnahmen Ost*, a special scheme created for Eastern Germany.

für Arbeit internet information service, June, 2002; figure excludes people in mark-work-schemes).

These problems were aggravated after 1990, especially in the eastern parts of Germany. After the fall of the Berlin Wall and during the process of unification, Helmut Kohl talked about 'flourishing landscapes' in East Germany within a time-span of five years. Of course, this was not meant as a threat to reverse the wheel of history and to turn the eastern parts into an agricultural society but rather as a promise to bring about a thriving economy and the concomitant welfare.

It is not possible here to depict in detail the fate of East Germany in the past decade[5]. The low productivity of East German firms, together with European Monetary Union (EMU) and the exchange of the DDR Mark for the Deutschmark (DM) at a rate of 1:1, led to an immediate breakdown of the markets in Central and Eastern Europe for East German firms. The new exchange rate led to a steep rise in export prices. At the same time, the unions were demanding a rapid growth of East German salaries to bring them closer to those of West Germany. As a result, roughly 3-3.5 million jobs (starting from 9.5 to 10 millions of employed persons immediately after the Wall came down) were lost within a few years and contributions and taxes were raised, often considerably. The public deficit increased from DM 1,049 billion in 1990 to DM 2,343 billion in 2000 (Statistisches Jahrbuch der Bundesrepublik Deutschland, various issues). Roughly 10% of the GDP are transferred annually from West to East Germany (Czada, 1998, p 39).

What has been the role of labour market policies in this process? As a result of initial optimism, the most widely used measure in 1990 and 1991 was *Kurzarbeitsgeld* (literally 'short time work payments', huge state subsidies paid to employers to cover wages for employees in firms with allegedly 'temporary' difficulties who might otherwise be laid off. It was granted to 1.7 million people in 1991). However, other measures had to be taken when it soon became clear that there was little hope that these enterprises could be saved from bankruptcy, or that they had to lay off huge numbers of their employees (Table 4.2). From 1992 onwards, the steps taken were measured out to keep the number of unemployed persons fairly constant at an average level of 1.1 to 1.2 million (after 1997, this was allowed to raise to 1.3 to 1.4 million). These steps consisted of:

- a huge programme of early retirement (*Vorruhestandsgeld* and *Altersübergangsgeld*) that wiped about one million persons aged 55+ from the labour market;
- all-encompassing training programmes allegedly rendering the 'backward' East Germans fit for the new world they were supposed to enter;
- 'make-work schemes' or 'job-creation measures' (*Arbeitsbeschaffungsmaßnahmen)*, substantial wage subsidies (between 30% and 75%, and, in exceptional circumstances, even 100%) for formerly LTU who work on tasks of 'public interest'[6].

Table 4.2: Reduction of unemployment figures in East Germany by selected measures (1990-2000) (in 000s)[a]

	1990	1992	1994	1996	1998	2000
Short-time work	341	189	39	29	13	11
Make-work schemes	5	540	363	355	246	237
Further training, re-training	6	383	214	205	146	137
Vorruhestandsgeld[b]	180	295	126	0	0	0
Altersübergangsgeld[b]	10	516	524	186	1	0
Others	(difference between sum and measures above)					
Total	542	1933	1282	788	420	405

[a] These figures do not show the number of persons directly affected by the different measures, but rather their estimated effects on reducing the number of unemployed.

[b] *Vorruhestandsgeld* and *Altersübergangsgeld* are payments for older people who quit their jobs before they are entitled to old-age pensions.

Source: Autorengemeinschaft (2001, p 27)

As a consequence, it is assumed that a potentially growing group of workers develop so-called 'labour market measure careers'. They participate in (perhaps several) measures either to be entitled (at least temporarily) to unemployment benefits, or simply to be kept busy, or finally as a 'test' concerning their willingness to work. In other words, such measures have the same effects as have early retirement programmes or, for that matter, special training programmes for youths without an apprenticeship contract that were prominent especially in the mid-1980s. They do not aim at re-insertion in the labour market; rather they free the labour market from the 'redundant' low-productivity workers.

Summing up these developments, then, we can say that social security citizenship has been maintained to some degree, both in West and in East Germany, but that its nature has changed. Until the mid-1970s, social security citizenship had two equally respectable faces: re-insertion into the labour market for those still in the working age, and retirement for those who had contributed enough to the pension fund in order to 'deserve' (that is, to have 'earned') their own old-age pension. Since the 1980s, re-insertion has not been abandoned, at least not completely, but for many of working age, the idea of reintegration has been given up and replaced by measures that represent more a pseudo-integration and at the same time keep the unemployment figures low. Retirement has also been devalued. Whereas formerly an old-age pensioner was someone looking back on a long working life that had provided him or her with income, status, and prestige, now increasingly an old-age pensioner, especially in early retirement, is someone who has been discharged because of low productivity, because of his or her inability to keep pace with the current demands of working life.

Discontinuities: the creation of a new type of citizenship – 'welfare (dependency) citizenship'

The developments described earlier may be grist to the mill for those who argue against state intervention precisely because of its double nature – expensive and inefficient. However, those measures that aimed at propelling labour market policies in a different, allegedly neoliberal direction were no more successful. Two aspects deserve particular attention because of the importance that was attached to them by the Christian Democratic-Liberal government and its critics.

Deregulation

In neoliberal discourse unemployment is brought about by the 'tight' regulations, among other things, that inhibit the development of a truly 'free' labour market. One rule has been attacked especially – the proscription of 'hire and fire' policies on the part of companies by erecting rather high obstacles against layoffs (at least formally), especially for firms with more than five employees. In each of these firms, which account for the majority of firms and, therefore of course, for the vast majority of employees, the duration of labour contracts in principle was unlimited, with only a few exceptions. In 1985 these exceptions were transformed into the rule, with the circumstances that permitted limited or fixed-term labour contracts being enlarged considerably; since 1996, all new labour contracts can be fixed-term (up to two years).

The increase in the number and proportion of fixed-term contracts, however, was very moderate (there are no data available concerning any change more recent than 1985), and most observers doubt that the deregulation of labour contracts had any effects on employment (and therefore, on unemployment; Bielenski, 1998; for earlier assessments and discussions see Büchtemann, 1990; Büchtemann and Neumann, 1990)[7]. At least two reasons exist for the very small increase in fixed-term contracts. On the one hand, even before the change in legislation it had always been possible to lay off employees for 'economic' reasons, for instance if they were redundant due to a decrease in a company's order inflow. On the other hand, fixed-term contracts do not fit the German Coordinated Market Economy; that is, companies that want to develop a close relationship with their workers will usually give them an unlimited contract. Therefore, fixed-term contracts were acceptable mainly to smaller businesses in the peripheral sectors of the economy (see Ganßmann and Haas, 1999, p 131). However, deregulation also had an ideological underpinning: if what was declared an important barrier to employment had been abandoned, by way of implication those still unemployed had to be lacking 'employability' – or perhaps even 'willingness to work'. Such notions were further supported by a second measure: cuts in benefits.

Cuts in unemployment benefits

One of the first measures implemented by the Conservative government was a reduction of compensation level and of eligibility criteria. A number of observers feared that this would entail a *Neue Armut*, or 'new poverty' (see Balsen et al, 1984; Lompe, 1987). Indeed, the number of households receiving (means-tested) basic welfare assistance payments (*Sozialhilfe*) as a consequence of unemployment increased dramatically during the 1980s (from about 100,000 in 1981 to almost 700,000 in 1993). It is less clear, however, to which extent this strong relationship between unemployment and poverty is a result of the cuts in unemployment benefits, or if it was simply caused by the high number of unemployed persons, especially long-term unemployed.

There was also an ideological dimension. These developments were accompanied (and justified) by increasing accusations that the unemployed were abusing benefits and were unwilling to work. Indeed, there were occasional expressions of contempt for the unemployed, or of 'blaming the victim', not least by Helmut Kohl himself (most famously when he spoke out against 'holiday park Germany'). Such notions gained strength during the 1990s. For instance, during the second half of the 1990s, regulations forced the unemployed to contact the local labour office regularly, a measure intended to restrict 'welfare fraud' (through receiving unemployment compensation without actually being willing to work). In the final analysis, however, this only burdened both the unemployed and the staff of the labour office. The measure has since been abolished by the Social Democratic/Green government. Also, in earlier times, job seekers were in some ways protected from having to accept jobs that paid significantly less or were inferior in other respects to their former jobs. These regulations have been changed to the effect that even a highly trained and experienced unemployed person must accept virtually any job so long as the salary is not lower than the current unemployment benefit (on penalty of receiving no more compensation payments). This, however, only applies in principle, since the number of 'bad' jobs available is far outweighed by the number of applicants with a corresponding lack of vocational training.

The cuts in unemployment benefits, and the slowly but steadily increasing number of long-term unemployed that had to rely either on *Arbeitslosenhilfe* or *Sozialhilfe* (or both) in the final analysis led to the creation of a new type of 'citizenship' that I term *welfare dependency citizenship*. Very few, if any, of the long-term unemployed living on *Arbeitslosenhilfe* or *Sozialhilfe* are under the illusion that they will be reintegrated in the economy. This has been especially so since 1993, when training measures have been granted only if a job placement is a prospect, and the subsidies for 'make-work schemes' have been reduced, thereby making them less attractive for employers[8]. Rather, it is made clear to the unemployed that their future is not bright *and* that they should be happy to receive welfare payments. At the same time it is repeated that many of them are 'work-shy' and use the allegedly generous benefits to live on other people's money. This is also emphasised by recent developments that add a touch of 'workfare'. Increasingly, *Sozialhilfe* and also *Arbeitslosenhilfe* recipients are forced to engage in community service (on penalty of first a reduction and finally a complete halt of all payments). In contrast to 'make-work schemes', community service is not a job with the concomitant social security payments (even though usually about one euro per hour is paid in addition to the basic *Sozialhilfe* or *Arbeitslosenhilfe* payments). Rather, it is understood as a compensation of the unemployed for the welfare support he or she receives (see Voges et al, 2000, on the different measures of local authorities).

The number of people affected is difficult to estimate. However, it is assumed that among the roughly 2.5 millions *Sozialhilfe* recipients, there are about one million single-parent families with small children who are exempted from workfare. By way of implication, this leaves about 1-1.5 million *Sozialhilfe* recipients plus an unknown number of *Arbeitslosenhilfe* recipients who may become subjects of 'workfare' measures. However, as the application of such measures is an affair of local authorities (communities or local Labour Offices), no regular statistics are available. One recent estimate of the Deutscher Städte- und Gemeindebund (Association of German Municipalities) gives a figure of 400,000 people per annum (www.verbaende.com/news/ges_text.php4?m=9555). The decisive point, however, is perhaps not the number of people concerned but rather the message conveyed; that is, that the provision of the basic needs is not something one is entitled to but rather something that has to be 'earned'.

Prospects

German Chancellor Gerhard Schröder gave highest priority to the reduction of unemployment in his 1998 electoral campaign. The most important means to further this aim are:

- The *Bündnis für Arbeit, Ausbildung und Wettbewerbsfähigkeit* (Alliance for Jobs), a coordination scheme in which employers, trade unions, members of the federal administration and other interest groups are supposed to develop and coordinate measures to foster growth and employment. The *Bündnis für Arbeit* in the meantime has established several commissions but its effects are judged controversially (Schroeder and Esser, 1999).
- An immediate programme to reduce youth unemployment, called *Jugend mit Perspektive* (JUMP; 'Youth with a Perspective') or Jusopro (*Sofortprogramm zum Abbau der Jugendarbeitslosigkeit*), with state subsidies to employers willing to create jobs for unemployed youths. Between 100,000 and 140,000 jobs or training measures per year were subsidised through this scheme from 1999 to 2001 but it is less clear how many of these actually were new jobs.
- A reduction of state debts and of social insurance contributions, supposed to create both higher incomes on part of the households and an economic climate conducive to increased investments and innovations on part of the economy.

- Policies whose overt aim is to stop the increase of deregulated employment, most notably legislation to detect the 'apparently self-employed'; that is, persons who are formally self-employed but who work for one firm only and do so on a regular basis[9].

While some of these measures are in line with social democratic ideas of protecting workers, overall present policies and rhetoric seem to be based on the demonstration that a social-democratic government is more capable than the conservatives to make the economy flourish. This 'flourishing', it is suggested, is the best measure to reduce unemployment. Indeed, a temporary upswing during 1999 and 2000 apparently 'proved' the soundness of these policies and was supported, as far as unemployment figures are concerned, by a concomitant decrease of the labour force due to demographic causes. On the other hand, Schröder has increasingly propagated 'civil society' ideas, not surprisingly with the aim to proclaim the idea that the state is not responsible for everything, and his statement that there is no "right to idleness" in spring 2001 has made clear that he is preparing the field for "blaming the victim" policies. Such policies may well be necessary – it currently seems that his goal, declared in 1998, of reducing the number of unemployed below the figure of 3.5 million and of cutting down the social contributions below 40% of the wages until 2002 seems beyond reach. Plans for labour offices to 'get tougher' on the unemployed and to engage more in 'testing' their willingness to work by developing 're-insertion plans' – the violation of which will lead to cuts in or loss of benefits – were implemented in January 2002 under the premise of getting the unemployed back into work faster and more efficiently. More recently, following the disclosure of the Labour Office's considerable inefficiency concerning job placements, the role of private job placement agencies has been enlarged. Furthermore, state subsidies to low-wage jobs that had been put into practice in a few regions by way of model projects (*Kombilohn* or *Mainzer Modell*) have been made available throughout the country. As these measures have been introduced virtually overnight, they seem to indicate hectic attempts to demonstrate concern for the unemployment problem, rather than well-devised plans.

In addition, there is still the divide between West and East Germany. East Germany's share of overall employment is likely to continue to decrease (Bade, 1999). While observers point out that small and medium-sized businesses in the industry sector show tendencies of expansion, other sectors of the economy (such as construction, but also the partly overstaffed state administrations) will exhibit declining employment (Pohl, 1999). Furthermore, while the first wave of East–West migration has come to a halt, the fear of a brain drain remains, with the most resourceful young people leaving a society of 'losers' behind. While this picture is certainly an exaggeration, the problems of East Germany will continue to cast shadows on the brighter picture of the future of the German economy that is at the heart of Schröder's politics.

Notes

[1] I am grateful to Jochen Clasen and Knut Halvorsen for their helpful comments on an earlier version of this paper, and to Maria Haunerdinger who gathered large amounts of data for this report, not all of which made it into the final draft. Finally, my sincerest thanks to Manuela Thurner and Julia Möbius for preventing some crude attacks on the English language!

[2] A good overview of the developments until about 1990 can be found in Clasen (1994). Note that even though I am uneasy using the terms 'active' and 'passive', they are used here for reasons of brevity (and for lack of genuine alternatives).

[3] However, there are ceilings built into the system. Contributions are paid only for that part of the wage or salary that does not exceed a certain limit; accordingly, there is an upper limit to the benefits paid.

[4] See Schmid et al (1994) for a special programme for the most disadvantaged among the LTU; also Heinelt and Weck (1998, p 76) on training programmes in general; Buslei and Steiner (1999) for training programmes and subsidies.

[5] Detailed accounts can be found in Heinelt and Weck (1998) and Wiedemann et al (1999).

[6] Roughly another million persons 'relieved' the East German labour market either by moving to West Germany or by commuting from the East to work in West Germany.

[7] Recent research, however, suggests that one effect of fixed-term contracts is a decrease in wages and salaries (Groß, 1999). Fixed-term contracts, therefore, may have been one of the causes of the increasing gap between incomes of wage earners and those of self-employed and/or employers. The regulations concerning fixed-term contracts were changed by January 2001. Although it is too early to assess the effects of these changes, they are unlikely to alter the picture in any great way.

[8] Above all, this concerns West Germany. For East Germany, special measures have been created, notably the so-called *Strukturanpassungsmaßnahmen Ost* ('structural adaptation measures East').

[9] However, these policies perhaps were intended foremost to collect contributions to the social security system. This is most obvious in the case of petty jobs, as the employees do not get anything for the money the employers are paying into the old age pension funds (except if they back this money up by additional payments of their own). The justification for this was to make petty jobs so expensive for employers that they were compelled to transform them into regular jobs.

FIVE

France: the impossible new social compromise?

Pascal Ughetto and Denis Bouget

Introduction

Since the 1980s, France has been experiencing high rates of unemployment, which, in comparison to certain European countries, appear particularly difficult to reduce (see Chapter Two of this volume).

France is often stigmatised for the extreme rigidity of its economic framework and especially of its labour market, and excessive employment protection, in particular, which prevent companies from becoming more competitive and aggressive on international markets. However, it is an overstatement to say that France has not reformed its institutions. Liberalism-driven programmes, to be discussed in this chapter, have renewed institutional settlements. Nevertheless, formal macro compromises seem difficult to engineer, although the state (especially under the socialist governments) tried to foster collective bargaining.

This chapter shows that the country has indeed tried to reform its institutions towards a certain liberalisation but that, at the same time, it has made sure that the market has not been allowed to govern all aspects of life. This results in a somewhat harsh and conflicting path of institutional reform which may be specific to France. However, it can be said that France is not necessarily condemned to rigidity but is building its own way to flexibility.

Unemployment patterns in France

For two decades, Europe has faced severe problems of unemployment, particularly in comparison to the US. French social history often stands as the most illustrative of these difficulties. Unemployment has risen constantly from less than 3% in 1974 to 10.5% in 1987. Following a dip in 1988 and 1989, it rose again in the 1990s and reached about 12.5% in 1995-97 (Figure 5.1). Its rapid decline since 1998 – down to 8.6% in 2001 – was subsequently halted, and it creeped back up to 9.1% in April 2002.

During these decades, unemployment stemmed from frustratingly slow growth in the employment level compared to the increase in the size of the labour

Figure 5.1: The unemployment trend in France from 1970 (%)

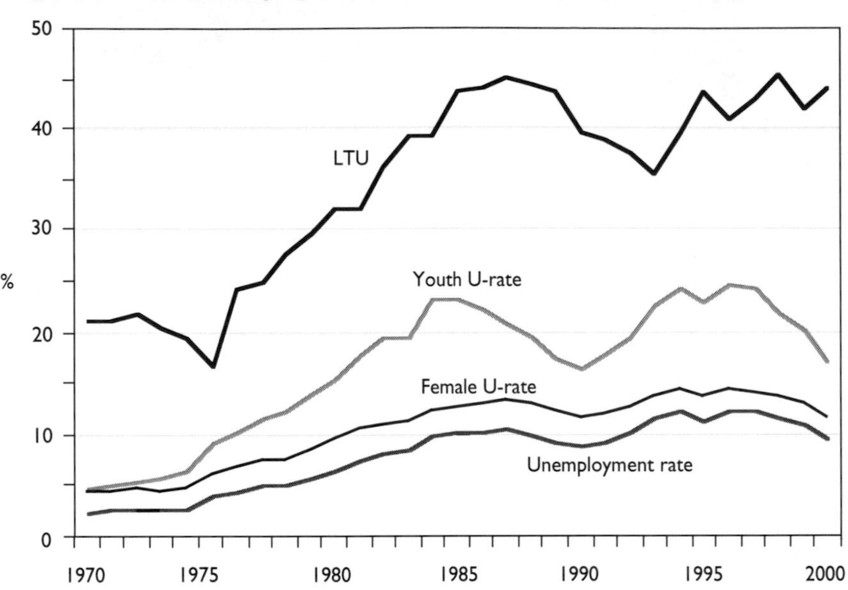

LTU: more than one-year unemployment.

Youth U: unemployed aged less than 25.

Source: Institut National de la Statistique et des Etudes Economiques (INSEE)

force. The latter is mainly the result of growing female participation (and demographic change), which more than offset declining economic participation in early and late working life. In France, young people enter the labour market at an average age of 21; the legal retirement age is 60, and early retirement has often been a way for firms to cut back on staff without social disturbances. As a result, France has a rather low economic participation rate, combined with a low employment rate, which mainly originates in low participation and employment of the young and elderly (see also Chapter Two of this volume).

French unemployment is characterised by a rather high average duration, which also increases as employees get older: 8.1 months for 16-24 age group; 13.3 for 24-49 age group; 22.7 for 50-65 age group (CGP, 1997). As Figure 5.1 illustrates, long-term unemployment grew dramatically from 15% of total unemployment in 1975 to 45% in the mid 1980s and also after the mid 1990s. Furthermore, its exposure to business cycles can also be observed. This pattern explains how long-term unemployment has been interpreted as the leading factor in social exclusion, and it has placed one series of employment policies more or less in the field of social exclusion: training for unskilled workers and the young, social security contribution relief for several employers, and so on.

The French labour market has specific selective effects (Cohen and Dupas, 1999), especially when compared to the US, in that finding a new job takes rather a long time and, once it has been obtained, the job is more precarious.

As a matter of fact, if insiders are more protected than in other countries such as the US, workers who have recently been settled into a new job are far less protected than their counterparts in the US.

Therefore, economic recession in France has produced and combined precariousness with unemployment. The resulting 'atypical work' gathers different types of working conditions; that is, several categories of 'under-' or 'poorly' employed people, discouraged workers and part-time workers wanting full-time jobs. Discouraged workers, early-retired citizens and involuntary part-time workers account for a population of two million individuals (compared to three million unemployed in the mid-1990s).

Until the 1970s, French society had lived with the futuristic ideology of a poverty-free society. Nevertheless, in the early 1980s, new impoverishment factors were described as a 'new poverty' and later as 'social exclusion' (Paugam, 1996). Most of the roots of the increasing poverty for this decade were to be found in the economic field. Precariousness of workers (Paugam, 2000) encompasses precariousness at work (new types of uncertain jobs, stress, pains, and so on) and precariousness in employment (unemployment, long term unemployment, non-permanent work and the low paid process for vulnerable groups).

Precariousness and social exclusion are temporal processes which afflict several vulnerable groups: the unemployed, young people, wives, single mothers, immigrants, and so on. Nevertheless, there are, at the same time, several differences compared with past poverty. Firstly, in France, the elderly are not considered as a vulnerable group. In fact, the senior citizen and retirement policies since the 1960s are, from a social integration or citizenship point of view, an unqualified success (although this is much more controversial from an

Figure 5.2: Trend of unemployment and precariousness

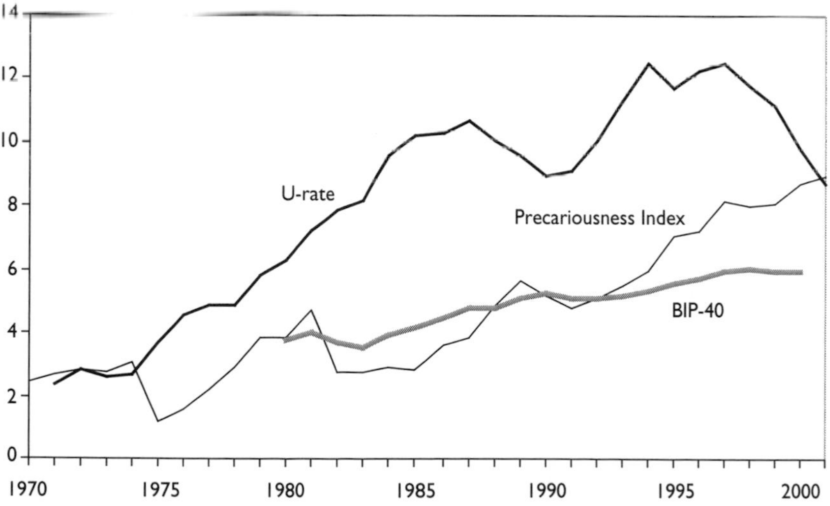

Source: CERC-Association (2002) databases

economic perspective). Secondly, social exclusion is less of a rural phenomenon than an urban one. Thirdly, the time-related process of social exclusion creates a generational poverty, in that young people seem to be increasingly vulnerable. Fourthly, poverty largely affects isolated people (many recipients of minimum incomes in France live alone).

Réseau d'alerte sur les inégalités (RAI) – a group of statisticians – have created a French index of poverty (BIP-40) partly inspired by the Human Development Index. Figure 5.2 shows the trend of the global index (BIP-40), the rate of unemployment rate and the trend of precariousness (part-time, under-employment, percentage of women in the part time). An opposite trend in the mid 1990s is the most striking facts. Despite a decreasing rate of unemployment, we can note ever-growing precariousness.

Liberal reforms: policies oriented towards adapting the French economy to a new competitive context

The French unemployment situation, the OECD often claims, is due to persisting excessive rigidities, a lack of trust in the market, competition and individual initiative, both equally hindered by the proliferation of rules. This does not do justice to the actual process of adaptation by the French economy and society, initiated in the 1980s and largely favoured by the state and accepted in seemingly less adversative industrial relations (Dufour and Hege, 1997). In particular, orthodoxy (supply policies tackling inflation, and so on) has clearly been the name of the game in macroeconomic policy, completed by policies aiming at adapting the most vulnerable populations to the new modes of unemployment and work.

Since 1982/83, a twofold strategy has been implemented to surmount unemployment. On the one hand, macroeconomic policy has focused on improving French competitiveness; the idea being that creating jobs requires the ability to take on international competition successfully. As far as the companies' situation is concerned, results have been obtained beyond expectations: wages in the 1980s and 1990s rose less than productivity, inflation slowed down from 14% in 1982 to a steady 1% in the 1990s, the trade surplus has been growing since 1992, and profits as well as the capacity to invest are now both very high. On the other hand, labour market policy has been targeted to accompany macroeconomic policy by facilitating the adaptation of the French labour force. During its initial stage, between 1982 and 1992 (DARES, 1997; Holcblat, 1998), it was mainly a matter of making the adaptation of French economy to international competition more acceptable for the more fragile section of the population; that is, retraining programmes, early retirement, actions favouring first-time access or return to the labour market by young people and/or the long-term unemployed, particularly through social contribution exemptions. This was interpreted as a 'social treatment of unemployment'. However, besides this policy, the Ministry of Labour was also promoting actions in favour of up-grading skills and work organisations oriented towards the quality of the products within the framework of a 'contractual training policy' negotiated with bodies at branch level. The state has also been active in improving the capacity of labour supply and demand that has to be met. Emphasis is now on reinforcing employability through training programmes while many forms of subsidised jobs have aimed at enabling people with low employability (low-skilled young people) to integrate into more traditional jobs. Moreover, the labour law has been reformed in order to make it less binding (easier layoffs, and so on). The deregulation of the labour market was probably the main concern, not forgetting the attempt to support firms' non-price competitiveness strategies.

In the 1990s, the main routes of the labour market policy partly shifted towards an increasingly liberalist one. Part-time work has been boosted since 1992 by more flexible legal rules and by incentives given to employers (tax exemptions). Conservative and socialist governments have tried to promote service jobs to individuals by tax cuts. The 1993 recession brought more unemployment and reinforced the liberal instigation of the labour market policy by focusing attention on the common arguments:

- wage cost would be exorbitant, in particular for low-wage jobs (which would yield low-skilled worker unemployment);
- unemployment benefits would have disincentive effects;
- passive spending would have to be turned into active spending, and so on.

One of the most liberal-inspired reforms is probably the law on employment (*loi quinquennale sur l'emploi*, 1993) which focused on the reduction in the non-wage cost. This law was explicitly based on the idea that excessive labour cost was the main reason for the unemployment among the less productive workers (see also Chapter One of this volume).

Employers are now exempted from paying social taxes on low wages:

> Exemption is thus activated by the job characteristics and not those of the employed person. The cut in labour cost no longer deals with offsetting a specific disability on the market but with influencing the amount of jobs offered. (Holcblat, 1998, p 2)

Economists generally have difficulties identifying clear outcomes of this policy but there is considerable consensus regarding the idea that it is a necessary remedy to the possible exclusion of the less skilled (Pisani-Ferry, 2000).

Besides, France also experienced a process of successive stages of reduction in the eligibility criteria for unemployment benefit throughout the 1980s and 1990s. The amount of benefit was also reduced. This process of reduction comes from the decisions of the *Union nationale pour l'emploi dans l'industrie et le commerce* (UNEDIC), the national institution which manages unemployment benefits. The employers argued on this occasion that it was necessary to create incentives to move on from unemployment, although the trade unions refused to follow such a rationale. In the future, there could be a new step forward in the process of liberalisation. The longer the duration of the unemployment the less unemployment benefit could be claimed. Indeed, this legal rule is a 'negative' incentive to work and a kind of sanction for being unemployed.

As a result, the liberalisation of French labour market has been significant in that it really has become more flexible. For example, most hiring is now carried out for insecure jobs. This has firmly helped to improve the 'employment content of economic growth': 2.3% of GDP growth is insufficient to boost job creation. In so doing, France has gradually implemented certain 'activation' strategies in a similar manner as other European countries. Only since 1997 has France appeared to explore specific non-liberal ways. In fact, the Jospin government (1997-2002) completed the inherited policy by two reforms: a reduction in working-time was implemented (the legal duration of work was shortened from 39 to 35 hours a week; Jefferys, 2000), and transitory public jobs are today being developed for young people in order to create activities and professions tackling new social needs that the market cannot satisfy spontaneously. Nevertheless, this is more an extension to previous policies than a radical shift or a scrapping of some kind of liberalism.

Without a significant labour market policy, the French economy would spontaneously have been unable to increase employment or even to keep it steady (Figure 5.3). In addition, only subsidised jobs succeeded in keeping jobs available at their constant average level, and only early retirement and training provided for the unemployed resulted in lower unemployment. Finally, we can note that labour market policy includes a number of individuals that remain at the same level as the unemployed population.

These policies show that the liberal doctrine has actually been influential, despite the reluctance shown by certain politicians. In fact, the liberal rationale has expanded and been implemented by successive stages.

However, criticisms from economists persist due to the over-pronounced liberal definition of economic policies. Some critics insist that institutional reforms towards liberalisation, although they can prove to have real effects in an economy (such as the US), must be considered very carefully.

In France especially, an unduly restrictive monetary policy, linked to the convergence criteria of the Maastricht Treaty, has kept economic growth below its potential level, while the US, on the other hand, chose a less restrictive policy mix (Atkinson, 1993). Some smaller European countries found other specific ways. Furthermore, national restrictive policies were chosen without any European political coordination. In fact, these non-cooperative strategies deepened each national economic recession. Finally, macroeconomic variables were more significant than microeconomic ones, such as wages (Husson, 2000; IRES, 2000). Real wage, for instance, rose in Europe by 0.9% per year between 1990 and 1998. Although this figure is quite similar to the 0.8% increase in the US, Europe created far fewer jobs. As a result, wages can hardly be the cause of unemployment. Moreover, Europe's increase in productivity (1.7%) was faster than in the US (0.9%), which means that wages had been kept under much

Figure 5.3: Components of the potential labour force (000s of persons)

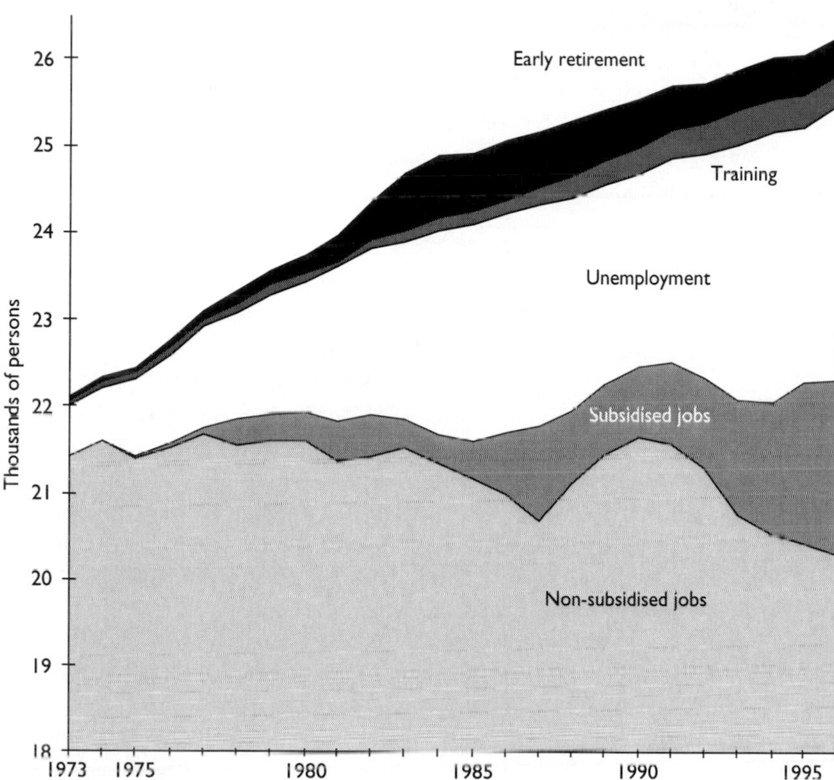

tighter control in Europe than in the US. Indeed, "paradoxically, it is the area that has provided the biggest efforts in terms of wage restraint that has created the least jobs" (IRES, 2000, p 18).

France experienced a dramatic decline in the share of wages within the national added value of the 1980s (a percentage that steadied in the 1990s and that is much more substantial than that of the US, for example). French wage earners appear to have taken part to an implicit social compromise based on serious efforts in wage moderation but the results in terms of reduction in unemployment are definitely not self-evident.

An analysis such as this could lead us to certain uncommon but suggestive interpretations. Unexpectedly, evidence shows that France was much more orthodox than what is commonly said and more so than several other countries. Conservative and socialist governments constrained the country to an almost general orthodoxy. For example, inflation converged toward a low common European level and even France, which had been traditionally one of the most inflationary countries, became less inflationary than the EU, Germany (in some years) and the UK (which remained less concerned about this criterion). Wage cuts, though not formally negotiated in a macro-compromise, were extended and made much more acute than in a country like Germany, thereby squeezing domestic purchasing power and forcing the economy to find sources of demand on the external markets. Another example is that monetary authorities kept to the target of a hard currency (*franc fort*) throughout both decades with the aim of imposing on firms the discipline of seeking competition – not devaluation (a situation converse to the US in the late 1980s and early 1990s, Italy and the UK in 1992). Contrary to the US, France refuted the idea of a deficit in its trade balance and also followed orthodox lines in this area. In this respect, French unemployment derived from an extensive orthodox policy with no tolerance for disequilibrium and the recent improvement in the situation comes seemingly from the breathing space offered by the fall in the euro.

Economic growth and the decline in unemployment between 1998 and 2001 seem to prove that the rate of economic growth in curbing unemployment is a relevant and crucial argument. Contrary to the liberal argument that unemployment is related to microeconomic rigidities and not to accelerating growth with a Keynesian macroeconomic policy, it has shown that unemployment rapidly decreases when growth accelerates. Against the dominant school of thought in the 1990s – that France had a 'preference for unemployment' because it chose not to destabilise the position of the insiders – certain Keynesian economists asked why economic policy had waived growth (Atkinson et al, 1994)? They stated that Europe, and France in particular, had special problems because they had chosen macroeconomic policies detrimental to growth.

The erratic way of French institutional reforms

The path to liberalisation is paved with numerous obstacles that reveal how difficult it is for the French élite to accomplish its social acceptance. As a consequence it is forced to follow a path that seems somewhat erratic and complicated as compared with other countries where formal compromises exist at a national level. When implementing reforms, France finds it very difficult to explicitly state the terms of a project of liberalisation and to discuss them.

The liberal trend in France is not linear because, as the liberal instigation has become more influential, it has increasingly met with certain kinds of resistance. One section of society has combated this extension of liberalism, sometimes inspired by conservatism, sometimes to avoid the various pitfalls arising from economic development, especially social exclusion and an impoverishment of the vulnerable people. Furthermore, several reforms have been inspired more by collective willingness, based on solidarity among individuals or citizenship.

Despite the liberalism pattern in the discourse and the willingness by the right wing political parties, its real implementation within society must be questioned. The liberal discourse is all pervading but its implementation sometimes seems to fall far short of the intentions. Briefly, the implementation of liberal policies was checked by several types of opposition on the one hand,

and by reforms inspired by other societal values which lay emphasis on the social cohesion in society on the other.

Several reforms failed because of popular resistance and opposition to the extension of economic liberalism in a country that has a long historical heritage of an 'administrated' society in a strong unitarian state and also because of the frequent changes of political majority in the 1980s and the 1990s. For instance, the Balladur government was forced to waive the creation of a special (and lower) minimum wage for young people by a widespread protest movement in 1994. In November-December 1995, a large strike rejected several items in the Juppé plan on social welfare system (pensions). In 1997-98 the protest movement by the unemployed highlighted several inequalities between minimum incomes (Bouget, 2002). The law on the creation of a funded pensions scheme (1997) was not implemented.

If reforms are not completely abandoned, those that appear too purely liberal generally fail to be implemented unless they come with restrictions. An example is the recent reform of the unemployment benefit system. In 1999-2000, MEDEF, the main employer's union, negotiated with trade unions and imposed a contract called the *Plan d'aide au retour à l'emploi* (PARE). According to this contract, the labour market institutions pledged to do their utmost to find the person a job who, in return, promised to accept the jobs or training he/she was offered. This means the introduction of workfare logic in France; that is, receiving subsidies is not a social right acquired in previous job situations, but dependent on mutual commitments. However, many argue that the agreement is unbalanced: only the unemployed were called to prove their efforts (and the state to help them) whereas employers received no special obligation. This led to two trade unions refusing to sign the agreement and to the state rejecting the first versions of this agreement. A compromise has been found in having this agreement accepted by the state but with no obligation for the unemployed to sign a PARE. The PARE is now based on free acceptance induced by its advantages (it allows the unemployed to perceive benefits at a constant rate throughout the duration of his/her unemployment).

In this context, institutional reform is often a combination of formal guarantees that social concerns will not be sacrificed in favour of deregulation, or a search for the means that would allow public authorities to get round such undertakings and reform institutions indirectly. For example, the age of retirement will remain 60 years-of-age but, due to the difficulty to ensure pensions payment in the new demographic context, entitlement will be rendered more restricting in the private sector. Indeed, to be entitled, people will have to be employed for a longer time so that, combined with the trend of young people entering the labour market later, workers will increasingly be compelled to work beyond the age of 60 if they want to have access to a full pension. Furthermore, the '35 hours' law not only has a social meaning – an equally important fact is that it has created the opportunity to introduce more flexibility into the organisation of working time and to reduce labour costs by tax cuts for some firms.

In short, the greatest difficulty for French élite (including trade unions, Socialist governments and so on) seems to be to clarify the direction it tends to give to institutional change. This generally leads to not purely liberal institutional arrangements. Changes do occur but in a more implicit and 'underground' manner (some trade unions, for example, have accepted changes at the corporate level that they formally refused in the national discourses). Institutional reform is not 'blocked' but, more exactly, it follows a path featuring the difficulty to accept both explicit new social compromises and the use of indirect ways.

Such specificity is understandable if we measure the strength of a certain reluctance of French society to let the market govern economic and social life without regulation. France is not incapable of sharing the shift towards more liberalisation but it does it with specificities. An example is given by the so-called 'activation' of labour market expenditure and policies. In a way, France has not been awaiting the official emergence of this injunction to obtain policies geared towards improving the ability of people to find new jobs (training, integration, and so on). However, until the late 1990s, the distinction had always been made between this type of action and the employment subsidies without a possible link between the two social policies; that is, of making subsidies conditioned by the entrance into employability-improvement programmes. In other words, if France had active policies, it had no idea of activating non-active expenditure by conditioning subsidies to efforts in finding a new job through contractual commitment. According to academia, as well as to one's common sense, unemployment is more a systemic problem than an individual one: French unemployment sociology (Demazière, 1995) stresses the fact that people who remain unemployed are often trapped in individual trajectories which combine different types of handicaps and which prevent them from finding their way back to employment in a selective labour market.

France does not seem easily permeable to an individualistic logic that casts the unemployed people as a group naturally tending to take advantage of public subsidies and refusing work. Nor is there the idea of a community having duties vis-à-vis vulnerable people but also being entitled to ask one to account for one's efforts in finding a job[1]. Therefore, adapting the institutions of the labour market and of other fields can hardly come from a general negotiation (like the Wassenaar Agreement in the Netherlands) where the idea clearly appears as an individual contract between the unemployed and the rest of society, and between employers and the employees. The process is doomed to be much more reiterated, made up of *coups de force* from the employers to dismantle inherited rules and of protest by employees and unions against the danger of un-ruled industrial relations (protests which can be, by reaction, extremely corporatist and conservative). This provokes state intervention in order to preserve certain basic rules. A succession of adversative[2] and partial negotiations is the typical route to more flexible institutional arrangements in France (IRES, 2000).

Liberalism and social citizenship

The common historical reference used to define the notion of citizenship remains the French Revolution. The 'philosophy of enlightenment' provided the basis for democratic citizenship as a reaction against monarchy. The Third Republic (1870-1940) implemented most of the public and civil dimensions of citizenship. History and political philosophy produced a typical type of citizenship often called 'republican citizenship', mainly based on the principles of equality and public interest (Bouget and Brovelli, 2002). This French concept has been elaborated by wide-ranging doctrinal debates and has been generalised by democratic political life and the creation of public services throughout the entire country. Its ideological power has been produced by the specificity of the public policy of education throughout the entire population. However, this doctrine did not include the domain of social risks, except for vulnerable or poor people (local social assistance).

In 1945, a large system of *Sécurité sociale* was instituted. The governmental decisions were partly influenced by Beveridge. From a doctrinal point of view, the system was supposed to meet the principles of universality and unity. The policy makers of the system expected to create a *démocratie sociale* based on principles of universality and unity within the administration. They expected that full employment would reduce poverty, and would narrow the sector of assistance to the poor (*aide sociale*). They also expected that harmonisation between benefits would lead to a single administrative body. However, the French government refused to impose uniformity; that is, the delivery of flat social benefits.

Instead, the creation and the extension of the social welfare system were not closely linked to citizenship until the 1970s. The implementation of the system was based on 'Bismarckian' principles (Baldwin, 1990; Dupeyroux, 1995; Clasen, 1997), that is, on the worker status. The French welfare system was created on the principle of compulsory social insurance schemes covering social risks (pensions, family benefits, unemployment benefits and health services). The basic principle was the equality of workers (and the members of their family) confronted by risk, non-discrimination between risk classes, and within each group of insured persons. It was based upon social security through full-time paid work contributions (Dupuis, 1995). The recipients of benefits were also the contributors within a framework of worker solidarity. Most cash benefits were income-related, and usually proportioned in accordance with earnings (pensions, unemployment benefits and daily sickness benefits), but family benefits and health services do not obey this rule today. This social insurance system was extended to the risk of unemployment in 1958.

The creation and extension of this system have been described as linked to social citizenship, through the idea of *démocratie sociale* and the rules of 'paritarism' between employers and employees. This term defines the principle by which salaried-workers and employers mutually finance and manage different social welfare schemes in France. However, this notion of *démocratie sociale* falls short of the prevailing conception of the expression today, either in terms of Marshall's definition or in terms of Nordic model of universalistic welfare rights (Esping Andersen, 1990, Abrahamson, 1999, Kautto et al, 1999, among others). In fact, the notion of republican citizenship remained pertinent and powerful in the political field and the provision of public services. However, the dramatic expansion of the social welfare system based on Bismarckian principles expounded largely out of this French notion of citizenship and also produced some confusion in the meaning of social citizenship.

From 1945 until the late 1970s, the French social protection system experienced a universalistic trend following a strong 'path dependency' on the model of social insurance, but, since the 1980s, this doctrinal basis of the social insurance framework has failed for several reasons. Firstly, the industrial partnership-based management failed to assume the total responsibility of the management of social insurance schemes. Gradually, the state – or, more precisely the government – increased its regulatory power in order to improve the system, to harmonise benefits and also to decide the new criteria of eligibility and the rate of social contributions. The gap between the huge jurisdictional power of the State and its narrow funding power created a contradiction within the French system. Secondly, the social insurance scheme was unable to sufficiently cover the risk of unemployment. Furthermore, the increasing unemployment and the chronic economic recession gradually diminished the share of wages in GDP (Darnaut, 1997, p 210). While the demand of social benefits rose, the revenues from social benefits became insufficient even after several increases in the rate of social contribution. This meant that the taxation of wages increased as the recession bit harder. Faced with the difficulty of further increases in the rate of social taxation, and in the name of citizenship, a reform was introduced in 1991 – the *contribution sociale généralisée* (generalised social contribution). It created an earmarked proportional income tax on an income basis larger than wages.

In the early 1980s, the crisis of the state and the social welfare system shook the traditional institutions. The state developed new social policies and tried to extend citizenship into the social fields mainly through the reference to social fundamental rights to protect poor people in society. As it became obvious that the social insurance system did not cover the whole population and that a new safety net was needed, a law establishing a minimum income, called the *revenu minimum d'insertion* (RMI), was carried unanimously by the French parliament at the end of 1988 (see Box 5.1).

In January 2000, one million households were receiving RMI (equal to approximately two million individuals, or 3.2% of the population). Fifty-eight per cent of the recipients were single people, and 20% were single parents. The recipient population is becoming increasingly younger (48% of the recipients are aged below 35).

If we add up all recipients of all kinds of minimum income, the percentage rises to 3.3 million, that is to say 11% of the French population (Amrouni et al, 1997).

Box 5.1: Minimum incomes in France and *revenu minimum d'insertion* (RMI)

The RMI is defined as a minimum income which contains three different dimensions:

1. A means-tested allowance for every poor person (over 25 years-of-age) in France which is based on the idea of a negative income tax; the full monthly rate in January 2002 was €405 for a single person.

2. Certain social entitlements such as health services, housing benefits or local tax exemption; recipients of the allowance become claimants of these social rights in the same way as the social insured.

3. A socioeconomic integration within the labour market or social integration through individual social action; the granting of the RMI is conditional to a beneficiary consent to sign a *contrat d'insertion* (social integration contract) with a professional, medical or social objective. Such a programme can be either job-seeking, vocational training or comprise other activities designed to enhance the recipient's social autonomy.

The RMI has often been described as a social policy based on a citizenship doctrine, opposed to a liberal conception of social protection. However, the analysis shows the ambiguity of its contents. Firstly, the allowance is not a basic income (that is, a total unconditional benefit), but a means-tested benefit. Secondly, the RMI defines an individual contract between the recipient of the allowance and state administration in terms of social integration, but it has led to diverging interpretations. On the one hand, it is used as a pedagogical instrument for the improvement of citizenship and expresses the idea of the link between rights and obligations within national solidarity. On the other hand, this individual contract is incomplete and asymmetrical. The frequent failure of the real individual economic integration either empties the contract of any substantive content, or turns it into a new pattern of state control of poor people in accordance with a conservative position known as 'social obligations of citizenship', by which the contract becomes an eligibility condition in welfare administration (Meads, 1986). Thirdly, today, the RMI has also to be partly included in the unemployment solidarity scheme (Belorgey, 2000); that is, 90% of the recipients of RMI who are unemployed do not receive any unemployment benefit. This means that RMI has gradually become the 'third component' of the unemployment benefit system in France.

In the 1980s and the 1990s in France, as unemployment increased, the social dimension of employment and of work became obvious and politically sensitive. The failure of the labour market legitimated the state not only to create a new minimum income (the RMI) but also to implement a wide range of employment policies. The problem is that, on the one hand, the full-employment objective of economic policy was more or less relinquished and, on the other hand, employment was defined as a fundamental right as in the law for tackling social exclusion (Act No 98-657, 29 July 1998). Immediately one can see the ambiguity between the principles and the empirical possibility of applying them in a world which works on contradictory rules. The globalisation of the economy and the economic doctrine of European institutions promoted the market doctrine (and obviously, the labour market) as a societal value and as a social institution. Simultaneously, however, more and more people were demanding jobs, conceived of as a public good, and often as a local public good.

In very general terms, the French social protection system embodies two dimensions: the occupational dimension, which founded the French system of social security for the employees (and their family), and the state, which oversees assistance to the poor. The dual structure of French social protection, the social security system and the system of national solidarity (in fact, public assistance for the most in need), reinforces the stigmatisation of the poor especially since the institution of social security (for the employees) has failed to absorb the institution of public assistance.

A tension in society comes from some contradictory trends between universalism on the one hand, and liberalism on the other. The economic crisis in the 1980s and the 1990s did not dismantle the system of social protection; rather, it destroyed its Bismarckian unity. The new social policies were introduced by reference to a patchwork of doctrines: a universalistic doctrine for some part of health care, a vertical redistribution for poor families and poor people, an occupational solidarity (Bismarckian doctrine) for pensions and unemployment benefits, as well as a market doctrine for private pensions. Therefore the reforms cannot be interpreted solely as a general shift toward social citizenship. Broadly speaking, the multiple references to citizenship in studies and discourses illustrate the frequent lack of a clear definition and its frequent use with an ideological objective. This gradual extension toward social citizenship has simultaneously blurred its meaning.

Conclusion

Esping-Andersen (1997) notes that, faced with more serious unemployment, European countries have produced responses defining a new typology which is based on the welfare-employment nexus. This includes:

- the 'labour reduction model' prevalent in much of continental Europe (and especially in France);
- the 'employment maximising' model (that is, 'active labour market' training favoured by Scandinavian countries);
- the market clearing 'low wage model';
- the de-regulation approach of the liberal welfare states.

For two decades, France experienced a high level of unemployment, an extension in all kinds of atypical jobs which simultaneously increased social exclusion and impoverished an increasing number of households. Rigidities arising from the French institutions are often stated as the main causes. However, contrary to what is commonly said, France has not avoided liberal reforms. The point is that the French debate encounters difficulties to explicitly state the growing liberal instigation of French élite but without preventing them from implementing rather liberal changes. A succession of adversative and partial negotiations is the typical route to more flexible institutional arrangements in France. Consequently, if France had to be seen as following a specific path, it is not in its refusal of liberalisation which is unduly asserted by some institutions, but rather in the adversative way it chooses to build new institutional arrangements.

Social policies, including unemployment benefits, simultaneously tried to alleviate the social consequences of economic recession on the one hand and were constrained by an increasing implementation of the liberal economic doctrine on the other hand. However, path dependency in social protection often constrained reforms to remain within a general pattern of social insurance. Indeed, popular resistance succeeded in preventing government decisions from any practical implementation and values such as solidarity or universalism also maintain the legitimacy of collective institutions. The social protection system exhibits limitations due to its male-breadwinner model. In fact, those who have not (nor have not had) a contract with an employer (in particular young people) are often excluded from social benefits. The RMI has tried to counterbalance these limitations but this would require a more global rethinking of the system to take into account the forms of precariousness which did not exist at the end of the Second World War when the system was implemented. However, the difficulty to lead employers, unions and the state to explicitly state a new consensus is such that the reexamination is being led only through partial reforms, so that unemployment continues to feed exclusion.

Notes

[1] Each logic is depicted by d'Iribarne (1990) concerning the Anglo-Saxon and the Scandinavian countries. Furthermore, each one could perhaps explain how they can converge on the idea of active labour market policies.

[2] Conflicts are more often concealed than explicit: the number of strikes in France has fallen dramatically since the 1980s, except in specific companies or industries (the rail industry, for example) and areas of particularly angry disagreement.

SIX

Labour market participation in the Netherlands: trends, policies and outcomes

Wim van Oorschot

Introduction

The Netherlands is no exception to the general European trend towards the activation of unemployed people and may even be seen as one of its forerunners. When Wim Kok, the former Labour prime minister, came to power in 1994 and declared 'work, work, work' as the central guiding slogan for his government, he only intensified a general policy aimed at increasing the (re)integration of the unemployed that had already been installed in the 1980s by Ruud Lubbers, his Christian-Democratic predecessor. From the early 1980s onwards, the country had been plagued by high numbers of (long-term) unemployed for nearly 15 years. In recent years, however, unemployment has decreased steadily, at present being back at the low levels of the prosperous early 1970s, and employment has skyrocketed. It is generally believed that Dutch activation policies and wage moderation have contributed significantly to this 'Dutch miracle' (Visser and Hemerijck, 1997).

In this chapter Dutch activation measures taken in the field of social security and labour market policies are critically reviewed. On the basis of an initial sketch of developments in Dutch (un)employment over the last three decades, the main trends in social security and labour market policy will be discussed, as well as the most important of the actual activation measures taken. Subsequently the nature and extent of the Dutch success story will be subjected to a critical analysis.

Developments in Dutch (un)employment

Following the oil crisis of 1973, unemployment increased from about 50,000 to 200,000 in 1975. This number was unacceptable to the then current government. After the second oil crisis, unemployment figures reached an all time high of 800,000 in 1984. From then on the numbers dropped gradually

Social security

The economic crisis made it clear that the Dutch system of social security could be overloaded and could eventually collapse. The initial reaction was to try to keep social expenditures under control by lowering the duration and level of insurance benefits and by 'freezing' the level of assistance and the state pension. This reaction was known as 'price policy', because it was mainly directed at keeping the system affordable. By 1990, however, the number of employees insurance beneficiaries had increased by over 300,000 from 1982, which more than offset the decline in the number of social assistance beneficiaries during this period. Subsequently, the emphasis was put on 'volume' policies which were aimed at reducing the accessibility of schemes and gaining control over the inflow of beneficiaries. Among the measures taken were:

- the sharpening of work record requirements for unemployment insurance;
- a limitation of the duration of earnings-related disability and unemployment benefits;
- a restriction of the concept of disability and a re-examination of the disability-status of 400,000 disabled workers according to the new concept;
- a nearly full privatisation of sick pay;
- a differentiation of employers' disability benefit contributions;
- the exclusion of young people from social assistance benefits.

The reconstruction of national insurance also reflected changes in Dutch society and culture. Some revisions were aimed at modernising the schemes by making them consistent with changing role patterns of men and women, particularly the increased participation of women in the labour force. Where modernisation implied an increased coverage, and therefore conflicted with the general aim of cutting back on social expenditures, means-testing was introduced to keep total expenditures under control, as was the case in the old age and survivors pensions.

There is no doubt that the measures have contributed to reducing social security expenditures – from 20% of GDP in 1980 to 13% of GDP in 1999 (SCP 2000, p 332). The system's collapse was prevented. At present, there is no prospect for a further rapid and substantial decrease in benefits expenditure, due to the very high number of disability benefits (nearly one million claimants) and the structural long-term unemployment among social assistance claimants. The ageing of the Dutch population can be added to this as a factor that most probably will lead to increasing demands for social protection (and health) expenditures in future.

Overall the level of citizens' social protection has declined. This, however, has not affected everybody to the same degree. Part of the decrease in protection offered by the collective system has been 'repaired' for workers in newly bargained collective labour contracts. The loss of collective social protection is also compensated at the household level as a result of the increased labour market participation of women: more often the misfortunes of one partner can be compensated by the other partner's means. Clearly, however, those who have lost most of their social protection are people with weaker or no ties to the market for paid labour. These include workers on flexible contracts, young workers, workers with repeated unemployment spells, and beneficiaries who have little chance of returning to the labour market, such as pensioners, disabled workers, long-term unemployed and single parents.

Employment and labour market policies

In a first reaction to the initial increase in unemployment in the 1970s, a Keynesian approach to stimulate the economy, and thus labour demand, was tried. Extra investments in housing, for instance, were stimulated, unprofitable industries were supported and employment in the (semi-)government sector extended. When these measures had no direct impact on unemployment, a strategy directed at reducing labour supply was soon adopted. Early retirement of older workers was stimulated, older unemployed were no longer subjected to a work test and many redundant older workers were 'shoved aside' into the then easy accessible disability benefits program.

The measures taken, however, were no match for the economic effects of the oil crisis of 1979. The idea took hold that the Keynesian approach was part of the problem. It had resulted in an increasing budget deficit and growing collective expenditures, and therefore in high interest rates and wage costs, which both blocked economic recovery and employment growth. The period of 'price' policy, of major cutbacks on collective and social expenditures, began. Curtailing wage costs was regarded as the prime effective instrument for stimulating employment. The benefit cutbacks had to result in lower contributions, and therefore in lower wage costs, but the main emphasis was placed on wage moderation. The Wassenaar Agreement of 1982, under which social partners, pressed by the central government, agreed on a moderate development of wages, is seen by some as a central and effective event in Dutch (un)employment policy making (Visser and Hemerijck, 1997). Others see it merely as a formalisation of a trend that was already present, since real wages had decreased from the late 1970s onwards, due to increased unemployment and the weakening position of Dutch unions (SCP, 2000, p 290). In any case, the agreement had no immediate effect on (un)employment.

It was only with the improvement of the global economy from 1985 onwards that the ranks of unemployed started to shrink. This process was markedly gradual, however, and the problem of long-term unemployment persisted. This gave rise to the idea that the unemployment problem was not only based on a lack of jobs, but also on the characteristics and behaviour of the unemployed and employers themselves. Therefore, the government's attention shifted from a macro approach, to a more micro-directed approach. Labour market participation of unemployed people was given top priority, and various means were applied.

On the whole, the activation of beneficiaries and social security entitlements became more closely interlinked. In the beginning of the 1990s, in particular, activating 'sticks and carrots' were introduced in unemployment, sickness and disability insurance, as well as in social assistance. Work came to be seen as a better means of social protection than benefits[1].

A closer look at Dutch activation measures

In the course of the past two decades, numerous activation measures have been taken. A distinction is made between activation measures proper and work-related benefit criteria. The first can be defined as measures that are directly and explicitly aimed at the (paid or unpaid) labour participation of unemployed people or at preventing employed people from becoming unemployed. Introducing and tightening work-related criteria for benefit entitlements has an indirect (but mostly not unintended) activation effect: they make unemployment less attractive for workers and result in higher pressures on unemployed people to find work. (Measures aimed at the [re]integration of disabled workers are discussed separately: disabled Dutch workers have no formal obligation to find work, but their labour market participation has become a major concern.)

Activation measures

Since the second half of the 1980s, there has been an 'explosion' of activation measures (see van Oorschot and Engelfriet, 1999, for a detailed review of measures). Prior to this period, the main scheme was *Loonsuppletie*, which offered a temporary wage supplement for all categories of unemployed willing to accept a job with a wage below their previous wage level. The newly added measures specifically were aimed at young and the (very) long-term unemployed, who by then formed a large segment of total unemployment. However, three groups with notoriously bad labour market chances – the older unemployed, women and ethnic minorities – have been conspicuously absent as explicit target groups for activation measures. There are specific schooling and training programmes for these groups, and within the measures for long-term unemployed they are sometimes seen as groups deserving extra attention, but apparently the government has hesitated to design any explicit measures for them. No public statements on the reasons for this could be found, but it could have to do with a fear of (further) stigmatising unemployed women and people from ethnic minorities in the eyes of employers. It might also be related to government sensitivity to public opinion, which is not in favour of positive discrimination of ethnic minorities and women (van Oorschot, 1998b). With respect to the older unemployed, the situation is different. It was among the first reactions to the economic and budgetary crisis of the early 1980s to exempt unemployed of 57.5 years-of-age or older from the obligation to seek work as a means of creating more opportunities for younger cohorts. It was only very recently, in 1999, when unemployment has dropped substantially, that this exemption has been abolished. In other words, the older unemployed have most emphatically not been among the priorities for activation.

Only few activation measures are solely aimed at the unemployed individuals themselves: wage supplement for those accepting a job with a lower wage level, reorientation interviews aimed at designing individual re-insertion plans (*heroriënteringsgesprekken*) and 'social activation' (unpaid, so-called *Melkert III* jobs). These are the only measures that do not require the immediate cooperation of employers. All other schemes do, in the sense that they try to encourage employers to employ long-term unemployed mainly by means of temporary or permanent wage subsidies and reduction of taxes and social security contributions. Apparently, the perceptions and attitudes of employers, and their related selection behaviour, is seen as more of a concern than the motivations and qualifications of the unemployed. Studies have indeed shown that by far the largest segment of all unemployed individuals is very eager to find a job (for example, Kroft et al, 1989; Hoff en Jehoel-Gijsbers, 1998) and that employers are prejudiced against (long-term) unemployed people (van Beek, 1994; Zwinkels en Besseling, 1997).

There is a mix of measures aimed at employment in additional and in regular jobs. Both types of job can be realised in either profit or non-profit organisations. Paid additional jobs are mainly created for the very long-term unemployed (*Banenpool*, *Melkert I* and *II* jobs) when such jobs are the only way of avoiding the strong barriers for this group, consisting of their stigmatisation among employers, their above-average age, their below-average skill level and the higher proportion of ethnic minorities. In the case of the young unemployed, additional jobs under the Youth Work Guarantee (JWG) scheme have replaced the right to social assistance benefit.

Schemes vary in the number of people participating in them. Generally, the participation rate, as the percentage of participants relative to the total target group, is very small. In 1988, for instance, about 7,000 young unemployed participated in the forerunner of the JWG, while nationally about 45,000 met the criteria. The *Vermeend-Moor* Act, which offers payroll tax reduction, covered 170,000 people in 1987, but only 6,000 participated (SCP, 1992). Even the 'larger' schemes, like *Banenpool* (23,000 participants) and *Melkert I* (40,000) and *Melkert II* (20,000) only cover small parts of their target groups of a few hundred thousand long-term unemployed.

Finally, most of the various measures have recently been integrated into two framework laws. One, the Act on the Integration of Jobseekers (*Wet Inschakeling Werkzoekenden* [WIW]) administered by municipal social services, is aimed at the participation of long-term unemployed in additional jobs. It incorporates both the JWG and *Banenpool*. The other, the Act on Reducing Contributions (*Wet Vermindering Afdracht* [WVA]) integrates schemes aimed at other types of unemployed or employed people, mostly schemes offering reductions and subsidies to employers. Government reasons for integration vary:

- there was overlap between some of the measures, and at some points even competition;
- clients and administrations had difficulties in distinguishing between the various conditions and target groups;
- there was lack of overall coordination.

Work-related benefit criteria

From the mid 1980s work-related benefit criteria and conditions have been introduced and tightened. Initially they mainly served the purpose of cutting back on social expenditure, later they are explicitly motivated by government on the basis of their activating effects. Work-related benefit criteria and conditions make unemployment less attractive for workers and result in higher pressures on unemployed people to find work.

With regard to unemployment insurance two moves were made. The 1996 new Law on Penalties and Measures (*Wet Boeten en Maatregelen*) intensified the sanctioning policies of social security administrations in order to activate unwilling unemployed more strongly. Formerly, issuing penalties for non-compliance with job-search obligations was a 'competence' of administrative bodies, some of which acted quite lenient, but with the new law, sanctioning is an obligation, penalties are nationally prescribed per type of misbehaviour and administrations are policed on their implementation. Secondly, during the 1980s and 1990s the work-relatedness of eligibility and entitlement criteria has increased significantly, mainly through linking them (more strongly) to a person's work record. Where benefit eligibility before 1987 depended on having worked at least 130 days in the year previous to unemployment, this has been changed in a number of steps into a combination of 26 weeks of work in the previous 39 weeks and having worked during four out of the last five years. The combination of these criteria means that nowadays only about 45-50% of workers will be entitled to the standard wage-related benefit would they become unemployed. Those who only meet the criterion of 26 out of 39 weeks are entitled to a short-term benefit of 70% of the minimum wage, and others will have to rely on means-tested social assistance. Maximum duration of the standard benefit has extended from 2.5 years to a maximum of 7.5 years, but this only counts for those with a very long work record. For those with smaller work records it has become more difficult to get benefit for more than half a year. On average being unemployed now means lower benefits, and for shorter periods. Consequently, keeping or finding paid work has become more important and compelling to workers.

Being the safety net of the Dutch social security system, the means-tested social assistance scheme has no work-related requirements regarding benefit eligibility. Benefit level and duration are independent of work record criteria too, but in practice they may vary according to whether clients conform to work related obligations or not. Non-compliance may result in penalties (of

5-20% of the amount of benefit) or a withdrawal of the full benefit (for maximally one month). Work-related obligations have not changed in the last decades but, as in case of unemployment insurance, the previously mentioned Law on Penalties and Measures (applied to assistance since 1997) has resulted in a more rigid and systematic implementation. Relevant changes are:

- for young people under 21 entitlement to benefit was replaced by a job entitlement through the JWG;
- single parents with children over five instead of 12 years-of-age became subjected to work obligations;
- the standard of 'suitable work' has been broadened, implying that beneficiaries are expected to accept work well below their educational and former job level;
- for each client with a reasonable labour market chance the municipal social service, that administers social assistance, has to design and implement an individual re-insertion plan.

Since it has been recognised that nearly half of the social assistance beneficiaries have very little real chances of finding a job municipalities have been given the possibility of implementing 'social activation' policies to prevent social isolation and apathy; that is, to stimulate clients to do voluntary or community work in exchange of exempting them from the work obligations.

Workers with disabilities

Traditionally, the (re)insertion of workers with disabilities has had little attention in Dutch social policy. There were (and there still are) sheltered workplaces for a limited number of disabled people, and the disability benefit scheme offered some possibilities for adjusting workplaces to additional needs, but structural and effective measures were not taken. This all changed, however, when the number of disability benefit claimants kept growing and stayed at very high levels, even after the economic recovery of the late 1980s. A variety of measures were taken to try and stimulate labour market participation of workers who were (at least partly) disabled (see van Oorschot and Boos, 2001, for details).

A first significant revision took place in 1987, with regard to long-term disability. Unemployed people without a job and who were partly disabled used to receive a full disability benefit on grounds of their very low labour market chances, but with the revision their benefit was proportioned to the degree of their disability. For the unemployment part they became entitled to unemployment insurance or assistance, and were therefore subjected to work obligations. In the early 1990s a 'bonus-malus-system' was introduced under which employers received a subsidy for employing a worker with additional needs for at least a year. In addition to this one-off subsidy, a 20% wage subsidy was also provided. Employers had to pay a fine or 'malus' in case an employee suffered a disability at work and was fired as a result. Next to this the reference standard for the assessment of the degree of disability was broadened from work 'suiting' one's educational and former job level into 'generally accepted work', a standard not connected to these criteria. As a result more jobs became regarded as being available for the workers with disabilities. At the same time, every disability claimant aged less than 50 years-of-age was reassessed according to the new standard, resulting in a (partial) withdrawal of benefit in 50% of all reassessed cases. The people concerned were declared to be partly or fully unemployed and had to rely on work-tested unemployment insurance or assistance. In 1995 the 'bonus-malus' system was abolished after it had met strong resistance among employers unions and administrative bodies. To carry further the 'battle' against the volume of workers with disabilities, new financial incentive measures were taken:

- an extension of the wage subsidy for employers;
- a wage supplement for disabled workers in case they lose income when accepting work;
- a guarantee for workers aged over 50 years of age and with disabilities that they will get their previous benefit level back if they have to stop working again;
- the possibility of working in a 'try out' job without loss of benefit rights.

Just recently, in 1998, an attempt was made to influence the behaviour of employers in such a way that they feel an individual responsibility for the prevention of disability as well as for the (re-)insertion of workers with disabilities. This is done by differentiating previously uniform premiums according to the number of disability claims that are generated in individual firms and sectors of industry. And by offering individual firms the option to leave the collective system and assume responsibility for the disability and subsequent benefits that it generates. (Some large companies have already chosen to 'opt out', but the first signs are that only few will follow.)

In the meantime, the Dutch government acknowledged that all the measures taken were still not effective (and were even contra-productive in some respects, as we shall see). It therefore introduced still further measures: employers get a fixed budget in case a job is offered to a worker with additional needs from which they are expected to pay the necessary workplace adaptations and access improvements. If costs are less than the budget the surplus does not have to be reimbursed. If costs exceed the budget an extra amount is possible. Furthermore, sickness pay for an employee with a disability will be paid from the national sickness fund, rather than the employer. Finally, an employer can get a reduction on his disability benefit contributions if 5% or more of his wages is paid to employees with additional needs.

With regard to short-term disability benefit, or sickness pay, measures taken were far more drastic. In a series of steps the sickness insurance scheme has been (nearly) fully privatised. The scheme still exists, since it still covers the sickness risk of specified categories (estimated at 15% of the previously covered population), such as pregnant women, workers who are (at least partly) disabled, people on temporary contracts and apprentices. But for the largest part of the Dutch workers it is replaced by the employer's duty to keep on paying wages during sickness leave. Either employers now pay wages for sick employees directly, or like most of them did, reinsure the risk with private insurance companies. Reducing sickness absenteeism is now in the employer's interest.

In short, the labour market participation of workers with long-term and short-term disabilities has been the subject of major policy concern. Access to the schemes is restricted, more work is seen as suitable for people with disabilities, partly disabled unemployed have stronger work obligations, and a number of financial incentives have been introduced for unemployed, but mainly for employers.

A critical view

Having sketched trends in (un)employment and activation policies, let us now address the question of the policies' successfulness on the basis of two questions: to what extent is there a 'Dutch miracle'? And how effective are the activation measures with regard to the (re)insertion of unemployed and disabled people?

A Dutch miracle?

The 'Dutch miracle' of strong job growth and steady decrease of unemployment figures of the past years gets admiring attention from academics and policy makers alike. It is generally believed that corporatist wage moderation – wage moderation explicitly agreed on between government and social partners – is at the heart of the success. We feel that this straightforward view on the Dutch success story needs to be put into perspective.

Firstly, regarding employment growth, it is true that in terms of the number of employed persons the second half of the 1990s witnessed an explosive increase: the working labour force grew with nearly 900,000 people from 1994 to 1999. However, in terms of the total of hours worked annually in the Dutch economy, the growth was much less impressive. After 1970 the number of hours worked decreased steadily to 90.6 in 1985 (indexed at 100), from which moment on it started to increase – but it did not reach the level of 100 before 1994. Until 1999 it increased to only 109.8 (SCP, 2000, p 280). In other words, the Dutch miracle comes down to an increase of the total of available work of 10% only, compared to 1970. Clearly, the discrepancy between the large growth in persons with a job and the much smaller growth in hours worked annually can be explained by the fact that the largest part of the new jobs (65%) are part-time. Most of these part-time jobs are occupied by women, which entered the Dutch labour market en masse in the 1990s. One could conclude that the Dutch jobs-machine mainly consisted of a giant redistribution of the work available. Grossly put: fulltime jobs held by men in an industrial economy have been replaced by service economy part-time jobs held by women.

Secondly, now unemployment is very low at about 3%, it looks as if a situation of full employment – as in the early 1970s – is near. However, the 3% concerns registered unemployment, that is, people without a job, who have registered at the Labour Office, who want to work for at least 12 hours a week, and who are directly available for work. This is a very strict definition of unemployment, compared both to the ILO standardised unemployment definition (that counts persons seeking any hours of work) and the number of registered job seekers as such. In 1998 there were about 300,000 registered unemployed in the Netherlands, about 425,000 people who were unemployed according to the ILO standard, and about 700,000 registered job seekers (SWZ, 2000b, p 28). Clearly, there is more real unemployment within the 'Dutch miracle' than the official figure suggests.

Thirdly, the suggested prime importance of Dutch corporatism and wage moderation needs to be put into perspective too. During the 1980s, Sweden was the exception when in most European countries unemployment was high. It was believed then that this was due to Swedish corporatist policy making, in which social partners and government agreed upon important industrial, employment and labour market policies. In the 1990s, however, Sweden has high unemployment rates of 7-10%. Is corporatism gone, or is it not such a strong guarantee for low unemployment after all? In this respect it should be noted that in the 1980s Ruud Lubbers, the then Dutch prime minister, complained about the 'Dutch disease' – he meant that the tradition of consensus building between social partners and government was a major obstacle for taking necessary policy measures aimed at reducing unemployment. At least, then, there are various interpretations possible of the relation between corporatist policy making and combating unemployment. Anyway, corporatism is not the only road to success. There are other countries in Europe that have succeeded in bringing their unemployment rates down significantly in the 1990s, like Denmark (8.5% to 5.2%), Ireland (13.2% tot 5.8%), Portugal (7.6% to 4.6%) and Norway (5.3% to 3.2%) (OECD, 2000a). Especially in the case of Portugal and Ireland, explanations for success – other than corporatism – are valid.

Regarding Dutch wage-moderation it can be questioned whether the so-called Wassenaar Agreement of 1982, in which government and social partners agreed on a moderate development of wages in return for employment creation measures, had such an important effect as Visser and Hemerijck (1997) suggest. Firstly, since the fundamental shift from strong wage increases to more moderate levels already occurred in the second half of the 1970s (SCP, 2000, p 290), worsening (un)employment had already turned the tide. And secondly, the real growth in employment took place after 1994, more than 12 years after the agreement. Although the effect of corporatist agreement on employment development is questioned here, it does not mean that wage moderation as such had no role. On the contrary, there is a broad consensus in the Netherlands that it had (Bovenberg, 1997; Van der Ploeg, 1998). The processes involved, however, may differ from the 'corporatist agreement' hypothesis. An alternative explanation of the continuous Dutch wage moderation over a period of nearly 20 years is that high unemployment rates suppressed wages, since they weakened the position of Dutch unions, and that the strongly increased female labour participation compensated at the household level the negative effect that wage moderation had on household incomes (SCP, 2000).

In short, the 'Dutch miracle' contains less employment growth than suggested by the growth in the number of people in paid work. Furthermore, it conceals a high degree of hidden unemployment, and corporatist agreements seem not to have played a prime role.

The effectiveness of activation policies on reinsertion of unemployed people and people with additional needs

Many individual people have found a job with the help of activation measures. For instance, about 60,000 have been employed in additional jobs (SCP, 2000, p 288), and the 'SPAK-measure' (*Speciale Afdrachtskorting*, Special Tax Deduction) that reduces employers' taxes and premiums on low wages is estimated to have created between 44,000 and 76,000 extra jobs (Van Polanen Petel et al, 1999). However, while the number of jobs grew from 1994 to 1999 with about 900,000, the total number of beneficiaries under 65 years-of-age decreased in that period with only 225,000 beneficiaries, of which 60,000 through additional jobs. Whether this decrease in beneficiaries is a direct effect of activation measures only remains difficult to assess. It is for example difficult to separate it from the effects of other factors, like employment growth due to economic revival or the effects of social security restructuring. Labour market participation of unemployed is influenced further by the degree to which measures are actually implemented, by selection behaviour of employers, the willingness to work of unemployed and their 'reintegration ability'.

Although it is impossible to say whether or not the situation would have been worse if activation measures had not been taken, I think that a reserved position towards their real effectiveness is justified.

Firstly, in a recently published report in which various types of Dutch and foreign activation measures are compared, the Nederlans Economisch Instituut (NEI) concluded that (easy to administer, fiscal) measures aimed at reducing wage costs for employers (like SPAK) are most successful in terms of reinserting the unemployed on the regular market of paid labour (NEI, 1999). For measures creating additional labour, however, it concluded that they mostly result in only a very few participants flowing into regular jobs. Once in an additional job, there seems to be a lack of possibilities and motivation to move on, since it was found that the flow from subsidised to regular jobs is smaller when the subsidy period lasts longer, and when the subsidised jobs are in the public sector. The NEI report, which is as critical on the effectiveness of most activation measures as two comparative OECD studies (OECD, 1996a; Martin 2000), shows finally that reinsertion of older people and lowly educated people is least successful, despite measures focusing explicitly on these groups. Another review of activation evaluation studies concludes that it is standard practice that administrations that want to show impressive success rates tend to cream their clientele – that is, concentrate their efforts on those with the highest labour market chances, among which many would have found a job without the assistance of a specific measure. Also, in many cases of additional labour, the jobs that are created are in effect pushing away other people's regular jobs (SCP, 1992).

Secondly, would the total of Dutch activation measures have had a significant effect, then the 'outflow probability' of unemployed people would have increased strongly in the years following the mid-1980s, which was the period in which the number of measures increased strongly. Table 6.1 shows that this is hardly the case. In the early 1990s the outflow chance of unemployed people even decreased, most possibly because of the second recession of the early 1990s, and at present the chances are at the same level still as in the early 1990s. It is not without reason that the first government of Wim Kok in 1994 declared that 'work, work, work' would be its leading slogan, since it started from the assumption that existing measures were not effective enough.

Thirdly, despite the measures taken there is still a large proportion of long-term unemployment. With the favourable developments in the labour market the contours of a relatively large group of people who are seen as very difficult to integrate, if at all, become visible. According to the Social and Cultural Planning Office (SCP) this counts for as much as two-thirds (n=1,100,000) of all people on unemployment insurance, unemployment assistance and disability benefit (n=1,600,000) on the basis of legal criteria (SCP, 2000). These criteria exclude people from the legal work obligation on grounds of older age, medical and social reasons, care tasks and so on. However, many of the reintegration measures are intended to promote the labour market participation of these people only. On subjective grounds – that is, when the unemployed and disabled people were asked how they experienced their labour market chances – four-fifths were very negative. That is, only one-fifth had the idea that there would be jobs available, and that soon they would find one (Research voor Beleid, 1998). Also according to administrative criteria the number of 'reintegratable' unemployed is very low. When unemployed people register at the Labour Office their 'distance to the labour market' is assessed in terms of 'phases', on grounds of their personal qualifications, the labour market situation in their profession and so on. Phase 1, 2 and 3 clients are regarded to be 'reintegratable';

Table 6.1: Outflow probability[a] of Dutch unemployed people and disability claimants

	1992	1993	1994	1995	1996	1997	1998	1999
Unemployment insurance	35.8	32.6	31.9	35.2	33.7	36.1	36.5	35.4
Unemployment assistance						16.0	15.2	
Disability insurance	4.4	4.4	5.8	6.1	3.7	3.2	3.5	

[a] Terminated benefits due to resumption of work, as a proportion of the number of benefits at the end of year *y-1* and the number of new benefits in year *y*.

Source: SCP (2000, p 341)

phase 4 clients are not. Significantly, of all disability benefit claimants, as well as of all social assistance clients, 45% belongs to phase 4 (Research voor Beleid, 1998). The SCP study concludes, on grounds of these figures, that there is a "stagnation of reintegration" in the wider context of job growth and decreasing overall unemployment, and it is therefore critical on the effectiveness of reintegration measures. It considers the process of reintegration as "very laborious" (SCP, 2000, p 288). The study mentions several factors that can explain this stagnation for long-term unemployed, social assistance clients and workers with disabilities. One is that employers prefer younger, healthy, 'Dutch' people, who are not stigmatised by a (long) period of benefit dependency (see also Van Beek, 1994; Zwinkels and Besseling, 1997), another that the fast increase in female labour participation prevented the long-term unemployed from filling the many places that became vacant in recent years. The fact that most of the new jobs are part-time plays a role here too: part-time wages are mostly too low for beneficiaries to overcome the poverty trap, while they are attractive as a second household income for women.

In the case of workers who are (at least partly) disabled, the conclusion that measures taken are ineffective and even contra-productive can be drawn without much reserve. The privatisation of sickness benefit and premium differentiation in the disability insurance scheme have created a remarkable tension between the intended activation impact of these measures and their actual effects. For, the incentives for employers are set such that they profit from having a workforce with a minimal disability and sickness risk. A number of evaluation studies (CTSV, 1996, p 199; Schellekens et al, 1999, Van der Giezen and Jehoel-Gijsbers, 1999; Schoenmakers and Merens, 2000) have shown that chronically ill people and (partially) disabled people nowadays even have more, in stead of less, difficulties in (re-)entering employment. This is because employers screen new employees more stringently on their health status – therefore, the chances of being fired have increased for workers with a poor health status. The number of temporary labour contracts, as a means of prolonging the period of screening employees on their 'sickness leave behaviour', nearly doubled between 1993 and 1995 from 11% to 20% of all labour contracts. Hiring workers via employment agencies, to reduce the risk of sickness pay, rose in the same period from 4% to 9%. Furthermore, while 20% of job applications from people with additional needs in 1991 led to an interview, this had decreased to 11% in 1998.

On grounds of these findings one would expect that the 'outflow probability' of disabled people would have gone down in the second half of the 1990s, after the introduction of privatisation and premium differentiation. This is precisely what is shown in Table 6.1.

To conclude, although many thousands of people got a (additional) job through activation measures, the aggregate effect of such measures on the labour market participation of unemployed people seems not to be very strong. In the second half of the 1990s the decrease in the number of beneficiaries has been much lower than the explosive growth in the number of jobs, the outflow chances of unemployed people have not improved and those of disabled people have even worsened. The reintegration of the most vulnerable groups is 'stagnating'. Overall it seems that on aggregate activation measures have at best further facilitated the labour market participation of those who might have got a job anyway in the period of strong job growth.

Brief discussion

In this chapter we have described developments in Dutch (un)employment, as well as general trends in social security and labour market policies, and we have critically discussed the successfulness of activation policies. The Netherlands suffered from high unemployment for nearly 15 years, but at present the socioeconomic situation seems very favourable. Registered unemployment is about 3% and back at its pre-recession 1970 level. Employment has grown explosively over the last six years. The main problem now seems to be a mismatch between labour qualifications asked and supplied, since unfulfilled vacancies add up to 2.5% of the working labour force.

We have seen, however, that actual unemployment is much higher than what is officially registered, that employment has mainly grown because of a large-scale redistribution of the work available, and that there is a large proportion of part-time work. Furthermore, the 'Dutch miracle' failed to improve the labour market situation of the most vulnerable groups, while social security restructuring worsened their social protection rights.

If the Dutch economy continues to do well and employment increases further, the labour market situation of vulnerable groups might improve. It is much more likely, however, that in that case other sources of available labour supply will be used first, like a further increase in women's (full-time) labour participation, since there is the reality of the mismatch between preferences of employers and characteristics of those who are regarded as 'not reintegratable'. The stagnation of reintegration might harden.

If the Dutch success story comes to an end, as is feared on grounds of increasing price inflation, and unemployment increases significantly, Dutch society will fully experience for the first time the consequences of the decline in social protection rights. Large proportions of the newly unemployed will be on means-tested social assistance immediately, while the non means-tested benefits for others will expire quickly. The miracle could turn into a nightmare.

Note

[1] With the linkage of benefit and participation policies, the need for administrative coordination and cooperation increased. To this end, new regional Centres for Work and Income (CWIs) were implemented in the course of 2001. They function as 'one-stop' service organisations, combining participation and benefits assessment. The idea is that benefits assessment and payment takes place only after possibilities for participation are assessed. The CWI format should also promote participation in active labour market policies during benefit dependency.

SEVEN

Is high unemployment due to welfare state protection? Lessons from the Swedish experience

Bengt Furåker

This chapter examines the unemployment patterns in Sweden over the last 25 years. It does not aim to give a full explanation as to why these patterns have developed the way they have. Such a task would require a thorough analysis of Sweden's economic history and policies, of international business cycles, the development and globalisation of world markets, and so on. Rather, this chapter examines Swedish unemployment patterns in relation to welfare state protection. It seeks to find out whether or not high unemployment levels can be explained by labour market 'rigidities' or 'sclerosis' due to welfare state arrangements[1].

Three types of measure will be examined, all of which are directly related to the problem of unemployment. The first type is employment protection legislation, which intends to protect workers from being too easily dismissed from jobs and, from there, into unemployment. Strict regulation may also have other consequences, however, and is therefore much debated[2]. It is a common argument that severe regulation makes employers unwilling to recruit workers, since they consider it too costly to get rid of them again in case they are not well suited for the job tasks or if the company needs to downsize.

A second type of welfare state intervention provides unemployment benefits for those who cannot find a job to earn their living[3]. A crucial aspect is the generosity of the benefit systems in terms of replacement rates and duration of payments. For one thing, the reservation wage – that is, the lowest wage at which individuals accept a job – may be affected. If the unemployed are well provided for, they may have little incentive to find employment quickly. It is often concluded that generous benefits prolong unemployment spells.

Finally, attention is drawn to active labour market policies, aimed at helping the unemployed to a job[4]. These include public employment services, training programmes, and job creation programmes. Sweden is something of a forerunner here, since this kind of state intervention has been used extensively in the country for a considerable length of time. A critical factor is whether or not active labour market policies help lowering unemployment and, if so, whether they do this to reasonable costs. And even should open unemployment be reduced there may be 'dead-weight', substitution or displacement effects, taking

The distribution of unemployment across social categories

Unemployment is not equally distributed across social categories. Therefore, it is important to examine its spread across the population (see also Chapter Two of this volume)[5].

Two main dimensions are dealt with: gender and age. Table 7.1 presents three different ratios of unemployment rates for the period 1976-2001: the first is concerned with gender, and the other two with age. In the period 1976-80, the female/male ratio clearly exceeds 1.0, which means that women's unemployment rates are higher. During most of the 1980s, however, we find rather small gender differences. In the 1990s figures plunge below 1.0 – and from 1992 we can observe 0.7 for three years in a row indicating that women's unemployment rates make up less than three-quarters of the male rates. The reason is of course that the recession during these years mainly hit male-dominated industries (such as manufacturing and construction). From the mid-1990s the gender ratio has been 0.8-0.9.

Table 7.1 also provides two different ratios with respect to age. First, unemployment rates among youth (aged 16-24) are divided by those among prime-age people (aged 25-54). The second ratio describes the relationship between the oldest part of the labour force (aged 55-64) and the prime-age category.

Youth unemployment rates were three to four times higher than those of the prime-age category for almost every year prior to 1987. The ratios then tend to decline, due to the ambitious labour market programmes for unemployed young people. Compared to most other countries, labour force participation among the older working-age population is high in Sweden. The ratios between unemployment rates among the older and among the prime-age labour force usually exceed 1.0, although they were lower for several years in the beginning of the 1990s.

Sweden's distribution of unemployment across social class and educational categories is very similar to that of many other countries. Despite having become more prevalent among white-collar workers in recent years, unemployment is still very much a working-class phenomenon. Blue-collar workers typically run higher risks of becoming unemployed than white-collar workers. This is a common pattern and Sweden is no exception (OECD, 1994a, pp 15, 18). Also, generally speaking, the further an individual has pursued education, the lower is his/her risk for unemployment (OECD, 1999b, pp 237-9).

Another dimension is ethnic background and citizenship. Immigrants have clearly higher levels of unemployment than 'native' Swedes. For example, in 2001 the average unemployment rates among non-Nordic citizens and Nordic non-Swedish citizens were 13.0% and 6.6% respectively, compared with 3.6% among 'native' Swedes (SCB, 2002).

Table 7.1: Gender and age category ratios of unemployment rates in Sweden (1976-2001)

	Female/male	Age 16-24/25-54	Age 55-64/25-54
1976	1.7	3.4	1.4
1977	1.5	3.5	1.1
1978	1.2	3.4	1.2
1979	1.3	3.6	1.4
1980	1.4	3.6	1.1
1981	1.1	3.5	1.1
1982	1.1	3.5	1.4
1983	1.1	3.3	1.6
1984	1.1	2.7	2.1
1985	1.0	3.0	2.1
1986	1.0	3.0	1.8
1987	1.0	2.9	1.3
1988	1.1	2.8	1.3
1989	1.1	2.9	1.2
1990	0.9	3.1	1.2
1991	0.8	2.8	0.9
1992	0.7	2.5	0.7
1993	0.7	2.6	0.8
1994	0.7	2.4	0.9
1995	0.8	2.3	1.1
1996	0.9	2.2	1.1
1997	0.9	2.2	1.0
1998	0.9	2.0	1.0
1999	0.9	2.0	1.2
2000	0.9	2.0	1.4
2001	0.8	2.4	1.3

Source: SCB database

Long-term unemployment

An important aspect of unemployment is the duration of each unemployment spell. Presumably, the longer it takes for a person to find a job, the more likely it is that he or she will suffer economically, socially and psychologically. If an unemployed individual is able to get a job quickly, he/she is not necessarily very much affected. There are therefore very good reasons to pay attention to long-term unemployment.

It is common to present figures on the proportion of the unemployed that are long-term unemployed (see Chapter Two of this volume). Instead, this chapter examines data that are not by definition dependent upon the general level of unemployment. Therefore, Figure 7.2 presents long-term unemployment

Figure 7.2: Long-term unemployment (LTU) rates in Sweden (1976-2001) (% of labour force)

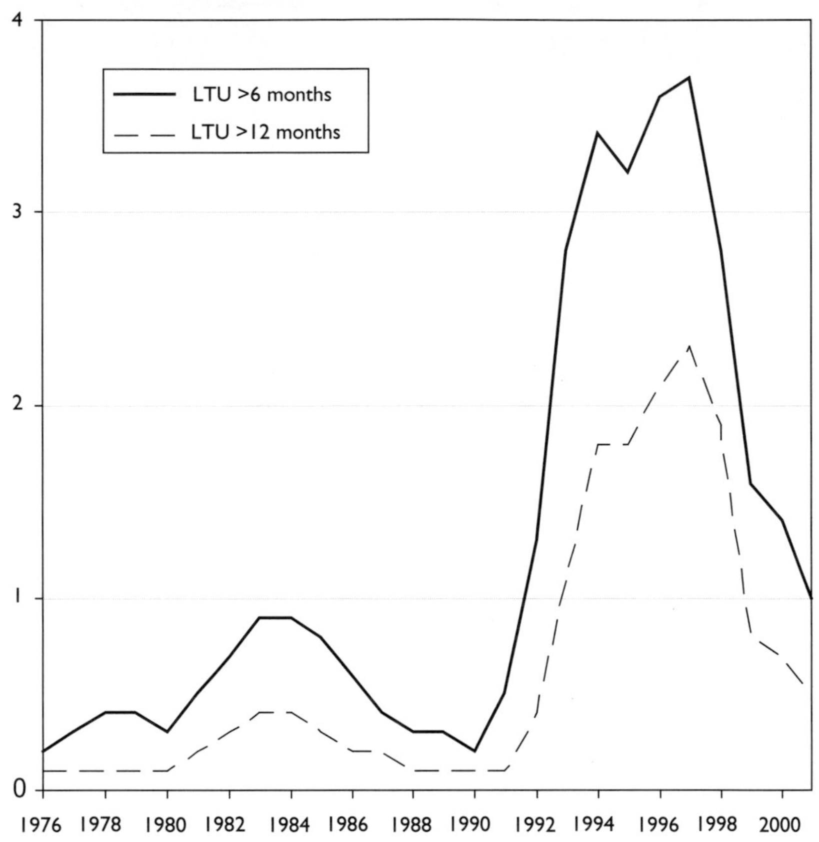

Source: SCB database

(LTU) rates as a proportion of the labour force. Two different measures are used:

- long-term unemployment lasting more than six months;
- long-term unemployment lasting more than 12 months.

The general shape of the two long-term unemployment curves is similar to that of the standardised unemployment rates. Most strikingly, both curves show a spectacular rise and decline in the 1990s. In spite of the recent labour market improvement, long-term unemployment rates have not come down to the levels of the 1970s and 1980s.

The labour force surveys also provide another relevant measure. Individuals defined as unemployed were asked how long they have been searching for a job; thereby we obtain information on the duration of ongoing unemployment.

Without going into details in this respect, it can be observed that the data are very much in line with the picture in Figure 7.2. Above all we find that periods of unemployment were dramatically prolonged during the recession in the 1990s. The average duration of ongoing unemployment was less than 15 weeks in 1990, but it soon nearly doubled – reaching 29 weeks in 1997 (SCB, 1991, 1998).

Hidden unemployment

Let us focus on people who are neither employed nor unemployed. Table 7.2 shows – for selected years after the mid-1980s – the percentage of the population aged 16-64 outside the labour force. Starting with the totals, we find a slight decrease between 1987 and 1990, when the economy was booming – from 16.8% down to 15.5%. Then figures quickly went up to a level more than five percentage points higher already in 1993 (20.9%) and the proportions for 1996, 1999 and 2001 were even higher. There was just a slight decline in the end of the period, although open unemployment rates decreased markedly. For all the years in Table 7.2, women have higher proportions outside the labour force than men. In most cases this difference exceeds four percentage points.

The recession in the first half of the 1990s led to rising open unemployment, but, moreover, it was accompanied by an increase in the number of people who neither had a job nor were looking for one. But what do people outside the labour force actually do? Table 7.2 reveals some information on their main activities, divided into three categories: housework, education, and other. Housework is almost exclusively a female business. There are men for whom such tasks make up their primary activity, but their proportion reaches only 0.1% for four of the years. An interesting fact is that the proportion of women primarily doing housework has declined substantially during the period. In

Table 7.2: Proportions not in the labour force by main activity (selected years 1987-2001) (% of population aged 16-64)

	Not in the labour force			Main activity					
				House work		Education		Other	
	Males	Females	Total	Males	Females	Males	Females	Males	Females
1987	14.6	19.1	16.8	0.1	6.1	6.9	6.6	7.6	6.4
1990	13.4	17.7	15.5	0.1	4.3	6.4	6.4	6.9	6.9
1993	19.1	22.8	20.9	0.1	3.9	8.9	9.0	10.1	9.9
1996	20.0	24.4	22.2	0.1	3.0	9.3	9.8	10.6	11.5
1999	20.5	25.2	22.8	0	2.1	9.7	10.4	10.7	12.7
2001	19.5	23.8	21.6	0	1.8	8.7	9.2	10.8	12.8

Source: SCB database

other words, the recession has not generally meant that women have returned to their traditional tasks.

Instead, in a situation with low demand for labour, the educational system has attracted more people and this pattern is similar for both men and women. The proportion of the population mainly engaged in educational programmes continues to be rather high also in the 2000s. Education seems to have become more important no matter how the business cycle develops. Still, the impact of changes in the demand for labour must not be underestimated.

With respect to the category 'other' (consisting of pensioners, long-term sick, people living abroad, and so on) we find a similar picture as that for education, although with even somewhat larger increases. After relatively small changes between 1987 and 1990, the proportions of both the male and the female working-age population belonging to this category strikingly turned upward. In particular women, but also men, show much higher figures during the later part of the period covered in Table 7.2, also after the recession was over. This indicates that the recent improvement of the Swedish labour market is limited.

In dealing with hidden unemployment we must also consider two other categories: involuntary part-time workers and discouraged workers. The first category refers to people who work part-time and would like to work longer but cannot do so because of labour market reasons. To a very large extent it consists of women, which is not surprising since women work part-time much more often than men do. The second category refers to people outside the labour force who do not look for a job, although they would like to have one and are in a position to take one. They refrain from job seeking because they regard their chances of becoming successful as negligible. Discouraged workers are not included in the labour force.

Sometimes, a measure of total 'slack' is calculated. This concept is supposed to be a summary measure of open and hidden unemployment. It can be calculated in different ways. The definition used here adds up the number of people in open unemployment, the number of discouraged workers, and 50% of the involuntary part-time workers. This sum is then taken as a percentage of the sum total of the labour force plus the discouraged workers (OECD, 1995, p 81).

In Table 7.3 we can first observe the proportions of involuntary part-time workers of the labour force. This type of underemployment is much more common among women than men. The percentage of involuntary female part-timers decreased between 1987 and 1990 (7.6% down to 5.9%), and then doubled in a few years (peaking at 12.1% in 1996), before declining again toward the end of the period. The male pattern is rather similar, although figures are much lower. It can be noted that the OECD (1995, pp 67-71) has found some positive correlation between rates of open unemployment and proportions of involuntary part-time work.

The next two lists of figures give the proportions of male and female discouraged workers relative to the sum total of the labour force and the

Table 7.3: Proportions of involuntary part-time workers, discouraged workers and total 'slack' (selected years 1987-2001) (%)

	Involuntary part-time workers		Discouraged workers		Total 'slack'		
	Males	**Females**	**Males**	**Females**	**Males**	**Females**	**Total**
1987	2.5	7.6	0.9	1.3	4.1	7.0	5.5
1990	2.6	5.9	0.8	0.9	3.6	5.3	4.4
1993	4.8	11.0	3.2	3.1	15.0	14.8	14.9
1996	4.7	12.1	3.9	4.2	14.4	17.2	15.7
1999	3.9	10.0	3.2	3.3	10.8	13.2	12.0
2001	3.2	8.2	2.8	2.7	8.5	10.2	9.4

Source: SCB (selected years)

discouraged workers. There are no large gender differences. Between 1987 and 1990 figures decreased, but then they rose considerably, eventually to turn downward again. As in the case with involuntary part-time work, therefore, the proportion of discouraged workers seems to increase when unemployment goes up and vice versa. This is also confirmed in an OECD study (OECD, 1995, pp 47-9).

Total 'slack' is estimated at 5.5% in 1987 according to Table 7.3, whereas, for the same year, open unemployment was just above 2%. 'Slack' then decreased to 4.4% in 1990, but with the recession in the beginning of the 1990s it rose dramatically. The 1993 and 1996 totals are more than three times higher than that for 1990. Finally, there is a decline in the end of the period.

There is also a gender pattern. With only one exception, women show the highest figures, whereas female rates of open unemployment have been lower since 1990 (see Table 7.1). In other words, when the hidden dimensions of unemployment are taken into account, this picture is generally reversed.

A third way of treating hidden unemployment is to look at the number of participants in labour market programmes. These individuals are normally classified either as employed (in subsidised jobs) or as outside the labour force (in training programmes), but some of them are embraced by the concept of standardised unemployment.

To begin with, a distinction should be made between two different kinds of programmes. The first consists of policies aimed at counteracting the effects of recession and structural change in the labour market; in other words, they are abolished or diminished when the demand for labour increases. The second type includes measures – such as sheltered workshops – for people with handicaps of various kinds. These measures are socially motivated and have little to do with business cycles. For each of the two kinds of programmes, Figure 7.3 provides the number of participants relative to the labour force. We must be aware that all these participants do not belong to the labour force, so this is just a matter of finding a measure to use.

Figure 7.3: Participants in labour market programmes (LMP) relative to the labour force in 1976-2000 (%)

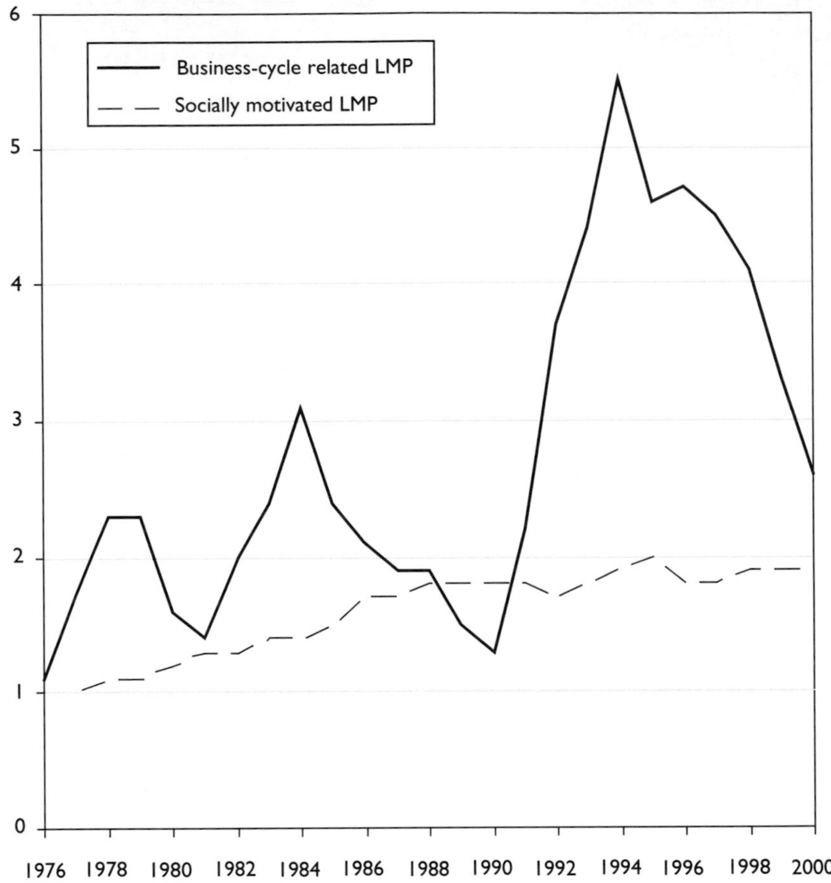

Sources: AMS database; SCB database

One conclusion to be drawn from Figure 7.3 is that the socially motivated measures seem to be independent of business cycles. Over the years, there is a trend of slowly increasing proportions of participants in these programmes – from about 1% of the labour force to almost 2%. In contrast, we find a great deal of variation concerning measures related to business cycles. Figures go from a low of about 1% of the labour force to a high of between 5% and 6%. The pattern reminds us of the unemployment rates, but how the two are related to each other is an issue which will be discussed later in this chapter.

Summarising what has happened with unemployment in Sweden since the mid-1970s, we can point to three features:

- For the whole period up to the beginning of the 1990s, Sweden did very well at least in comparison with most other OECD countries. During these years, the annual average of open unemployment never reached 4% of the labour force.
- There was a dramatic turn of events in the early 1990s, when hundreds of thousands of jobs were lost in a very short time. Unemployment rapidly rose to a very high level and remained there for a number of years.
- Toward the end of the decade, however, it started to decrease and this development has continued in the 2000s.

The proportions of hidden unemployment – whatever definition of that concept we adopt – can be added to these features, as well as the duration of unemployment spells, which increased substantially during the recession in the 1990s. Apparently such changes are rather normal, but they were very pronounced in Sweden in this period. Regarding the distribution of unemployment across social categories we can note that the recession made male rates exceed female rates – earlier it was the other way around. The reason for this is that the economic crisis mainly affected male-dominated industries, in particular in its early phase. Furthermore, unemployment among the youth has clearly been higher than for the prime-age labour force, which is the common pattern also in other countries. More recently, however, this gap has narrowed somewhat in Sweden, due to a great extent to extensive labour market policy measures directed to young people.

Institutional arrangements

This section relates the development of unemployment in Sweden to the welfare state arrangements mentioned earlier in this chapter. First, there is legislation aimed at protecting employees from being easily laid off from their jobs. A second type of welfare state intervention is unemployment benefit for those who cannot find work. Thirdly, attention will be paid to active labour market policies aimed at getting people into jobs either directly or via training programmes.

Employment protection legislation

It is sometimes argued that restrictive employment protection legislation makes employers hesitant to recruit new workers since it can be rather costly to get rid of them if, or when, necessary. However, it has been difficult to demonstrate any clear effects of restrictive employment protection legislation on unemployment. Having reviewed a body of other studies and carried out its own analysis, the OECD (1999b, p 88) recently concluded that employment protection regulation seems to have very little, if any, effect on overall unemployment. However, the demographic composition of the unemployed may be affected. Stricter rules probably contribute above all to lowering unemployment rates among prime-age males, and it is assumed that other groups, in particular young people, therefore get higher rates.

The principal legal framework concerning employment protection in Sweden is the *Employment Protection Act* (1974). Without going into all of its specifications, we can observe that it starts out from the assumption that a job is permanent unless something else is agreed upon, that is, social citizenship includes the right to a certain degree of job security. Employers are allowed to discharge workers in case of a 'just cause' (shortage of work, for example, is considered a just cause). However, certain rules do apply. Notice must be given at least one month in advance for the youngest (below the age of 25), two months for those aged 25-29, and so on, up to six months for the oldest workers (aged 45+). A main principle is 'first in, last out' – that is, those who have been employed most recently must be the first to leave when downsizing occurs. In other words, seniority means having a more secure job. However, in 2000 the parliament passed a bill allowing small firms to exempt two employees from this rule.

Even though the employment protection legislation has been modified in some other respects too – above all, it has become easier to use temporary contracts – the general rules have been rather much the same for a quarter of a century. There are also other laws that affect employment protection. For example, the *Codetermination Act* (1977) gives the unions the right to negotiate with the employer regarding all significant changes in the workplace, such as changes in the size of the workforce including the closure of the workplace.

The employment protection legislation is optional; that is, the unions and the employers can agree upon other rules than the ones provided by the law. In the absence of such agreements, however, the law must be followed. A key issue in relation to unemployment is the rules concerning fixed-term contracts or temporary employment. This is where the most significant changes have taken place.

There are several studies comparing employment protection in various countries, and which often use different methods of classification. The OECD (1999b, pp 66-7) has summarised the outcome of the most important of these studies, covering the late 1980s and the late 1990s. Each country is given a score supposed to measure the strictness of employment protection legislation. The criteria cover different aspects, for example, notice, severance pay, difficulties of dismissal, and regulation of temporary employment. Sweden received a score of 3.5 for the late 1980s – ranking it 15th out of 19 countries. The US is considered the least strict country (0.2) and Portugal and Italy the strictest (4.1).

For the late 1990s, another seven countries were included in the comparison, amounting to a total of 26. This time two versions of the employment protection score are given. The first is the same as for the 1980s and the second one is a weighted score. Sweden gets 2.2 in the first case and 2.6 in the second, ranking 16th and 18th respectively among the 26 countries. Obviously, the Swedish employment protection is judged to have become less strict. The reason for

Figure 7.4: Standardised unemployment rates and proportion of temporary workers of all employees (1987-2001) (%)

Sources: SCB database; OECD (2001a, p 252), and database

this has reference to temporary employment. It has become easier to make longer fixed-term contracts and temporary work agencies are now allowed to operate.

Certain changes in the formal rules have thus taken place, but they must be regarded as rather limited. The application of rules may be another story, but it is difficult to know exactly what happens within individual companies. One way of dealing with this issue is to look at the proportion of temporary contracts among workers. We have data on this from 1987 and they are presented in Figure 7.4, together with standardised unemployment rates.

First of all we see that the proportion of temporary contracts was relatively high in 1987 (12%) but decreased in the late 1980s. Then, with the recession in the early 1990s, the rate curves upward, resulting in the highest figure yet –

almost 16% in 1999. The general relationship between the two variables in Figure 7.4 is positive; that is, the higher the rate of unemployment, the higher the proportion of temporary workers.

We must be cautious in establishing a causal relationship between the variables, but a possible mechanism would be the following. When demand for labour increases in relation to supply, competition between employers in the labour market becomes greater. One way to be successful in that competition is to offer permanent jobs. In a recession employers do not have to provide such offers. This argument can at least help us explain part of the pattern in Figure 7.4, but we also need to consider other changes that have taken or are taking place in the labour market. For example, unions seem to have become generally weaker, especially within certain industries, making it easier for employers to set the terms of employment contracts.

One other aspect deserves to be commented upon. Table 7.1 illustrated that youth unemployment has been relatively high in Sweden – a fact that might be interpreted as an outcome of restrictive employment protection legislation. However, there are good reasons to be cautious in this respect. Examining the country with the least restrictive employment protection of all – the US – we find that the ratio between youth and prime-age unemployment was 3.1 and 3.0 in 1999 and 2000 respectively (OECD, 2001b, p 214). In other words, it is far too simplistic to reason that high rates of youth unemployment are due solely to restrictive employment protection regulation. There must also be other explanations why it is relatively difficult for young persons to find a job.

Cash benefits for unemployed people

The unemployment insurance and other cash benefits for the unemployed make up a crucial type of welfare state measure when people cannot provide for themselves because they fail to find work. From a social citizenship perspective we can observe that the unemployed have the right to be supported but also the duty to be available in the labour market.

Sweden has one the most generous unemployment benefit schemes in the world. The system consists of two parts: basic insurance and a voluntary income-related insurance. The latter is based upon funds organised by the trade unions (the so-called Ghent system) but controlled and heavily subsidised by the state. There is a waiting period of five days (one working week) before benefits are paid. Having fulfilled certain membership and work requirements, unemployed members of the voluntary funds will receive 80% of their previous income up to a ceiling. They can be supported via the unemployment insurance for 60 weeks and re-qualify for another period by participating in labour market programmes. Benefits are lowered after 100 days of payment and when no more benefits are available, people have to rely on social assistance.

In 1988 the maximum compensation of the unemployment insurance was set at 90% of the previous income (up to the ceiling). Before that it was possible to get 91.7%. During the recession in the 1990s the maximum level was lowered first to 80% (1993) and then to 75% (1996). The waiting period that had been taken away in 1988 was also reintroduced in 1993. Since 1998, 80% is again the highest level of compensation.

Taken in its entirety (that is considering replacement rates, ceilings, qualification rules, duration, and so on) the Swedish unemployment benefit system is clearly more generous than the European average. And it has been so for a long time, throughout periods with very different labour market developments. There is therefore simply no way that the high Swedish unemployment rates in the 1990s can be blamed on the generosity of the benefit system. For many years before the recession people could get 90% or more of their previous wage up to a ceiling, and this was fully compatible with exceptionally low levels of unemployment.

When the recession had started in Sweden in the early 1990s, the unemployment insurance was reorganised to be less generous. It might be argued that unemployment would have been even higher in the following years had not the level of compensation in the benefit system been lowered. This is, however, only a hypothesis. And even if the generosity of the benefit system means longer unemployment spells, this can only explain a minor part of the total level of unemployment.

There is another aspect to be brought up in relation to the unemployment insurance, namely the pressure put upon people to take existing jobs. Strict work tests may be important to shorten unemployment spells (see, for example, Nickell and Layard, 1999, pp 3070-1). In a study by the Ministry of Finance in Denmark (Finansministeriet, 1998), an attempt is made to judge the strictness of work availability criteria in 19 OECD countries. Several indicators are being used:

- demands on job search activity;
- availability during participation in active labour market programmes;
- demands on occupational mobility;
- demands on geographical mobility;
- extent of valid reasons for refusal of job offers;
- benefit sanctions in case of self-induced resignation;
- benefit sanctions in case of refusals without valid reasons;
- benefit sanctions in case of repeated refusals.

On each of these dimensions, countries were given between one and five points according to the strictness of rules. There was also a weighting procedure, based on the assumed effects of the demands on job availability.

The total score ranged from a high of 25.25 (Luxembourg) to a low of 11.25 (Ireland). With a score of 23.5, Sweden is the third most restrictive system. It is of course difficult to make realistic judgements regarding the different work availability criteria, but in addition to the simple benefit levels there is a story to tell which takes rules and their implementation into account. Although criticised by the OECD for having nothing to say about implementation

(OECD, 2000a, p 138), the Danish study provides important information. One hypothesis might be that the legitimacy of high compensation rates is dependent on the strictness of work tests.

In addition, prolonged unemployment spells due to generous benefits for the unemployed may not be as negative as we tend to think. It is not always in the individual's best interest to accept the first offer that appears in the labour market. Taking the first possible job without considering what is suitable may mean a mismatch resulting in dissatisfaction on the part of both the worker and the employer. This increases the likelihood that the person has to find a new job soon again. It may then be better if the unemployed have the chance to wait for a suitable job opening.

Active labour market programmes for unemployed people

Active labour market policy can be regarded as an expression of political ambitions to achieve full employment or at least to avoid open unemployment. The general purpose is to get people without jobs (back) into work through public employment services or through job creation or training programmes. This is related to the participation aspect of citizenship and the idea that having a job promotes the individual's social integration.

The OECD has pointed out that the success of active labour market policies must imply a commitment to 'effective management of' – and not just to 'spending on' – such programmes (OECD, 1994b, Part II, p 108). In this context, Sweden is mentioned as an example of a success story during the 1970s and the 1980s. A crucial issue is whether there are macroeconomic policies helping to create a demand for labour and whether active measures are coordinated with these policies. Measures that fit well in a recession may not be so well suited to periods of economic upturn, and vice versa (OECD, 1994b, Part II, p 108). Moreover, people may not be very active in searching for jobs when participating in training and job creation programmes, and the benefits or wages paid in connection with these programmes may of course also affect participants' reservation wage. In other words, we should be aware of the risk of counterproductive elements in active policies.

There are many different kinds of active programmes, and the programmes in Sweden have undergone many changes over the years – it seems to be an urgent concern among Swedish politicians to find ever-new solutions. Let us concentrate here on how the business-cycle related programmes and unemployment rates are connected to each other. Figure 7.5 shows the number of participants in these programmes relative to the labour force and standardised unemployment rates.

The main impression given by Figure 7.5 is that the business-cycle related policies actually coincide with the ups and downs of the economy. The two curves follow each other fairly well, although there is a large gap between them after 1992. Then obviously the number of participants in active programmes could not keep pace with the unemployment rates. However, it

Figure 7.5: Standardised unemployment rates and participants in labour market programmes relative to labour force (1976-2000) (%)

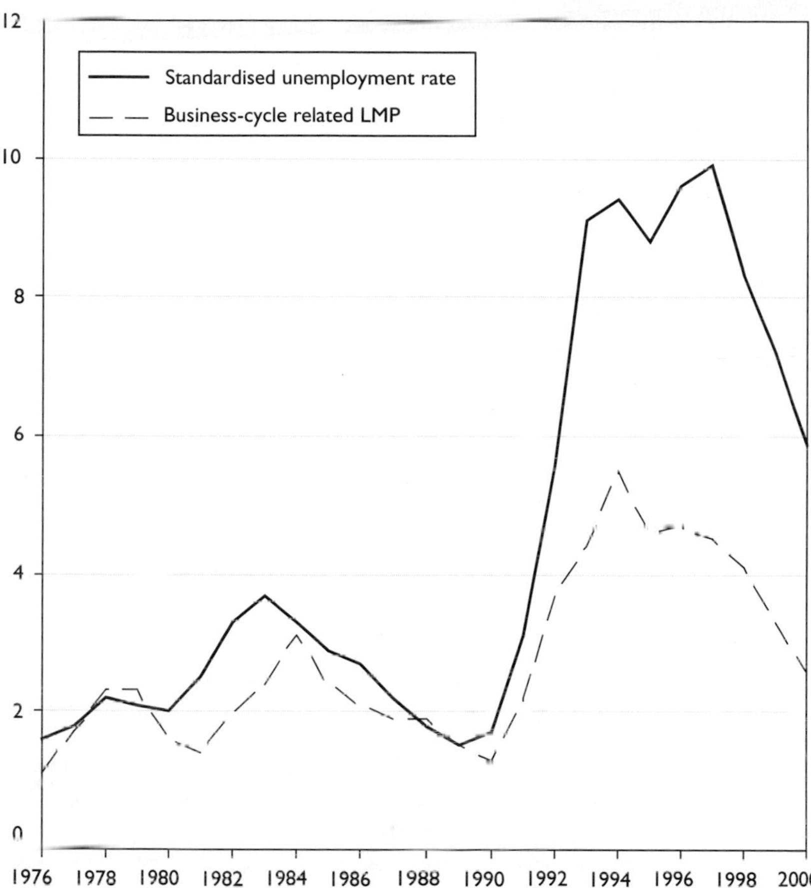

Sources: AMS database; OECD (1997d, A25; 2001a, p 252; and database); SCB database

was never an intention that active policies would confront such high levels of unemployment.

Moreover, we find a tendency that the proportion of participants in business-cycle related programmes increases *after* unemployment starts to rise, and declines *after* unemployment starts to decrease. In other words, there is a time lag between the two indicating that these labour market policies are to a large extent reactive measures, even if institutionalised beforehand. Of course, it can be said that people stay longer in programmes than necessary, since programmes do not shrink as unemployment decreases. On the other hand, it is difficult to imagine a system with no delay at all in this respect.

Conclusion

Unemployment rates have been low in Sweden on the past 25 years, but there have been some fluctuations, among them the spectacular rise in the 1990s. It may be considered even more remarkable, though, that Sweden was able to maintain very low unemployment levels for such a long time before this latest recession. And there now seems to be a notable improvement in the labour market.

The Swedish unemployment patterns have been examined in the light of three kinds of welfare state protection – employment protection legislation, unemployment benefits, and active labour market policies. It was emphasised from the outset that these arrangements can at most be ascribed a limited role. Although they are often blamed for increasing the level of unemployment, they can by no means be regarded as having any principal impact in this respect. The changes in supply and demand in the labour market must above all be explained in terms of other factors – economic developments including those of world markets and international business cycles. Also, when we examine the changes in the welfare state arrangements in question and relate them to unemployment patterns, it is difficult to establish any clear connections.

Employment protection legislation in Sweden has been subject to some reforming since it came into force in the mid-1970s, and the application of rules has been relaxed. Temporary contracts are more common today than at the beginning of the 1990s. Therefore the system has become somewhat more liberal. On the whole, however, the rules have been very much the same both in periods with increasing and in periods with decreasing unemployment rates.

Are the decreasing unemployment rates at the end of the 1990s related in some way to the increasing proportion of temporary jobs? To say yes would be to argue that were employment contracts to become less of a long-term commitment, employers would be more willing to hire. It seems premature to explain the improvement in the Swedish labour market by this simple argument. The whole history from 1974, when the *Employment Protection Act* was adopted, speaks in favour of an entirely different interpretation. The employment protection regulation in Sweden has been fully compatible with very low, as well as very high, levels of unemployment.

In spite of certain significant changes, unemployment benefits have not been fundamentally altered since 1974. There were no preceding important reforms that might account for the sudden and dramatic rise of unemployment in the early 1990s. During the recession the system was made less generous. It is difficult to know whether this led to lower unemployment than there might otherwise have been. Even if there was some effect of this kind, it could not explain very much at all of the total figures, and unemployment started to fall in 1998 when the 80% compensation level was restored.

The analysis of active labour market policies tells us a somewhat different story. There have been many changes in these measures, but participation in business-cycle related programmes generally follows the development of unemployment. An important observation is that active programmes tend to be reactive. Once institutionalised, their size is determined by the level of unemployment; that is, they are expanded when unemployment rises, and vice versa.

Without doubt, it is possible to reduce the number of unemployed with the help of active programmes, but the positive consequences are often clearly smaller than expected or intended, due to 'deadweight', substitution or replacements effects. Moreover, active labour market policy was never aimed at solving the kind of mass unemployment that appeared in Sweden in the 1990s. The marginal utility of programmes is likely to be dependent on the number of participants, and the costs per individual are much higher than for unemployment benefits. Nevertheless, it may be worthwhile letting people participate in labour market programmes rather than being idle, both from a social and a labour market point of view.

Sweden is characterised by having both comprehensive social protection and relatively strong requirements on people to take jobs available or to participate in active labour market programmes. Social citizenship therefore involves a combination of rights and duties. There has been a persistent ambition to provide people with paid work, concomitant with a generous safety net for those who fail to find employment. For a long time the Swedish model was associated with low unemployment, but in the 1990s something changed and unemployment levels rose dramatically. This turn of events cannot be blamed on the social protection system; rather, it must be explained with the help of other factors. And we should observe that, without very large changes in the welfare state policies, unemployment in Sweden has started to decline substantially. Whether the Swedish citizenship model is a successful integration regime or not may be an open question, but provided that participation in the labour market is to be attributed a significant role for integration there are good reasons to pay attention to it.

Still we must be cautious when it comes to drawing conclusions. Welfare state policies can be related to the functioning of the labour market in various ways – this chapter has studied but one particular case. For example, the generosity of unemployment benefits may have very different consequences if combined with strict requirements concerning availability for work than with relaxed demands. Therefore, supposing that there is a lesson to be learnt from this analysis, it does not go beyond the specific Swedish set-up of welfare state protection. With this limitation, the picture presented gives us no ground for believing that less restrictive employment protection legislation, less generous unemployment benefits, and less ambitious active labour market policies would make any great difference for the better.

Notes

[1] As well as Chapter Two of this volume, see also Lindbeck (1994); Nickell (1997); Siebert (1997); Nickell and Layard (1999); Esping-Andersen (1999, pp 120-42); Esping-Andersen and Regini (2000).

[2] There are quite a few studies on the subject of employment protection legislation. See, for example, Buechtemann (1993); Grubb and Wells (1993); Scarpetta (1996); Gregg and Manning (1997); Nickell (1997); Nickell and Layard (1999); OECD (1999b, pp 47-132).

[3] See, for example, Atkinson and Micklewright (1991); Layard, Nickell, and Jackman (1991); Atkinson and Mogensen (1993); Calmfors (1994); Reissert and Schmid (1994); Nickell (1997); Nickell and Layard (1999); Martin (2000); Sjöberg (2000).

[4] For an overview, see OECD (1993, pp 39-80); Calmfors (1994); Calmfors and Skedinger (1995); Scarpetta (1996); Martin (2000); Robinson (2000); Martin and Grubb (2001).

[5] All the data are taken from the Swedish labour force surveys and are based on the national definition of unemployment, in contrast to the data used in Figure 7.1.

EIGHT

Denmark: from the edge of the abyss to a sustainable welfare state

Jørgen Goul Andersen

Introduction

At the beginning of the 21st century, Denmark ranks among the European countries that have recovered quite convincingly from the employment crisis. Around 1980, Denmark was described as balancing on the edge of the abyss, but 20 years later, it is sometimes held up as a 'model country' for a European third way in a globalised economy (Auer, 2000). Indeed the Danish experience has demonstrated that there are alternatives to the market-oriented reforms advocated by OECD (1994c, 1997b) and others. The Danish experience also seems to speak against the very idea of structural or a natural level of unemployment as a guide to policy – or at least against the estimation and interpretation of it. Until the mid-1990s, structural unemployment was normally estimated at around 10% (Finansministeriet, 1993, 1996, 1999; OECD, 1997a), indicating that nearly all unemployment was structural. From 1993 to 1998, however, the standardised unemployment rate declined rapidly from 9.6% to 4.9% (Chapter Two, Table 2.1 of this volume) without inflationary consequences. And the improvement has been stable – by mid-2002, the unemployment rate was 4.2%.

As this economic turn has happened concurrently with the adoption of new labour market policies, it would be tempting to suggest a relationship. However, whereas the Danish experience clearly seems to speak against the necessity of die-hard market oriented reforms, it is contested what exactly explains the improvements:

- Active labour market policy (as emphasised by the Social Democratic government)?
- Tightened eligibility criteria (equally important, according to the Ministry of Finance)?
- Danish 'flexicurity' – the combination of liberal employment protection and generous protection of the unemployed (Madsen, 2002)?

- Employment-friendly financing of welfare almost exclusively through general taxes, without social contributions (Scharpf, 2000)?
- The switch to 'sound' economic policies (Goul Andersen, 2002c)?
- Innovative technology (for example environmental technology), and organisation (modern corporate governance)?
- Luck (Schwartz, 2000) – including quite significant oil revenues?

There are counter-arguments against most of these explanations. Individual-level evaluations of activation effects have been rather negative (Larsen, 2002a), tightening has after all been quite moderate (see below) and the problem with explanations referring to 'flexicurity' or 'employment-friendly financing' is that these characteristics were also there during the crisis ten years earlier.

Leaving aside the question of which combination of factors exactly triggered the turn, however, it remains that it has been possible to move from 'vicious circles' to 'good circles' in the economy, but without higher wage inequality, lower basic social protection, or similar market-oriented reforms (Goul Andersen, 1997a, 2000c, 2002c) – although not entirely without cutbacks (Korpi, 2002). This contradicts the idea that welfare states in a globalised economy face a dilemma between equality and employment, or a trilemma between employment, equality and budget balance (Iversen and Wren, 1998). The compensation rate for unemployment benefits has remained 90%; economic inequality has not increased and is probably the lowest in the EU (Det Oekonomiske Raad, 2001; Finansministeriet, 2002; see also Chapter Two, Table 2.17 of this volume); and even public expenditure has gone down from a peak 63% of GDP in 1993 to about 53% in 2000 (Goul Andersen, 2002c)[1], despite a growth in public services of nearly 20% in real terms from 1992 to 2000. Although there are reservations about this 'economic miracle', it certainly speaks against current diagnoses of the problems of the welfare state, and it also seems to question the concept – or at least the measurement of – structural unemployment as a guidance to policy.

Not surprisingly, it has been claimed that much of the decline in unemployment is nothing more than 'window dressing', as people have just been moved from unemployment to activation or early retirement. Therefore, this chapter begins with an examination of the validity of such claims. It then provides a brief overview of changing economic and labour market policies and the underlying processes, pointing out firstly that corporatism has played a very limited role, and secondly that, somewhat paradoxically, it is the economic upswing, more so than economic crisis, that has led to a termination of several welfare programmes, including the Danish leave arrangements of the 1990s, due to concerns about the labour supply. The final section discusses the effects of the 'active line', as well as the changing conceptions of citizenship underlying this policy change.

Table 8.1: Unemployment in Denmark: (approximate) register definitions and Labour Force Survey (ILO criteria) (first two quarters of 2000)

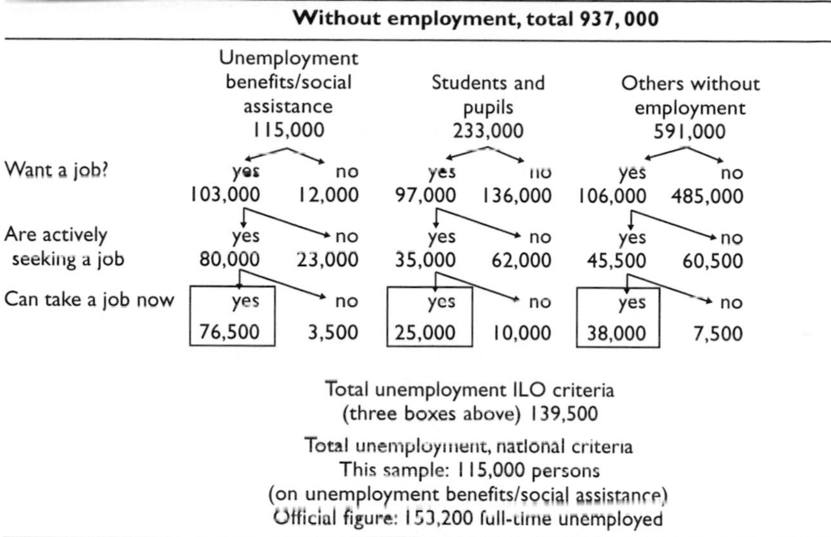

Without employment, total 937,000

	Unemployment benefits/social assistance 115,000		Students and pupils 233,000		Others without employment 591,000	
Want a job?	yes 103,000	no 12,000	yes 97,000	no 136,000	yes 106,000	no 485,000
Are actively seeking a job	yes 80,000	no 23,000	yes 35,000	no 62,000	yes 45,500	no 60,500
Can take a job now	yes 76,500	no 3,500	yes 25,000	no 10,000	yes 38,000	no 7,500

Total unemployment ILO criteria
(three boxes above) 139,500

Total unemployment, national criteria
This sample: 115,000 persons
(on unemployment benefits/social assistance)
Official figure: 153,200 full-time unemployed

Sources: Labour Force Statistics (basis for Eurostat and OECD figures) 2000, p 44, p 47. Average of first two quarters, 2000 (occasionally rounded to have figures match). Official unemployment: same series (2000, p 20, p 32)

Real improvement of unemployment or just 'window dressing'?

Comparative and national labour market statistics

As Chapter Two has already pointed out, small changes in definitions and methods have a significant impact on the picture of the level and structure of employment and unemployment. In the Danish case, the correspondence at the individual level between unemployment according to official registers and according to the Labour Force Survey is surprisingly low (Table 8.1). Aggregate figures are similar: 153,200 and 139,500, respectively (first two quarters of 2000) and trends are largely parallel. However, the persons are often not the same. Among those counted as unemployed according to the survey (who fulfil the three criteria of not having, seeking and being available for a job), only 76,500 (55%) are formally unemployed (receiving unemployment benefits or social assistance)[2], and nearly one-fifth are students. And among the 153,200 full-time unemployed in the unemployment statistics, the survey only records 115,000 persons[3], among whom 12,000 do not even want a job, 23,000 are not actively looking for a job, and 3,500 are not available. This leaves only 76,500 (50% of registered unemployment, or 67% of those formally unemployed in the sample) who fulfil the ILO criteria of unemployment.

Not surprisingly, this discrepancy has been the subject of debates about abuse of unemployment benefits. Others have pointed at hidden unemployment. However, there is not much evidence to support such claims, and in the Danish case, figures based on administrative registers are the most reliable because:

- even allowing for a few people on activation in the group it is normally misleading to count students and pupils as unemployed;
- 'unemployment' among people outside the labour force may be an artifice of the questionnaire. In Denmark, labour force participation is insensitive to the business cycle, and there are few 'discouraged workers' who do not care to register;
- a panel survey of long-term unemployed reveals that subsequent transition to work does not depend at all on whether they fulfil the ILO criteria (Bach, 1999); only in the very long term is a small effect discerned (Goul Andersen, 2001b; Larsen, 2002b). Even most indicators of willingness to be flexible, including reservation wage (the lowest wage people are willing to accept for a job) appear to have no effect.

The level and structure of unemployment

As compared to registered unemployment, the standardised figures (as in Chapter Two of this volume) are too low. But as the first two rows in Table 8.2 show, trends are parallel. Both series peaked in 1993, and both series for 2000-02 reveal the lowest unemployment since 1975. From 1981 to 1995, registered unemployment oscillated around 10%, and at the culmination of the economic upswing in 1986/87, it was only down to 7.9%. Therefore, the figures around 2000 clearly indicate a break. It also seems sustainable: inflation has remained low, and the balance of payment shows a solid surplus.

The low incidence of long-term unemployment also speaks against the idea of structural unemployment equilibrium. By 1994, a marked increase in registered long-term unemployment to 5.5% of the labour force seemed to support the claims about generous welfare leading to unemployment traps and 'hysteresis'; that is, a sedimentation of people who would not be employable when the business cycle turned. However, long-term unemployment nearly halved already during the first phase of the upswing from 1994 to 1996. This supported the predictions based on survey data that a very large group among the long-term unemployed could relatively easily get back to work, even though register-based information on their employment history indicated a bad prognosis (Finansministeriet, 1995; Goul Andersen, 1995, 1996). By 2000, long-term unemployment was only 1% of the labour force.

The Danish unemployment figures reflect that many people were affected by unemployment spells, but for short periods. From 1980-2000, between 20% and 30% of the labour force were affected by unemployment within a calendar year. This indicates high flexibility, which in turn reflects low employment

Table 8.2. Unemployment and employment in Denmark (main indicators)

	1980	1984	1986	1990	1992	1993	1994	1995	1996	1997	1998	1999	2000	2001
1. Standardised unemployment rate	–	–	–	7.2	8.6	9.6	7.7	6.8	6.3	5.3	4.9	4.8	4.4	4.3
2. Official unemployment rate	7.0	10.1	7.9	9.7	11.3	12.4	12.3	10.4	8.9	7.9	6.6	5.7	5.4	5.2
3. Labour force participation rate	78.9	79.9	80.5	80.3	79.8	79.6	79.4	78.9	77.8	77.4	77.5	77.5	77.5	
4. Employment rate	73.1	73.0	75.5	73.6	71.7	71.7	70.3	71.0	71.5	71.9	72.8	73.9	74.2	
5. Labour force (000s)	2,746	2,834	2,873	2,908	2,910	2,910	2,908	2,896	2,872	2,863	2,868	2,874	2,878	
6. Affected by unemployment	611	746	699	737	795	842	818	783	756	697	657	606	560	542
7. LTU (Long-term unemployment)	54	95	66	95	121	144	159	114	85	77	51	37	38	33
8. LTU % of labour force	2.0	3.4	2.3	3.3	4.2	4.9	5.5	3.9	3.0	2.7	1.8	1.3	1.3	
9. Registered unemployed	184	276	220	272	318	349	343	288	246	220	183	158	150	145
10. Activation (total)	–	–	–	–	–	(116)	(84)	71	74	76	77	87	81	79
11. Leave from unemployment + transitional allowance[a]	–	–	–	–	–	4[b]	33	68	83	66	58	44	31	26
12. Gross unemployment	–	–	–	–	–	469	460	427	402	362	317	288	262	250
13. Full-time employment (private sector)	–	–	(1,877)	1,834	1,800	1,759	1,750	1,769	1,792	1,812	1,839	1,864	1,882	1,892
14. Full-time employment (public sector)	–	–	(761)	771	768	771	770	770	781	795	812	821	823	827

[a] Transitional allowance is a pre-early retirement programme for 50-59-years-old long-term unemployed (to be phased out).

[b] No information on leave but it was negligible.

Sources: 1. OECD (2002a); 2, 6, 7, 8, 9, 10, 11 *Statistics Denmark: Unemployment Statistics*; 3, 4, 5, *Statistics Denmark: Register-based Labour Force Statistics*; 13, 14 Statistics Denmark, National Accounts (Statistisk Tiårsoversigt and Statistiske Efterretninger. Arbejdsmarked, various issues). LTU defined as more than 80% unemployment during last 12 months

protection (Madsen, 2002), and high job turnover (OECD, 1998a). Unlike the figures in Chapter Two, which are inflated by job-seeking students[4], register-based data show low youth unemployment (among the 16- to 24-year olds) since 1993 – even below general unemployment. In 1999, the figure was only 3.7%. Further, register-based data show that despite high minimum wages, the decline in unemployment between 1993 and 2000 was most significant among the unskilled (Table 8.3), mainly because the number of unskilled labourers in the 1990s declined even faster than the demand for unskilled labour power (Finansministeriet, 2000).

In contrast to the theory of 'hysteresis', which predicts a sedimentation of 'unemployability' among the unskilled (who will not return to the labour market during an economic upturn), the data conform with the classical observation that unemployment among the unskilled simply follows the business cycle more closely than unemployment among other groups. The unskilled, quite simply, are 'last in' and 'first out'.

To some extent, this applies to immigrants as well. Until recently, Denmark performed poorly as far as employment among the immigrant population is concerned (Craig, 2001; OECD, 2001c). Among non-Western foreigners (men and women), employment rates were down to one third in the second half of the 1990s (Mogensen and Mathiessen, 2000), and even by 1999, it was only 41% (Mogensen, 2001). Next to the Netherlands, Denmark had the lowest labour force participation rate in Europe among male immigrants in 1998 (OECD, 2001c, p 49), and next to the Netherlands, Sweden and Belgium, Denmark had the highest share of foreigners among the unemployed, relative to their share of the labour force (OECD, 2001c, p 52). Still, in accordance with the last in/first out interpretation, the situation has improved. In 1994, unemployment among foreigners peaked at 34.3%; by 1999, it had declined to 15.4%.

Table 8.3: Unemployment in Denmark, by education

	1990	1991	1992	1993	1994	1995	1996	1997	1998	1999	2000
None	11.2	12.0	12.7	14.0	14.5	11.9	10.0	8.8	7.2	6.3	5.7
Apprenticeship level	7.6	8.7	9.5	10.7	10.0	8.1	7.0	6.3	5.2	4.5	4.4
Higher, three years or less	5.5	6.0	6.4	6.7	6.6	5.4	4.7	4.7	3.9	3.2	4.0
College level	3.4	4.0	4.4	4.9	4.6	3.6	3.1	3.2	2.7	2.4	2.5
University degree	4.9	5.6	6.1	6.3	6.4	5.2	4.3	4.4	4.0	3.3	3.2
Total	8.8	9.6	10.3	11.4	11.3	9.2	7.7	6.9	5.6	4.9	4.6

Source: Statistics Denmark (2001), this statistic is based on a slightly different delineation of unemployment than the registered unemployment

Net and gross unemployment

It has been claimed that not all unemployed were 'really unemployed', or that there is no real improvement of unemployment. Official figures have been accused of 'window dressing' as employment rates have not increased correspondingly. Even Auer (2000) argues (but with appreciation) that unemployment would have been much higher if thousands of people had not been inactivation, on leave, or in an early retirement scheme. According to Table 8.2, this was partly true in the mid-1990s, but not some years later. Between 1993 and 1996, unemployment rates declined by 3.5 percentage points (103,000 persons). Education and parental leave from unemployment went up by 37,000, however, and transitional allowance (pre-early retirement for long-term unemployed from the age of 50) by 42,000 – that is, 79,000 in total. So, real improvement was modest. Furthermore, early retirement allowance (from the age of 60) accounted for another increase of 12,000 persons, and the number of disability pensioners went up by a similar figure. This also adds up to 103,000 persons. Even though activation declined, employment rates went up only by 0.4 percentage points. Therefore, until 1996, improved employment could to a large extent be seen as 'window dressing'.

Between 1996 to 2000, however, the improvement was genuine. Unemployment declined by another 100,000 persons: activation was stable; leave from unemployment declined by 31,000 and nearly disappeared; transitional allowance went down by 21,000; even disability pensioner figures shrunk by 6,000. Only early retirement allowance continued to increase. In all, there was a significant increase in employment rates from about 71.5% to about 74.5%. In short, improvements were exaggerated by the figures on unemployment between 1993 and 1996, but between 1996 and 2000, the opposite occurred. Over the entire period, there was a largely parallel decline in official and 'gross' unemployment. The conclusion is clear: improvements in unemployment are not window dressing.

Still, after seven years of recovery, employment rates by 2000 had not yet reached the pre-recession level from 1986. It must also be noted that employment in the public sector accounts for a large share of the improvement (see Table 8.2). After years of zero growth, public employment went up by 76,000 from 1993 to 1999. Private sector growth was only 56,000. Compared to 1986, the growth in private sector employment was zero; only the public sector reveals a growth of some 65,000. At the same time, working hours have been reduced, and part of the increasing employment consists of students. Women's transition from part-time to full- or almost full-time labour pulls in the opposite direction – part-time (less than 30 hours) has nearly disappeared for women in their 30s from more than one-third in 1982 to 4.5% in 2000 (Goul Andersen, 2002c). Otherwise, figures on labour market participation change considerably when we count the high employment rates among students and pupils. Therefore, it was found (Goul Andersen, 1999) that the labour force participation rate of 82.5% among working age men in 1998 dropped to 73.4% when students and pupils are excluded. This corresponds with the observation made in Chapter Two that participation rates among prime age men are by no means exceptionally high in Denmark.

Negative interpretations of these figures should not be taken too far. True, employment in the private sector has been stagnating in Denmark; in fact the 1999 figure is no higher than in 1948 – for half a century, the public sector was the only long-term job generator. Still, the system works. The economy was more sustainable in 2000 than in 1948; macroeconomic surroundings were healthier than ever; and public expenditures had declined markedly. A good circle between declining unemployment and declining public debt has replaced the vicious circle of the 1970s and early 1980s (Goul Andersen, 2002c). The figures above only serve as a warning that improvements are not *that* great, and as a reminder that employment in the private sector remains a major challenge in the Danish welfare state.

Termination of leave arrangements and other welfare policies

As pointed out elsewhere (Goul Andersen, 2000c, 2001a, 2002b), the dominant policy paradigm in Denmark changed, after a long learning process, from a Keynesian, demand-side paradigm in the 1970s, over a more export-oriented (but still demand-side) paradigm in the 1980s, to a supply-side paradigm in the 1990s. Even though competitiveness was emphasised in the 1980s, it was believed that unemployment could gradually be eliminated if wage competitiveness could ensure a sufficiently high export-driven demand for labour power. However, from 1989, attention was directed to the 'inflexible' wage structures, disincentives, 'poverty traps' and so on – in short, to the "structural problems on the labour market" (Regeringen, 1989). At first, nothing really happened, but in the following years, the diagnosis of *structural unemployment* (see Chapter One of this volume) was accepted with surprisingly few reservations by nearly all actors; that is, the major parties and interest groups.

This meant that labour market policies, which had remained nearly untouched under the Conservative-Liberal coalition government (1982-93), became a key instrument in the economic policy after 1993. During the 1970s and 1980s, the unemployment benefit system had nearly approached a basic income system (see Figure 8.1). In terms of *access*, it required only one year's membership of a union and six months' (normal) employment to achieve full entitlements. *Duration* was eight to nine years, as entitlement to 2.5 years of unemployment benefits could be prolonged twice for another 2.5 years via participation in a job programme. The *compensation level* of 90% (which has not changed) was very favourable to low-income groups; except for a very small income interval, unemployment benefits became in practice a flat-rate benefit. *Controls* were lenient: the unemployed were formally required to be actively job seeking and available for a job. In recession periods, however, not much was done to ensure effective works test, and sanctions were left in the hand of the unemployment insurance funds. In short, the unemployment system of the 1980s constituted a kind of 'ultimate universalism' that had moved quite far towards a basic income system.

This was supplemented by early retirement arrangements, which included not only ordinary disability pension, but also (from 1979) early retirement allowance open for everybody aged 60+ (conditional only on 10, later on 20 years' membership of an unemployment insurance fund), and (from 1993) a pre-early retirement transitional allowance for long-term unemployed aged 55+. Early retirement allowance was equal to maximum unemployment benefits for 2.5 years, and 80% of maximum benefits after that.

The Labour Market Reform of 1993 not only introduced new active labour market policies; it also completed the generous benefit/retirement system by

Figure 8.1: The Danish Unemployment Benefit/Early Retirement System, and the new leave arrangements by 1993/94

Unemployment benefits by 1993/94

1. **Easy access:** One year of membership in Unemployment Assurance Fund, 26 weeks of employment within the last three years.
2. **Long duration:** 2.5 years but right to participation in a job project twice, with entitlement to benefits for another 2.5 year period. Total entitlement: more than eight years (from 1994 fixed to seven years).
3. **High Level of compensation:** 90% of former wage, with a relatively low ceiling. In practice close to a flat-rate benefit. No differentiation according to family situation, seniority or duration of unemployment.
4. **Lenient control:** with active job seeking, depending on the business cycle.

Early retirement by 1993/94

5. **Early retirement allowance:** 60- to 66-year-olds who had been insured against unemployment for at least 20 years were entitled to leave the labour market. During the first 2.5 years, they received maximum unemployment benefits; for the remaining period 80% of that amount.
6. **Transitional allowance:** Pre-early retirement allowance, introduced in 1992, granting 55- to 59-year-olds long-term unemployed (from 1994 also 50-54 year-olds) right to an allowance (80% of maximum unemployment benefits) until early retirement allowance from the age of 60.
7. **Disability pension:** The traditional early exit pathway.

New Leave Schemes from 1993/94

8. **Parental leave:** Up to 52 weeks, with 13 weeks as unconditional right, for each child aged less than nine years.

   Siblings less than three not allowed to public daycare, others only half-time. Eighty per cent of maximum unemployment benefits (UB) + minor municipal subsidy (voluntary for municipality). Equal access for unemployed.
9. **Educational leave:** Up to 52 weeks, conditional on acceptance by employer. One hundred per cent of maximum unemployment benefit (+ supplements in some collective agreements). Equal access for unemployed.
10. **Sabbatical leave:** Up to 52 weeks, conditional on employers' acceptance and job rotation. Eighty per cent of maximum unemployment benefits.

    Maximum unemployment benefits (2002 level) about €20,000 per year (taxable income).

extending the transitional allowance to 50-54-year-olds, and by introducing new leave arrangements – parental, education and sabbatical leave – aimed at improving work–life balance and stimulating skill enhancement. Two of the leave schemes were introduced by the Conservative-Liberal government already in 1992, but were significantly improved. In particular, parental leave for parents with children of up to eight years-of-age was extended from 36 to 52 weeks of which the first 13 weeks became a *right*, not conditional on employers' acceptance. The allowance was 80% of maximum unemployment benefits, but many municipalities provided additional support. Educational leave remained conditional on employers' acceptance, but was improved so that the allowance was 100% of maximum benefits. Significantly, both arrangements were open also to unemployed, who typically constituted about one-half of the persons on leave (and more than that in months, as leave periods of those unemployed were longer). Finally, a sabbatical leave was introduced on the same economic conditions as parental leave, but conditional on job rotation and employers' acceptance. This allowed people to take a sabbatical for whatever reason (for example, travelling).

Combined, the unemployment benefit system and the early retirement and leave schemes represented a very generous and decommodified welfare system, and it is remarkable that it was the economic upturn rather than the economic crisis that put these arrangements under pressure. The reforms for a while nourished a government discourse about new philosophies of work and education, and of the changing relationship between family and work life. But they were also used to 'break the unemployment curve', and as unemployment declined, these programmes suffered a backlash. By 2002, all the new programmes had been terminated or marked for phase-out (Figure 8.2). Retrospectively, this was presented as a labour market reform in three stages (and a half). Rather than a 'master plan', however, it was a gradual adaptation to changing economic and political realities.

Parental leave created bottleneck problems from the very beginning, as nurses and others with zero unemployment did not want to miss out on this opportunity of a lifetime. Therefore, it was decided already in the 1994 'check up' negotiations on the Labour Market Reform that compensation for parental leave would be gradually lowered from 80% to 60%, and that sabbatical leave would be closed from 1995 and phased out by 1999. In return, both parental and educational leave were made permanent. But few things remain permanent in politics. From 1999, access for unemployed to educational leave was restricted to six weeks, and with effect from the end of 2000, the educational leave programme was abolished altogether along with a comprehensive reform of the further training system providing support for more 'ordinary' education, in particular for the employed[5]. After an initial explosion, the number of persons on leave almost halved, from 63,000 in 1996 to 34,000 in 1999. What was left in 2001 was a not very generous parental leave, which was mainly used as a prolonged maternity leave. In 2002, the new Liberal-Conservative government abolished parental leave for children born from 2002 in return for an extension of the maternity leave to 52 weeks. Finally, it was decided in the negotiations on the 1996 Budget to phase out the transitional allowance. In short, the transitional allowance and all the new leave arrangements were terminated or marked for phase-out in the late 1990s and early 2000s.

The active line

The main reason for the break with leave experiments was an increasing concern about provision of labour power, as unemployment declined rapidly. Debates about 'passive support' and an ageing population pulled in the same direction. This also affected the most significant policy change in the 1990s, which was the 'active line' in labour market and social policies. It was originally firmly rooted in the philosophy of structural unemployment, in particular in the idea of a mismatch between wages and labour productivity (Regeringen, 1993). To avoid lower minimum wages (and, accordingly, lower social protection) the labour movement preferred the functionally equivalent alternative of activation (education and job training), and to a lesser extent subsidised labour[6], even alongside somewhat stronger incentives and controls. It is the combination of activation and controls/incentives that came to characterise the 'Active Line' of the 1990s.

Formally speaking, active labour market policy in Denmark was not an entirely new phenomenon as such. Already from 1977, municipalities and counties were required to establish employment projects, education and courses for young unemployed, and in 1978, a 'job offer' programme was adopted for people in danger of dropping out of the unemployment benefit system after 2.5 years of unemployment. In 1981, the number of job offers (with entitlement to a new period of benefits) was fixed at two. Later on, this was supplemented

Figure 8.2: Labour market reforms in Denmark: closing the leave arrangements (1994-2002)

1994 **Check-up** (compromise on 1995 Budget).
Parental leave: allowance gradually reduced to 60% of maximum unemployment benefits.
Sabbatical leave reduced accordingly and decided to be phased out in 1999.

1995 **Labour Market Reform II** (Compromise on 1996 Budget)
Transitional allowance for 50-59-year-olds to be phased out; entrance closed from 31 January 1996.

1998 **Labour Market Reform III** (Compromise on 1999 Budget)
Access to educational leave for unemployed restricted to six weeks from 1999 and abolished from 2000.

1999 (Compromise on 2000 Budget)
58- to 59-year-olds may be exempted from activation requirements, on an individual basis.
Educational leave terminated ultimo 2000, in connection with
a comprehensive reform of the further training system.

2002 Extended maternity leave (to 52 weeks), in return for phasing out parental leave system.

Figure 8.3: Major labour market reforms in Denmark: the 'active line' (1990-2001)

1990-1992
Tightening for young unemployed on social assistance.

1993 **Labour Market Reform I**

Duration of unemployment benefits seven years (plus leave), right and duty to activation after four years, without earning entitlements to continued benefits.
Decentralisation of implementation to 14 corporatist regional boards.
Individual plans of action for long-term unemployed.

1994 **Check-up** (compromise on 1995 Budget)
Extended right to unemployment benefits for 50-to 59-year-olds.

1995 **Labour Market Reform II** (from 1996) (Compromise on 1996 Budget)
Duration unemployment benefits five years, right and duty to activation after two years.
Unemployed under 25 years without formal education are required to attend education after six months.

1998 **Labour Market Reform III** (from 1999) (Tripartite negotiations but not on early retirement + Compromise on 1999 Budget).
Duration unemployment benefits four years, activation after one year.
50-to 54-year-olds unemployed transferred to ordinary conditions.

Early retirement allowance reform: ear-marked contributions for at least 25 years. Ninety-one per cent compensation if retirement at 60; 100% if retirement at 62; cash premium to those who abstain from early retirement. Pension age lowered to 65 years.

1998 Law on social assistance replaced by new law complex, including 'Law on active social policy', stressing duty to activation.

2001 Law on disability pension, emphasising subsidised labour for disabled people; pensions improved.

by subsidies for education or to establish a private firm. The job offer programme in the 1980s counted roughly the same number of participants as activation did in the 1990s. According to OECD calculations, spending on active labour market policies went up from 1.1% of GDP in 1986 to 1.8% in 1997, as compared to an un-weighted EU average of 0.9% and 1.1% of GDP, respectively (Martin, 2000, p 85); only Swedish figures (2-3%) were significantly higher. In short, the system before 1993 was not exclusively characterised by 'passive support'. But it was rooted in other philosophies, and a major purpose was to maintain people in the non-stigmatising unemployment benefit system (the job offer programme replaced a temporary suspension of time limits of benefits in 1976).

Another important difference is the changing balance between rights and duties. The first stage of the 1993 reform was ambivalent on this issue. On the one hand, the maximum unemployment period was fixed at seven years of which the last three years from 1995 included 'right and duty' to activation (education or job training) without renewed entitlement to benefits. On the other hand, seven years (through leave occasionally extended to nine years) is a long time, and it only took 26 weeks of ordinary employment to become entitled to another seven-year period (Figure 8.3). Also, from 1993, the active labour market policy was decentralised to 14 regions where corporatist Labour Market Councils would direct policy implementation according to specific regional needs, as well as increase responsiveness to the unemployed. Furthermore, the reform demanded an 'individual action plan' for long-term unemployed and vulnerable groups in a dialogue between the unemployed and the employment office. The 'action plan' outlines the activation effort in accordance with the wishes and the abilities of the unemployed individual as well as the need of regional labour markets to maximise employment opportunity (Jensen, 1999). In principle, this constitutes a strengthening of rights, even though practice have not always followed the ideals (Olesen, 1999).

Duties were also emphasised, for example in the terminology: 'job offer' was replaced by 'activation', and 'social rights' by 'right and duty'. This emphasis on duties started long before the 1993 reform, namely for young social assistance claimants. Already in 1990, a 'youth allowance' was introduced for 18-19 year olds, which demanded early activation as a condition for social assistance. By 1992, this had been extended to everybody under the age of 25 (the 1998 Law on Active Social Policies, which replaced the law on social assistance, extended it to 25- to 29-year-olds). Emphasis on duties gradually increased from the mid 1990s, and activation was officially referred to as both an educational measure and a works test. In the 1995 compromise with the Conservatives on the 1996 budget, which was in effect the second phase of the reform, duration of benefits was cut to five years, with 'right and duty' to activation after two years. Entitlements to benefits now required 52 weeks of ordinary employment, and various other requirements regarding transport time and duty to take jobs outside one's field were formally tightened.

Some elements of the third phase, unlike the first and second ones, was negotiated with the social partners, but included in the agreement on the 1999 State Budget. Duration was now fixed at four years, with (as it turned out, a very costly) right and duty to activation after only one year, in principle for at least 75% of the time[7]. The 50- to 54-year-olds, who had until then been entitled to unemployment benefits indefinitely, were now transferred to ordinary conditions, whereas the special arrangements for 55- to 59-year-olds were maintained. The third phase also included a reform of the popular early retirement allowance, giving people a strong incentive to remain in the labour market until the age of 62 by otherwise reducing the allowance to 91% of the full amount. Finally, as part of this reform complex, the pension age will be lowered from 67 to 65 years (from 2004). As most people retire earlier, this was also a money saving measure. In addition, a quite expensive, earmarked early retirement contribution was introduced in addition to the ordinary fee to unemployment insurance, and early retirement was made contingent on 25 years' contribution. People who do not use their right to early retirement, but continue to work until the age of 65, receive a cash payment (approximately €14,000)[8]. None of these changes were negotiated with the unions.

As has already been mentioned, the Law on Social Assistance was replaced by a new law complex including the Law on Active Social Policy in 1998.

Both the title of the law and the wording of its paragraphs underline the duty to work and the loss of social assistance for those who refuse[9]. As elsewhere, the effects depend on street-level implementation; however, there have been indications of unintended effects among some of the weakest groups who are incapable of fulfilling any form of activation[10]. Finally, a reform of disability pensions in 2001 also emphasised the creation of subsidised jobs for the disabled along with improvements of the (flat-rate) disability pensions (related only to degree of disability).

Apart from a decision in 1999 to exempt, on an individual basis, 58-59 year-olds from activation[11], the intention of the reforms was to increase emphasis on the duty to work. This is partially based on a communitarian notion of work as the very core of citizenship and social integration, which has had effects of its own. Increasingly, however, the reforms have also been influenced by lower unemployment rates, making it more realistic to find a job and more necessary from an economic point of view to avoid bottlenecks and inflation, which could reverse the economic recovery. Still, it was a dramatic change from something resembling a basic income system to a system which, according to the government's 'benchmarking' of duty to work, (formally) places the requirements of the Danish system nearly on line with those of Sweden, where this was always a core element in social and labour market policy (Finansministeriet, 1999, pp 183-7; Regeringen, 1999, pp 290-1).

Why such changes?

All in all, we observe that significant (although mostly incremental) path breaking was possible. But, what explains this change? Unlike the underlying assumption in the otherwise insightful 'welfare retrenchment' literature (Pierson, 1998), pressures from the environment do not offer much explanation, at least not in terms of economic crisis. On the contrary, what could qualify as retrenchment or tightening of conditions mainly appeared towards the end of the period and was related to improved economic surroundings.

Turning to institutional explanations, it is important to note that there are few 'veto points' in the Danish system. First, the social partners are not in a position to block decisions. They were formally consulted on one occasion only, namely the third stage of the labour market reform in the autumn of 1998, and this did not even include the early retirement reform where the trade unions were as surprised and as dissatisfied as everybody else. Therefore, the labour market reforms in Denmark do not signify any revival of corporatism, even informal consultations with the trade unions seem to have been the exception. Second, with the early retirement reform in 1998/99 as a significant exception, there has been little resistance from the public at large. This may be ascribed to low saliency as well as to the fact that improvements and retrenchments were mixed. Third, it is an important institutional trait that nearly all reforms were part of package deals, typically related to the annual state budget negotiations and usually not presented as 'reforms' at all.

Negotiations were conducted among a narrow group of party leaders, over a few weeks (at least the publicly known part), and the content of the compromise was often unknown to the public until the very last moment. The same goes for the big tax/labour market reform in 1993, where negotiations mainly took place within the (majority) government. This leaves little opportunity for groups outside parliament to mobilise and, again with the exception of the early retirement reform, the package deals were furthermore highly complicated, both to the public and sometimes even to the party leaders themselves.

It appears that we should look for explanations in the motives of political actors, in their interest and their ideas. These ideas were, of course, influenced by discourses, especially by the economic discourse about structural unemployment, a national discourse about dependency ratios getting out of control, and a communitarian discourse about integration through employment (see also Cox, 2001). Why did the Social Democratic Party accept a policy containing numerous elements that the party had previously resisted so strongly?

- It was *willing to*, partly because Social Democrats have always emphasised employment, but also because of the influence of new ideas: a new economic orthodoxy, concerns about dependency ratios, and communitarian ideas of social integration through employment.
- It was *forced to* because of the political situation. In the mid-1990s, the Social Liberals, the coalition partner, found its raison d'etre in demanding institutional change, and for bourgeois parties, labour market reforms provided a well-suited target for routine budget negotiations.
- It enabled the party to *avoid a worse fate*. In order to maintain high compensation and long duration of benefits, the Social Democrats were forced to give in on tightening (see also Barbier, 2002).
- The Social Democrats were *not afraid* to tighten up as the labour movement maintains considerable control over street-level implementation. Little is known about the real effects of stricter requirements as to transport time or willingness to take any job; but most likely, there is a large discrepancy between formal rules and actual practice. Low unemployment and special rules for elderly unemployed reduced the risk of exclusion from the unemployment benefit system. Moreover, municipalities have strong incentives to provide temporary jobs in order to 're-circulate' long-term unemployed as they pay 100% of social assistance and 0% of unemployment benefits. Little is known about this, but at least until 2002, only a few thousand persons were excluded from the unemployment benefit system (Goul Andersen, 2002b).

Changing ideas and control over implementation seem to be the most important among these explanations. It is also a part of the story that even though the unemployed have not always considered activation beneficial for their employment chances, a large majority has always welcomed activation anyway (Madsen, 1999b; Hansen et al, 2001).

Effects and implications for citizenship

Denmark is among the countries with the largest decline in unemployment and at the same time among the countries with the most far-reaching change towards active labour market policies. But how strong is the *causal* relationship between these changes, and what are the implications for citizenship?

These are highly contested issues. As to the first question, the (relatively) high employment performance in Denmark seems more attributable to sound economic policies and to the basic labour market flexibility than to activation. Countless evaluations have been done and many different methods applied, especially to control for selection effects and deadweight losses, and the results are not very impressive. With a few exceptions, most forms of activation seem to have statistically significant effects on reemployment chances (Madsen, 1999b). Typically, however, the effects are very small (Arbejdsministeriet, 2000; Larsen, 2002a); that is, below 20% improvement in job chances. As is the case in other countries (Martin, 2000), the most efficient method is private job training; however, only a very small proportion (typically some 5-7%) is activated in the private sector. In terms of cost/efficiency, activation is generally not very successful, and like in Sweden in the early 1990s, it may even constitute an economic threat in case of a recession.

As to the causes for the rather small effects, we should probably not look for implementation problems, but rather for underlying assumptions about the causes and effects of long-term unemployment (Larsen, 2002b). The assumption of insufficient incentives does not find much empirical support. Assumptions about missing qualifications underlying the activation strategy are not too convincing either, as it is almost impossible to find any association between economic incentives, education, and transition to employment (Bach, 1999; Goul Andersen, 2001b; Larsen, 2002b). It appears that youth-targeted initiatives have been quite efficient, but it does not follow that this can be extended to other groups (Larsen, 2002b). Instead, we should recognise the diversity of persons and groups among the long-term unemployed, and look for effects of networks and contacts in gaining access to recruitment and in reducing prejudice and 'statistical discrimination'.

The effect of the 'active line' in terms of citizenship is equally contested. Both the old strategies and the active line are aimed at maintaining full citizenship, but each is built on a different philosophy. The strategies of the 1970s and 1980s were based on a classical notion of social rights and the aim of maintaining people as 'full citizens', even if they did not have a job, in particular by maintaining the unemployed in the benefit system (avoiding the stigmatisation and economic marginalisation associated with social assistance), and by maintaining equal social rights for employed and unemployed. This was visible:

1. in the prolonged duration of entitlements to unemployment benefits;
2. in the easy access to the system;

3. in the principle that wages during job training should follow collective agreements;
4. in the regaining of entitlement to benefits while in job training;
5. in the principle of equal access to leave arrangements for employed and unemployed;
6. and in the high level of benefits enabling people to maintain a decent standard of living.

From a social rights perspective, the active line has violated most of these rights:

1. duration was shortened;
2. access was restricted;
3. job trainee wages did not follow collective agreements;
4. unemployed did not regain entitlements through activation;
5. the unemployed's access to leave was restricted from 1999.

Only (6) relatively high compensation level for low-income groups and (1) an after all relatively long duration of benefits has been maintained. For instance, only 6% of those receiving social assistance by 1999 were people who had lost the right to unemployed benefits (Harsløf and Bach, 2001), and among those registered as unemployed, the proportion receiving social assistance has always been well below 20%. What after all counts as a strengthening of rights (or 'empowerment') are the individual action plans that emphasise dialogue between the unemployed and the employment officer.

Still, even though there are informal ways of modifying the effects of stricter requirements and shorter duration, from a social rights perspective, the 'active line' represents an erosion of citizenship[12]. However, while the Social Democrats were in office, the rationale of the active line was increasingly influenced by a communitarian notion of citizenship that sees employment as indispensable for citizenship. People who are excluded from the labour market are not full citizens as they are implicitly believed to be marginalised on all other arenas of social action (including democratic political participation), to become stigmatised, or even to develop 'un-civic' attitudes. From a communitarian perspective, a renewed emphasis on duties in return for rights is also welcomed. And the long-term ambition is not only to lower unemployment, but to ensure that all people of working age have, as far as possible, the 'right and duty' to a job. Therefore the next logical step is to try to provide jobs instead of 'passive support' for social assistance clients and workers with disabilities. Even if it does not bring them any further to ordinary employment, activation and other measures are considered – in official language – to contribute to 'stabilise' their situation' (Loftager, 2002). Although this normative debate cannot be reduced to empirical questions, it is obvious that it also rests on premises about the relationship between unemployment and citizenship that can be tested empirically. This has rarely been done (see, for example, Goul Andersen, 1996,

2002a; Gallie and Paugam, 2000), but just like the economic rationale for activation strategies and incentive strategies, it seems to rest on quite dubious assumptions.

Throughout its first six months in office, the new Liberal-Conservative government from 2001 kept a low profile on all these issues. Basically, it adheres to more neoliberal ideas, but apart from savings on activation expenditures, it has so far held back on labour market policies and welfare policies relating to the labour market. Even when it had launched a labour market reform in 2002, the proposals turned out to be quite modest and partly symbolic. At the same time, the communitarian rhetoric was downplayed in favour of a rhetoric of incentives. After negotiations with the social partners, the reform was adopted in October 2002 by all parties, except the parties to the left of the Social Democrats. It contained a wide array of incremental changes, including some tightening to make work pay for families receiving social assistance, but nothing fundamentally new.

Conclusions

Denmark's active line has sometimes been celebrated as an example of a third way solution to Europe's unemployment problem. This is an exaggeration. It does have positive employment effects, and from a citizenship perspective it is equally important that it is largely welcomed among the unemployed. But it would hardly pass a cost/effectiveness test, and it does contain potentially negative effects for both economy and citizenship if it is pushed too far. Probably, it will never be determined exactly what explains the significant recovery since the mid-1990s. Activation and education of the unemployed; tightened rules; the particular combination of low employment protection and generous (minimum) protection for unemployed; employment-friendly, almost exclusively tax-financed welfare – or other factors in the field of organisation and industrial innovation.

But the important point here is that Denmark has proved that it is possible to break out of more than two decades of mass unemployment without resorting to radical market-oriented welfare reforms, without increasing income inequality, and without increasing unemployment among the lower-skilled. On the contrary, rather than leaving a large group of 'unemployable' people behind, and in accordance with more classical orthodoxy, the economic upswing benefited the low-skilled most. Little is known about the implementation of the active labour market policies from a citizenship perspective. What we do know is that exclusion from the generous and non-stigmatising unemployment benefit system has, until 2002, been limited, and even though the number of (job-seeking) social assistance claimants has not declined at the same speed as the number of unemployment benefits, the latter still constitute the huge majority (some 80%) among the registered unemployed. Even though Denmark has moved far away from the citizens' wage path it once pursued, and even though activation requirements have been strengthened, the basic social protection has been maintained at a relatively generous level, at least for the lower income groups – and for Danish citizens.

Notes

[1] 'Total outlays' divided by GDP (1993) corrected for tax reform by +1.6% (from 1994, a number of transfers were changed from net to taxable income and were raised accordingly).

[2] People who receive social assistance are registered as unemployed only if they fulfil the ILO criteria.

[3] This deviance mainly derives from definitions: *unemployment* (calculated as full-time employed) does not refer to persons, unlike the number of unemployed *persons* in the surveys. According to ILO criteria, an individual is classified as employed if he/she has one hour or more of employment in the reference week, so deviance may be substantial. Register-based accounts of *employment status of persons* also produce lower figures (Statistics Denmark, 2000, p 7).

[4] Official figures, on the other hand, are deflated by the high number of students in the denominator.

[5] However, courses and education form the backbone of the activation system.

[6] The 'service strategy' deserves a special mention. It was a third functional alternative to create jobs for the 'surplus population' of less qualified workers. This strategy, based on subsidising labour-intensive household services, was developed by the Ministry of Industry and was implemented in 1993. It also became a 'pet project' of the minister, who was the leader of one of the small coalition parties (the Centre Democrats). It was strongly supported by the Welfare Commission in 1995, but only half-heartedly by the government, and it lost political and bureaucratic backing as employment opportunities for the unemployed improved. The calculation and the form of the subsidy changed on several occasions. By 2002, the subsidy was reduced to 40%, and the service (except for pensioners) was reduced to cleaning. According to the government, the sector employed some 5,000 workers before the 2002 reform.

[7] In practice, activation typically means education and job training in the public sector. By 1999, 26,000 out of 51,000 (calculated as full-time activated) were under education; 14,000 were in public job training; 3,000 in private job training, and 8,000 in various other programmes. Altogether 142,000 persons (including overlap/double counting) were involved in some kind of activation (Statistics Denmark, 2000, no 24, p 11).

[8] Unlike the other reforms, this reform generated widespread protest and almost halved support for the Social Democrats in opinion polls, also because it violated an explicit promise by the prime minister (Andersen et al, 1999). Along with lower protection for

the young and declining class-consciousness, the higher fees have also contributed to a significant decline in unionisation among the young.

[9] All who receive social assistance are obliged to accept activation. People aged less than 30 *must* be activated before 13 weeks, for at least 18 months. If they participate in a job programme, they receive about €1½ per hour in supplement to social assistance, which is 60% of maximum unemployment benefits for a single person. By 2000, about 88,000 people received social assistance as the dominant source of income. About three quarters of these were not registered as unemployed as they were considered by the municipality to have 'other problems beyond unemployment'. Still, the same rules of activation in principle apply to these.

[10] Apparently without much success so far, a number of programmes – flexible jobs, protected jobs, and so on – have been implemented for particularly vulnerable groups. It is the government's ambition to include as many groups as possible on the labour market by means of such subsidies.

[11] Unemployed aged 60+ have no right or duty to activation, but are entitled to 2.5 years of benefits including the unemployment period before age 60. After that, they will normally be transferred to early retirement allowance.

[12] Of course, this holds in particular for those receiving social assistance who are obliged to activation. Only half of those participating in job projects do not think this has any purpose apart from testing willingness to work. And 75% of those participating in activation do not consider that this qualifies them for ordinary work (Harsløf and Bach, 2001). As a reaction, an increasingly visible 'National Association of Unemployed' was formed in 1998. It considers itself a modern 'civic rights' movement; to save money it successfully exploits the Internet as the main form of communication and has a very professional and very frequently used website (www.ladk.dk).

NINE

Unemployment and (un)employment policies in Norway: the case of an affluent but oil-dependent economy: the paradox of plenty?

Knut Halvorsen

Introduction

Norway has a strong resource base, but a vulnerable industrial structure. The dilemma for this country is that a fast accumulation of wealth – created by exploiting its natural resource (petroleum) – cannot, in the long run, be a blessing but quite the contrary. This is the 'the paradox of plenty', which means that a country is unable to handle a sudden 'wealth shock'. Netherlands is used as an example: huge state revenues from gas resulted in high inflation, reduced competitiveness, concentration of resources in the oil sector at the expense of other sectors in the economy[1]. It turned out, for example, that it was difficult for the government to keep down expenses to social benefits. It contributed to the so called the 'Dutch disease' (Karl, 1997)[2].

For the purpose of this chapter, then, we must ask: is Norway, as a universalistic welfare state, economically sustainable and able to maintain full employment? So far, there has not been any *major* cut-backs in social benefits, but it has been suggested that it is necessary to reform part of its social security scheme in order to reduce the inflow into sickness benefits, disability pension and early retirement pension. In common with many other countries, Norway fears that that demographic changes (low increases of working-age and elderly populations) will make it difficult to meet the demand for workers, especially in the public sector (healthcare), without inducing inflation and reduced competitiveness for the private sector of the economy.

Are Norwegian institutions (especially the labour market and the welfare state) able to meet the challenges of a wealth shock coming from huge oil revenues, or for that matter new external 'negative' shocks coming from a drastic fall in oil prices, such as in 1988 and in 1998? This chapter attempts to answer this by looking at how Norway has managed the 1988-93 recession, and the boom that followed and continues to this day.

Norway's historical legacy

Countries such as Norway are often called 'labourers' societies' (Arendt, 1958) or 'employment regimes of the Scandinavian type', because paid work (wage labour) and a policy of full employment are regarded as cornerstones of the society in general and of the welfare state in particular. The Scandinavian welfare state contributes to a maximisation of job offers (*commodification)* through high public employment and demand-side policy, an active labour market policy (*recommodification*), and by creating the opportunities for temporary absence from work, by paid sick and parental leave (*decommodification*). The high labour force participation rate among women, combined with one of the highest fertility rates in Western Europe, testifies the success of the Norwegian welfare state.

The labour movement and social democratic parties (and governments) have been strong supporters both of the work ethic and the ideology of full employment. The obligation for the political authorities to create opportunities for employment was inserted into Norway's constitution in 1954.

The Norwegian welfare state is also based on a strong commitment to ideals of equality, social justice, social security, solidarity, and social integration. The work ethic is strong (Halvorsen, 1998; Svallfors et al, 2001), and full employment is still regarded as a central means to redistribute wealth, reduce inequality and poverty, to avoid dependency, enhance self-reliance, and secure integration into mainstream society of all non-disabled persons (NOU, 1992, p 26). Non-disabled persons not only have a right to work but an obligation towards society to work: to create economic growth, and, by paying taxes, contribute to the financing of a huge public sector and securing a decent economic support to those outside labour force.

The 1980s

International recessions and structural changes in the economy have (according to Norwegian standards) resulted in unemployment at unacceptably high levels between 1981 and 1983, and again between 1990 and 1993. Contrary to most other European countries, Norway did not experience macroeconomic external shocks due to drastic increases in oil prices. In 1983, the end of an international recession resulted in a boom in Norway due to increased export. The boom was reinforced by increased national demand, thanks to huge oil investments and an expansive finance policy. Of greatest importance, however, was deregulation of the financial and housing markets, which resulted in a strong increase in private consumption and investments in housing. Up to 1985, business cycles were identical with those of Norway's trading partners. Since then Norway's economic activity has been more independent of them and more dependent on domestic circumstances, especially oil investments (NOU, 2000, p 21). Huge wage increases – and reduction of working hours in 1987 – resulted in much higher wage costs than Norway's trading partners. In order to avoid a reduction in Norway's competitiveness, the Norwegian Crone (NOK) was devaluated several times. The end result was high inflation and interest rates. Besides, Norway was negatively affected by the dramatic fall in oil prices in 1986. This fall worsened the trade balance and public finances (NOU, 2000, p 21). A tight financial policy and a collapse in the housing market and problems for the financial industries at the same time, contributed to a recession starting in 1987, which was reinforced by the international recession from 1990. Despite the economic problems of the 1980s, it was nevertheless possible to keep the unemployment level low (on average 3.6% for the period 1980-90). Revenues from the oil sector enabled the government to keep unemployment levels low during most of the 1980s, despite a strong decrease in employment in the manufacturing industries by expansion of public sector employment (NOU, 1992, p 26).

The recession of 1988-93: from work to welfare

According to Norwegian standards, unemployment reached unacceptably high levels in 1990/93. However, thanks to a huge oil production and high oil revenues, the level of unemployment was in fact low compared with other OECD countries. Norway was nevertheless negatively affected by the international recession, which began in 1990 (see Chapter Two, Table 2.5 of this volume). The highest level of gross unemployment (registered unemployed plus persons taking part in labour market programmes) was reached in 1993 with 8.2% of labour force. Thanks to a huge expansion of higher education and public sector employment and an active labour market policy, persistent long-term unemployment (hystereses) did not occur. Yet, as with other countries, there was also a sharp fall in the labour force participation rate for men aged 55+, but not for women (St. meld. nr. 50 for 1998-99). There has been a strong tendency to early retirement from the labour market by older people, mainly through disability pension or early retirement pension schemes.

Some of these people are discouraged workers. Part of this discouraged worker effect is due to mergers, acquisitions, company close downs and retrenchments. The retrenched are regarded as early retirees and are no longer visible in the statistical figures of unemployed, and could even respond in surveys that they are neither interested in paid work nor actively seeking work.

Perhaps the best way of detecting withdrawal from the labour force is to study short-term *changes* in the labour force participation rate for various age categories or in the composition of persons *outside* the labour force. Seen in this way it turns out that Norway is the one OECD country with the greatest short-term and long-term flexibility in the labour force participation rate. With a 1% increase in the unemployment rate, the labour force participation rate falls to 0.9%. This means that if employment falls proportionally equal in all OECD countries, the increase in unemployment would be especially small in Norway, because the number of people in the labour force is strongly reduced (Colbjørnsen and Larsen, 1995). In 1992, it was shown that the labour force consisted of 160,000 fewer persons than had the labour force developed according to current trends. Almost half of this withdrawal consisted of persons taking part in education or labour market programmes (Larsen and Eriksen, 1995).

Young women are over-represented by this temporary withdrawal from the labour market (Ellingsæter, 2000a). Labour market programmes have worked to prevent long-term unemployed from becoming permanently excluded from the labour market (Colbjørnsen and Larsen, 1995). This development demonstrates that it is not necessary to liberalise labour laws in order to create a more flexible labour market, as long as state support schemes are linked to an activation policy (education and labour market programmes).

Based on a sharp increase in the number of persons on disability pension during the 1970s and 1980s, an exponential increase was forecasted for the coming years, so long as the eligibility rules remained unchanged. Nevertheless, in 1988 a negotiated *early retirement* scheme was introduced, partly financed by the government. It made it possible to retire at 65 years-of-age (while the ordinary pension age is 67).

Throughout the international recession, it was nevertheless possible to have positive economic growth thanks to the huge oil-producing sector of the economy. Public expenditures, jobs and investments increased in order to compensate for reduced private sector investments and the fall in household consumption. High oil tax revenues made this Keynesian policy possible. At the same time, a tight fiscal policy aimed at keeping the inflation low was put into effect in order to enhance the competitiveness. Yet even this could not prevent increases in unemployment levels.

Inspired by the Swedish labour market policy, an 'active' policy[3] means that the government has tried to reduce unemployment levels and keep the unemployed attached to the labour market by expanding labour market programmes during the recession. In 1993, active labour market measures cost 2.6% of Norwegian GDP (up from 1.1.% in 1991, but down again to 0.8% in 1999; NOU, 2000, p 21). So-called active measures constitute about 50% of total expenses, but varies according to the level of unemployment, which is in line with OECD recommendations (see Drøpping et al, 1998; Torp, 1999). The main labour market programme was and still is qualifying courses (AMO), accounting for 75% of all participants in 1998 (Moe, 1999). Of great importance also are practice placements, job clubs, wage subsidies and in-house work training, both for unemployed and for persons with vocational disabilities. The main purpose of labour market programmes is to increase the competitiveness of participants in the labour market, but in that respect it seems that during the recession the programmes have not been very successful (Opdal et al, 1997), although practice placements seem to improve job chances (Moe, 1999). On the other hand, participation in programmes seems to improve the quality of life as compared with staying unemployed, and also encourages (young) participants to take further or higher education.

To combat youth unemployment the government extended the capacity in higher education. It issued a *guarantee* for work, practice placements, or education for persons aged below 20.

There were not any major welfare cutbacks during the recession. In fact, the duration of unemployment benefits was gradually extended from May 1992 up to a maximum period of 186 weeks in 1993 (but later reduced to 156 weeks). This liberalisation was the result of political pressure from the labour union, which found that its members were becoming increasingly long-term unemployed. The unemployment benefit for a supported child was doubled in May 1992. The only exception was the establishment of stricter requirements before disability pension was granted: medical disability had to be the main reason for the reduced working capacity (social and economic problems are not legitimate entitlement criteria for a disability pension). Besides, a claimant's work capacity had to be measured against any work the claimant could do and anywhere in the country (geographical and vocational mobility). There was also a reduction in the percentage for calculation of supplementary pension benefits from 45% to 42%, and reduced compensation for high-income earners.

After the recession: from welfare to work

Development of the labour market

In addition to registered unemployed, gross unemployment includes participants in labour market programmes and persons vocationally disabled taking part in a programme. However, even gross unemployment has decreased even more since the recession of 1991-93, and was in fact negligible by 2000 (Table 9.1).

Only the numbers of persons with disabilities in vocational rehabilitation have increased since 1993, which is due to stronger enforcement of eligibility criteria for disability pension.

Unemployment rates are especially high among the youth; that is, persons aged less than 25 years-of-age, and both for men and women (see Chapter Two, Tables 2.6 and 2.8 of this volume). In Norway, there has been a deliberate

Table 9.1: Gross unemployment (1993-2001) (persons)

	1993	1994	1995	1996	1997	1999	2000	2001
Labour market programmes	57,260	53,174	42,145	34,765	23,024	8,000	11,000	10,000
Persons with disabilities in vocational rehabilitation	14,700	16,826	18,614	19,821	19,510	20,400	22,000	24,000
Unemployed	118,146	110,280	102,154	90,938	73,525	60,000	63,000	63,000
Total	190,106	180,280	162,913	145,524	116,059	88,400	96,000	97,000

Source: Directorate of Labour, and St.pr.nr. 1 (2001-02), Budget 2001 for Arbeids og administrasjonsdepartementet

policy to avoid unemployment among young persons in particular by increasing study capacities in higher education, or by providing young persons with the opportunity to take part in labour market programmes. In that manner one eases the burden of being unemployed, while at the same time improving the qualifications of young people, which is hoped to make them more employable. The main reason for the high level of unemployment among youth (even today) is that their main activity is education, while at the same time seeking part-time work (St. meld. nr. 30 for 2000-01).

The duration of unemployment is generally seen as a manifestation of the flexibility of the labour market (Ellingsæter, 2000b). However, the proportion of long-term unemployed (six months ore more) varies with unemployment levels – 10% in 1980. It was at its highest in 1993 with 38%, but, according to labour force surveys, went down to 16% in 2000. Long-term unemployment was 20.4% in 1990 according to Eurostat definitions (12 months or more unemployed), 16.0% in 1996 and down to 6.8% in 1999 (see Chapter Two, Table 2.10 of this volume). These figures indicate that high unemployment in the early 1990s was not structural, but Keynesian.

Since 1962, the total volume of work hours has not changed, even though at the same time 700,000 more people (mostly women working part-time) have entered the labour force (results not presented). An implicit work sharing has therefore taken place. In 2000 the labour force participation rate (16-74 years) had increased to 73.4%, the highest proportion ever measured[4]. Yet, in 1997 only 63.5% of the population in this age group regarded paid work as their *main* activity. Like in the other Scandinavian countries more and more women are now working full time, mainly because they have fewer children. What also matters, however, is improved parental leave, the provision of after-school childcare and more publicly financed childcare arrangements. Up to a certain limit approved childcare expenses are tax deductible. The separate taxation of spouses and the principle of individualisation of social and fiscal rights are also important, which means that women are treated as subjects with individual rights. On the demand side, the availability of part-time work, growth in private service sector employment and public employment has been of great importance.

When looking at the high Norwegian labour force participation rates, one has to take into consideration that for the majority of young persons under the age of 19 their *main activity* is schooling (81%)[5]. And among the 20-24 year-olds, 36% had studying as their main activity. One third of each category has at the same time some paid work, and is consequently included in the labour force. This means that in international comparisons the high participation rate in Norway is somewhat overrated. Furthermore, included in labour force participation rates are also persons temporarily absent from work, for example because of sickness or maternity leave[6]. It is also quite common to combine receipt of benefits with some paid work, which means that, for example some persons on disability pension are included in the labour force participation rates. On the other hand, people in the 65-74 age bracket are working. These are not included in comparisons of labour market participation in Europe (see Chapter Two, Table 2.4 of this volume). In 1998, 15% of men and 15% of women aged 65-69 years were working. The same was the case for 5% of men in the 70-73 age bracket. Most of them are combining old age pension with some paid work, but some also work full-time until they reach the mandatory *retirement* age of 70 years (while the pension age is 67 years). This development could explain that parallel with the higher proportion of long-term beneficiaries in the 1990s, the proportion of non-employed persons of the population aged 16-74 has been reduced. In 1972, 38% of the population aged 16-74 was outside labour force. By 2000, this figure had dropped to 26.6%.

In 1999, 59% of Norwegian women worked full time (up from 23% in 1980), 26% long part-time (more than 20 hours per week), and only 15% short part-time (less than 20 hours per week). Only 10% of men worked part time. Since long part-time work gives full social rights entitlements, it is normalised. The number of full-time *homeworking* women in the 16-66 age group has been reduced strongly during the 1980s and 1990s, and represented less than 100,000 women in 1998 (Statistics Norway, 2000a). This means that Norway is catching up with the other Nordic countries.

The proportion of employees with standard daytime work has been reduced from 80% in 1980 to 70% in 1997 (Statistics Norway, 1998). About 25% of all full-time workers had overtime work in 1999. This means that flexible-work time arrangements have been more widespread. Average working hours per year has been reduced from 1,511 in 1980 to 1,393 in 1997, while on average *full-time* workers are actually working only 1,500 hours per year (Statistics Norway, 1997).

Eight per cent of employed persons are temporarily employed, and this figure includes more women than men, partly due to the fact that a higher proportion of women than men take parental leave and are replaced by a substitute (Ellingsæter, 2000a). Many short part-time workers in particular are temporarily employed and 57% of the temporarily employed want tenure. Young people are over-represented. People entering the labour market often hold such contracts (Ellingsæter, 2000b). These contract workers are not marginalised, because a survey indicates that about half of those on temporary part-time contracts in 1989 had a permanent contract in 1993 (Skollerud, 1997).

Only few employees are outsiders with low pay[7], little protection, and in 'non-standard' jobs (causal short-term contracts), apart from persons of school-age.

The number of employed in the *public sector* has increased in Norway by 190,000 between 1980 and 1995, of which the majority are working in municipal health and social services (Statistics Norway, 1998). The public sector is comprised of 30.5% of the workforce, representing 26.4% of all working hours (St. meld. nr. 50 for 1998-99). This increase has been possible by mobilising female labour power. In 2000, 47% of all working women were employed in the public sector, in contrast to 21% of men (Statistics Norway, 2000b). The greatest decrease in employment has taken place in manufacturing, construction and agriculture. As a result the growth in *productivity* is very low in Norway, which means that it is more and more costly to finance the public sector. The results are fewer hands and greater wage pressure.

Yet, along with more and more people in paid work, there has been a worrying increase in the number of people on sickness benefits[8] (the figure has doubled since 1993), rehabilitation allowance, disability pension and early retirement pension. Due to high absence from work due to sick leave and maternity leave, the total working hours in Norway has been rather stable over the last 10 to 15 years, despite a 10% increase in the labour force. There is therefore no indication of 'end of work' due to introduction of new technology or for example increased competition because of globalisation, as was predicted by some authors (Rifkin, 1995; Aronowitz and DiFazio, 1995). Annual growth in labour productivity has mostly been lower than the annual economic growth. Economic growth and growth in employment still goes hand in hand (Henwood, 1998).

Hidden unemployment constitutes discouraged workers (persons outside the labour force who had given up job search because they did not think they would get a job; that is, early retired[9] or homemakers) and part-time workers wanting full-time work.

Underemployment is not normally included in figures of registered unemployment. In 1999, 69,000 persons were underemployed, and among this group, women were over-represented. We also find underemployment among part-time workers who want to work longer hours. The high level of underemployment persists even when there is a fall in unemployment levels. In 1996, partly-employed job seekers represented 2.9% of the labour force. The majority of the underemployed are women, but the proportion of underemployed among the partly-employed is in fact higher among men. According to labour market surveys four out of five partly-employed registered as underemployed in the first quarter of 1998, and had left this position one year later (St. meld. nr. 30 for 2000-01). Fears of hysterisis (unemployment as a self-reinforcing process because of skill deterioration) therefore seems to be unfounded. There is no sign of the development of a 'culture of dependency' among long-term unemployed or recipients of social assistance allowance (Halvorsen, 1999a, 1996b).

The figures presented earlier indicate that work sharing has made room for more people in the labour market. Yet Norway's social democratic government has refused to deliberately use work sharing as a central means of reducing unemployment, for example by getting rid of overtime or by reducing standard working hours. Neither has it accepted a de facto reduction in pension age, for example, by introduction of public early retirement schemes as a means of creating job opportunities for younger people. In fact, the government wishes to increase the de facto pension age of 60 by three years in the next 10-15 years in order to ease the future burden of high pension expenditures. It also fears that a planned reduction of the labour supply would increase labour costs and therefore reduce Norway's competitiveness in a global economy.

The composition of the population outside the labour force has changed. There has been a decrease in the proportion of persons privately supported, such as housewives, and an increase in the proportion supported by the welfare state (on a short or long-term basis), such as students, single mothers, persons with additional needs, early retired and old age pensioners. This represents a challenge for the government.

Policy for full employment

To create more jobs, a solidaristic wage policy had been negotiated between the social partners, that is, labour unions and the Employers' Association, with strong support from the social democratic government. The Norwegian bargaining system was by the end of the 1990s regarded as the most centralised in the OECD area (OECD, 1997e). In practice it is illegal to strike for higher wages in Norway (*tvungen lønnsnemnd*). Centralised collective bargaining has resulted in low unemployment levels compared to other OECD countries. In fact the national pay setting is export-led. Such a policy is necessary because of the 'paradox of plenty'. Wage moderation is obtained even though unemployment is low. This corporate system has resulted in smaller wage differentials than in countries such as the UK and US. It has been possible because of the high unionisation of employees (Freeman, 1997). Ellingsæter (2000a) concludes that strict employment protection, high levels of unionisation and generous unemployment benefits do not have serious implications for average unemployment, if combined with high levels of coordination in wage bargaining and pressures on the unemployed to take jobs. The centralised bargaining system has since been threatened by high salaries among chief executives and huge company profits, which are not reinvested but paid out as dividends to shareholders who take part in 'conspicuous consumption'. This break with an egalitarian tradition tends to undermine the legitimacy of the consensus formation between government and organisations about macroeconomic policy (Moene, 1999).

An active policy for restructuring Norwegian industries to meet increased global competition is also an essential element in the strategy for full employment. An example of this restructuring are efforts to privatise public companies and to make public sector services more market-oriented[10].

There has not been any major welfare cutbacks, apart from tightening the eligibility criteria of benefits (unemployment, disability and transitional allowance)[11] and enforcing more stringently the 'work-test'[12]. The tightening of the unemployment benefit scheme has been moderate, compared with what has happened in Finland and Denmark during the 1990s for example. It is also worthwhile mentioning that stricter eligibility criteria took place when there was an increasing shortage of labour. It is politically easier to tighten such schemes when the number of unemployed affected by stricter eligibility criteria is small and decreasing (Torp, 1999). The main changes in the disability pension scheme during the 1990s were moderate: in 1995 it stressed that lasting sickness must be the main cause of reduced work ability. In 1998 the lowest age of eligibility was raised from 16 to 18 years-of-age.

No *fundamental* change of the Norwegian welfare state has taken place during the 1990s. Mainly due to high oil revenues, it has not been an economic necessity to reform the existing welfare state arrangements. So far, it has also been impossible to get the necessary political support for any major welfare reforms.

Neither has there been a major shift towards supply-side policy. There has been no liberalisation of labour laws, for example, such as making it easier for fixed labour contracts or to layoff or dismiss employees (Ellingsæter, 2000a).

In order to avoid long-term unemployment and create a more flexible labour market, the 'work line' has been stressed (St. meld. nr. 2 for 1995-96). There is a fear that generous cash benefits, such as disability pension and unemployment benefits, could be a disincentive to keep a job or to get a new one if unemployed. Therefore, eligibility criteria have been tightened. Instead of 'passive' income support, the government wants to give 'active' support, for example, by offering or obliging the unemployed to take part in labour market programmes and the disabled to participate in vocational rehabilitation. While previously the right to work and the society's obligation to secure 'work for all' has been stressed, today more emphasis is put on the obligation of the individual to find paid work. This means, for example, that the unemployed must be prepared to relocate or to accept what the labour exchange offices regard as 'suitable' work. People have to be less 'selective' so that the mismatch between available jobs[13] and qualifications of available people can be reduced.

The labour market administration cooperates extensively with the county follow-up services to ensure that teenagers who do not exercise their right to upper secondary education are given the best possible offer. Teenagers who are not pursuing an education or do not have ordinary employment may be offered an apprenticeship. Between 1995 and 1997, persons aged 20-24 who had been without a job, in education or a labour market programme for more than six months, were either offered a job or a place on a labour market programme. Job seekers over the age of 19 may be eligible for participation in a 'job club' – this is a job placement measure where the search for a job takes place on a full-time basis.

For the time being, however, labour market policies have been more focused on job placement due to high labour demand and growing labour shortages. Mobility requirements are strictly practised to counteract bottleneck problems in the labour market, even if that means that the unemployed person will have to move from home or take a job, which is not in accordance with his or her qualifications. Due to a decline in unemployment, labour market measures have gradually been de-escalated.

'Work for welfare' ('workfare')[14] arrangements have become more popular among politicians. A new Social Services Act was passed by the parliament in 1991. A new clause was added: recipients of the means-tested social assistance, for example, are obliged to take suitable work for the municipality (relief work).

The target group is primarily non-disabled young recipients (Enjolras and Lødemel, 1999; Lødemel, 2001). They may be required to work a maximum of 15 hours a week for six months in individually adjusted work according to the circular from the ministry, but in practice these guidelines are violated by the municipalities. These persons are punished for their idleness, but an evaluation of the implementation of such programmes at 'the street level' demonstrates that the reality is much more complicated (Vik-Mo and Nervik, 1999). Nevertheless, in this way a strong employment commitment is sustained and the municipality saves money. It has to be mentioned, however, that so far very few persons have been subjected to this new workfare regime. Besides, cooperation between the labour offices, the health and social services and the social insurance offices has been given greater emphasis.

Part of an 'active' labour market policy has also been wage subsidies in order to encourage employers to hire unemployed persons, or persons with additional needs. To combat long-term unemployment, the government is subsidising study leave and childcare leave if an unemployed person is hired for up to ten months as a substitute for the person on leave. More emphasis is also put on vocational education and the creation of apprenticeships. Finally, in 1993 an entrepreneur grant programme, which was part of a national plan to reduce unemployment, was launched. The programme is open to anyone planning to establish a new business, but unemployed people, together with women and applicants from economically disadvantaged areas, are to be given priority. Grants are provided both for planning a business and for making the investments connected with starting a business.

In order to reduce labour costs, employers in Norway's three northern counties are exempted from paying their share of social expenditures. Some industries, such as shipbuilding and farming, are still heavily subsidised, which contributes to maintaining employment in these sectors. This is possible because Norway is not a full member of the EU, but only affiliated through the separate European Economic Agreement (EEA). This means that the degrees of freedom in maintaining high employment are somewhat greater for Norway than for the members of the EU.

In order to reconcile work and childcare the centre-right government (in power from September 1997 to March 2000) introduced a controversial *cash benefit* scheme in 1998, not tied to the employment contract[15] (in addition to a child allowance introduced already in 1946) for parents with children aged between one and two years-of-age (extended to three years-of-age in 2000), and who do not make use of public childcare arrangements[16]. This reform diverges from the main principle of social-democratic policies (Ellingsæter, 2000b). As a result about 20% of women with very young children have reduced their labour market participation (Statistics Norway, 2000; see also St. meld. nr. 43 for 2000-01). Furthermore, since 1998 it has been possible to retire at 62 years-of-age[17].

Outlook and challenges

The main challenge for the Norwegian government now is to combat inflation, high interest rates and to adjust the economy to fluctuations in oil prices. With a huge oil fund[18], and surplus in state budgets and in foreign trade balance[19], it is difficult to convince labour unions that it is in their own interest not to claim higher wages or more generous social benefits. This could make it more difficult to attract foreign investors. It is especially feared that the huge oil fund will bring about rent-seeking activities by economic actors. This huge wealth could also make room for growing discontent in the population who have rising expectations of higher personal welfare. The end result could be lower employment commitment and lower productivity (Isachsen, 2001). This is the paradox of plenty.

We have already seen a reduction of employment in the competing sector of the economy, especially in manufacturing industries exposed to international competition. Labour productivity in Norway is also lower than in many other OECD countries, mainly due to a huge public sector, while the wage increase over the last few years has been 10% higher than among its trading partners. There is also a price to be paid for high female labour force participation rates in terms of high paid absence from work (sickness benefits and maternity benefits). Modernisation of the public sector means restructuring[20], which inevitably results in more people on early retirement and disability pension. A future membership of the EU will mean a drastic reduction of a heavily subsidised agricultural sector, as well as creating problems for employers located in the three northern counties, and who are now subsidised.

It is also forecasted that there will be a low increase in the number of people of working age in the years to come. In addition, as of 2002 all workers are entitled to five weeks of paid holidays (six weeks for workers aged 60+). The government fears that Norway will experience a shortage of labour, particularly in the public sector as from 2010 (Arbeidsdirektoratet, 2000a)[21]. It has therefore been suggested that one has to discourage people to retire early by making it more profitable to stay in work until the pension age of 67 and to reduce the sickness benefit compensation level from 100% to 80%. It is proposed by the government that guest workers such as trained nurses should be invited to work in Norway for a period of time. The labour market authorities put more efforts into job placement in order to overcome skills and territorial mismatch and thus structural unemployment. The labour union has nevertheless proposed to reduce the standard working week to 35 hours as a first step towards a 30-hour working week, as well as a flexible pension age from 60 years.

Implications for citizenship

In line with OECD recommendations the government tries to avoid 'passive' measures and to prevent non-disabled persons from staying too long on income support. The work-line means that waged work would be the first and 'natural' choice for all persons who are able to support themselves. The goal of self-reliance is stressed, both by the former social democrat governments (Halvorsen, 1998), the centre-right government (up to March 2000) (St meld. nr. 52 for 1998-99), and the right-centre government as from September 2001. There are strong incentives to be employed, but not necessarily to work more. The Norwegian employment regime reconciles reproduction and work, but creates a two-tier model of parenthood/work life, one model for women and one for fathers (Ellingsæter, 1999).

This means that according to widespread opinions a full citizenship is only achieved through participation in the labour market. As a member of the labour force one has an undisputed status as a citizen where civic obligations correspond to rights according to mainstream thinking. One lives up to the principle of reciprocity according to the recent Clinton-Blair orthodoxy (Jordan, 1998). By taking an active part in society, self-respect and dignity is achieved. It is stigmatising to be on income support. That is especially the case for the means-tested social assistance allowance, which could undermine recipients' self-respect. One could question whether workfare is in consistence with the normative citizenship ideal of treating all citizens with equal concern and respect (Dworkin, 2000; see also Kildal, 2001).

As long as there is not any tendency to an increase in non-standard, precarious jobs and the number of outsiders/marginalised persons in the labour market, a strong work ethic makes it preferable for people to stay in paid work. There is, however, a risk that emphasis on the 'welfare to work measures' could create a form of *constrained* participation (systems of forced labour) which represents a threat to the goal for full citizenship of all the members of the society. Examples include single mothers who can be forced to take (low) paid work, and young people who have to work for the municipality in return for receipt of social assistance allowance. Among much else, their liberty to make choices as to what work to do is violated. Similarly for unemployed persons, who now are obliged to accept any job, even if it is poorly paid, if they want to claim unemployment benefits. Enforced, active participation does not necessarily mean inclusion or integration. A move from an 'opportunities approach' to a 'sanctions approach' (Kosonen, 1999), could for some categories represent an impediment for achieving full citizenship – at least in the short-term. The long-term implications for citizenship are dependent on future development of the labour market.

Tightening of the eligibility criteria for disability benefits has made the life circumstances worse, for women in particular, especially for those who are too sick to work, but too healthy to be eligible for disability pension. This is an example of implementing the 'work line' through *negative* measures. In general, however, women have been integrated in the labour market, and do not risk marginalisation to any greater extent than men. Parental leave, subsidised childcare and part-time work has also made it possible to for women to reconcile paid work and care. Motherhood is no longer a barrier to women's social citizenship. The right to care is part of the work contract (Ellingsæter, 1999b).

Married women, however, still experience a double burden of paid work and household responsibilities to a greater extent than married men do. However, Norway seems to be heading towards a 'dual breadwinner' society, to use Lewis' typology (1992). More and more women are entering higher education and a sectorial shift from industries to services (public sector) represents high demand for female labour (Ellingsæter, 1999b). A process of individualisation supports the development. The labour market is, however, still segregated on gender lines. Yet, through their (more continuous) participation in paid work women have earned access to social benefits (such as disability pension) as an individual right and have therefore gained some independence from men (their husbands). It has also been argued that women's citizenship should also include the right to time to care (Lewis, 1997; Lister, 1997). Extension of parental leave arrangements and cash benefits for those who take care of their own children under the age of two favours such ideas. Yet, single parents who are unable to work are heavily penalised economically through this work-centred approach to social protection. Their right to care has the price of not being available for paid work, which means that the children of single mothers are at risk of living in poverty.

An implication of tightening of eligibility criteria (stricter conditions for acquisition) and more stringent 'work testing' and ongoing public discourses about misuse of benefits may result in increased non take-up of benefits. This could especially be the case for persons who are in a 'grey zone': they are too healthy to be entitled to disability pension, but too sick to get an ordinary job. They risk a permanent precarious position in the labour market and, being low-income earners, they may be unable to take an active part in society as citizens and are at risk of being socially excluded. Besides, their identity and self-esteem can suffer from their position as a secondary citizen. In addition, newcomers to the labour market (especially young persons without a sufficient work record) could be harmed in their full social participation because they are not entitled to unemployment benefits, and have to rely on the stigmatising and needs-tested social assistance allowance.

There has been a move by the previous *centre-right* government towards a basic income through an increased minimum (not earnings-based) old age pension, while the earnings-related old age pension has been less generous in relative terms. Besides, cash allowance to parents with small children who do not make use of public childcare arrangements, also acknowledges that rights can be achieved without having to live up to the principle of reciprocity outlined earlier. It remains to be seen whether the new *right-centre*, minority government (in power since September 2001) will follow up this policy. It is not very likely that this government would give up its 'path of activation' in favour of a 'citizen wage path' (see Chapter Two of this volume), advocated for example by the social-liberal party (Venstre). The present government and labour market partners have for example signed a contract concerning an *inclusive working life* with the explicit purpose of reducing sickness leave and use of disability pension, and to make use of the labour resources of older workers and persons with additional needs in working life. As a consequence of this employers contributions to the social insurance scheme for employees aged 62+ are reduced by up to four percentage points as of 1 July 2002.

Conclusion

There have not been any fundamental changes – 'process of retrenchment' to use Pierson's formulation (1994), or 'restructuring' to use a formulation suggested by Van der Veen et al (1999) – of the Norwegian welfare state during the 1990s. The welfare state has not moved in a more residualist direction, although work conditionality has become an increasingly important determinant of eligibility to social protection schemes, with the exception of old age pension. The obligations of recipients of social benefits have also been more clearly defined and are more effectively supervised, but since the labour market has improved considerably since 1994, the negative implications for citizenship are negligible thus far. It is also safe to conclude that a policy of full employment matters, since the government was able to keep unemployment levels low during the international recession. This shows that the unemployment in early 1990s was mainly of the Keynesian kind. Structural unemployment was handled through disability and early retirement schemes. However, high absence from work is the price we have to pay for high labour force participation rates, especially for older people (and younger women with very young children). More and more working-age people are dependent fully or at least partly on social benefits.

Is the Norwegian welfare state sustainable? So far high economic growth, an international boom, low productivity and huge oil revenues have made it relatively easy to secure full employment, first and foremost by creating more jobs in the public sector. However, huge oil revenues and surplus in state budgets makes it politically difficult to keep public expenditures down. It is often difficult for people to understand the necessity of this in a situation where the oil fund is increasing with NOK 250 billion a year. State employees want higher wages, and employees in the private sector want lower taxes. And everybody wants more money spent on health care, education and public transport. This means strong wage pressures (especially in the public sector with shortage of labour), and difficulties in maintaining a solidaric wage policy. With a drastic fall in oil prices (say to less than $10 dollar a barrel), Norway will soon have to readjust to new economic realities. Its public sector has to be modernised and restructured. With an ageing population the dependency ratio is also worsening, which means that the burden on those of working age will have to be heavier. They will have to increase their labour productivity, and at the same time be prepared to pay more taxes[22]. In the near future there will be shortage of labour at the same time as the labour force is ageing. This means that the welfare state arrangements must encourage people to work. This might be achieved:

- by increasing the pension age in the early retirement scheme;

- making it less generous;
- making it more attractive for (old age and disability) pensioners to have some paid work;
- by encouraging housewives to take paid work;
- by importing guest workers.

But in case of new external shocks (such as a global recession or a drastic fall in oil prices), unemployment could raise to unprecedented high levels. With so many persons eligible for public support (unemployment benefits and disability pension), and fewer persons than ever dependent on private support since the two-earner family is the norm, it can be necessary to cut back benefits and pensions and tighten eligibility criteria.

Notes

[1] In 1996, oil and gas represented 16% of GDP, 1% of employment, 23% of investments and 38% of export (Thonstad, 2001).

[2] It has also been found that countries rich of natural resources have had a lower economic growth than countries with limited access to natural resources (Norman et al, 2001).

[3] A rather misleading conception since receipt of benefits makes it possible to live an active life. See Sinfield (1997).

[4] In 2000, 50.5% of the total population is in paid work, as compared with 47.4% in 1980 (own calculations).

[5] Mandatory school age now is 19 years-of-age (up from 16).

[6] In countries with high proportions of employed persons on leave, one tends to overestimate the labour force participation rate. For comparisons it is therefore better to compare *employment* rates.

[7] Collective bargaining has raised the earnings of low decile workers towards the median and produced a spread of earnings more compressed than in any country (Freeman, 1997).

[8] In 2000, an employed person was on average on sick leave for close to 25 days (St. meld. nr. 30 for 2000-01).

[9] In 1987, 6% of persons 16-66 years were outside labour force and on disability pension, early retirement pension or on rehabilitation allowance. In 2000, the proportion had risen to 9% (St. meld. nr. 30 for 2000-01).

[10] This modernisation can be very costly for the government in terms of more people on generous disability and early retirement schemes.

[11] There is for example still a 100% compensation for sickness leave for up to one year.

[12] In 2000, 12,000 claimants to unemployment benefits or 10% of all claimants were denied (further) benefits because they did not pass the "willingness to work test" or were unemployed due to their own fault (see Arbeidsdirektoratet, 2000b).

[13] Since the recession in the early 1990s the number of vacancies has doubled (St. meld. nr. 1 for 2000-01). In January 2001, the stock of job vacancies at the Labour Office was 23,000, while the number of registered unemployed was 65,000 (Arbeidsdirektoratet, 2001).

[14] See Kildal (2001); Lødemel and Trickey (2001) for definitions.

[15] Parents get paid in cash the amount equivalent to the state subsidy to a public childcare place.

[16] It amounts to NOK 3,000 per month per child. And since it is economically attractive to take care of own children, the labour supply has been reduced with between 3,500 and 4,500 man years (Langseth et al, 2000).

[17] Previously ad hoc company-based early retirement schemes have been widely used. Such schemes have also been used by the government to modernise public sector services such as post, telegraph and railways.

[18] By the end of 2001 it is estimated to be NOK 632 billion. By 2010 it could be as high as NOK 1,800 billion according to the National Bank's director Svein Gjedrem. With an average oil price of $25 a barrel the next 20 years it is estimated that the oilfund will be NOK 4,000 billion in 2020 (Norman, Roland and Reve 2001).

[19] In 2000, the trade surplus was NOK 224 billion (St. meld. nr1. for 2000-01).

[20] Since 1996, there has been a 36% increase in the number of disability pensioners among public employees (*Aftenposten*, 2001).

[21] Towards 2010, the demand for labour will increase by a forecasted 320,000, while expected supply is 140,000. Also by 2010, the working age population will be older: 150,000 more persons will be aged 60-65, while the 25-29 age group in the same period will be reduced by 50,000.

[22] Yet, in a globalised economy where employers and investors can threaten to move production or capital abroad, there is a limitation on the level of taxation of profits and wages.

TEN

Unemployment and unemployment policy in Finland

Heikki Ervasti

Introduction

This chapter analyses Finnish labour markets and labour market policies. Finland achieved a solid growth rate between the mid-1970s and late 1980s, averaging 3.2% per annum between 1976 and 1989. During this period unemployment was comparatively low. However, the dominant feature of the Finnish economic landscape of the last two decades has been the recession in the early 1990s. During its gloomiest years (1991-93), Finnish GDP sank by 12%. As a part of this deep recession, Finland faced unprecedented levels of unemployment. According to OECD statistics the Finnish unemployment rate reached more than 18% in the year 1994[1].

Sections two and three of this chapter describe in more detail the developments in the Finnish labour markets and the main features of unemployment in Finland. In particular, attention is focused on how the increasing levels of unemployment affected different segments of the population in Finland, with special emphasis on differences between age groups, between men and women and socioeconomic groups. In section four, attention shifts to Finnish labour policies. In the early 1990s the government adopted restrictive economic policies including austerity measures and cutbacks which probably further increased unemployment. The main target of the government was to reduce budget deficit and foreign debt as much as possible and to keep the inflation rate as low as possible, regardless of how high the unemployment rate rose. It would be easy to expect this type of policy to have dramatic social consequences such as increasing economic inequality or worsening social problems. However, in retrospect, Finland overcame the economic crisis with surprisingly low social consequences. The high levels of unemployment put a strong pressure on the Finnish welfare state. The need for social security benefits increased simultaneously with declining resources to finance it. However, the Finnish welfare state succeeded surprisingly well. Income differentials did not increase during the recession, nor did the relative poverty rate. However, a closer scrutiny at the national level reveals that the Finnish society is not the same as it was prior to the recession. As the country recovers from the recession, new social divides and even possible signs of polarisation of the population have emerged, mainly as a consequence of the policies that were adopted during the recession. Section five analyses the reasons for this unexpected development.

Unemployment in Finland since the 1970s

In contrast to other European countries, Finland did not experience any major rise in unemployment in the aftermath of the oil crises of the 1970s. During the 1970s, unemployment in Finland varied from 1.8% in 1974 to 7.2% in 1978. In the 1980s, Finland even enjoyed decreasing unemployment. In the early 1980s, the Finnish unemployment rate was around 5%, well below the EU average, and it had decreased further to less than 4% by the end of the 1980s. Note also that the Finnish employment rate was well over 70% in the late 1980s, significantly higher than the EU average (see Chapter Two of this volume).

In the early 1990s, following a period of sustained economic growth and low unemployment rates, the international recession hit Finland harder than any other country. Several things, each of which on its own had likely caused only a small decline in the economy, happened simultaneously. The international recession started around the same time, leading to the low international price of paper, a factor that has traditionally affected the Finnish economy adversely. Furthermore, the over-valued Markka decreased export demand. More unexpectedly, the sudden upheaval in the former USSR resulted in Finland effectively losing a market, which had accounted for as much as 100,000 jobs and 20% of Finnish exports[2].

The recession sent unemployment levels soaring more than six-fold between 1990 and 1993. After the year 1994, unemployment started to fall in response to the export-led recovery and subsequent increase in domestic demand. Since 1994, the Finnish economy has been recovering with GDP growing faster than in most EU countries. However, despite relatively strong economic growth, the rate of unemployment has remained above the EU average.

Main features of unemployment

Although the overall unemployment rate has been decreasing, the Finnish labour markets have still not recovered from the shock of the 1990s. However, as shown in Chapter Two, the levels of long-term unemployment are below the European averages but well above the Nordic levels. At its highest level, long-term unemployment constituted more than half of the Finnish total unemployment. Towards the end of the 1990s, as the overall unemployment rate started to decrease, the level of long-term unemployment also declined. In 1999, long-term unemployment constituted 30% of all unemployed people.

Another problem in the Finnish labour market has been the increase of the so-called 'atypical' employment. The number of fixed term contracts increased remarkably during the 1990s (see Nätti, 1993; Nurmi, 1999, pp 122-4; Kauhanen, 2000; Lodovici, 2000). According to Lodovici (2000, p 56), whereas 10.5% of the Finnish labour force had fixed term contracts in the mid 1980's, the figure had increased to 17.3% in 1996. Furthermore, the risk of becoming unemployed has increased among those in atypical jobs (Parjanne, 1998). The number of those employed on a part-time basis has always been clearly lower in Finland than in other Nordic countries; however, between 1998 and 1999, part-time employment also became more common in Finland.

The unemployment problem faced by various segments of the population, that is different age groups, socioeconomic and educational groups, and men and women, are increasingly differentiated. Moreover, the duration of unemployment spells clearly depends on age and education (see, for example, Mustonen, 1998).

Unemployment and age

As in many countries (see Chapter Two of this volume), the two most problematic age groups are the youngest and the oldest wage earners. The unemployment rate of the youngest age group (that is those under the age of 25) has always been considerably higher than in the other age groups. In the early 1990s, unemployment increased most rapidly among the youngest age group despite the increasing participation in education[3]. After 1995, however, youth unemployment has decreased significantly. Also the unemployment rate of the oldest age group (aged 55+) has been comparatively high especially in the latter part of the 1990s (see also Kautto, 2001, pp 84-85). The oldest wage earners are also more likely to have longer unemployment spells than the younger ones (see, for example, Mustonen, 1998; Ministry of Labour, 2000). However, it should be noted that, because of early-exit programmes, the labour force participation of the oldest age group is among the lowest in EU countries. Nevertheless, the 55-59 age group was the only one where unemployment continued to increase until the latter half of the 1990s. Since 1998, however, the employment rate of the oldest age group has improved clearly. The oldest wage earners have stayed in the labour market; in other words, the early-exit rate has started to decline. However, re-entry into employment is extreme rare in this age group (see Romppanen, 2000). In practice the early-exit programmes have offered the oldest age group the only way out of unemployment. Demand on the labour market has been primarily for young workers who have an up-to-date education and the skills required by the 'information' society.

Differences between socioeconomic groups

Traditionally, a high occupational status and a higher level of education in particular have provided a relatively efficient protection against unemployment. The risk of unemployment has always been highest among certain blue-collar occupational groups, especially construction workers. During the years of recession, however, unemployment became somewhat more common among the well-educated white-collar employees. A higher level of educational attainment no longer protected against the risk of unemployment. However, as the overall unemployment rate began to decline, those with upper secondary or tertiary level education were the first to find a new job. All in all, unemployment and especially long-term unemployment still depends on educational level. Those with the lowest level of education have the highest unemployment rate (see also Mustonen, 1998; Vähätalo, 1998, pp 140-1). However, in a comparative perspective the Finnish differences between socioeconomic groups are by no means intolerable.

Gender differences

Gender differences in unemployment have traditionally been comparatively small in Finland. Differences have remained, although the recession of the 1990s did not affect men and women equally. At the start of the recession, unemployment hit the male-dominated private industries like construction and manufacturing. As a consequence, the male unemployment rate rose more rapidly than the female rate. At a later stage, unemployment in the female-dominated sectors (healthcare, social services, administration and clerical work, private services) started to increase. The cutbacks in health, education and welfare services, as well as the crisis in the female-dominated banking sector increased female unemployment. Nonetheless, the recession did not force women out of the labour market permanently or en masse although the female labour force participation rate did decline for several consecutive years (Nurmi, 1999, p 106). However, the unemployment rate for women has decreased more slowly than that that for men after the recession. At the end of the 1990s, the unemployment rate among women was slightly higher than among men. Moreover, fixed-term employment is clearly more common among women than among men.

The difference between men and women's long-term unemployment has on the whole remained relatively small. During the recession, however, men's long-term unemployment increased more rapidly, as a result of which the gender gap increased. As the economy took an upturn, the differences started to narrow again (Nurmi, 1999, p 139).

Policies

Traditionally, Keynesian stabilisation policies and bridging strategies have not been pursued in Finland to nearly the same extent as in other Nordic countries (see Pekkarinen, 1992; Andersson et al, 1993). On the contrary, public expenditure has been cut during times of low economic growth and vice versa. The main characteristic of Finnish economic policies has traditionally been a strong emphasis on maintaining budgetary balance, international competitiveness, low inflation and high investment. Compared to Sweden for instance, low unemployment has been a less important policy goal in Finland[4].

Multiple explanations have been put forward for Finland's failure to adopt Keynesian economic policies. In their historical analysis Pekkarinen and Vartiainen (1993, p 144) show that the low commitment on Keynesianism was never consistently and indisputably explained by the policy makers. Typically the policy makers justified their policies by referring to budget constrains, stable exchange rate, structure of the economy, institutional rigidities and 'political realities'. A more plausible explanation is that political instability and the frequently changing governments made economic policy planning quite difficult until the 1980s. According to Pekkarinen and Vartiainen (1993, pp 343-6), however, the most important reason for the rejection of Keynesian policies was the powerful position of the banks and export industries in the Finnish version of corporatist power structures. Economic policies were subordinated to the special interests of banks and export industries (see also Uusitalo, 1990, p 304). Andersson et al (1993) characterise the Finnish model of economic policy making as a 'business-oriented corporatism' (p 20). Fiscal policies and the democratic process play a subordinate role in economic policy making, while the commercial banks and the central bank, together with the export industries, have orchestrated the working of the model rather independently of the political government. The neglect of aggregate demand management and the rejection of Keynesian stabilisation were logical since the political government's grasp of economic policy was always insufficient. As economic policy has been tailored for the needs of strong business groups, there has been no agent on the economic policy scene who would pay attention to the stability of aggregate demand.

Moreover, the low priority of low unemployment may be understandable since Finnish industrialisation took place comparatively late. Until the 1950s the country was predominantly agrarian. Since the late 1950s, a rapid growth in the industrial and service sectors increased the demand for labour force of which there was an over supply in agriculture. Until the 1970s unemployment was mainly caused by fluctuations in the timber industry and hit the rural areas hardest. Moreover, emigration to Sweden also helped keep the Finnish unemployment rates on a low level, especially after 1954, when the free Nordic labour market was established. Although active labour market policies were initiated in the late 1960s, the unemployment rate has varied closely in tune with macroeconomic variation.

Finland has reacted to all economic shocks in accordance with its traditional model of economic policy making. For example, in the recessions of the 1950s, 1960s or 1970s, there were no systematic attempts to use counter-cyclical means to bridge the recession. Only for a short period of the economically most successful years in the 1980s, did Finnish economic policies develop in a Keynesian direction. However this advancement was halted by the recession of the 1990s.

The policies pursued by the right-wing government during the first half of the 1990s also followed the traditional Finnish economic policy model. Once again, unemployment was not considered the primary problem of the economy. Keynesian economic policies to increase the aggregate demand were widely considered impossible. On the contrary, the government even tried to control the growing foreign debt and budget deficit by suppressing domestic demand. The right-wing government put these aims explicitly higher in the agenda than lowering unemployment. Fiscal policies were restricted and cuts in social security were introduced. These measures led to further increases in unemployment.

On the ideological level, the right-wing government strongly criticised the welfare state. It argued that the main reasons for high unemployment were rigidities of the labour market, the possible work disincentives created by the welfare state, and the excessively high wages set in centralised negotiations. In the public debate there has been concern about the effects of allegedly over-generous social benefits, and the negative impact of high wages has been emphasised more than in the past. Unemployment has been seen more as a consequence of individual choices than as a result of structural societal phenomena even in the kind of economical situation that prevailed in Finland in the beginning of 1990s. Not surprisingly, the government started to introduce cutbacks in social security. Furthermore, it put special emphasis on encouraging people to become entrepreneurs. In the area of labour market policies, the government stressed activating measures.

The social democratic government that has been in power since 1995 has pursued similar economic policies as its predecessor although, at least in rhetoric, it has paid more attention to reducing unemployment. Although it was widely considered unrealistic, the explicit aim of the social democratic government was to halve the level of unemployment during its first term. This aim was never reached, and in practice, the policies of the social democratic government did not differ that much from its predecessor's policies.

The Finnish welfare state therefore underwent notable changes during the 1990s, although the basic structure of the social security system remained unchanged. The cuts in social security changed the structure of public expenditure notably. A good indicator of the significance of the cutbacks is the estimation that public social spending in 2000 was approximately 8.5% less than it would have been in the absence of these cuts. Most of the changes in the social protection system have been negative, meaning that eligibility criteria have been tightened, duration of the benefits has been shortened, and the benefit amounts have been decreased. Table 10.1 presents the most important changes made to the social protection between 1992 and 1998. All of these changes reflect the emphasis on reducing the work disincentive effects of the social protection system.

Unemployment and family benefits have undergone the most severe cuts in relative terms. Basically the Finnish unemployment benefit system is very much alike those in other Nordic countries. All residents are covered by basic flat-rate unemployment assistance and earnings-related benefits may be obtained

Table 10.1: Changes in social protection in Finland (1992-98)

Benefit	1992	1993	1994	1995	1996	1997	1990
Unemployment benefit							
Labour market support					■●	●◆	⊠
Basic unemployment benefit		■●	●		■	●◆	⊠
Earnings-related	■◆					■	
Family policy							
Parent allowance	■	■❖	■		■	■	
Child allowance				■			
Home-care allowance				■	■	■◆	
Income support			■◆		■◆	■	◆
Pensions							
National pension			●		●		
Employment pension			■		■		

■ Decrease in the amount of the benefit paid.
⊠ Increase in the amount of the benefit paid.
● Decrease in the number of the benefits paid.
❖ Limitation of the duration of the benefit.
◆ Changes in the structures (for example, more incentives to work).

Source: Kosunen (1997, p 62)

by voluntary membership in an unemployment benefit fund as in the other Nordic countries that are similarly following the principles of the Ghent model. In accordance with the other Nordic countries, only those who have been members of an unemployment benefit fund and paid the required fee to the fund can obtain the earnings-related benefit. The earnings-related unemployment benefit system is governed by unemployment funds connected to the trade unions and subsidised by the state[5]. However, certain differences can be found in the Finnish system and the systems in the other Nordic countries. Most importantly, the Finnish system is more related to earlier income than its Swedish and Danish counterparts. In principle, there is no upper limit for the Finnish earnings-related unemployment benefit level.

Another peculiarity of the Finnish system is that, unlike in Sweden and Denmark, the flat-rate unemployment assistance is means-tested for unemployed individuals without previous employment record. Since 1994, the Finnish unemployment benefit system has included two types of basic flat-rate unemployment assistance. The basic flat-rate unemployment assistance is paid without a means test to persons with an employment record, but lack membership of a voluntary unemployment insurance fund. More precisely, unemployment assistance is paid to unemployed persons aged 17-64 who have registered as unemployed job seekers for a full-time job, and are capable of and available for work. Moreover, in order to obtain unemployment assistance the unemployed must fulfil a so-called employment condition which means that they must have been working for at least 43 weeks in a full-time job during the last two years, and that no work or training has been provided for them by the employment office. Persons in receipt of other benefits, such as sickness, maternity or parental allowance, are not entitled to the unemployment assistance. The benefit is taxable income and the maximum payment period is 500 days during four consecutive calendar years. In 2002, the level of the assistance is €22.75 per day and it is paid for five days a week. The level of the assistance is comparatively low, but it can be supplemented with social assistance.

For people without an employment record – for instance, those who leave school and cannot find any suitable work – the benefits are means-tested. This part of the unemployment assistance is called 'labour market support'. Labour market support is also paid to unemployed persons who have received basic or earnings-related benefits for the maximum period and to unemployed persons who are not entitled to unemployment assistance by reason of not satisfying the employment condition. Unlike the basic allowance, the labour market support is means-tested. A demonstrated need of financial assistance is also required and, for example, the income of the spouse of the applicant may reduce the amount of the labour market support. The highest level of labour market support is €22.75 per day. As in the case of unemployment assistance, it is possible to supplement the labour market support with social assistance.

The central starting point for the reforms was to move the focus from paying passive income maintenance benefits to supporting job applicants' active efforts in seeking work and in developing their occupational skills. The aim was to make active job seeking, and accepting short-term jobs in particular, more profitable than staying unemployed. The main reforms were:

- The waiting period of unemployment benefits was extended from five to seven days.
- The employment condition was prolonged from 26 to 43 weeks during the last two years.
- The amount of the earnings-related allowance was decreased by a new calculation method. At the same price indexation was suspended until the year 2002.
- Means-testing criteria for labour market support and social assistance were tightened.
- Tighter activation responsibilities were applied to social assistance, too. Where beneficiaries refuse to participate in the activation initiatives, social workers have discretionary powers to reduce income support by 20%, and in the case of repeated refusals by 40%.
- Comparatively strong measures were taken to encourage young unemployed to enter education and training courses. This system of 'forced education' was tightened gradually during the 1990s. At first, there was only a six-week waiting period for 17- to 19-year-olds who did not accept a study place offered by the employment authorities. Since 1994, under 25-year-olds with

no occupational education have been obliged to take part in vocational training.

All in all, it is easy to conclude that the living conditions of the unemployed were weakened in Finland during the 1990s. However, at the system level, the changes were not very radical. The basic structure of the Finnish social security system was not changed. Clearly, most changes in the social security system were motivated by willingness to cut costs. In this sense, the changes might, in Pierson's (2001) terms, be called cost-containment and rationalisation.

Income distribution, poverty and citizenship

It is well known that unemployment is one of the most important background factors associated with poverty. Furthermore, as unemployment tends to concentrate in particular segments of the population, it would be natural to expect increasing economic inequality in a country with high levels of unemployment. The macroeconomic difficulties obviously caused problems at the micro level also. Bread queues, soup kitchens, increased receipt of social assistance, and personal bankruptcies were all seen as evidence of increased ill being.

Interestingly enough, the picture presented by statistics is not that gloomy. Despite the fact that unemployment skyrocketed during the recession years, the distribution of disposable equivalent income among Finns did not change to any notable extent during the recession. The recession did not leave any population groups untouched and the decline in the disposable equivalent income occurred roughly the same way at different income levels and among different population groups.

Despite the fact that the median income for the poor decreased during the deepest recession, the income level of the poor in 1995 was approximately the same as it had been ten years earlier (see Halleröd and Heikkilä, 1999). The poor managed to maintain their income level as well as the population on average, while the opposite is true for most other countries. The social security system is to thank for that: although inequality in the distribution of factor income transfers grew, the increasing redistributive effect of social income transfers was able to compensate for such changes. Social security proved capable of preventing an increase in poverty and growth in the differences in disposable equivalent incomes. Although the overall unemployment rate and the share of the long-term unemployed grew in Finland during the recession to be among the largest in EU, the relative poverty rate remained stable among the employed and as well among the unemployed (Haataja, 1999). However, on average, the rich weathered the recession better than other groups and their incomes in 1995 were clearly higher than they had been in 1987.

Nevertheless, there are indications that the rapid economic growth during the latter part of the 1990s has changed the picture. Now the tide has lifted the 'best boats', while the poor have been left behind. Consequently, income inequality has increased in Finland and is back at the level of 25 years ago. There are several reasons for this. First, since the early 1980s there has been a slight tendency towards growing factor income inequalities. The trend became more obvious between 1993 and 1996, after which the increase levelled off. However, because of the growing redistributive impact of transfers, the growth of factor income inequality was counteracted and differences in disposable incomes did not increase until 1994. Since then the redistributive effect of income transfers (caused by cuts in benefits and increasing long-term unemployment) and taxes (lower tax rates for high-income earners) has decreased. The combination of these various trends has increased Finnish income inequalities to the level they were in the early 1970s (Uusitalo, 2000).

Even though I am painting a very positive picture, it must be taken into account that cuts have been made to the social security system throughout the 1990s. For the time being, these cutbacks have not resulted in an increase in disposable equivalent income differences. However, the effects of austerity measures accumulate in such way that their full force is felt only few years later. It has been estimated that the cutbacks made in the mid-1990s will widen the gap between population groups dependent on social security and other groups (Uusitalo, 1997, p 116).

The fall of average income, resulting from unemployment and cutbacks in social security, increased the need for social assistance in the 1990s. Altogether 11.7% of the Finnish population received social assistance in 1996. Since then, the number of social assistance claimants has declined in each consecutive year.

Despite the increase in income differentials during the recent years, relative poverty did not increase substantially between 1995 and 2000 (Uusitalo, 2000, p 45). Other measures of poverty (such as involuntary lack of basic necessities, subjective experience of poverty, over-indebtedness and receipt of social assistance) also yielded significantly lower poverty rates in 2000 than in 1995 (Ritakallio, 2002).

However, there is evidence suggesting that a qualitative change has taken place in Finnish poverty. Prior to the recession, Finnish poverty used to be temporary in nature; during the recession, however, it gradually became a more persistent problem. Quantitatively speaking there is less poverty in Finland than there was in the peak of the recession, but qualitatively speaking the persistency makes the problem more severe than it used to be (Ritakallio, 2002). Cutbacks in unemployment benefits and social assistance have worsened the situation of the unemployed. Moreover, the proportion of the unemployed receiving only the flat-rate unemployment assistance has increased. All in all, despite the macro-level indicators, there are signs of small groups ending up in more serious difficulties than before. As the unemployment rate is still high, there is a risk of polarisation of the whole population.

Concluding remarks

The recent history of the Finnish labour markets is the story of an economy in shock. As a part of the most severe recession in Finland's peacetime history, unemployment increased to unforeseen levels. The policies that were chosen were typical of the country's economic policymaking tradition but were also influenced by new ideological elements that advocated greater market orientation and dismantling of the welfare state. The most important aim of the Finnish business-oriented corporatism was to guarantee the profitability of export industries. At the beginning of the recession the rising unemployment was not a surprise to policy makers, rather it was a deliberate choice, although in the end unemployment reached a higher level for a longer period than was expected.

Towards the end of the 1990s, however, Finland succeeded in recovering remarkably well from the economic crisis. Measured by national economic indicators, the recession ended and the economy started to grow again in 1994. Economic growth recovered, competitiveness of the export industries was restored, and the balance of payment became positive again, public debt started to decline and budgetary balance was achieved. Unemployment started to decline and employment was increasing, although not as fast as was expected.

The standard interpretation of the labour market suggests that once the economy is hit by shock – such as the recession in Finland – and the unemployment rate increases notably, the effects of the shock remain even after the economy makes an upward turn. Gradually, unemployment becomes structural in nature. In Finland, the level of unemployment has stayed above the OECD average.

Does the recent history of Finland support the hypothesis of structural unemployment and hysteresis? As Chapter One outlines, the main sources of structural unemployment are the discrepancy between productivity and high minimum wages, the high reservation wages, the loss of qualifications and the decline of work motivation associated with long-term unemployment.

Seen from the point of view of the unemployed, the argument of structural unemployment receives very little support. Empirical evidence does not support the view of over-inflated reservation wage in Finland. According to Punakallio (2001) the reservation wages among the majority of the Finnish unemployed are clearly low enough not to form obstacles for re-employment. Recent surveys on the Finnish unemployed (such as Kortteinen and Tuomikoski, 1998; Vähätalo, 1998; Ervasti, 2002) do not support the argument about low work motivation either. These surveys report consistently that work motivation even among the long-term unemployed has not decreased and that most unemployed in Finland suffer from both economic and psychological strain, and therefore have incentives to search for a job. All in all, the structural approach or the hysteresis argument can only account for a very small part of the problem.

Very few signs of structural unemployment can be found in Finland. The most important source of structural unemployment in Finland is the age structure. As we have seen, the youngest and oldest age groups in particular, and those with the lowest occupational status and/or educational level, have been the most likely segments of the population to suffer from unemployment. The oldest unemployed probably face the biggest problems. The older generations in the Finnish labour force are very badly educated. The level of educational attainment is one of the lowest in the EU, whereas the younger generations have the highest educational levels in the world. This generational gap in education makes it almost impossible to employ the older members of the Finnish labour force, and it appears that the only option is to let them take various early exit routes out of the labour market.

However, it is important to note that the problems of the Finnish case look quite different at the national level and in international comparisons. Although, at the national level, the main problem in the Finnish labour market is connected to the age structure of the labour force, in a comparative perspective this problem is not unexceptional. Chapter Two has already illustrated that Finland's distribution of unemployment by age does not differ from that of the other OECD countries.

In fact, comparative and national perspectives provide quite different views of the overall success of the Finnish economy. In a comparative sense, economic balance has been achieved and, at the macro level, the consequences of the economic shock appear surprisingly smooth. Seen from a comparative perspective, even the rise in unemployment in Finland during the early 1990s was not particularly bad. Compared to Sweden, for instance, the relative increase of unemployment was equal in these two countries (Kautto, 2001). Seen from the OECD level, the growth of employment has been above the OECD average since 1995 (see Kasvio, 2001).

Still, at the national level, Finland's recent history illustrates the risks associated with policies advocated by the OECD. The clearest implication is that the policies that were chosen did not reduce the level of unemployment. More generally, from the point of view of citizenship, the development has not been straightforward, either. In the aftermath of the recession, an obvious risk of polarisation of the population has emerged. Although economic inequality and poverty rates did not increase to notable extent during the recession, income differentials started to increase after the recession.

Comparisons with other countries and especially Sweden lead to the conclusion that, had it implemented different policies, Finland might have survived the economic crisis with less severe implications for its labour market. Sweden was hit by almost as hard an economic crisis as Finland. In Sweden, too, tighter budgetary policies and cutbacks were introduced, although somewhat later than in Finland. However, there were clear differences in the way in which adjustment was designed. In Finland the primary aim was to balance the budget and to achieve low inflation, even if this meant increasing unemployment. The Swedes on the other hand took a greater risk with the state budget in order not to increase unemployment. The cutbacks appeared more stringent in Finland and, together with rapid economic growth after the recession, were extensive enough to quickly reduce the GDP share of social protection expenditure close to the EU average (Kosonen, 1998, pp 341-52; Kautto, 2001, pp 62-3).

The current Finnish unemployment figures are still above the OECD average. However, most authors estimate that unemployment will decrease significantly in the near future. The main reason for expecting declining unemployment lies again in the country's age structure. From the year 2005 onwards the exit rate from the labour market will exceed the entrance rate of new age groups (Tiainen, 2001). This may even mean that, instead of an unemployment problem, there will be labour shortages in the near future.

Notes

[1] The standardised unemployment rate of the OECD gives even a more moderate picture of the situation. According to the Ministry of Labour, the monthly unemployment rate in January 1994 was over 20%.

[2] Milner (1994, p 177); Jäntti and Ritakallio (1999, p 67); see also Bordes et al (1993).

[3] Participation in education rose in the under-20 age group to around 70% in 1996 from around 60% in 1990 (Laaksonen, 2000, p 3).

[4] Indeed, according to Pekkarinen (1992, p 326) "unemployment was deliberately used as a means to provide workers with a lesson of the consequences of excessive wage claims and to give the economy room to expand".

[5] Each union has its own unemployment benefit fund. However, a wage earner may be a member of the unemployment benefit fund without being a member of the union. In practice, however, most wage earners belong to both the fund and the union. There are also a few unemployment benefit funds not connected to any trade union. The market share of these independent funds is, however, marginal.

ELEVEN

Slovenia's navigation through a turbulent transition

Miroljub Ignjatović, Anja Kopač, Ivan Svetlik and Martina Trbanc

Introduction

Slovenia is a small European country situated between Italy, Austria, Hungary and Croatia, with a population of two million people. It is also one of Europe's newest countries, and its geographical location and culture are more Central than Southern European. Slovenia only became independent in 1991. The decision to break from the former Yugoslavia involved making a radical break with the past in political and economic terms. In the politics sphere, the transition included:

- a shift from a one-party system to political democracy and a legal state;
- approaching international organisations as an independent state;
- applying for full membership of the EU.

In the economic area, in particular the transition included:

- a shift from a planned to a market economy;
- privatisation in terms of substituting well-defined private owners for the previous ownership of nobody and the state;
- a shift from predominantly internal to external markets.

Several changes started parallel to this and caused the biggest social turbulence in the postwar era. The most important issue was how to navigate the country through the treacherous waters of a crisis in order to open again the doors of prosperity that had been closing before transition started (see Svetlik, 1992; Fink-Hafner and Robins, 1997).

Ten years later, a success story (see also Svetlik, 1998) has unfolded that can be summarised thus:

- Slovenia has been recognised as an independent state and become a member of the most important international organisations, such as the UN and the

World Bank (WB). It leads a group of countries set to become new members of the EU.
- Several institutions have been created anew, restructured or abolished in order to put political democracy on firmer grounds. The fourth democratic elections in 2000 gave power to a centre-left coalition.
- Institutional backing of the market economy has been provided. Legal barriers to free entrepreneurship have been removed, and the number of new enterprises has more than tripled. Most prices have been liberalised. The Slovenian currency (tolar) has been made convertible. The deep economic crisis was over in 1993. Gross domestic product (GDP) per capita exceeds $10,000 ($15,000 in purchasing power parity). Investments, productivity and real wages are increasing. However, hard currency reserves that exceeded the debts and the budget deficit that was below 2% in the 1990s have again become problematic. Inflation remains at about 8%.
- The economy has been mainly privatised, with the banking, insurance and public utilities sectors lagging behind. A special feature of Slovenia is that workers and managers have majority shares in over half of all enterprises.
- Industry has been restructured. This involves downsizing, contracting-out, closing down, technological changes, shifts to more demanding markets, the fragmenting of industrial structure in terms of a falling number of big enterprises and an increasing number of small ones, a shift towards services and so on. Slovenia exports over one third of its GDP, and of this nearly two-thirds goes to the EU. Foreign exchange is well balanced.

The turbulence caused by transition has also affected the labour market. The number of jobs was reduced due to the loss of most Yugoslav markets and many markets in Eastern Europe. The transition from a planned to a market economy revealed many unviable production facilities that had to be closed down, and many employees with no real jobs became redundant. In 1989, hidden unemployment was estimated to cover 46,000 employees (Mencinger, 1989), representing some 5% of the workforce. Liberalisation of employment relations is shifting away from the job security guaranteed by law and the full employment that prevailed until the late 1980s.

However, in spite of Slovenia's turbulent unemployment, it has not reached the high figures witnessed in most other transition countries. It is even lower than in some EU member states. This chapter explains the extent to which Slovenia's relatively favourable development can be ascribed to the specifics of transition or the specifics of employment policies.

A changing labour market

At the EU15 average, with older workers moving out of the labour market

Slovenia's labour market very much resembles the EU15 average[1]. As the tables in Chapter Two illustrate, the labour force participation rate (68.4%) remains constant over time and is close to the EU15 average. Slovenia's rate resembles most the rates of Portugal, France and Germany. While the female labour force participation rate (63.8%) exceeds the EU15 average, and is comparable to that seen in the Netherlands, Germany and Austria, the male labour force participation rate (72.9%) is below the average, as it is in Italy, France, and Belgium also.

Both the labour force participation rate and employment rate among the younger generation (63.5% of 20- to 24-year-olds) and the older generation (47.3% of 55- to 59-year-olds) are significantly lower than the average for the EU15. The younger generations are increasing their full-time participation in initial education and training. This is understandable in light of the worsening employment opportunities given that better educated workers find work more easily. Young people see their futures in investment in human resources.

The older generation was pushed out of the labour market via the relatively generous early retirement scheme applied in the first half of the 1990s, when unemployment occurred in significant numbers for the first time after the Second World War. In addition, it left the labour market with the help of generous disablement pension practices and the pension system, which allowed men to get a full pension at the age of 57 and women at the age of 52 (if they had 40 and 35 years of service, respectively). The effect of these buffer measures on labour activity is presented in Figure 11.1. They prevented any dramatic raise of open unemployment, but also maintenance of the labour force

Figure 11.1: Four main reasons for terminating labour market activity (number of people)

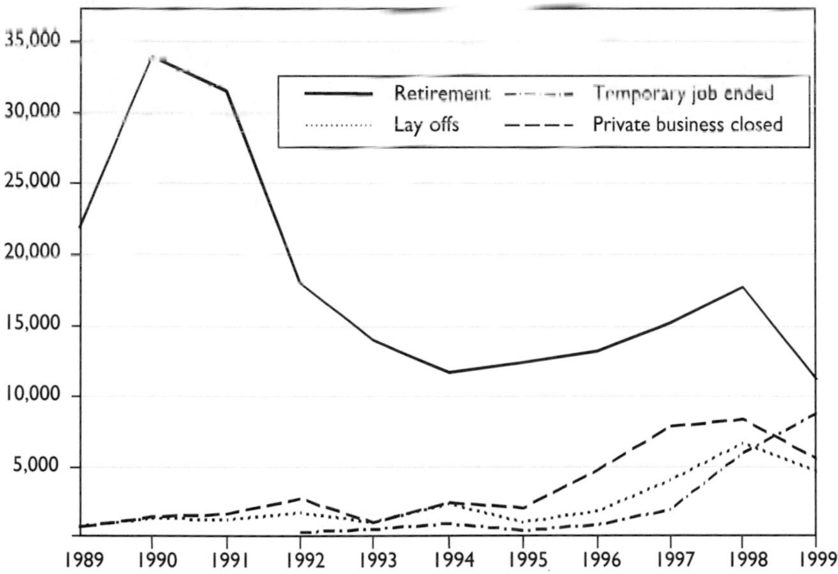

[a] Expected number for whole year, based on the first five months.
Source: SORS (1999)

participation rate. This policy changed in the second half of the 1990s when the pension fund underwent crisis. However, the effects on the labour force participation rate are still visible.

The unemployment rate in Slovenia culminated in the mid-1990s and stabilised afterwards. Measured by the labour force survey according to the ILO's standards (5.9%; SORS, 2001c), it remains below the EU15 average level. The comparison is especially in favour of Slovenian women, whose unemployment rate only slightly exceeds that of men. This relatively positive situation can be explained by the gradual transition to a market economy, by the measures applied in the pension and education systems, and by the active employment policy measures. However, employment policy measures have been relatively ineffective in the case of long-term unemployment, which is very high compared to the EU15. Around 56% of all unemployed have been unemployed for more then 12 months. A similar evaluation may be given in the case of policies against youth unemployment. This characteristic can be partially explained by labour market rigidity, which even before the transition protected the employed population at the expense of the unemployed and new entrants. In this respect, Slovenia is a typical representative of the continental welfare state, where inflexible labour market causes insider/outsider divisions.

Although Slovenia's labour market fits relatively well into the EU15 average, we would like to point out two idiosyncrasies that contribute some features to European employment.

The puzzle of the unemployment rate

A striking feature of Slovenian unemployment is the difference between the two unemployment rate figures (see Table 11.1). One, counting the number of unemployed registered with the Employment Service of Slovenia (ESS), has come to reveal almost twice the level than the measure derived from the Labour Force Survey (LFS). The discrepancy can be explained in different ways[2].

- The labour market situation is worsening for individuals. Registration with the ESS provides not only some kind of shelter and cash benefits for some of those registered, but also access to a number of employment programmes, health and old age insurance payments, and assistance in preparing job applications. Therefore, many people register even though they may not be job seekers, or are already employed in the informal economy.
- Monitoring the behaviour of the registered unemployed did not exist until the late 1990s. Therefore, some people benefited from legislation that allowed them to register with the ESS without actively seeking jobs. This was also made possible because, rather than strictly apply the rules, ESS officials prefer to express sympathy with the unemployed.
- Along with increasing unemployment, the ESS has rushed through the introduction of various employment programmes which are not always prepared and administered in the best possible way. For instance, employers

receive subsidies if they hire registered unemployed persons (tax deductions, subsidised work places and training). It was reported informally that some employers made employees redundant in order to hire them afterwards and collect these subsidies.

Unemployment benefit recipients are allowed to earn money while receiving benefits if their income is below the benefit level. The aim is to reduce the unemployment benefit by the sum earned. However, this cannot be controlled effectively. Asked if they had worked for pay/profit for at least one hour last week, and the unemployed answer 'yes', they are counted as actively working.

Many workers registered with the ESS continue to work informally and have two sources of income. This reveals a specific feature of transition countries, which widely tolerated the informal economy in socialist times and can only gradually break with this practice. In 1993 the informal economy in Slovenia was estimated to be between 16.8% and 21.3% of GDP (Kukar, 1993).

In Figure 11.2, the comparison between the two categories is shown for 2000. One could speculate that the difference between the LFS and the registered unemployment reveals the discrepancy between real job seekers and those registered with the ESS just to attain the status of the unemployed and to be eligible for cash and other benefits. There is also a significant number – 12,000 (17.4%) – of ILO-defined unemployed, who are not registered and who may be in a relatively difficult social situation. One may nevertheless conclude that most individuals and employers have adjusted much faster to the new situation than has the state's employment administration.

Temporary employment 'yes', part-time employment 'no'

For many years lifelong full-time employment was the only existing form of employment. The expectations of workers and employers, as well as the

Figure 11.2: Comparison between the registered and LFS-defined unemployed 2000 (ESS, 2001)

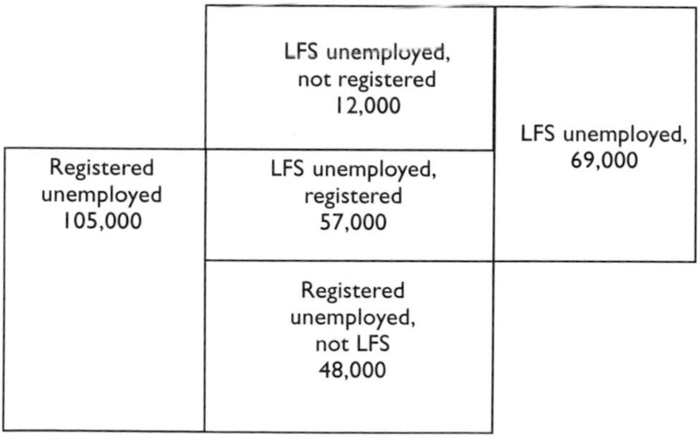

LFS unemployed, not registered 12,000

LFS unemployed, 69,000

Registered unemployed 105,000

LFS unemployed, registered 57,000

Registered unemployed, not LFS 48,000

Table 11.1: Unemployment (aggregate figures) and unemployment rates in Slovenia (1975-2001)

	1975	1980	1988	1990	1991	1993	1995	1997	1999	2001
Annual numbers of registered unemployed[a]	11,663	12,227	21,342	44,623	75,079	129,087	121,483	125,189	118,951	104,316
Unemployment rate (registered unemployed)	1.6	1.5	2.2	4.7	8.2	14.4	13.9	14.4	13.6	11.8
Unemployment rate (LFS criteria)	–	2.2[1]	2.6[2]	4.9	7.3	9.1	7.4	7.1	7.4	5.9

[a] The numbers displayed are annual numbers of unemployed people according to the national definition of unemployed persons (that is, the registered unemployed).

Sources: Svetlik and Trbanc (1991); Ignjatović et al (1992); SORS (2000); ESS (1999, 2000, 2001)

assumptions underlying most policies and benefits related to employment, were set in line with this form of work. For immediate social cost and social peace reasons, several policies remain in place today, focussing on job preservation. However, recent changes to the legal framework and active employment policy prepared by the government are directed towards increasing the flexibility of the labour market.

Self-employment is the most common form of flexible employment. It has stabilised close to the EU15 average, that is, at about 12% of all employment. The share of temporary employment has been constantly increasing in the last ten years and has exceeded 10% of total employment. In 2001, 72.4% of new employment was temporary. Employers use this form on a large scale to protect themselves against potential redundancies, which are time-consuming and costly due to the legislative protection of employment. Temporary employment is used especially for first job seekers as a kind of probation before a permanent job is offered. Although some young people prefer temporary arrangements, the number of those who have become second-class citizens on this basis has increased. For instance, they have difficulties obtaining bank loans when resolving their housing problems.

Part-time employment in Slovenia is at a much lower scale than in more developed EU countries. In 2001, part-time employment accounted for just 6.6% of all employment. The demand for part-time jobs is very low: only 2.5% of unemployed people were seeking or had already got part-time jobs and slightly more than 10% of those who were seeking full-time employment were ready to accept part-time job should a full-time job not become available. The supply of part-time jobs is also very low. There is no tradition of part-time work in the country, either among employees or employers. This also includes social security arrangements which do not favour it, meaning that all social rights are proportional to the length of working time. Part-time employment is used primarily to ease the transition to retirement for older workers and to keep workers with disabilities employed.

The number of women working part-time in Slovenia only slightly exceeds that of men (7.8% and 5.6%, respectively). This is the heritage of socialist regimes that followed the policy of equal opportunities for men and women, particularly in the field of employment. Full-time and part-time employment was not considered to be equal. In addition, equal opportunities of women were provided by the development of subsidised public childcare services, generous maternity leave, paid sick leave for caring for ill children and similar. This has led to a high labour force participation rate among women which, in terms of working hours, exceeds that of Scandinavian countries. However, the high share of women full-timers also has its dark side. Taking into account employment and household chores, some analyses show that they are overburdened with work (Černigoj-Sadar, 2000).

In the circumstances described, it is difficult to expect women in Slovenia to shift from full-time to part-time employment. This would be perceived as discrimination: affecting income, quality of jobs, work-based rights and benefits and social security arrangements for women. Rather than part-time work for women, shortening general work time and a more equal division of household tasks between partners have been proposed.

Social protection during unemployment: greater control and fewer rights

The social insurance system for the unemployed in Slovenia has been regulated similarly to the German legislation pattern since 1974. The rights given to unemployed persons, especially income-related rights, were generous for the whole period, ensuring a high social security level. The right to an unemployment benefit was mainly used by those who were hard to place in employment or incapable of work, and therefore supervision was not demanding. To maintain social harmony, the 1991 legislation again ensured a high level of social security for the unemployed. A lack of control over actual fulfilment of the obligations related to active job seeking by unemployment benefit recipients has become a key problem under the conditions of mass unemployment.

Due to rising unemployment rates it became financially impossible to maintain such a high social security level. The arguments that the privileges and long-term eligibility to unemployment benefit kept the unemployed from re-entering the employment were gaining weight (Vodopivec, 1996).

In light of these arguments, the definition of an unemployed person has changed throughout. The objective and subjective availability to work is emphasised much more while the sanctions have become much tougher. Apart from that, the duration of unemployment benefits has been shortened for most unemployed from a maximum of two years to a maximum of one year. The responsibility of the ESS has been tightened through the obligation to prepare individual employment plans in cooperation with each unemployed person. The employment plans have been deliberately shaped according to the British model. They define precisely the measures that must be taken by the ESS and the activities of an unemployed person to re-enter the labour market.

Social security schemes: Central European

The unemployment insurance scheme is codified in the Employment and Unemployment Insurance Act (EUIA), which has been revised and amended[3] several times. The last changes came into force in 1998[4]. Unemployment benefit and unemployment assistance are determined by the EUIA. Apart from this, unemployed persons are entitled to a mobility allowance and have:

- the right to participate in programmes preparing the unemployed for employment;
- the right to health, pension and disability insurance.

The unemployment insurance scheme covers all employees who have signed an employment contract for a fixed or unlimited period and are working full-time or part-time, but at least half of full-time (that is, 20 hours). All these employees are compulsorily insured. Self-employed people can be insured against unemployment on a voluntary basis.

The basis for calculating a person's benefit is the average monthly gross wage in the twelve-month period prior to unemployment. The benefit is 70% of this amount in the first three months and 60% thereafter. However, the amount may not drop below the guaranteed minimum income, and cannot be higher than three times the lowest possible benefit.

The duration of an unemployment benefit depends on the working/insurance record and the age of the claimant. It is paid between three months and two years (see Table 11.2).

The unemployment assistance is a benefit which the unemployed, who were insured against the risk of unemployment and are in need, may receive after termination of their unemployment benefit. Unemployment assistance is defined within the unemployment insurance scheme, but it has the nature of a right to social protection.

Unemployment assistance is a flat-rate benefit amounting to 80% of the guaranteed minimum income and can be paid for a maximum of 15 months. The possibility of prolongation is offered to an unemployed person who lacks a maximum of three years to reach retirement age. Such an unemployed person may receive unemployment assistance until retirement.

The figures displayed in Table 11.3 show the numbers of unemployment benefit and unemployment assistance recipients. At the beginning of the 1990s, the share of recipients of both benefits among all the registered unemployed was above 40%, before dropping below 30%. This happened because unemployment is becoming long-term and the duration of unemployment benefit has shortened. Stricter conditions for the acquisition and keeping of benefits that were recently introduced already influence a further reduction of the eligible unemployed.

Table 11.2: Maximum duration of unemployment benefit relative to the working/insurance record and age (EUIA, 1998)

Working/insurance record and age duration of the unemployment benefit	Maximum
One to five years of work/insurance record	Three months
Five to 15 years of work/insurance record	Six months
15 to 25 years of work/insurance record	Nine months
Over 25 years of work/insurance record	12 months
Over 25 years of work/insurance record and over the age of 50	18 months
Over 25 years of work/insurance record and over the age of 55	24 months

Table 11.3: Recipients of unemployment benefits (UB) and unemployment assistance (UA), Slovenia (1991-2001)

Year	Recipients of UB (December each year)	Recipients of UA (December each year)	Total number of recipients and UA of UB (December each year)	Recipients of UB and UA as a % of average monthly registered unemployment
1991	31,818	14,110	45,928	40.0
1993	42,582	20,052	62,634	43.1
1995	28,305	5,936	34,241	30.3
1997	37,152	3,734	40,886	32.6
1999	31,227	3,283	34,510	31.0
2000[a]	23,585	3,818	27,403	29.4
2001[a]	20,305	4,416	24,721	24.0

[a]The figures for 2000 and 2001 are for November.

Sources: ESS (1999, p 82, 2000, 2001, 2002)

Besides the unemployment benefit and assistance, the unemployed may also receive non-contributory (cash) social assistance, which is defined in the Social Protection Act[5]. The general social assistance scheme provides a benefit for persons in need. It aims at alleviating the situation of those individuals who do not have the essential means of living. It is means-tested and applies to families.

The duration of (cash) social assistance is limited (that is, to three, six months or one year), but in certain cases the duration can be also unlimited (for example, in the event of a permanent inability to work). The number of beneficiaries is rising quickly from year to year. In 1995, 24,908 people received a cash allowance, in 1998 the number was 33,017[6] and in 2001 it was 37,129. The amount of money spent on cash allowances is also growing. In 1993, it amounted to 12.4% of all the money spent on social security benefits, while in 1998 it rose to 29.8%. The weaker the unemployment insurance scheme the more social assistance must step in.

The unemployment benefit and unemployment assistance are financed partially from the compulsory contributions paid by the employees (insured persons) and their employers. Employees pay 0.06% of the gross wage and employers pay 0.14% of the same base. The total amount of money collected through these contributions does not cover expenditures. In 2001, the funds gathered by compulsory contributions amounted to as little as 13.6% of all the finances necessary for cash benefits. The deficit is covered by the state from the national budget (ESS, 2002, p 15).

The benefit offered by the general social assistance scheme is totally financed out of the national budget and administered by the community centres for social work.

The unemployment insurance and social security schemes in Slovenia are administered similar to other developed countries. In conditions of a relative budget deficit and high unemployment, the entitlement to unemployment benefit and unemployment assistance has become more limited. Several changes may be observed:

- the number of entitlement criteria to be met by individuals to qualify for unemployment status has increased;
- the entitlement criteria are described in much more detail;
- the application of criteria by employment officers has become stricter;
- the meeting of entitlement criteria during an unemployment period has been monitored more often and in new ways;
- in cases where the unemployed fail to meet the criteria the immediate loss of benefits and/or deleting off the register occurs;
- financial sanctions for misbehaviour of the unemployed have been introduced;
- higher flexibility and activity of the unemployed have been demanded;
- the unemployed in further education and public works programmes have been given the status of students and temporary employees, respectively.

There are rules for dealing with the unemployed that are applied by employment officers. The unemployed are expected to commute longer distances to and from work and to accept lower paid, part-time and temporary jobs. They are also expected to participate in the employment policy programmes offered and to act according to personal employment plans. Employment officers also have wider competence in relation to sanctioning unemployed persons' behaviour. However, this stricter sanction and supervision regime is not always implemented for different reasons (that is, organisational culture, objective circumstances in which the front-line officers work, individual values and attitudes, legally determined discretion, and so on). The lack of experience in terms of sanctioning clients' behaviour is the most important element contributing to the gaps seen in the implementation process[7].

Apart from the possibility of a total loss of the right to cash benefits, an unemployed person who does not accept suitable employment or temporary work in the case of natural disasters can lose 50% of cash benefits for a period of two months. He/she also has to accept suitable temporary or periodic work of a humanitarian nature or public work if he/she does not want their cash benefits to be reduced by 30% for two months.

In short, the social security policy is shifting from the insurance to the activation principle. So-called passive employment policy is increasingly in line with the principles of active employment policy.

EU-oriented active employment policy measures

The first active employment policy measures in Slovenia were introduced in the late 1980s when the unemployment rate started to rise. As experience from other countries has been gained, the number of programmes has grown and they have become more focused and refined. The existing programmes can be broken up into four groups:

- education and training programmes;
- support for self-employment of unemployed people;
- public works;
- other programmes, such as subsidies and the payment of contributions for new jobs, programmes focused on the disabled workers, for example training and sheltered workshops, labour funds and so on.

Education and training programmes: tackling structural inconsistencies

Education and training programmes are considered to be vital in the conditions of increasing structural inconsistencies. A variety of these programmes focusing on the unemployed and permanently redundant workers are in place: programmes assisting professional career planning and job seeking, programmes of psycho-social rehabilitation and personal development, short vocational training and retraining programmes, especially for the unskilled, on-the-job training and so on.

The majority of training programmes is of a shorter duration. However, there has recently been an attempt to bring people without vocational training, especially young drop outs and others who did not finish formal education, back to school. The so-called 'Programme 5000' enabled 5,288 individuals to be enrolled in basic vocational training and other education programmes in 2000/01. Unemployed participants of the programme acquire the status of pupils or students.

As regards participation in education and training programmes, priority is given to the long-term unemployed, young people under the age of 26 and unskilled persons. The practical rule is to involve the unemployed in the training and education programmes according to their employment plans. The numbers of unemployed persons participating in education and training programmes in the last seven years are shown in Table 11.4.

In 2002, the ESS carried out an evaluation of all education and training programmes for 2001. Table 11.5 shows how effective different education and training programmes were with regard to finding a job after completing the programme[8].

The evaluation showed that those participants who found jobs after training most often succeeded in the first three to six months after the end of the training programme. Later, the share of those finding jobs falls relative with time.

The relatively high shares finding regular jobs should be taken with some reservation. In the evaluation analysis, windmill[9], creaming[10], substitution[11] and other possible and undesirable side-effects were not controlled for (Schmid, 1996).

Table 11.4: Participants in education and training programmes by type of programme[a], for 1994-2001, in absolute numbers

	1994	1995	1996	1997	1998	1999	2000[b]	2001[b]
Functional training[c]	5,550	10,290	11,559	8,442	14,433	11,113	10,754	10,324
Occupational education/ training	1,312	2,224	2,235	1,955	7,736	6,359	4,854	5,711
On-the-job training	2,555	2,753	3,491	4,057	6,350	5,040	7,557	7,715
Training without a job	315	283	92	119	350	291	251	272
Training for lower vocational qualification	1,036	906	790	444	358	215	–	–
Total	10,768	16,456	18,167	15,017	29,227	23,018	23,416	24,022

[a] Since most training programmes are of a shorter duration, an unemployed person can participate in more than one programme in a year.

[b] The classification and structure of education and training programmes available for the unemployed changed (termination of the programme of training for lower vocational qualification; the main stress is on Programme 5000 and various possibilities of on-the-job-training programmes; new programmes were introduced – called work trials).

[c] Includes all programmes of shorter training in job-seeking methods, planning a professional career, motivation programmes, programmes of psycho-social rehabilitation and personal development, and so on.

Sources: ESS (2000, p 62; 2001, pp 53-9; 2002, pp 60-8)

Support for self-employment and entrepreneurship

This is an important measure for stimulating employment and promoting creativity and active problem-solving among the unemployed. The most common programmes are:

- informative seminars;
- introductory seminars;
- in-depth training and workshops;
- training for small businesses;
- introduction of the Co-operatives Programme and the Self-Employment in the Countryside Project (ESS, 1999, p 47; 2002, p 72).

These programmes focus on unemployed persons who want to develop their business ideas and meet the conditions and possibilities for their realisation. In the middle of the 1990s, over 3,000 unemployed people per year became self-employed with the help of these programmes. Later on, the number levelled off to about 1,700 per year (ESS, 2002).

Table 11.5: The effectiveness of different types of education and training programmes in 2001

Name of programme	Number of participants	Job placement rate for participants (%)
Additional training and educational programmes	4,214	39.2
Work trials	1,497	73.9
On-the-job training (without employment)	272	29.4
Job clubs[a]	2,043	58.0

[a] The figures refer to 2000.

Source: ESS (2002)

A survey of the survival of the self-employed after the first two years of operation was carried out and the results show that most previously unemployed people, who started their own businesses with the help of the programmes, remain in business. Self-employed people usually work individually, but family companies are slowly emerging as well. Important information for assessing the positive effects of the self-employment support measure is that, on average, self-employed people employ 1.5 people in addition to themselves. Many of the surveyed self-employed would choose to start their own business again, even though the original reason for becoming self-employed was mostly that there was no regular job available for them and they had to make ends meet. The survey also revealed that most persons who became self-employed with the support of this employment measure were contemplating self-employment long before they became unemployed. This confirms that the long-term unemployed people are rarely potential business people (ESS, 1999, p 48; 2002, p 73).

Public works: against long-term unemployment

Public works were introduced in 1991 in Slovenia. Over the last few years, public work programmes have become an important instrument. Their most important aim is to engage the long-term unemployed and those unemployed people who are difficult to employ in work activities; that is, to provide them with work experience (thereby making them more attractive to potential employers) and to integrate them socially. Public works have both an employment and social function.

In 2001, 2,247 public work programmes were run in nearly all Slovenian municipalities. They involved 9,374 unemployed people (9.0% of all unemployed people in Slovenia). According to the EUIA, which pinpoints public works as an increasingly important measure of employment policy, participation in public works may not exceed one year, but may be extended if the unemployed person cannot be provided with a suitable job. The status of public works participants has also been converted from the unemployed to the temporarily employed. This means they are deleted from the unemployment register and enjoy all the rights of temporary employees according to labour legislation including a regular initial salary.

Public work programmes are carried out in the areas of public administration, culture, education and tourism, social and health care, public utilities infrastructure and environmental work, agriculture and forestry.

In 2001, 1,260 unemployed people (13.4% of all participants) found regular jobs through public work programmes. The numbers of participants in public works that find jobs are growing from year to year, which shows such programmes do have an employment function. In fact, many public work programmes have, in terms of content and organisation, grown from being simply an employment policy measure into a regular activity. For instance, some homecare services started in the form of public works. After some years, by which time the programme had ceased, they have continued to exist as a partially community subsidised and partially commercial service. This is one of the approaches to the creation of new services and new jobs in the social economy.

Relationship between 'active' and 'passive' employment policy measures

Figure 11.3 shows the proportion of the annual budget of the ESS transferred to the 'passive' and the 'active' employment policy measures in the last four years. It shows a trend visible in most European countries: expenditures for passive measures are falling. This is caused by several factors:

- the prolonged duration of unemployment pushes many individuals out of unemployment benefit entitlements;
- there are stricter conditions of entitlement to unemployment benefit and unemployment assistance and more effective control over fulfilment of obligations of the unemployed;
- the required previous working record has been prolonged, and the maximum duration of an unemployment benefit shortened, from 24 to 12 months for non-elderly unemployed persons.

Giving advantage to 'active' employment policy measures over the passive ones in recent years has changed the structure of spending on each programme. However, despite the changes in favour of active employment policy measures approximately 50% of the annual budget went to unemployment benefits and unemployment assistance in 1998, and only 16% went on active employment policy measures. In 2000, for the first time, more than 20% of the ESS annual budget was spent on active employment policy measures, and less then 50% for unemployment benefits and unemployment assistance. This trend was obvious also in 2001, when the amount of money spent on active employment policy measures was even higher (25% of the annual budget). A large proportion of

Figure 11.3: Breakdown of the ESS annual budget by purpose in the period (1998-2001)

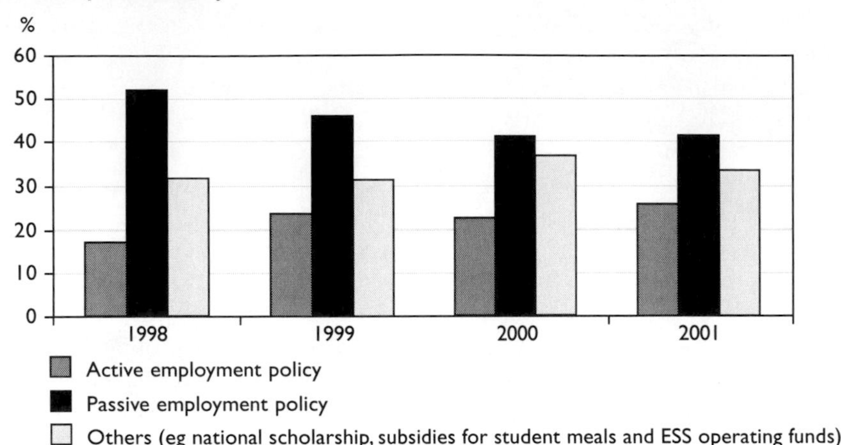

Sources: ESS (1999, 2000, 2001, 2002)

the ESS annual budget is also allocated for the purpose of financing national scholarships, and student meals, which in Slovenia is situated within the ESS structure.

Increasing European and decreasing social citizenship?

Up until its transition, Slovenia pursued a policy of full employment. It was successful from an employment perspective in guaranteeing parallel lifelong employment and reasonable social security and welfare to workers and their families. Employment offices were not abolished in the socialist period. They were established in their current form in the mid-1960s. They dealt with people that were 'hard to place' in employment, especially people with additional needs, and developed extensive programmes of occupational guidance for youth. Unemployment insurance has been offered since that period on as well. This was made possible by the quite favourable position of the Slovenian economy within the protected markets of former Yugoslavia. However, a relatively high price was paid for this high security in the long run. The labour market was increasingly rigid and the economy inefficient. It lagged behind developed countries in terms of technological development, productivity and the quality of products. A self-management system, based on workers' participation and nobody's ownership, was more redistribution- and consumption-oriented, rather than productivity and economic efficiency oriented. It was unlikely that workers would sack themselves in the event of redundancies. At the end, it was no longer possible to maintain the then existing welfare system and social security. The system's legitimacy was shaken.

Independence and transition put Slovenia into a much different context.

The economic prosperity of a small country can only be assured by its openness to the world market, integration with the EU and high flexibility. This also holds to the labour market. By the end of 1980s, unemployment was knocking on the door; in response, the first active employment policy measures were created, while unemployment insurance started to be used more extensively. The ensuing developments can be summarised as follows:

- The unemployment insurance system has become less insurance-based and more social assistance based, as well as less contribution-financed and increasingly tax-financed. The duration of benefits has shortened and the maximum payment decreased. The insurance scheme is becoming more redistributive, aiming at the provision of basic security rather than the maintenance of living conditions of those losing jobs at the level that they had as employees. Priority has been given to people in a more difficult position, such as older workers.
- The subsidiary nature of cash benefits is strongly emphasised. The aim to provide social security via employment has come to the fore. However, employability is replacing the concept of full employment. The ranking of priorities is as follows: (1) employability; (2) work; (3) basic (redistributive) social security; (4) (full) insurance. Employment policy is becoming less ambitious and perhaps more realistic.
- The rights of workers have become more closely related to their responsibilities. The payment of insurance contributions is by no means a sufficient condition for one to receive benefits. Compliance with a number of other rules set by the state is necessary. The right of an unemployed person to free choice of employment is no longer guaranteed.
- An increasing stress is on the active and activating, rather than passive, measures, which have also been increasingly applied in an active way. A much higher level of individual's activity is required.
- In the initial phase, employment programmes were more demand-oriented; that is, focused on employers. Gradually they have been shifting to the supply side, that is, to individuals. Training as a means of adjusting to labour demand is at the fore.
- Employment policy programmes have become more refined, more selective and more precisely focused on target groups. They have become more concerned with costs and effectiveness. Increasing attention is paid to their side effects, monitoring and evaluation.
- Employment policy is becoming increasingly individualised; that is, adjusted to the needs and special position of every individual. So-called tailor-made employment plans prepared for individuals are put into practice. Employment offices are expected to prepare employment plans in cooperation with the unemployed within three months of one being registered. Unemployed people should participate in the preparation of a plan and sign it to confirm their responsibility to act accordingly. Certain job-searching activities and/or enrolment in employment programmes are previewed and reporting on

those determined. Services provided by the employment offices – and their adjustment to the individual's needs – are expected to be levelled off by their activity and contractual responsibility.

- Creation of employment programmes from below and their adjustment to the needs of regions have become accentuated.
- National employment policy is increasingly influenced by the EU directives and guidelines. It is becoming supra-national. Slovenia has prepared its National Action Plan and Mid-Term Employment Strategy (MLFSA, 1999) structured around the four pillars of the EU's employment policy.
- In spite of the complex employment and social policy, not all paid work provides eligibility to participate in its programmes. Certain forms of part-time and contractual work are excluded and do not guarantee any social security.

One may conclude that several factors have contributed to the relatively favourable development of employment seen in Slovenia. The economy was quite developed at the start of transition and quickly adjusted to the demanding global markets. Well-organised trade unions contributed to the gradual liberalisation of the economy and the rejection of any shock therapy. This also stands for the employment policy, which shifted in the direction of active measures at the beginning of transition.

The development of employment policy, however, also has its darker sides. Tightening of employment measures in the late 1990s pushed a reasonable number of the unemployed off the register. Decreasing unemployment, which is becoming structural and long-term, remains unevenly distributed in spite of the variety of programmes. There are big regional differences in unemployment. In 2000, the unemployment rate according to the register in the best-off municipality was 2.6% and in the worst-off one 19.8% (ESS, 2002). Some social groups have very limited chances of getting jobs, especially the more stable ones. Those groups are the unskilled and semi-skilled, school drop outs in primary and secondary education, older workers and people with disabilities. A lack of at least basic vocational skills, physical disabilities and age seem to be the main reasons why people are, or are considered by employers to be, less productive and less flexible.

The long-term unemployed people can, after the expiry of their rights to unemployment benefit and unemployment assistance, receive (cash) social assistance. However, the real value of the (cash) social assistance is low and in most cases hardly covers the costs of basic survival. Unless the long-term unemployed can count on the help and solidarity of family and other networks of civil society, they are in a very difficult situation. As the analysis of household expenditure data for the period 1997-99 shows (SORS, 2001b), the most vulnerable and at a high risk of poverty in Slovenia are:

- single households, especially elderly persons and elderly couples, but also families with three or more children below the age of 16, and single-parent families;
- households without work-active persons;
- households whose reference person (or head of the household) is poorly educated;
- households whose main sources of income are pensions and other social transfers;
- households living in non-profit and social housing units.

Practically the same categories of households were at a high risk of poverty in 1993 (MLFSA, 1999). Obviously, labour market inactivity of a longer duration is one of the main predictors of financial and consumption deprivation, especially when combined with other factors often causing deprivation such as low education and old age.

Marginalisation in the labour market is very often connected not only to lack of financial resources and low consumption levels, but also to deprivation in other spheres of life, for example in housing, access to important social and public services, health services, and so on. This is especially true because, in the areas of housing, public, social and health services, the role of the state has changed in the last decade and a substantial part of the resources has been left to the market regulation. Of course, the state still guarantees the coverage of basic needs in all mentioned areas (that is non-profit and social housing units, basic health services and so on), but for higher quality or higher level services individual financial contributions are demanded.

This overlapping of deprivation, marginalisation and obstacles in access to resources in different areas of life is especially problematic since it can lead (especially if combined with the low support of social networks) to social exclusion. Slovenian Quality of Life Survey data for 1994[12] indicated that as many as 13.7% of respondents suffered severe disadvantages – namely, disadvantages in four or more out of six observed areas of life[13] (Trbanc, 1996, p 108). The unemployed were over-represented among respondents with multiple disadvantages (24.6% of unemployed respondents versus an average of 13.7% among all respondents).

The formula used in socialism – every citizen must work, and every worker and his/her family member is socially insured – is being dismantled. However, is the complex of employment policy measures, focused directly on the individuals, developing in a similar direction? New measures are not necessarily less coercive than those under socialism when directing people to active economic life. The role of work is increasingly emphasised. The labour market and paid employment are seen as the principle means for conferring citizenship and the best way to tackle poverty and social exclusion (Clasen, 2001). The so-called activation trend can be recognised and the concept of *de-commodification* introduced by Esping-Andersen (1990) is gradually being replaced by *re-commodification* (Lødemel and Trickey, 2001). It seems that full employment has been preserved as a hidden scenario. In addition, the management of the complex set of employment programmes may become quite expensive.

Slovenian independence is a recent phenomenon, and so, therefore, is Slovenian citizenship. However, social citizenship rights are gradually fading away in comparison to the socialist period and social responsibilities are increasingly being put on the shoulders of individuals and their families. It seems that integration with the EU – that will make political and social citizenship, including employment policies, increasingly supranational – may amplify these trends. Member states will have to follow the agreed directives, guidelines and other policy provisions. However, there could be less room for nationally specific programmes that may go beyond the agreed minimum because of tight economic policies, such as those set within the monetary union.

In the long run, the accent on employability, training and new forms of working time arrangements will contribute to the redefinition and redistribution of work. In the first case, education and training as well as jobs in the social sector are coming into the paid-work horizon. As some programmes indicate, workers sent on longer training enjoy the rights of employees including the right to return to their employers if unemployed persons are meanwhile placed in their jobs. Social rights could therefore be based not only on work but also on training.

In the second case, a variety of new working time arrangements have been proposed and used. For most workers, they bring shorter working hours and make room for the unemployed to get paid work. The important point is that these new arrangements link work, although temporary, part-time, precarious and so on, to the social security system. In principle, any type of work could yield a proportional entitlement to social rights. If this does not happen, it could lead to an increasing differentiation among employees. So-called key workers, whose social rights are in less jeopardy, could be given 'first-class' citizenship as opposed to others in the 'second class'.

These changes do not move work from the centre of social institutions. Instead, they extend the logic of paid work to previous non-work activities. Therefore, social citizenship can be increasingly linked to work.

Notes

[1] The figures in brackets apply to 1999 and can be found in tables in Chapter Two of this volume.

[2] The reader is reminded of the problems which can also occur in relation to the ILO criteria. See Chapter Two of this volume.

[3] Official Gazette RS, nos 5/91, 17/91, 12/92, 71/93, 2/94, 38/94, 69/98.

[4] Official Gazette RS, no 69/98.

[5] Social Protection Act (SPA), Official Gazette RS, nos 54/92, 42/94 and 32/01. The last changes were adopted in April 2001. Prior to them, two different schemes were defined: cash assistance and cash allowance. The first was offered to people permanently incapable of work and persons aged 60+, who did not have other means of survival. The second was offered to people in need if their own as well as their family income situation made them eligible. However, now only one benefit – the so-called cash social assistance – is defined. The main eligibility condition remains the same – that is the lack of necessary means of survival.

[6] The data refer to the previous benefit – that is, cash allowance.

[7] In 1999, only 358 supervisions were completed, while in 2000 their number rose to 1,300 (ESS, 2000, 2001). Nevertheless, the number of violations discovered is still quite low (in 1999, 11% of unemployed were removed from the register and 1.4% lost the right to cash benefits; in 2000 the share grew to 21.4% and 2%, respectively). In 2000, job counsellors deleted – for various reasons – from the register some 10,000 unemployed.

[8] The figures are displayed only for those educational and training programmes where more or less a direct link between them and job placement can be established.

[9] A windmill effect occurs if the programme encourages employment, training and so on, of those who would have been employed, trained and so on without it, as was the case with subsidising of employment of graduates in Slovenia.

[10] The creaming effect indicates the tendency of employment offices and/or programmes to give priority to those unemployed persons who have the least difficulties finding jobs.

[11] The substitution effect occurs in the case of subsidising employment, training and so on, for some employers who, due to their lower costs, push unsubsidised workers out of employment.

[12] In May 1994, the Faculty of Social Sciences, Centre for Welfare Studies, carried out the Quality of Life Survey in Slovenia. The sample is representative of the resident population of Slovenia aged 18+. The sample size was 2,517 persons (of whom 1,806 persons were actually interviewed).

[13] The areas which were observed in the analysis of the 1994 Slovenian Quality of Life Survey data were the following: housing, access to services in the resident environment, educational attainment (and functional literacy), consumption, employment (work activity), interpersonal integration (integration in the interpersonal networks: family, friends, neighbourhood). The highest percentages of respondents with serious problems are in the areas of housing (43.1%) and education (45.1% – low educational attainment; low functional literacy; Trbanc, 1996, p 105). Only 17.2% of respondents do not have problems in any of the observed areas, while 52.3% have problems 'localised' in one or two areas (Trbanc, 1996, p 106).

TWELVE

Unemployment and unemployment policy in Switzerland

George Sheldon

Introduction

Unemployment in Switzerland is low, by international standards. In 2001, unemployment averaged a mere 1.9%, compared to 7.8% in the EU and 4.8% in the US[1]. Swiss unemployment, however, has not always been this low. In fact, starting from 0.5% in 1990, the unemployment rate rose to 5.2% in just four years and topped off at an unprecedented 5.7% in the winter of 1997, before decreasing to its present level. Not even during the Great Depression in the 1930s did unemployment rise that high in Switzerland.

While the recent rapid decline in Swiss unemployment was remarkable by international standards, the unemployment rate nevertheless failed to fall back to its pre-recession level of 0.5%. In this respect, the time path of baseline unemployment[2] in Switzerland has risen in a step-like fashion from one business cycle to the next, a pattern repeated in other European countries. By contrast, the unemployment rate in the US tends to fluctuate around a stationary baseline level of about 6%, rising above this mark in a cyclical downturn and falling below it in an upswing.

A high level of baseline unemployment is costly both to the unemployed as well as to society as a whole. Depending on the amount of turnover in unemployment and on the generosity of unemployment insurance (UI) benefits, a high baseline level of unemployment subjects the unemployed to significant financial and emotional stress. Moreover, it leads to a loss of output, lowering the standard of living available to all. Furthermore, it strains the government budget by raising spending (on income support schemes, for example) while at the same time lowering tax revenues.

The following contribution examines the causes and consequences of the increase in baseline unemployment in Switzerland. Section two of this chapter documents the rise in baseline unemployment, while section three discusses the causes of this increase. Section four then assesses the policy response to the unemployment increase. Conclusions are drawn in section five.

Rise in baseline unemployment

A number of signs exist which point to an increase in baseline unemployment in Switzerland. One such piece of evidence is the unemployment rate itself. Its time path from 1970 to the present is documented in Figure 12.1. The unemployment rate in Switzerland has risen sharply on three occasions in the last 30 years: in the mid-1970s and early 1980s, following in the wake of the two large OPEC oil price hikes, and again at the start of the 1990s as a result of a restrictive monetary policy adopted to combat a sharp rise in inflation in Switzerland at the end of the 1980s. Exports – accounting for almost 50% of Switzerland's GDP –also faltered on two instances during this period, further weakening aggregate demand and hence adding to unemployment.

More important than these sharp rises in unemployment, however, is its weaker decline during subsequent economic upturns. As Figure 12.1 illustrates, at the end of every recovery period the unemployment rate has come to rest at a point higher than its pre-recession level. Consequently, the long-term or baseline unemployment rate has risen continuously from roughly 0% in the 1970s, to about 0.3% in the 1980s, to 0.5% in the 1990s, and currently to about 2.0%. While these numbers are low by international standards, they nevertheless point to a trend increase that has resulted in unemployment now beginning to rise from a base four times higher than it was ten years ago. This development does not bode well for the future.

Another sign that baseline unemployment has risen in Switzerland can be seen in the repeated outward shift of the so-called Beveridge Curve, presented

Figure 12.1: Unemployment rate (1970-2002)

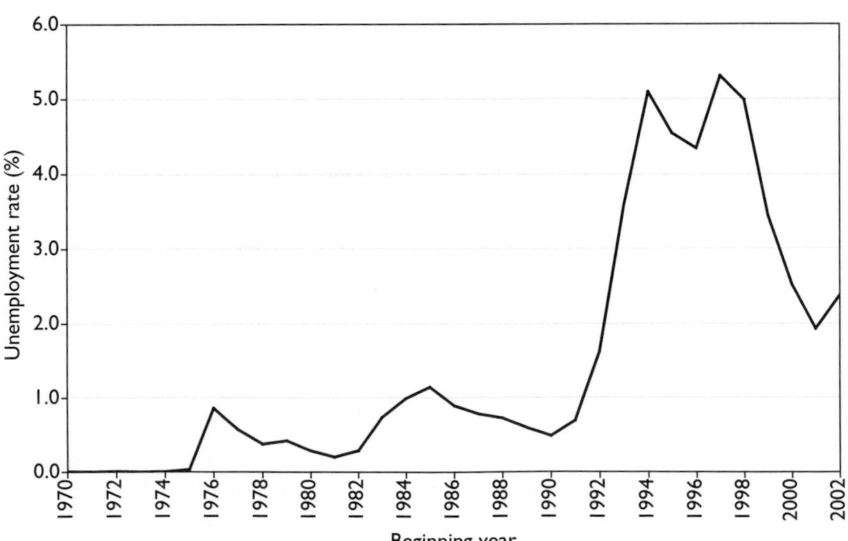

Source: Swiss Unemployment Statistics, State Secretariat for Economic Affairs, Berne, various issues

Figure 12.2: Beveridge Curve (1970-2001)

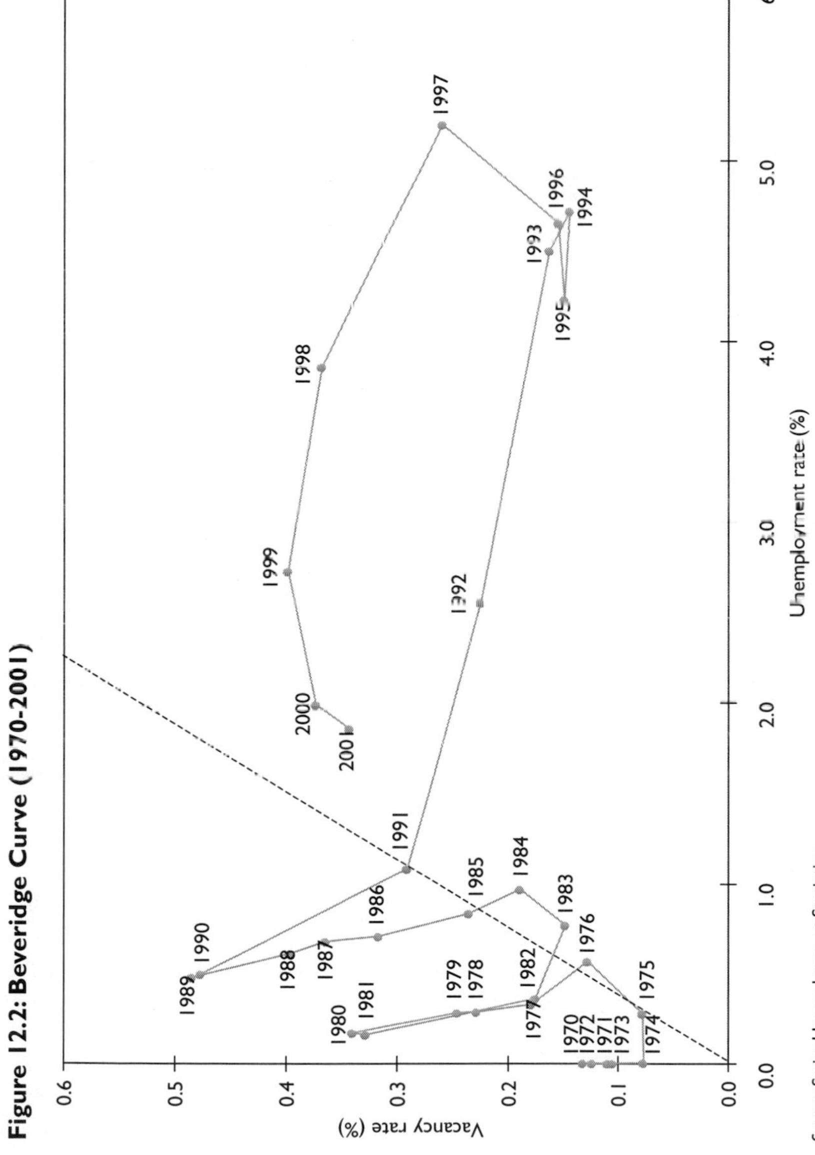

Source: Swiss Unemployment Statistics

in Figure 12.2. The Beveridge Curve describes a hyperbolic relationship that exists between the number of job openings and unemployed over the business cycle[3]. In an economic downturn job, openings decline and job seekers increase in number; the opposite occurs in an upturn. This inverse relationship is clear to see in Figure 12.2. The chart also reveals that the Beveridge Curve has shifted outwards from the origin over the years, the last shift taking place in 1997. A movement of this sort is generally interpreted as a loss in labour market efficiency as it implies that an ever larger stock of job openings is needed to lower unemployment to a given level. For example, according to the figures in the chart, roughly twice as many job vacancies were required in 1999 than in 1992 to achieve an unemployment rate of roughly 2.5%. Many forces can lie behind such a shift: increased mismatch between the structure of jobs and unemployed, decreased market transparency, or weakened job search efforts, to name just a few.

The dashed line in Figure 12.2 represents the current vacancies:unemployed ratio that is thought to prevail at full employment in Switzerland. The point at which this ray intersects the Beveridge Curve gives an estimate of the baseline rate of unemployment. Latest estimates put that unemployment rate at just over 2.0%, which conforms to the level of baseline unemployment that Figure 12.1 suggests.

Sources of the increase

What has led to the increase in the baseline rate of unemployment in Switzerland? An immediate cause is a decrease in the cyclical flexibility of labour supply. In the past, the size of the labour force has closely followed changes in the level of employment, falling when the number of jobs decreased during a recession and rising when they rose again in an economic upturn. As a result, job losses have not translated into commensurate increases in unemployment. This was particularly true in the mid-1970s when employment fell sharply in response to the first OPEC oil price shock, as Figure 12.3 demonstrates.

The chart shows how the number of employed, officially unemployed, and unemployment participating in active labour market measures (AM) have evolved since 1970 (unemployed participating in active labour market measures conventionally are not included in the official unemployment statistics in Switzerland). The sum of these three groups constitutes the labour force. As the graph verifies, unemployment dropped dramatically in the mid-1970s, falling by roughly 8%, the largest decline in jobs witnessed in any OECD country at the time. Yet employment never rose above 1% because the labour force declined by almost as much. As the chart shows, however, the responsiveness of the labour force to dips in employment has since declined. For example, the unemployment rate rose well above 1% in the 1990s (Figure 12.1) although employment fell by far less than in the 1970s. In short, one reason that baseline unemployment has risen is that, today, contractions in employment are more

Figure 12.3: Employment and unemployment (1970-2001)

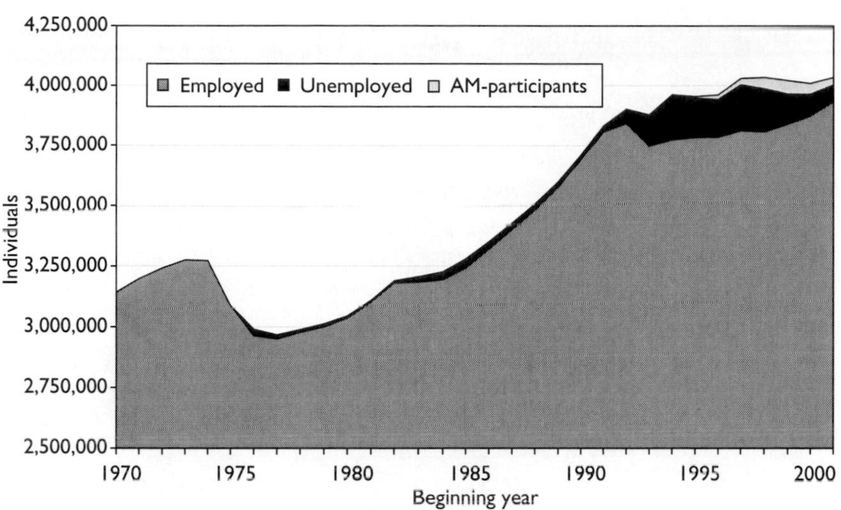

Source: Swiss Employment and Unemployment Statistics

fully reflected in the unemployment statistics. On the other hand, Figure 12.3 also indicates that an increasing number of the unemployed are beginning to disappear once again from the statistics as a result of participating in active measures. Without this effect, the Swiss unemployment rate would currently be a third higher, putting it at around 2.5% instead of 1.9%.

Two major factors lie behind the decreased responsiveness of the labour force to changes in employment opportunities:

- the introduction of widespread compulsory UI in April 1977;
- the increasingly sedentary nature of the immigrant labour force in Switzerland.

Before UI became compulsory in 1977, only 20% of the active labour force was insured against unemployment. Without entitlement to unemployment benefits, most workers who lost jobs chose not to register at the local placement office (where the unemployed are required to register in order to draw UI benefits) and therefore did not enter the unemployment statistics. Since they were not employed either, they (statistically speaking) exited the labour force. The incentive for the unemployed to report to a placement office and be counted as unemployed obviously rose with the introduction of compulsory UI, increasing the level of measured unemployment solely for statistical reasons. The urge to report increased further in 1984 with the enactment of the national UI Law. Previously, one only had to have been employed and paid premiums in six of the last 12 months prior to unemployment to receive benefits, whereas after the enactment of the new law six of the last 24 months sufficed.

Consequently, more unemployment became eligible for benefits and therefore registered their unemployment[4].

The increased permanency of the immigrant labour force has also detracted from the flexibility of labour supply. In the early 1970s only about a quarter of the non-Swiss workers in Switzerland had a permanent visa allowing them to remain in the country without a job (see Figure 12.4). All other non-Swiss employees had an annual or seasonal permit, or were cross-border commuters from the neighbouring countries of Austria, France, Germany and Italy. Since their work permits were only temporary, valid for a year at most, with the possibility of renewal if employment was found, immigrant workers had to return home when they lost their jobs and therefore did not enter the ranks of the unemployed. Over 80% of the job loss suffered in the 1970s recession was absorbed by the departure of immigrant workers[5]. Today the situation is different: almost 60% of immigrant workers have permanent residency status, and as a result, a larger share of immigrant workers remain in Switzerland and register at the placement office when they become unemployed.

The impact on unemployment of wider UI coverage and an increasingly sedentary immigrant labour force has not been simply superficial. They have also had fundamental effects on the level of baseline unemployment.

A large share of the immigrant workers in Switzerland are not only settled, but they are low-skilled as well. According to Swiss census figures almost half of all immigrant workers (principally annual and permanent permit holders) residing in Switzerland in December of 1980 were unskilled. At the time of the 1990 census, the share of unskilled immigrant labourers still equalled 45%,

Figure 12.4: Non-Swiss national labour force by permit category (1960-2001)

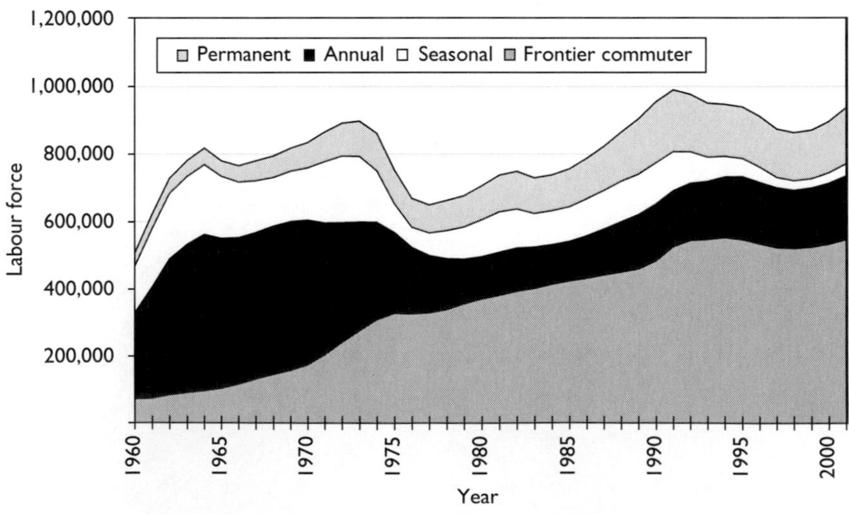

Source: Swiss Foreign Worker Statistics (August figures); Swiss Federal Aliens Office, Berne, various issues

down a mere five percentage points, whereas the share of unskilled among Swiss workers had fallen from 25% to below 15% in the same time span.

This situation improved in the interim. Even today, less than 20% of all new work permits are issued to persons taking on a high-skill position, where high-skill jobs are defined as positions in academia, research, information and communications technology, or upper-level management, and this despite an apparent shortage of skilled workers in Switzerland. (Since Swiss migration data do not register the skill of immigrants, but rather the type of jobs taken, we must resort to this indirect measure of skill.)

The disproportionate share of the low-skilled among immigrant workers reflects a failed immigration policy. The employment of immigrant labour is of course controlled in Switzerland: the federal government sets limits on the number of new permits that may be issued in a given year according to the needs of the labour market. Yet these quotas only apply to about 20% of the yearly influx of immigrants into Switzerland. They do not apply to the entering family members of immigrant workers with annual or permanent visas. Nor do they apply to the seasonal workers who, having worked four consecutive eight-month seasons in Switzerland, have a right to an annual permit (an entitlement wrung from Switzerland by the Common Market members in the early 1970s). Dhima (1991) estimates that as much as two-thirds of the stock of permanent non-Swiss residents in Switzerland consist of former seasonal workers and their families, whose numbers are not controlled and who can generally be expected to be low-skilled.

The effect of a rising share of low-skilled workers in Switzerland on unemployment is illustrated in Figure 12.5. The figure compares the relative

Figure 12.5: Share of annual and permanent work permit holders in the labour force and the stock of unemployed (1975-2000)

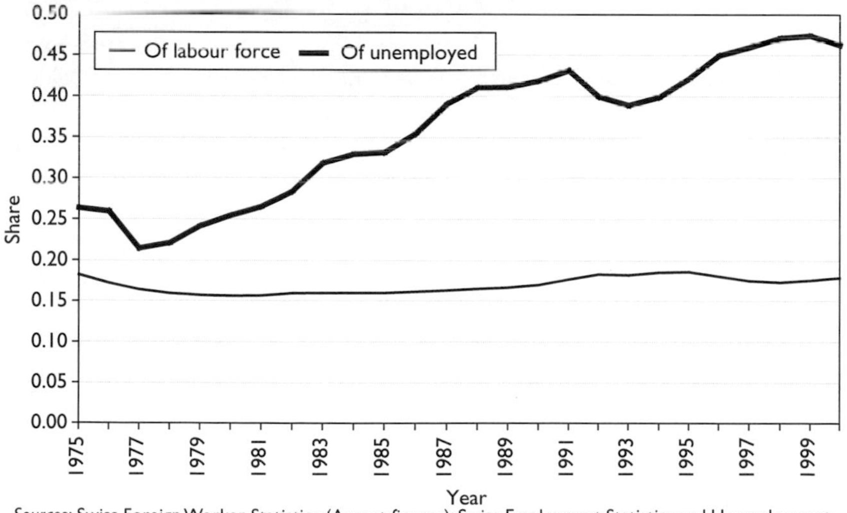

Sources: Swiss Foreign Worker Statistics (August figures); Swiss Employment Statistics and Unemployment Statistics

share of holders of annual and permanent work permits in the labour force with their share in the stock of unemployed. Clearly, the proportion of annual and permanent work permit holders in the labour force has fluctuated around a relative constant rate of 18% since the mid 1970s, whereas their share in the stock of unemployed has climbed steadily to almost 50%. In other words, almost every other unemployed person in Switzerland today is an immigrant, although less than one fifth of the labour force is made up of non-Swiss nationals. The cause of the disproportionate share of immigrant workers among the unemployed is that the risk and duration of unemployment are inversely related to skill levels, as is found in all OECD countries.

The large share of low-skilled immigrant workers in Switzerland also has a second drawback. Sheldon (2000a) shows that technical change in Switzerland is skill-using[6], meaning that technical progress increases firms' demand for high-skilled workers and lowers that for low-skilled labourers, be they non-Swiss nationals or otherwise. In such a situation, ready access to an abundant supply of low-skilled immigrant workers weakens the economic incentives for firms to invest in new skill-using technologies, thereby slowing the rate of technical progress and stunting economic growth[7]. Accordingly, immigrant workers in Switzerland are concentrated in industries with below-average economic and employment growth and, in the case of seasonal workers, also with sub-average growth in labour productivity. These industries include clothing, textiles, construction, mining and quarrying, metalworking, as well as hotels and restaurants.

One of the reasons that so many immigrant workers in Switzerland are low skilled is that the social costs these workers create in the form, say, of increased unemployment are not borne by the permit-issuing authorities or the employing firm. As a consequence, more low-skilled immigrant workers are demanded by firms and given permits than would be the case if the parties involved had to bear the full costs of their actions. The UI system redistributes these costs by assessing all firms the same insurance premium irrespective of the amount of paid-out insurance benefits their layoffs generate. Sheldon (2000b) calculates that the construction and hotel/restaurant industries, where a majority of immigrant workers are employed, finance less than half of the paid-out benefits that arise out of their layoffs. During the 1990s, these cross-subsidies totalled almost 300 million euro or roughly 10% of UI benefits (see Table 12.1). If UI premiums were experience-rated[8], firms' demand for low-skilled immigrant labour would be less inflated.

The UI system has also had a fundamental effect on the level of baseline unemployment. Every increase in the number of unemployed has in the past led to a prolongation of the maximum duration of benefit entitlement. During the recession of 1975-76, benefit entitlement was extended from 15 to 25 weeks, during the next recession from 25 to a maximum of 50 weeks[9] and in the last recession from 50 to 104 weeks (or two years). To be sure, the extension of UI benefit entitlements has been more a reaction to than a cause of increasing unemployment. Yet as Figure 12.6 indicates, extensions have remained in place

Figure 12.6: Unemployment and UI benefit entitlement (1970-2000)

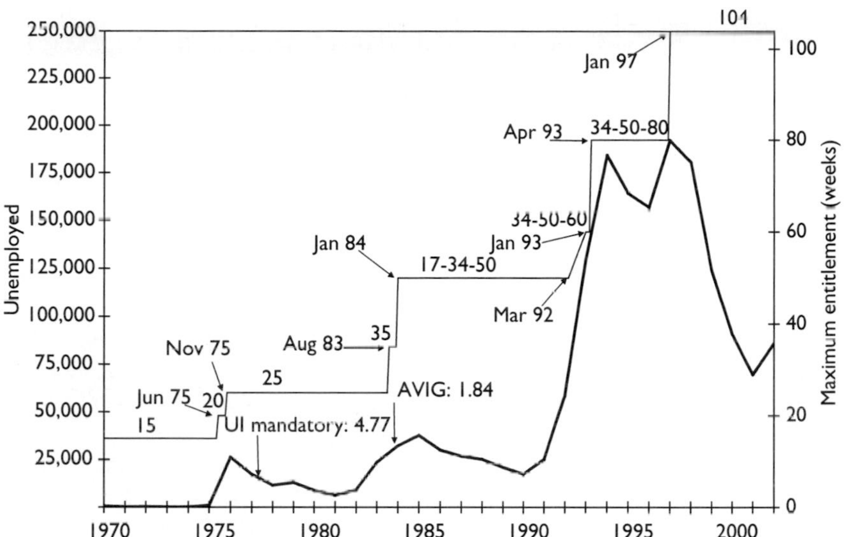

long after their causes have vanished, while unemployment has failed to return to its pre-recession level. The graphical evidence therefore suggests that UI changes have not only arisen in reaction to increasing unemployment but have themselves affected unemployment by increasing its long-term or baseline level.

A number of econometric studies have investigated this issue, controlling for the problem of reverse causality (see Gersbach and Sheldon, 1996; Sheldon, 1996, 1999a, 1999b, 2001). The latest study (Sheldon, 2001), which covers the period 1990-99 and therefore also includes a phase of economic recovery, shows that the three extensions of benefit entitlements in the 1990s increased the duration of unemployment by about a third, the share of long-term unemployed (conventionally defined here as unemployment lasting more than one year) by two-thirds and the baseline rate of unemployment by half[10]. In addition, it was discovered that the benefit extensions neutralised the employment-supporting effects of active labour market measures. Furthermore, it was found that long-term unemployment is relatively unresponsive to both active measures and economic recovery. Combined, these results suggest that prolonging benefit entitlements in response to mounting unemployment runs the risk of creating a large stock of long-term unemployed whose chances of finding employment are impervious to counter-cyclical measures or to a general improvement in economic conditions. In other words, extending benefits can transform cyclical unemployment into structural unemployment – the so-called hysteresis effect.

The studies also indicate that the extension of benefits was both expensive and inefficient (see Figure 12.7). The extension of support increased UI benefit outlays[11] by about €833 million, of which €563 million (or two thirds) were due to an insurance-induced weakening of search efforts ('moral hazard')[12]. In turn, a third of this €563 million went to support short-term unemployment, which is not generally considered to be a serious problem in need of added support. Viewed from this angle, more than a fifth of the additional UI outlays arising from extending entitlements was 'wasted' on the short-term unemployed.

Extending benefit entitlements in the face of increasing unemployment is of course understandable: the authorities fear that not to do so would subject the unemployed to financial distress. However, econometric studies (see Sheldon, 1999a) of the labour market exclusion of former unemployed in Switzerland on the basis of social security records provide scant support for this position. Instead they show that an equally large share of persons who exited unemployment found jobs in the 1980s and 1990s, although job growth expanded in the 1980s and languished in the 1990s. Moreover, post-unemployment wages continued to equal pre-unemployment wages on average in the 1990s. Furthermore, every second unemployed person moved up at least one income decile within four years after being re-employed. These results do not point to an increased economic and social exclusion of the unemployed in Switzerland in the 1990s despite the sharp rise in unemployment.

On the other hand, the econometric studies also show that a third of the unemployed suffered wage losses by accepting work and that these losses had not been fully recouped even after four years of employment. Accepting wage cuts did improve these individuals chances of securing permanent work, however.

Figure 12.7: Financial effects of benefit extensions (1998)

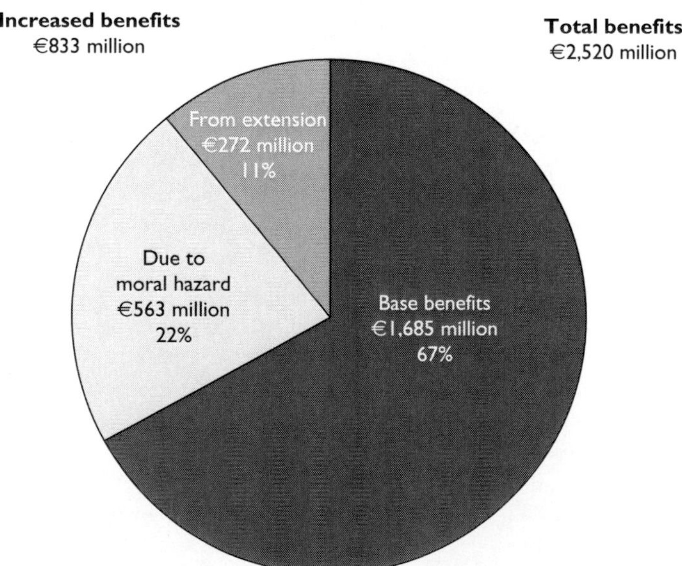

Source: Sheldon (2001)

The permanency of the wage losses combined with the stability of post-unemployment work together implies that the income loss suffered by these individuals resulted from changed labour market conditions that could not be avoided. In such a situation, extending benefits does not help solve the problem, but merely delays the inevitable.

The distribution of income did not become more unequal in the 1980s and 1990s either, suggesting the working poor problem has also not increased in Switzerland in recent years. Figure 12.8 shows how the various income deciles evolved in relationship to median monthly wage earnings in Switzerland from 1984 to 1994[13]. As the figure clearly shows, the relative distribution of wage earnings barely varied across the sample period, although the Swiss economy boomed in the 1980s and declined in the 1990s. As OECD (1996b) reports have shown, Switzerland shares this pattern with Denmark, Italy, Norway, and Sweden. In other words, the increased income inequality experienced in the US is not a general phenomenon common to all OCED countries.

Policy responses

The policy response of Swiss lawmakers has not been solely to extend benefit entitlements. In 1997, the UI Law was revised with the aim of placing greater emphasis on the re-integration of the unemployed. The revision brought several changes. For one, the 3,000+ unemployment registration offices were re-organised into roughly 150 regional placement centres. Up until then, greater

Figure 12.8: Relative deviation of deciles from median monthly earnings (1984-94)

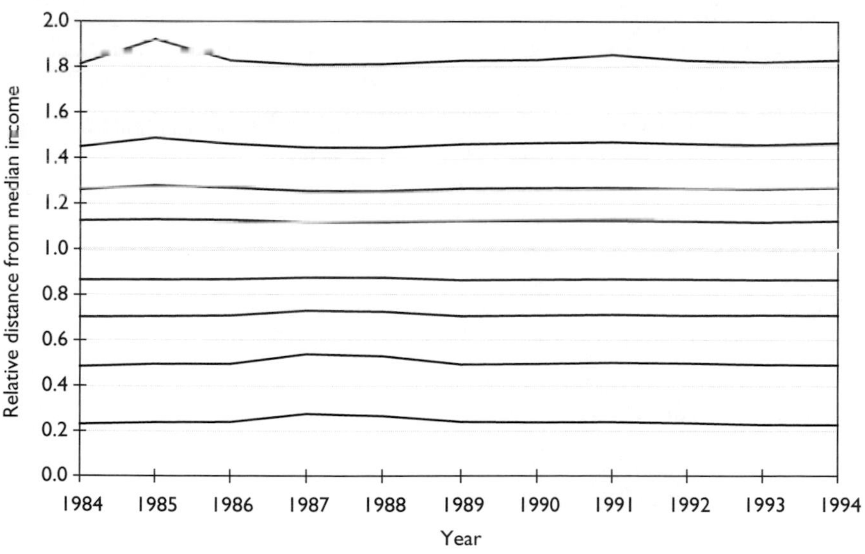

Source: 100,000 sample from the Swiss Social Security records (own calculations)

emphasis was placed on monitoring the employed rather than on placing them. In fact, in some small rural communities the local police station, for lack of personnel, served as the unemployment registration office. Today, the placement centres, rather than unemployment, are monitored. The centres are judged on their success in reintegrating the unemployed and are awarded accordingly: canton administrations, which run the centres, receive an additional 5% funding from the UI if their placement centres significantly outperform the national average, while they lose 5% if their centres significantly fall short.

The revision of the UI Law also placed greater demands on the unemployed. To draw benefits for more than 30 weeks, the unemployed are now required to participate in active measures such as training or work programmes after 30 weeks. The increased emphasis on active measures is reflected in the outlay structure of the Swiss UI system, presented in Table 12.1. As the table indicates, the share of spending on active measures has increased dramatically since the mid-1990s. Unfortunately, recent econometric studies of the effectiveness of the active measures have yielded sobering results[14]. It seems that most measures have been unsuccessful in getting the unemployed back to work more quickly or permanently. This may result from poor targeting: 30 weeks of unemployment is a very rough guide of which measures the unemployed need in order to regain employment.

A further revision of the UI Law is now in the pipeline. Breaking with the previous tradition of repeated entitlement prolongation (Figure 12.6), the planned revision envisions shortening the maximum duration of benefit entitlement from 104 to 80 weeks for all unemployed aged less than 55. However, the recent increase in unemployment and past political experience make one sceptical that the planned reform will come into being: a previous act of parliament in 1997 to lower the benefit level[15] by a mere 2% provoked a national referendum revoking the act.

Switzerland is also in the midst of revising its so-called Aliens Law with an eye to improving the average skill level of immigrant workers, a subject debated at length in various issues of the *Swiss Political Science Review* throughout 2001. The proposed revision foresees eliminating seasonal and annual permits and replacing them with so-called short-term and normal permits, respectively. Short-term permits could be issued up to one year and renewed once for a

Table 12.1: UI outlays on the unemployed (€million) (1993-2000)

	1993	1994	1995	1996	1997	1998	1999	2000
UI benefits	3,517.5	3,189.5	2,649.9	2,994.7	3,385.6	2,628.8	2,007.1	1,440.9
Active measures	91.1	214.7	330.9	537.1	1,157.5	669.0	611.4	370.1
Total	3,608.6	3,404.1	2,980.8	3,531.9	4,543.1	3,297.8	2,618.5	1,811.1
% active measures	2.5	6.3	11.1	15.2	25.2	20.3	23.3	20.4

maximum of two years. Thereafter the individual would have to leave Switzerland for an as yet unspecified length of time. The holder of a short-term permit could be allowed to bring in his or her family, but would not be entitled to do so. Nor would a short-term permit holder be entitled to a long-term permit, no matter how long the individual had worked in Switzerland. In contrast, holders of a long-term permit would be entitled to have their families accompany them and would have the right to a permanent visa after residing in Switzerland for ten years, five of which with a long-term permit. Long-term visas would have no fixed, but nevertheless a limited period of validity. The issuance of work permits to non-EU or EFTA nationals[16] would have to serve the general long-term economic interests of Switzerland and not merely meet current local needs. Moreover, in the case of long-term permits, skill versatility, language capabilities, and age would have to ensure the sustained integration of the applicant.

The revised law foresees exceptions to these guidelines, however, if the applicant:

- is an investor or entrepreneur expected to create jobs;
- is a renowned performer in the arts, sciences, or sports;
- possesses unique occupational skills in demand;
- is required to be in Switzerland to maintain important international business relations.

Critically, the success of the revised law will hinge on its ability to stop the large influx of low-skilled immigrant workers into Switzerland. The elimination of the entitlement of seasonal workers to longer-term work permits and the increased emphasis on an applicant's skills and potential for sustained integration in the Swiss labour market are surely steps in the right direction, but it is questionable whether they will suffice.

For one, local canton authorities issue the majority of work permits, and it is questionable whether they are capable of judging whether or not the issuing of a particular permit is in the general economic interest of Switzerland. And even if they could, it is doubtful whether the cantons would subordinate local interests for the good of the nation. Past experience does not leave one to expect them to do so. In addition, few local authorities are probably in a position to judge the skills of an applicant. Moreover, the proposed revision leaves a lot of room for interpretation. Almost anybody can be viewed as having 'special occupational capabilities that are in demand'. In fact, unique skills, because of their very uniqueness, make sustained labour market integration less likely. The fact that so many special interest groups rejected the original proposal of applying a rigid and objective list of criteria for issuing permits, as happens in Canada, for example, implies that interest groups hope to be granted exceptions. Giving cantonal authorities room for interpreting the law and introducing exceptions makes them susceptive to local pressure groups, who probably do not have the general economic interests of Switzerland in mind.

The only way to ensure that immigrant worker employment serves the general long-term interests of Switzerland is to take the decision to issue work permits out of the hands of local authorities. Yet the political resolve to do this is currently missing in Switzerland.

Conclusions

Our discussion has shown that the baseline level of unemployment in Switzerland, as in most European countries, has risen in the last 25 years. This is due to three basic factors:

- a decline in the responsiveness of labour supply to cyclical fluctuations in employment resulting from the introduction of compulsory UI and an increasing share of immigrant workers with permanent residency status;
- the build-up of a large stock of low-skilled immigrant workers;
- repeated extensions of the maximum period of UI benefit entitlement.

Policy changes have taken place with the aim of lowering unemployment. For one, public employment services have been completely reorganised and given financial incentives to improve their effectiveness. For another, greater emphasis has been laid on placing the unemployed as opposed to merely administering them. In turn, the unemployed are expected to participate in active labour market measures if their unemployment persists.

Additional reforms are underway. The Aliens Law is in the midst of being revised with an eye to stemming the flow of low-skilled immigrant workers into Switzerland. In addition, a proposed revision of the UI Law foresees rolling back some of the extensions to UI benefit entitlements. Whether these planned reforms will ever come into being or have the intended effects is open to debate.

Despite these reservations, it should nevertheless not be overlooked that the Swiss labour market exhibits a number of features, not discussed in this short contribution, which support a low baseline level of unemployment, among others: non-restrictive employment protection rules, low taxes, decentralised wage negotiations and an absence of strikes. Econometric studies by Nickell (1997) and Blanchard and Wolfers (2000) indicate that these factors contribute importantly to explaining international differences in baseline unemployment rates. Hence, although baseline unemployment is on the rise in Switzerland, no signs exist suggesting that it will reach the 8% level that EU countries currently average.

Notes

[1] The figures for the EU and the US are based on the latest OECD figures, which do not currently include figures for all EU member countries.

[2] Baseline unemployment is the level of unemployment that persists across a business cycle; that is, the unemployment that emerges after adjusting for cyclical effects. If unemployment does not exhibit a trend, then baseline unemployment corresponds to long-term average unemployment. It is roughly akin to the theory-based concepts of the natural rate of unemployment or the non-accelerating inflation rate of unemployment (NAIRU) addressed in Chapter One of this volume.

[3] The chart plots vacancy and unemployment rates. The denominator in both cases is the same: the number of active workers, unemployed and employed. In short, the active labour force.

[4] Since 1991, the figures for unemployed are also gathered by an annual telephone survey conducted in the second quarter of each year. Currently, both counting procedures yield very similar results.

[5] On the other hand, immigrant workers that lost their jobs and re-migrated also took their demand with them, which explains why employment decreased more in Switzerland than in any other OECD member country in the 1974-75 worldwide recession.

[6] Kugler and Spycher (1992) found that this also held in an earlier study. The skill bias of technical change is a common finding in OECD countries. Kugler et al (1989) demonstrate this for Germany.

[7] Note that stunting growth – that is, slowing the *change* in economic activity – in no way contradicts the fact that immigrant labour, be it unskilled or otherwise, is needed to maintain the current *level* of economic activity in Switzerland. Stunting growth means that the current level of economic activity could have been higher had immigrant labour been more skilled.

[8] Experience rating means that a firm's insurance premium is linked to the amount of paid-out benefits its layoffs cause. Interestingly, premiums for occupational disability insurance are commonly experienced rated in Europe: clerks, for example, pay lower rates than construction workers. Yet, UI premiums are not. This is all the more surprising given that experience-rated UI premiums were introduced in the US to meet the demands of unions, who see experience rating as an instrument to discourage layoffs. Empirical studies – such as Feldstein (1978), Saffer (1982, 1983), Topel (1983, 1984, 1985), Anderson (1990), Anderson and Meyer (1994, 1998), Card and Levine (1994) among others – show that experience-rating does indeed reduce layoffs.

[9] From 1984 to and including 1996, the duration of benefit entitlement was linked to the length of UI contributions. From 1984 to 1992, 18 months of contributions over the two years prior to unemployment gave entitlement to 50 weeks of benefits, 12 months to 34 weeks and six months to 17 weeks. The maximum entitlement was raised twice thereafter before graduation was abandoned, and benefit entitlement extended to 104 weeks for all.

[10] This strong impact of the extension of UI entitlements on long-term unemployment in Switzerland may seem to contradict the casual observation that benefit entitlement in some countries are even longer than in Switzerland and yet long-term unemployment is lower. Such a comparison is misleading, however. The results presented here are based on an inter-temporal comparison within a given country holding institutional conditions constant, whereas a simple international cross-sectional comparison controls for nothing. Recent international econometric studies, such as those performed by Nickell (1997) and Blanchard and Wolfers (2000), which do control for country-specific differences yield the same results as here: longer benefit entitlements generally increase unemployment.

[11] Although UI benefits include all income support schemes, in addition to standard unemployment benefits also those applying to short-time work, for example, the UI benefits in Figure 12.7 pertain only to unemployment and not, say, to short-time work.

[12] Moral hazard refers to the negative side effects that any insurance has on the behaviour of the insured. In general, the insured invest less effort in avoiding risks and damages when these are insured. As a result, increased insurance coverage often leads to a rise in the very risks and damages it is intended to insure.

[13] The social security data do not control for work time. Hence the extremely low wages in the lower deciles result in part from part-time work.

[14] See Gerfin and Lechner (2000) and Lalive and Van Ours and Zweimüller (2000). On the other hand, Sheldon (2000c) finds that the reorganisation of public employment services did increase placement efficiency by six percent.

[15] UI benefits are quite generous by international comparison. Benefits currently amount to 80% of previous gross earnings up to a limit of €4,747 monthly, if the recipient is married, has dependents to support, aged 55+, or is handicapped. All others receive 70% of previous earnings up to a maximum of €4,153. Benefits are subject to social security contributions and income tax, the latter varying by canton and community.

[16] Since the bilateral agreements between Switzerland and the EU went into effect on 1 June, 2002, the Aliens Law no longer applies to citizens of EU or EFTA countries. Until then, about 70% of the permits issued annually went to EU or EFTA nationals.

THIRTEEN

Work, welfare and citizenship: diversity and variation within European (un)employment policy

Jochen Clasen and Wim van Oorschot

Not so long ago mass unemployment seemed to be a universal and typically European problem. From the early 1980s onwards most Western-European countries were plagued by unemployment figures that permanently and by far exceeded those of other industrialised countries, notably the US. Early socioeconomic policies, that tried to stimulate domestic demand, increase international economic competitiveness and redistribute labour, had no clear and lasting positive effects. The idea then took hold that unemployment in Europe was a structural phenomenon strongly connected to the relatively generous welfare systems of European countries and their rigid labour market institutions. This image of 'Eurosclerosis' – of European welfare states being caught in structures of inflexibility, preventing the solution of the problem of mass unemployment – contrasted sharply with the image of the liberal US welfare state, where flexible labour markets and low social protection fuelled the jobs machines of its service economy. In more detail, the standard interpretation of the European problem of structural unemployment saw two main causes: the gap between wages and productivity for low-skilled workers, and the inflexibility of and distortions to the smooth functioning of labour markets. Solutions advocated broadly in national and international policy discourses included increasing wage flexibility; increasing productivity levels and employability of workers; flexibilisation of labour contracts and working-time; and changing incentive structures for employers (subsidies, tax credits), but of course also for the unemployed (lower and shorter benefits, stricter work tests, workfare type obligations). At present ideas and dialogues of this kind, based on the standard interpretation of the unemployment problem and asking for a shift from equality and protection to employment, still dominate the work and welfare policy nexus.

However, as Chapters One and Two have illustrated, actual developments in European employment and unemployment rates since the second half of the 1990s defy the pessimistic Eurosclerosis image of structural mass unemployment. In recent years many European countries have experienced a decisive decline in unemployment, notably Denmark, the Netherlands, Portugal, Ireland, Austria,

Sweden and the UK. In fact, these countries of the EU15 outnumber those with still high and persistent unemployment, for example Germany, France, Italy, Finland and Spain, which means that the standard interpretation has no universal empirical validity. What is more, several European countries now have unemployment rates below that of the US (and poverty rates that have been persistently lower), which shows that adequate levels of equality and social protection can be combined with high employment levels.

It has been shown in Chapter Two that most of the expectations about differences in unemployment rates between types of 'employment regimes' and groups of unemployed, as derived from the standard interpretation of the unemployment problem, are not supported by empirical findings. With the exception of long-term unemployment, levels and structure of unemployment do not follow expected patterns; also non-market oriented welfare systems have positive employment records, and no structural or 'natural' levels of unemployment have been found.

The purpose of this book has not been to develop an alternative theory of (un)employment and its possible solutions. For now, casting grounded doubt on the standard interpretation that has been around for so many years, and which has been so influential, suffices as a first step. The sincere aim of the book, in fact, justified by precisely this doubt, was to have a closer and empirical look at what exactly happened in individual European countries in the last decade and to provide an updated overview of their unemployment and employment policies, specifically from a citizenship perspective. Since Marshall's famous essay on citizenship rights (1949) the central goal of the welfare state has often been formulated as to strive for the ideal of full citizenship, conceived of as full participation of all in all spheres of social life. In the context of high unemployment in Europe this rather broad view has been narrowed down to equating full citizenship with labour market participation. This relation, however, can be questioned in its generality and remains an empirical matter for which several indicators have been applied in the country-specific chapters (Chapters Three to Twelve).

There is clearly a high level of national diversity. Despite the existence of similar socioeconomic and political challenges and common pressures, the stories told in each of these chapters reflect national paths of reform which display a considerable degree of variation. Many chapters also illustrated the considerable recovery within these countries' respective labour markets which often began in the first half of the 1990s. They provide ample evidence that solutions derived from the standard interpretation of the (un)employment problem, such as further deregulation of labour markets, reducing employment rights and lowering standards of social protection, are but one type of strategy among several which can lead to lower unemployment and rising employment levels. From a citizenship perspective these countries also indicate that the path based on the standard interpretation might not be the most desirable. Clearly, there are alternative ways to fight unemployment. Furthermore, relatively generous social protection does not appear to be a decisive obstacle to economic and employment recovery, and such recovery is compatible with quite different designs of social protection systems.

Secondly, despite the wide variation, however, there seems to be a common attempt to redraw the link between work and welfare. This attempt might best be summed up as 'towards activation'. There is, of course, diversity in the use of types and degrees of activation measures, and stimulating the unemployed to work and optimising conditions for their labour market integration has implications for citizenship rights to different degrees, but the common trend is there. Finally, attention will be paid in this chapter to the future prospects of work and welfare relations by discussing the sustainability of the various models of labour market recovery.

Towards activation

Within the past 10 years or so, the approach common in many countries in the 1980s – keeping overt unemployment down by diverting jobless people into alternative roles (early-retiree, recipient of sickness or disability benefits, care) has been superseded by the single most important goal of boosting employment and transferring benefit recipients to gainfully employed tax payers. A range of policies have been employed across western welfare states in order to achieve this goal, accompanied by an often bewildering phraseology such as 'activation', 'insertion', raising 'employability' or making benefits 'more employment friendly'. What these phrases have in common is their character of signalling a stronger emphasis on supply side oriented labour market policies combined with a stricter degree of conditionality attached to the receipt of social security transfers for working age claimants. At times these policies have increased the level of compulsion within benefit systems, in the sense that entitlement rights have been more closely linked to obligations on the part of benefit claimants to participate in training or work schemes. Some have interpreted this trend as the introduction of 'workfare' or of 'workfare-like elements' within social security policy for the jobless (Gilbert and Van Voorhis, 2001; Lødemel and Trickey, 2001).

There is some scepticism about the effectiveness of activation policies in particular, and labour market programmes as a whole. Indeed, applying a narrow measure of labour market integration, activation policies do not seem to be impressively successful. Also at times of a more favourable labour market development, it is certainly difficult to assess the degree to which activation policies have actually contributed to the decline in unemployment. As the Danish experience of the 1990s has shown, for example, a large part of the decline in open unemployment was reflected in the rising number of participants in various labour market programmes. In the Netherlands, there are doubts about the net contribution of activation measures particularly regarding the improvement of labour market chances of the weakest or 'hardest to place' groups. However, activation policies seem more easily justified when unemployment is already declining and when policies are put in a broader context, which includes aims such as a reconnecting unemployed people with the world of work or raising human capital.

The stronger emphasis on activation (of working-age benefit recipients) has certainly brought with it a blurring of the traditional division between the policy areas of social protection and labour market policy (Esping-Andersen et al, 2001). This trend is perhaps the most common denominator found in the ten countries reviewed in this book. It applies to countries which have successfully overturned a previously bleak labour market situation (the Netherlands, the UK or Denmark), to those which always have had comparatively low levels of unemployment (Norway, Switzerland), to those with stubbornly high levels of unemployment in the 1990s (France, Finland and Germany) and to those where unemployment levels have fluctuated (Sweden, Slovenia).

It is tempting to connect such cross-national similarities to external influences such as EU guidelines on employment policies, for example, which at times formulate concrete policy aims and require member states to demonstrate steps of implementation towards reaching them. For example, the European Council meeting in Luxembourg (the 'Job Summit') in November 1997 stipulated that the age of 25 years should be a cut-off point in the sense that younger people should be offered new employment or training within six months of unemployment. However, the role of the EU should not be exaggerated. In this particular incidence, European countries outside the EU have also introduced policies depending on age. Young people under the age of 25 are a special target group for employment reintegration in Norway, for example. Moreover, individual member states had already singled out younger age groups for activation programmes long before 1997, such as young social assistance claimants in Denmark and the Netherlands in the early 1990s, for example.

By the late 1990s it had become clear that activation policies (without using the same terminology) played a major part of actual policy making and policy legitimation particularly in the 'success countries', that is those which turned a bleak employment situation into one of sustained improvement. The introduction of the New Deal programmes in the UK, for example, was the central element of the welfare reform policy which Tony Blair's Labour government heralded as one of its major policy aims during its first term of office after 1997. The approach was similar to the one adopted by previous Conservative Party policies of increasingly stepping up requirements on the part of the unemployed (job seeking, for example). The Labour government went further, however, by establishing a closer connection between labour market and social policy with the explicit aim of reducing the level of dependency on social security for working-age benefit claimants by increasing the labour market integration rate. Less geared towards long-term or young unemployed, 'work, work, work' was the slogan which accompanied many direct and indirect (for example directed at employers) Dutch measures aimed at raising the employment rate. A special problem was, and remains, the high number of disability claimants, with an alleged high degree of hidden unemployment.

The British policy rhetoric, if not the policy detail, echoed very much the one which the Danish social democrats employed for justifying the introduction of labour market reforms after 1993. In turn, it can be argued that Denmark adopted the Swedish 'work line' which, having been in place long before the 1990s, might be seen as an 'activation forerunner' and which, consequently, did not undergo any major changes despite the upheavals in the Swedish labour market in the first half of the decade. This differs from Finland, where a range of measure were introduced with the explicit notion of making the unemployment policy regime less 'passive' and more 'active', such as tighter entitlement rules and lower benefit levels. However, also countries with low unemployment have introduced similar policies. Norway's policies amounting to the 'work line' explicitly expect claimants to be reintegrated in the labour market. Placement efforts have also been stepped up in Switzerland for example, where some unemployed groups are now expected to participate in labour market programmes.

Activation policies introduced in the remaining countries also indicate their relevance from a citizenship perspective. In Slovenia, for example, a trend has been identified which can be described as strengthening the 'activation' principle at the expense of the 'insurance' principle. More concretely, this implies that benefit entitlement is becoming less governed by past behaviour in terms of employment and contribution record (determining access to benefits, training, suitable job offers, and so on) and more by the current and future behaviour as job seekers (stipulated in individual employment plans which prescribe participation in labour market programmes, public work, and so on). Structurally, the Slovenian unemployment benefit system is very close to the German system. Moreover, the policy trend in Germany bears a close resemblance to Slovenia: the rights of job seekers (for example in terms of having to accept certain job offers) are decreasingly determined by their prior status and earnings and increasingly by the state of the labour market in general.

The French discourse on activation can be said to have started in the early 1990s when passive benefit expenditure was regarded as in need of being turned into active spending. However, there are two important differences to similar policy debates in other countries. First, the turn towards a more active approach in benefit policy has occurred in a much more adversarial policy environment compared with the Netherlands or Denmark, for example. Second, underlining the relevance of rhetoric and discourse in the French polity (see Hay and Rosamond, 2002) activation policies were introduced despite a general rejection of the notion of increasing flexibility, deregulation, or anything which might resemble the introduction of workfare. The latter in particular is regarded as an Anglo-American attempt of blaming the unemployed for their predicament, which is contrary to the French emphasis on a 'social treatment of unemployment' based on the idea of unemployment as a 'systemic' problem beyond the control of the individual.

And yet, while not declared as such, French reforms during the 1980s and 1990s introduced labour market reforms which increased flexibility, made hiring and firing of employees easier, and raised the number of jobs which can be considered as insecure. There was even the implementation of a 'workfare logic' with PARE in the sense that, as in many other countries studied in this volume, the right to benefit was to be governed less so by past contributions and increasingly by contractual commitments between the unemployed and the employment office regarding steps to take for a return to paid employment.

Finally, as Ervasti illustrates, the Finnish trend towards activation has not so much resulted in 'workfare' but in 'training fare'. Particularly younger benefit claimants without qualifications have increasingly been required to make applications for training courses. While this might be regarded as a particular form of activation, it is the other end of the labour market where actual problems of reintegration can be found. For older unemployed workers with low education levels there seems indeed very little chance to return to paid work in the Finnish labour market.

Citizenship rights

From a citizenship perspective the examples of policy trends discussed earlier are important since they indicate a re-balancing and redefinition of rights and obligations on the part of unemployed benefit claimants. If one aspect of citizenship rights is predicated on the notion that all those who seek a job should be able to find employment, certain trends in many countries reviewed in this volume should be welcomed. In some countries, such as France, Finland or Germany, unemployment levels remained stubbornly high or declined at a much slower rate than elsewhere. Many other countries, however, witnessed an impressive decline of rates on unemployment and long-term unemployment and raised employment levels considerably, without deteriorating their commitment to high levels of social protection or compromising low levels of poverty (see Gallie and Paugam, 2000a). Denmark and the Netherlands, for example, have maintained relatively generous benefit levels for most unemployed groups, except for lower rates which might apply to younger claimants. As discussed, the quid-pro-quo has been a much more explicit degree of conditionality attached to the receipt of social security support. The terms have required a more pro-active job search, the enhanced willingness to participate in training and other labour market programmes and the introduction of a stricter work test in general. Sanctions for non-compliance have been toughened. In general, the 'work-relatedness' of benefit entitlement has also become more pronounced in many European welfare states during the 1990s (Clasen et al, 2001).

A potential effect of such policies could be an increase in the scope of benefit exclusion. However, such a risk is, for the time being, relatively small due to favourable employment conditions particularly in those countries in which activation policies have been extended. For example, due to a tougher work line in Norway, any threats to citizenship rights are merely theoretical because of the low unemployment levels. In addition, policies are targeted at some groups only, such as younger people on social assistance benefit, or have not been implemented at local level. Also, there has been no erosion of labour market standards in Norway given that there are few workers with little protection, a very low share of 'non-standard' jobs and no flexibilisation of labour law. This is almost the reverse situation as in France where precarious forms of employment have grown despite a rhetoric that suggests otherwise. Equally, unless one considers the introduction of Revenue Minimum d'Insertion as the measure which fully preserved full citizenship rights, the effect of persistently high levels of unemployment and the much lower efficiency of the primary form of unemployment compensation have resulted in a decline of citizenship rights for job seekers in France.

By contrast, the much improved employment prospects and changes in patterns of labour market participation in the Netherlands from a household perspective (towards the 'one and a half earner couple') meant that changes to social protection have not been felt. However, should labour market conditions deteriorate, this situation might change. Also, citizenship rights for weaker and hard-to-place unemployed people (such as those with additional needs) have not improved due to the persistence of problems of entering the labour market. Nevertheless, the Dutch model, which is based on a proliferation of part-time jobs, is interesting from a citizenship perspective, not least because part-time employment is not discriminated against within the social security system. This is very different in other countries, such as Slovenia for example, where the expansion of part-time work is hampered by the concomitant decrease of citizenship rights for part timers in terms of access to welfare benefits, benefit levels and also the types of job which are available.

Unlike the Dutch model of increasing part-time work (and not only among women), the Danish model rests on a declining share of women working part-time. From a citizenship perspective, a clear shift has occurred over the past two decades. In the 1970s and 1980s, keeping people integrated in society meant first and foremost maintaining social rights to insurance based benefit, preserving income levels and opening access to opportunities (for example, to training or leave arrangements). Such a quasi-universal system was replaced in the 1990s with a system with a high level of conditionality attached to benefit entitlement and much increased obligations on the part of job seekers. Benefit levels have remained generous in comparative perspective, but, as in the UK, the participation in paid work has become an explicit source of citizenship. As Goul Andersen states (in Chapter Eight), this policy shift amounts to the adoption of a 'communitarian notion' of citizenship with employment as an indispensable element.

It could be said to some extent, that Denmark has adopted the Swedish model, not in the sense of employment protection, but in the sense that citizenship rights are now as in Sweden based on a dual strategy of a comparatively generous benefit system coupled with a fairly strict work test. Indeed, compared with the radical change in Danish labour market policy since the early 1990s, the Swedish system has remained rather unchanged, with limited reforms in unemployment compensation and labour market efforts which have followed the business cycle. From a citizenship perspective, it is immigrants in both Sweden and Denmark who seem to be losing out as their disproportionate unemployment rates signify, while the rise in both underemployment and non-employment (for example due to early-retirement, sickness, and so on) during the 1990s has brought Sweden in line with many other European countries where hidden unemployment has grown since the 1980s.

Foreign citizens play a particular role in the Swiss labour market and it is not the recent trend towards activation which has affected their citizenship rights, but the very model within which the Swiss labour market operates. In short, because unemployment is heavily concentrated on non-Swiss workers, it is unemployment per se which affects the position on immigrant workers in Switzerland. On the other hand, and despite the recent rise and the increase in the unemployment baseline over time, unemployment has remained very modest in international comparison. The citizenship position of Swiss unemployed people also has been relatively unaffected. The level of social protection during unemployment is fairly generous and the chance of re-employment has remained almost unchanged, even though for some unemployed the wages might be below those in previous employment.

Elsewhere it seems that the social rights of those who, for one reason or another, cannot be placed within the 'first' (that is, non-subsidised) labour market seems to have been neglected within the overriding policy drive towards increasing participation in paid work as the major source of citizenship. Perhaps more so than anywhere else, this is the impression at least of the British case. As in Denmark, the communitarian notion of paid work as the core of citizenship and social integration has become all but omnipresent in social security policy generally and in benefit policy for working age claimants which has undergone a substantial degree of re-balancing of rights and responsibilities with introduction of 'workfare elements' in particular (Trickey and Walker, 2001). Almost in its shadow, and without parallel in any other country covered here, access to social security rights based on universal or social insurance principles has all but vanished for working-age citizens while targeted means-testing (in the form of cash benefits or tax credits) has become ever more dominant.

Finally, German society has long been portrayed by mainstream political parties and perceived by the wider public as a 'work society', with participation in (full-time and permanent) waged work (for men) as the central institution for securing family income and social rights, and as transferring status and fostering a sense of identity. Traditionally, welfare benefits and labour market policies were regarded as mechanisms for attaining or regaining secure jobs within this 'work-based' citizenship model. However, the persistence of high levels of unemployment has threatened to turn this model upside down. Unemployed people, and particularly those claiming social assistance, are increasingly required to work for the public good or engage in labour market programmes in order simply to maintain their right to benefits. This is due to a number policy changes introduced in the 1990s which imply that for some unemployed at least, the hope of a return to the labour market (work-based citizenship) has been replaced with a life on benefits, interrupted only with spells of participation in make-work programmes and community service. As Ludwig-Mayerhofer argues in Chapter Four of this volume, these might be considered as signs of the emergence of a new form of 'welfare dependency' citizenship, which includes 'a touch of workfare'.

Prospects for the future?

Perhaps the most sustainable models of labour market success are to be found in those countries which never have experienced high levels of unemployment, at least within the time span covered here and in relation to other countries reviewed in this volume. Nevertheless, the basis of their models might have changed, as well as actual or potential impacts on citizenship rights.

From the latter perspective, the Swiss model has remained volatile for foreign workers in two respects. First, economic downturns in the past, and in the 1970s in particular, were not reflected in rising unemployment because of redundant foreign workers dropping out of the workforce by ways of leaving the country (see also Bonoli, 2001). Today this option of absorbing unemployment is no longer available because of the increasing number of immigrants with permanent residency status. However, the on average lower skill level is the second reason why the degree of labour market and thus social protection which immigrant workers enjoy continues to be well below that of Swiss citizens. Half of all unemployed people in Switzerland are immigrant workers, yet they represent only one in five employees. In short, even if many would stay in the country, a sudden rise in unemployment is likely to affect non-Swiss national workers much more drastically than their Swiss counterparts.

Norway is the other non-EU country with a remarkable low unemployment record. Here, wage moderation, high unionisation, strict employment protection and generous benefits are counterbalanced by central wage coordination and the application of a strict work test. Ideologically similar to Sweden in combining generous welfare benefits with a tough 'work line', Norwegian policies have emphasised 'commodification, de-commodification and re-commidification' (Halverson in Chapter Nine of this volume). For example, the policies promote a high employment rate, various options for temporary leave from work (for example for education or child care), and a range of programmes aimed at reintegrating those who have become unemployed. Oil reserves seem to be a major factor which should help to secure the medium-term sustainability of this particular model, having enabled the public sector to become a large employer and, through subsidies for public and private child care, allowed women in particular to reconcile working careers with family life.

The UK is one of the success stories of the 1990s in the sense that an answer seems to have been found to what appeared to be intransigently high levels of unemployment, interrupted by brief recoveries accompanied by strong inflationary pressure. The labour market recovery which began in 1993 has not only continued for almost ten years now, but has not been accompanied by rising inflation or public deficits out of control. Unlike in the 1980s and early 1990s, some of the contributing factors behind this development are now based on a broad consensus across the two major parties. That is, the need to create a flexible labour market with relatively little employment protection, buttressed by a modest level of minimum wage combined with the use of tax subsidies paid to low paid workers. Apart from the potential problems of poverty traps, the emphasis on labour market integration has done little to address the problem of those for whom the labour market is not an option and have to continue to rely on welfare state benefits as their main or even only source of income. Within European comparisons, levels of inequality and poverty remain high, even though there has been some improvement in recent years (Howard et al, 2001). The concentration of unemployment and inactivity at individual and household basis in particular geographical areas are major factors here, as international comparisons show which demonstrated that the link between unemployment and risk of poverty is very strong in the UK (Gallie and Paugam, 2000a). There are signs that the New Deal programmes have made an impact, but the effect of accompanying policies facilitating labour market participation for some groups (for example provision of or subsidies towards childcare) has remained relatively small (Millar, 2002).

One of the longest and apparently persistent revivals of labour market performances has occurred in the Netherlands. Recently there have been positive assessments as to the sustainability of this models which rests on a strong expansion of part-time work (Visser, 2002). Whether the labour market recovery is sustainable in the long run, however, might be questionable since the external factors that have contributed to the success of the Dutch 'miracle' might easily change and have strong negative effects. Wage moderation, for example, which may have helped to turn things round, has been succeeded by currently strong wage demands and high inflationary pressure. The Dutch labour market has become a bit more flexible, however, with people adjusting more easily to working part-time, which might result in a buffer against suddenly increased high unemployment. From a citizenship perspective, a marked increase of unemployment would quickly put the spotlight on the issue of social rights given that most newly unemployed people would have to resort to social assistance fairly quickly.

Both the Dutch and the Danish 'welfare-to-work' approaches have been identified as core elements in increasingly coherent third-way supply-side strategies (Green-Pedersen et al, 2001). Both economies have attempted to mesh an increased degree of labour market liberalisation with maintaining high levels of social protection and avoiding poverty and inequality ('flexicurity'). Each has also implemented innovative labour market policies, such as particular job creation schemes in the Netherlands or various labour market sabbaticals and job rotation programmes in Denmark. While questions have been asked in both countries about the effectiveness of such approaches in a narrow job generating sense, from a wider perspective (raising employability and reconnecting people with paid employment) some of those programmes have been truly innovative, creating interest also in other countries. But there are also crucial cross-national differences. There is no Danish equivalent to Dutch neo-corporatism, and while female part-time work is on the decline in Denmark it has risen considerably and become a crucial cornerstone for the success of the Dutch model. After little net employment growth in the Danish labour market in the first half of the 1990s, the further recovery in the second half of the decade combined with a sound public budget (despite the continuous use of public sector employment) seems to have put the Danish model on a sustainable path, at least for the time being.

Despite some similarities in the use of active labour market policy and 'activation' strategies, and the ability to largely stem increasing rates of poverty and social exclusion, the Swedish model differs considerably from the Danish in many other respects. Most of all, the Swedish labour market is much more regulated than the Danish. The experience with mass unemployment in the 1990s has not been as prolonged as in other countries, yet it could be argued that the Swedish model has proved to be one which is compatible with both low and high unemployment. After a traumatic economic and labour market turmoil in the first half of the 1990s, Sweden has also recovered considerably in recent years. Hence, ten years after the sudden and steep increase in unemployment, and against pronouncements of its demise, the Swedish model (that is, the combination of generous welfare rights with principles of a 'work line') seems to be alive and kicking. It appears to be an alternative to the 'flexicurity' approach adopted in Denmark or the Netherlands on the one hand, and the Anglo-American deregulated low-wage strategy on the other. The same cannot be said about Finland where cutbacks have been deeper and unemployment has declined somewhat, but remains stubbornly well above the EU average.

Apart from Finland, France and Germany are the other two countries reviewed here where unemployment levels have remained high or declined at a much slower pace than elsewhere. A recent rise in unemployment in Germany indicates that the country is somewhat out of step with many other European countries. Irrespective of the unique implications arising from German unification, high non-wage labour costs, payroll taxes as the funding basis of large parts of social protection and other problems of expanding service sector employment have frequently been mentioned as major problems for a more sustained adaptation to a changed socioeconomic environment (Manow and Seils, 2000b). In contrast to the Netherlands, radical reforms are much more difficult to implement because of institutional constraints and the different set-up of corporatist structures (Hemerijck et al, 2000). As a result, for better or worse, welfare state institutions have largely remained intact. Nevertheless, small incremental changes have started to erode the previous citizenship model of social security and labour market support for unemployed people.

Despite some changes with respect to financing welfare and steps towards labour market liberalisation the French policy repertoire has remained rather traditional with massive expansion of early retirement, tax cuts and subsidising low wage employment. In the 1990s, this was complemented by major efforts in terms of working time reduction and temporary job guarantees for younger people. It is clear that, at this macro-economic level, the French model is very different from the one in the UK. However, from a citizenship perspective, and despite much French rhetoric to the contrary, the French and the British model have also much in common as far as the rights and obligations on the part of the unemployed are concerned (Clasen and Clegg, forthcoming).

Conclusion

This volume has shown that high levels of unemployment are no longer a universal and typical European phenomenon. Many countries, especially the smaller economies, have recovered remarkably well and sometimes surprisingly rapidly. The paths they followed seeking a way out of unemployment differ to a great extent, but their success has two important implications. Firstly, the diagnosis of structural 'Eurosclerosis', of European welfare states being caught in structures of inflexibility leading to 'natural' mass unemployment, has proved to be invalid generally. And secondly, recovery has in most cases been attained without social 'dumping', implying that it is possible to combine high employment levels and adequate social protection. To what extent policy experiences are transferable from successful countries to less successful ones remains an open question. The detailed information from the country-specific chapters (Chapters Three to Twelve) seems to indicate that not only the effects of measures are highly dependent upon national social, economic and institutional contexts, but also the possibility or feasibility of certain types of measure. Typically, what are known as 'conservative' welfare states, such as Germany and France, are the least successful, as are the 'Mediterranean' welfare states of Italy and Spain. At the same time these are larger economies and larger countries; what is it exactly that makes them more vulnerable to higher unemployment? The character of their social protection systems, the structure and nature of their economies, or scale-effects regarding governance potentials?

Although it seems by all means justified to speak of a successful recovery of employment in case of the smaller European economies, honesty would not mistake this with downright success in terms of citizenship rights. It has been shown that even in the most successful countries there remains considerable levels of hidden unemployment, non-employment, large differences in unemployment rates along dimensions of gender, age, health status, ethnicity, and educational level. And although ruthless social dumping has not been a path followed by any of the countries analysed, there are countries in which the balance between rights and duties of unemployed people has been restructured quite drastically.

References

Abrahamson, P. (1999) 'The Scandinavian model of welfare', in *Comparing social welfare systems in Nordic countires and France*, Copenhagen conference vol 4, Paris: Direction de la recherche, de l'evaluation et des statistiques, Coll. Mire, pp 31-60.

Aftenposten (2001) *Statlig omstilling gir flere nfere*, Oslo: Aftenposten.

Alcock, P. (1991) 'The end of the line for social security: the Thatcherite restructuring of welfare', *Critical Social Policy*, vol 30, pp 88-105.

Amrouni, I., Concialdi, P. and Math, A. (1997) 'Les Minima Sociaux : 25 ans de transformations', *La Note du CERC-Association*, no 6, June.

Andersen, J., Borre, O., Goul Andersen, J. and Nielsen, H.J. (1999) *Vælgere med omtanke*, Aarhus: Systime.

Anderson, P. (1990)'Linear adjustment costs and seasonal labor demand: evidence from the retail trade industry', *Quarterly Journal of Economics*, vol 108, pp 1015-42.

Anderson, P. and Meyer, B. (1994) *The effects of unemployment insurance taxes and benefits on layoffs using firm and individual data*, NBER Working Paper 4960, Cambridge, MA, December.

Anderson, P. and Meyer, B. (1998) *Using a natural experiment to estimate the effects of the unemployment insurance payroll tax on wages, employment, claims, and denials*, NBER Working Paper 6808, Cambridge, MA, November.

Andersson, J.O., Kosonen, P. and Vartiainen, J. (1993) *The Finnish model of economic and social policy – From emulation to crash*, Åbo: Meddelanden från ekonomisk-statsvetenskapliga fakulteten vid Åbo Akademi, series A:401.

Andriessen, S. et al (1995) *Risicoselectie op de Nederlandse arbeidsmarkt*, Zoetermeer: CTSV.

Arbeidsdirektoratet (1993) *Arbeids- og bedriftsundersøkelsen*, Bergen: NSDArbeidsdirektoratet.

Arbeidsdirektoratet (1999) 'Utviklingen i antall uføretrygdede 1985-1998', *Kvartalsrapport om arbeidsmarknaden*, vol 4, pp 21-27.

Arbeidsdirektoratet (2000a) *Kvartalsrapport 1/2000*, Oslo: Arbeidsdirektoratet.

Arbeidsdirektoratet (2000b) *Annual report*, Oslo: Arbeidsdirektoratet.

Arbeidsdirektoratet (2001) *Labour market statistics*, Oslo: Arbeidsdirektoratet.

Arbejdsministeriet (1999) *Arbejdsmarkedsreformerne. Et statusbillede*, Copenhagen: Ministry of Labour.

Arbejdsministeriet (2000a) www.am.dk/arbejdsmarkedet/Noegletal/januar_2000.htm.

Arbeitskreis AFG-Reform (1995) *Memorandum für ein neues Arbeitsförderungsgesetz*, Düsseldorf: Druckerei Johannes Plum.

Arendt, H. (1958) *The human condition*, Chicago: The University of Chicago Press.

Aronowitz, S. and DiFazio, W. (1995) *The jobless future: Sci-tech and the dogma of work*, Minneapolis: University of Minnesota Press.

Atkinson, A.B. and Micklewright, J. (1991) 'Unemployment compensation and labor market transitions: a critical review', *Journal of Economic Literature*, vol 29, pp 1679-727.

Atkinson, A.B. and Mogensen, G.V. (1993) *Welfare and work incentives. A North European perspective*, Oxford: Clarendon Press.

Atkinson, A.B., Flemming, J.S., Fitoussi J.P., Blanchard, O. and Malinvaud, E. (1993) *Competitive disinflation: The mark and budgetary politics in Europe*, Oxford: Oxford University Press.

Atkinson A.B., Blanchard O.J., Fitoussi J.P., Flemming, J., Malinvaud, E., Phelps, E. and Solow, R. (1994) *Pour l'emploi et la cohésion sociale*, Paris : Presses de la Fondation nationale des sciences politiques.

Auer, P. (2000) *Employment revival in Europe. Labour market success in Austria, Denmark, Ireland and the Netherlands*, Geneva: ILO.

Autorengemeinschaft (2001) 'Der Arbeitsmarkt in der Bundesrepublik Deutschland in den Jahren 2000 und 2001', *Mitteilungen aus der Arbeitsmarkt- und Berufsforschung*, vol 34, pp 5-27.

Bach, H.B. (1999) *Længerevarende ledighed – jobsøgning og beskæftigelseschancer*, Copenhagen: SFI, (99:12).

Bacon, J. (2002) 'Moving between sickness and unemployment', *Labour Market Trends*, vol 110, no 4, pp 195-205.

Bade, F.-J. (1999) 'Regionale Entwicklung der Erwerbstätigkeit 1997-2004', *Mitteilungen aus der Arbeitsmarkt- und Berufsforschung*, vol 32, pp 603-17.

Baldwin, P. (1990) *The politics of social solidarity. Class bases of the European welfare state 1875-1975*, Cambridge: Cambridge University Press.

Balsen, W., Nakielski, H., Rössel, K. and Winkel, R. (1984) *Die neue Armut. Ausgrenzung von Arbeitslosen aus der Arbeitslosenunterstützung*, Cologne: Bund Verlag.

Barbier, J.-C. (2002) 'The welfare states in the age of globalisation: activation policies, workfare and "insertion". Lessons from Europe and the USA', in J.-C. Barbier and E. van Zyl (eds) *Globalisation and the world of work*, Paris: L'Harmattan, pp 129-46.

Barth, E. (2000) 'Er lønnsforskjellene for små?', *NOU 2000: 21. En strategi for sysselsetting og* verdiskaping, Oslo: NOU, pp 421-44.

Beatty, C., Fothergill, S. and MacMillan, R. (2000) 'A theory of employment, unemployment and sickness', *Regional Studies*, vol 34, no 7, pp 617-30.

Belorgey, J.M. (2000) *Minima sociaux, revenus d'activité, précarité*, Paris: Commissariat Général du plan.

Bender, S. and Karr, W. (1993) 'Arbeitslosigkeit von ausländischen Arbeitnehmern. Ein Versuch, nationalitätenspezifische Arbeitslosenquoten zu erklären', *Mitteilungen aus der Arbeitsmarkt- und Berufsforschung*, vol 26, pp 192-206.

Bertola, G., Boeri, T. and Cazes, S. (1999) *Employment protection and labour market adjustment in OECD countries: Evolving institutions and variable enforcement*, Employment and Training Papers 48, Geneva: Employment and Training Department, ILO.

Bielenski, H. (1998) 'Enttäuschte Hoffnungen, enttäuschte Befürchtungen. Praktische Erfahrungen mit der Deregulierung des Rechts befristeter Arbeitsverträge', in B. Keller and H. Seifert (eds) *Deregulierung am Arbeitsmarkt. Eine empirische Zwischenbilanz*, Hamburg: VSA, pp 56-70.

Bielenski, H., Bosch, G. and Wagner, A. (2001) *Employment options for the future: Actual and preferred working hours. A comparison of 16 European countries*, Dublin: European Foundation for Living and Working Conditions.

Bivand, P. (1999a) 'Jobs figures reveal New Deal success', *Working Brief* (April), Unemployment Unit, pp 22-23.

Bivand, P. (1999b) 'Ethnic inequality in New Deal jobs', *Working Brief* (October), Unemployment Unit, pp 8-9.

Blanchard, O. (2000) *Employment protection, sclerosis, and the effect on unemployment. Lionel Robertson Lecture*, London School of Economics, October, (www.mit.edu/faculty/blanchar).

Blanchard, O. and Katz, L.F. (1996) 'What we know and do not know about the natural rate of unemployment' *Journal of Economic Perspectives*, vol 11, no 1, pp 51-72.

Blanchard, O. and Summers, L. (1986) 'Hysteresis and the European unemployment problem', in S. Fisher (ed) *NBER Macroeconomics Annual*, vol 11, Fall, pp 15-78.

Blanchard, O. and Wolfers, J. (2000) 'The role of shocks and institutions in the rise of European unemployment: the aggregate evidence', *Economic Journal*, vol 110, no 1, pp C1-33.

Blossfeld, H.P. and Hakim, C. (eds) (1997) *Between equalization and marginalization. Women working part-time in Europe and the United States of America*, Oxford: Oxford University Press.

Blundell, R. (2000) 'Work incentives and "in-work" benefit reforms: a review', *Oxford Review of Economic Policy*, vol 16, no 1, pp 27-44.

Blundell, R and Hoynes, H. (2001) *Has 'in work' benefit reform helped the labour market?,* NBER Working Paper 8548, Cambridge, MA.

Bonoli, G. (2001) 'Switzerland: stubborn institutions in a changing society', in P. Taylor-Gooby (ed) *Welfare states under pressure*, London: Sage.

Bonoli, G., George, V. and Taylor-Gooby, P. (2000) *European Welfare futures: Towards a theory of retrenchment*, Cambridge: Polity.

Bordes, C., Currie, D. and Söderström, H.T. (1993) *Three assessments of Finland's economic crisis and economic policy*, Suomen Pankin Julkkaisuja, Sarja C, Helsinki: Bank of Finland.

Born, A. and Jensen, P.H. (2001) 'A second order reflection on the concepts of inclusion and exclusion', in J. Goul Andersen and P.H. Jensen (eds) *Changing labour markets, welfare policies and citizenship*, Bristol: The Policy Press, pp 257-81.

Bouget, D. (2001) 'Mouvements des chômeurs, institutions sociales et pouvoirs publics: l'épisode du Fonds d'urgence sociale (1998) dans les départements', *Revue Française des Affaires Sociales*, vol 55, no 1, January-March, pp 51-75.

Bouget, D. (2002) 'The movements by the unemployed in France and social protection: the *Fonds d'urgence sociale* experience', in J. Goul Andersen and P.H. Jensen (eds) *Changing labour markets, welfare policies and citizenship*, Bristol: The Policy Press, pp 209-35.

Bouget, D. and Brovelli, G. (2002) 'Citizenship and social policies in France', *European Societies*, vol 4, no 2, pp 161-84.

Bovenberg, L. (1997) 'Dutch employment growth: an analysis', *CPB Report* 2, The Hague: Central Planning Office, pp 16-24.

Bradshaw, J. (1993) 'Social security', in D. Marsh and M. Rhodes (eds) *Implementing Thatcherite policies: Audit of an era*, Oxford: Oxford University Press.

Buchele, R. and Christiansen, J. (1999) 'Do employment and income security cause unemployment?', in J. Christiansen, P. Koistinen, and A. Kovalainen (eds) *Working Europe. Reshaping European employment systems*, Aldershot: Ashgate, pp 33-56.

Büchtemann, C.F. (1990) 'Kündigungsschutz als Beschäftigungshemmnis? Empirische Evidenz für die Bundesrepublik Deutschland', *Mitteilungen aus der Arbeitsmarkt- und Berufsforschung*, vol 23, pp 394-409.

Büchtemann, C.F. and Neumann, H. (1990) *Mehr Arbeit durch weniger Recht? Chancen und Risiken der Arbeitsmarktflexibilisierung*, Berlin: Edition Sigma.

Buechtemann, C.F. (ed) (1993) *Employment security and labor market behavior: Interdisciplinary approaches and international evidence*, Ithaca, NY: ILR Press.

Buslei, H. and Steiner, V. (1999) *Beschäftigungseffekte von Lohnsubventionen im Niedriglohnbereich*, Baden-Baden: Nomos.

Buslei, H. and Steiner, V. (2000) 'Beschäftigungseffekte und fiskalische Kosten von Lohnsubventionen im Niedriglohnbereich', *Mitteilungen aus der Arbeitsmarkt- und Berufsforschung*, vol 33, pp 54-67.

Calmfors, L. (1994) 'Active labour market policy and unemployment – a framework for the analysis of crucial design features', *OECD Economic Studies*, no 22, pp 7-47.

Calmfors, L. and Holmlund, B. (2000) 'Den europeiska arbetslösheten', *NOU 2000: 21. En strategi for sysselsetting og verdiskaping. Vedlegg 4*, Oslo: NOU.

Calmfors, L. and Skedinger, P (1995) 'Does active labour-market policy increase employment? Theoretical considerations and some empirical evidence from Sweden', *Oxford Review of Economic Policy*, vol 11, no 1, pp 91-109.

Card, D and Krueger, A. (1995) *Myth and measurement: The new economics of the minimum wage*, Princeton, NJ: Princeton University Press.

Card, D and Levine, P (1994) 'Unemployment insurance taxes and the cyclical and seasonal properties of unemployment', *Journal of Public Economics*, vol 53, pp 1-29.

Carling, K., Holmlund, B. and Vejsiu, A. (2001) 'Do benefit cuts boost job finding? Swedish evidence from the 1990s', *The Economic Journal*, vol 111, no 474, pp 766-90.

CERC-Association (2002) 'Le BIP 40, un baromètre des inégalités et de la pauvreté', *Alternatives Economiques*, no 202, April, pp 48-55.

Černigoj-Sadar, N. (2000) 'Spolne razlike v formalnem in neformalnem delu (Gender differences in formal and informal work)', *Dru•boslovne razprave* (Review of Slovene Sociological Association), no 34-35, pp 31-52.

CGP (1997) *Chômage : Le cas français*, Paris: La documentation française.

Clasen, J. (1992) 'Unemployment insurance in two countries – a comparative analysis of Great Britain and West Germany in the 1980s', *Journal of European Social Policy*, vol 2, no 4, pp 279-300.

Clasen, J. (1994) *Paying the jobless. A comparison of unemployment benefit policies in Great Britain and Germany*, Aldershot: Avebury.

Clasen, J. (ed) (1997) *Social insurance in Europe*, Bristol: The Policy Press.

Clasen, J. (2000) 'Motives, means and opportunities: Reforming unemployment compensation in the 1990s', in M. Ferrera and M. Rhodes (eds) *Recasting European Welfare States*, (*West European Politics*, vol 23, no 2, special issue), pp 89-112.

Clasen, J. (ed) (2002) *What future for social security? Debates and reforms in national and cross-national perspective*, Bristol: The Policy Press (originally published in 2001 in hardback by Kluwer Law International).

Clasen, J. and Clegg, D. (forthcoming) 'Unemployment protection and labour market reform in France and Great Britain in the 1990s: solidarity versus activation?', *Journal of Social Policy*.

Clasen, J. and Taylor-Gooby, P. (2000) 'Unemployment and unemployment policies in the UK', Paper presented to the COST A13 Working Group on Unemployment, November 3-4, Brussels.

Clasen, J., Kvist, J. and van Oorschot, W. (2001) 'On condition of work: increasing work requirements in unemployment compensation schemes', in M. Kautto, J. Fritzell, B. Hvinden, J. Kvist and H. Uusitalo (eds) *Nordic welfare states in the European context*, London: Routledge, pp 198-231.

Claussen, B. (1999) 'Arbeidslinja og uførepensjonen: hva ble effektene av innstrammingen i 1991', *Søkelys på arbeidsmarkedet*, vol 16, pp 41-46.

Cm 3805 (1998) *New ambitions for our country: A new contract for welfare*, London: The Stationery Office.

Cohen, D. and Dupas, P. (1999) 'Une comparaison des trajectoires individuelles sur les marchés du travail français et américain', *Lettre de la régulation*, no 29, pp 1-7.

Colbjørnsen, T. and Larsen, K.A. (1995) *Arbeidsløshet i en oppgangstid*, Rapport 1995:6, Oslo: Arbeidsdirektoratet.

Commission on Structural Labour Market Problems (1992) *Rapport fra Udredningsudvalget om arbejdsmarkedets strukturproblemer*, Copenhagen: June.

Cornetz, W. and Schäfer, H. (1999) 'Arbeitsmarktwende durch einen Niedriglohnsektor', *Wirtschaftsdienst*, pp 548-54.

Cox, R.H. (2001) 'The social construction of an imperative: why welfare reform happened in Denmark and the Netherlands but not in Germany', *World Politics*, vol 53, no 3, pp 463-98.

Craig, G. (2001) 'Ethnicity, racism, and the labour markets: a European perspective' in J. Goul Andersen and P.H. Jensen (eds) *Changing labour markets, welfare policies and citizenship*, Bristol: The Policy Press.

CTSV (College van Toezicht Sociale Verzekeringen) (1995) *Kroniek van de sociale verzekeringen 1995*, Zoetermeer: CTZV.

CTSV (1996) *Augustusrapportage*, Zoetermeer: CTSV.

Czada, R. (1998) 'Vereinigungskrise und Standortdebatte. Der Beitrag der Wiedervereinigung zur Krise des westdeutschen Modells', *Leviathan*, vol 26, pp 24-59.

DARES (1997) *La politique de l'emploi*, Paris, La Découverte.

Darnaut, N. (1997) 'Reform of social security system in France: challenges and prospects', *European Economy*, no 4, pp 193-236.

De Beer, P. (1996) *Het onderste kwart: Werk en werkloosheid aan de onderkant van de arbeidsmarkt*, Rijswijk: Sociaal en Cultureel Planbureau.

De Grip, A., Hoevenberg, J. and Wiillems E. (1997) 'Atypical employment in the European Union', *International Labour Review*, vol 136, no 1 (Spring).

Dean, H. (1999) 'Citizenship', in M. Powell (ed) *New Labour, New welfare state? The 'third way' in British social policy*, Bristol: The Policy Press.

Dean, H. and Taylor-Gooby, P. (1992) *Dependency culture. The explosion of a myth*, London: Harvester Wheatsheaf.

Demazière, D. (1995) *Sociologie du chômage*, Paris: La Découverte.

Det Oekonomiske Raad (2001) *Dansk oekonomi, Efteraar 2001*, Copenhagen: Det oekonomiske raad.

Devine, T. and Kiefer, N. (1991) *Empirical labour economics – The search approach*, Oxford: Oxford University Press.

Devine, T. and Kiefer, N. (1993) 'The empirical status of job-search theory', *Labour Economics*, vol 1, pp 3-24.

Dhima, G. (1991) *Politische Ökonomie der schweizerischen Ausländerregelung*, Chur: Rüegger.

D'Iribarne, P. (1990) *Le chômage paradoxal*, Paris: PUF.

Drøpping, J.A., Hvinden, B. and Vik-Mo, K. (1998) 'Activation policies in the Nordic countries', in M. Kautto, M. Heikkila, B. Hvinden, S. Marklund and N. Ploug (eds) *Nordic social policy*, London: Routledge.

DSS (Department of Social Security) (1999) *Memorandum submitted by the Department of Social Security (CP24), to the Select Committee on Social Security*, Minutes of Evidence, House of Commons, 13 December.

Dufour, C. and Hege, A. (1997) 'The transformation of French industrial relations: glorification of the enterprise and disaffection on the streets', *European Journal of Industrial Relations*, vol 3, no 3, pp 333-56.

Dupeyroux, J.J. (1995) *Droit de la sécurité sociale*, Paris: Dalloz.

Dupuis, J.M. (1995) *Le financement de la protection sociale*, Paris: Presses Universitaires de France.

Dworkin, R. (2000) *Sovereign virtue*, Cambridge, MA: Harvard University Press.

DWP (Department for Work and Pensions) (2002) *Opportunity for all: Fourth annual report 2002*, Cm 5598, London: The Stationery Office.

Eardly, T., Bradshaw, J., Dietch, J., Gough ,I., and Whiteford, P. (1996a) *Social assistance in OECD countries: Synthesis report*, DSS Research Report 46, London: HMSO.

Eardly, T., Bradshaw, J., Dietch, J., Gough, I., and Whiteford, P. (1996b) *Social assistance in OECD Countries: Country reports*, DSS Research Report 47, London: HMSO.

Economic Council (Det økonomiske Råd) (1988) *Dansk økonomi*, June, Copenhagen: Det økonomiske Råd.

Ellingsæter, A.E. (1999a) *Gender mainstreaming and employment policy. Norway report*, ISF Rapport 99:11, Oslo: Institute for Social Research.

Ellingsæter, A.E. (1999b) 'Women's right to work: the interplay of state, market and women's agency', *NORA*, vol 7, nos 2-3, pp 109-23.

Ellingsæter, A.E. (2000a) 'Welfare states, labour markets and gender relations in transition – the decline of the Scandinavian model?', in T. Boje and A. Leira (eds) *Gender, welfare state and the market – Towards a new divison?*, London: Routledge.

Ellingsæter, A.E. (2000b) 'Scandinavian transformations: Labour markets, politics and gender divisions', *Economic and Industrial Democracy*, vol 21, pp 335-59.

Ellingsæter, A.E. and Wiers-Jensen, J. (1997) *Kvinner i et arbeidsmarked i endring*, ISF Rapport 97:13, Oslo: Institute for Social Research.

Elmeskov, J. and MacFarland, M. (1993) 'Unemployment persistence', *OECD Economic Studies*, vol 21, pp 59-88.

Employment Observatory (1998) *Sysdem Trends*, no 30, Brussels: European Commission, Employment and Social Affairs.

Employment Observatory (1999a) *MISEP policies*, no 66, Brussels: European Commission, Employment and Social Affairs.

Employment Observatory (1999b) *Sysdem Trends*, no 32, Brussels: European Commission, Employment and Social Affairs.

Enjolras, B. and Lødemel, I. (1999) 'Activation of social protection in France and Norway: new divergenced in a time of convergence', in P. Abrahamson et al (eds) *Comparing social welfare systems in Nordic Europe and France*, Paris: Mire-Drees.

Ervasti, H. (2002: forthcoming) 'Työttömien elämäntilanne', in O. Kangas (ed) *Laman jäljet: Suomalainen yhteiskunta 1990-luvun lopulla*, Helsinki: Kela.

Esping-Andersen, G. (1990) *The three worlds of welfare capitalism*, Oxford: Polity Press.

Esping-Andersen, G. (1996a) 'After the Golden Age? Welfare state dilemmas in a global economy', in G. Esping-Andersen (ed) *Welfare states in transition. National adaptations in global economies*, London: Sage, pp 1-31.

Esping-Andersen, G. (1996b) 'Welfare states without work: the impasse of labour shedding and familialism in Continental European social policy', in G. Esping-Andersen (ed) *Welfare states in transition. National adaptations in global economies*, London: Sage, pp 66-87.

Esping-Andersen, G. (1997) 'Do the spending and finance structures matter?', in W. Beck, L. van der Maesen and A. Walker (eds) *The social quality of Europe*, The Hague: Kluwer Law International, pp 121-26.

Esping-Andersen, G. (1999) *Social foundations of postindustrial economies*, Oxford: Oxford University Press.

Esping-Andersen, G. and Regini, M. (eds) (2000) *Why deregulate labour markets?*, Oxford: Oxford University Press.

Esping-Andersen, G., Gallie, D., Hemerijck, A. and Myles, J. (2001) *A new welfare architecture for Europe?*, Report submitted to the Belgian presidency of the European Union.

ESS (Employment Service of Slovenia) (1998) *Annual Report 1997*, Ljubljana: ESS.

ESS (1999) *Annual Report 1998*, Ljubljana: ESS.

ESS (2000) *Annual Report 1999*, Ljubljana: ESS.

ESS (2001) *Annual Report 2000*, Ljubljana: ESS.

ESS (2002) *Annual Report 2001*, Ljubljana: ESS.

EUIA (1991) 'Zakon o zaposlovanju in zavarovanju za primer brezposelnosti in njegovi popravki ter dopolnila' ('Employment and Unemployment Insurance Act and its revisions and amendments'), *Official Gazette of the Republic of Slovenia*, no 5/91, 17/91, 12/92, 71/93, 2/94, 38/94, 69/98.

European Commission (1994) *Growth, competitiveness and employment: The challenge and the ways forward into the 21st century*, Luxembourg: European Commission.

European Commission (1995) *Employment in Europe, 1994*, Brussels: European Commission.

European Commission (1998) *Employment in Europe 1998*, D.-G. for Employment, Industrial Relations and Social Affairs, Luxembourg: Office for Official Publications of the European Communities.

European Commission (2000) *Employment in Europe 1999*, Brussels: European Commission.

European Council (2002) *Presidency conclusions*, Barcelona European Council, March 15-16, Barcelona, http://ue.eu.int/pressData/eu/ec/69871.pdf.

Eurostat (1997) *Part-time work in the European Union*, (Statistics in Focus 13), Luxembourg: Statistical Office of the European Communities.

Eurostat (1998) *Statistical Yearbook 1998*, Luxembourg: Office for Official Publications of the European Communities.

Eurostat (1999) *Social protection expenditures and receipts, 1980-1997*, Luxembourg: Office for Official Publications of the European Communities.

Eurostat (2000) *Eurostat Yearbook 2000*, Luxembourg: Office for Official Publications of the European Communities.

Evans, M. (1998) 'Social security: dismantling the pyramids?', in J. Hills (ed) *The state of welfare*, Oxford: Oxford University Press, pp 257-303.

Evans, M. (2001) 'Welfare to work and the organisation of opportunity: European and American approaches from a British perspective', in J. Clasen (eds) *What future for social security? Principles and reforms in national and international perspectives*, The Hague: Kluwer Law International, pp 211-34.

Faculty of Social Sciences (1984-1994) *The quality of life project.*

Fagan, C. and Rubery, J. (1999) 'Gender and labour markets in the EU', Paper presented at the COST workshop, 'Gender, labour markets and citizenship', Vienna, 19-20 March.

Faulks, K. (2000) *Citizenship: Key ideas*, London: Routledge

Fay, R.G. (1996) *Enhancing the effectiveness of active labour market policies: Evidence from programme evaluations in OECD countries*', Labour Market and Social Policy Occasional Papers No 19, Paris: OECD.

Feldstein, M. (1978) 'The effects of unemployment insurance on temporary layoff employment', *American Economic Review*, vol 68, pp 834-36.

Ferrera, M. (1996a) 'The southern model of welfare in social Europe', *Journal of European Social Policy*, vol 6, no 1, pp 17-37.

Ferrera, M. (1996b) 'Modéles de solidarité, divergences, convergences: perspectives pour l'Europe', *Swiss Political Science Review*, vol 2, no 1, pp 55-72.

Ferrera, M. (2000) 'Reconstructing the welfare state in Southern Europe', in S. Kuhnle (ed) *Survival of the European welfare state*, London: Routledge, pp 166-82.

Ferrera, M. and Gualmini, E. (2000) 'Reform guided by consensus: the welfare state in the Italian transition', in M. Ferrera and M. Rhodes (eds) *Recasting European welfare states. West European politics*, (Special Issue), vol 23, no 2, pp 187-208.

Ferrera, M. and Rhodes, M. (2000) 'Recasting European welfare states: an introduction', in M. Ferrera and M. Rhodes (eds) *Recasting European welfare states. West European politics*, (Special Issue), vol 23, no 2, pp 1-10.

Finansministeriet (Ministry of Finance, Denmark) (1993) *Finansredegørelse 1993*, Copenhagen: Finansministeriet.

Finansministeriet (1995) *Finansredegørelse 1995*, Copenhagen: Finansministeriet.

Finansministeriet (1998) *Availability criteria in selected OECD countries*, Working Paper 6, Copenhagen: Finansministeriet.

Finansministeriet (1999) *Finansredegørelse 1998-99*, Copenhagen: Finansministeriet.

Finansministeriet (2000) *Finansredegørelse 2000*, Copenhagen: Finansministeriet.

Finansministeriet (2002) *Fordeling og incitamenter 2002*, Copenhagen: Finansministeriet.

Fink-Hafner, D. and Robbins, J.R. (1997) *Making a new nation: The formation of Slovenia*, Aldershot: Dartmouth Publishers.

Finn, D. (1997) 'The stricter benefit regime and the New Deal for the unemployed', Paper presented at the Social Policy Association, 31st Annual Conference, University of Lincolnshire and Humberside, 15-17 July.

Finn, D. (1999) *From full employment to full employability: New Labour and the unemployed*, Conference paper WS/69, 15-16 April, European Forum, Florence: European University Institute.

Fitzenecker, B. and Speckesser, S. (2000) 'Zur wissenschaftlichen Evaluation der aktiven Arbeitsmarktpolitik in Deutschland', *Mitteilungen aus der Arbeitsmarkt- und Berufsforschung*, vol 33, pp 357-70.

Freeman, R.B. (1995) 'The limits of wage flexibility to curing unemployment', *Oxford Review of Economic Policy*, vol 11, no 1, pp 63-72.

Freeman, R.B. (1997) 'Are Norway's solidaristic and welfare state policies viable in the modern global Economy?', in J.E. Dølvik and A.H. Steen (eds) *Making solidarity work? The Norwegian labour market model in transition*, Oslo: Scandinavian University Press.

Freeman, R.B. (1998) 'War of the models: which labour market institutions for the 21st century', *Labour Economics*, no 5, pp 1-24.

Freeman, R.B. and Schettkat, R. (1999) 'Zwischen Fastfood und Excellence. Die Beschäftigungslücke in Deutschland im Vergleich zu den USA', *Hamburger Jahrbuch für Wirtschafts- und Gesellschaftspolitik*, vol 44, pp 95-113.

Freeman, R.B. and Schettkat, R. (2000) *Skill compression, wager differentials and employment: Germany vs the US*, NBER Working Papers No 7610, Cambridge, MA.

Fridberg, T. and Ploug, N. (2000) 'Public attitudes to unemployment in different European welfare regimes', in D. Gallie and S. Paugam (eds) *Welfare regimes and the experience of unemployment in Europe*, Oxford: Oxford University Press, pp 334-48.

Friedlander, D., Grenberg, D.H., and Robbins, P.K. (1997) 'Evaluation of government training programmes for the economically disadvantaged', *Journal of Economic Literature*, vol 35, no 4, pp 1809-55.

Friedman, M. (1968) 'The role of monetary policy', *American Economic Review*, vol 58, pp 1-17.

Friedmann, P. and Pfau, B. (1985) 'Frauenarbeit in der Krise – Frauenarbeit trotz Krise?', *Leviathan*, vol 13, pp 155-86.

Friedrichs, H. and Wiedemeyer, M. (1998) *Arbeitslosigkeit – ein Dauerproblem. Dimensionen. Ursachen. Strategien*, Opladen: Leske and Budrich.

Fryer, D. and Paine, R.L. (1984) 'Proactivity in unemployment. Findings and implications', *Leisure Studies*, vol 3, pp 273-95.

Furåker, B. (2000) 'Unemployment and welfare state arrangements in Sweden', Paper presented at seminar in COST A13 Working Group Unemployment, Brussels, 3-4 November, Gothenburg: Department of Sociology, University of Gothenburg (see Chapter Seven in this book).

Galbraith, J.K., Conceicao, P. and Ferreira, P. (1999) 'Inequality and unemployment in Europe: the American cure', *New Left Review*, vol 237 (September-October), pp 28-51.

Gallie, D. (2000) 'Unemployment, work and welfare', Paper presented at the seminar 'Towards a learning society: innovation and competence building with social cohesion for Europe', Lisbon, 28-30 May.

Gallie, D. and Alm, S. (2000) 'Unemployment, gender, and attitudes to work', in D. Gallie and S. Paugam (eds) *Welfare regimes and the experiences of unemployment in Europe*, Oxford: Oxford University Press, pp 109-33.

Gallie, D. and Paugam, S. (eds) (2000a) *Welfare regimes and the experience of unemployment in Europe*, Oxford: Oxford University Press.

Gallie, D. and Paugam, S. (2000b) 'The experience of unemployment in Europe: the debate', in D. Gallie and S. Paugam (eds) *Welfare regimes and the experience of unemployment in Europe*, Oxford: Oxford University Press, pp 1-22.

Gallie, D. and Russell, H. (1998) 'Unemployment and life satisfaction', *Archives Européennes de Sociologie*, no 39, pp 3-35.

Gallie, D., Jacobs, S. and Paugam, S. (2000) 'Poverty and financial hardship amongst the unemployed', in D. Gallie and S. Paugam (eds) *Welfare regimes and the experience of unemployment in Europe,* Oxford: Oxford University Press, pp 41-68.

Ganßmann, H. (2000) 'Labor market flexibility, social protection and unemployment', *European Societies*, vol 2, pp 243-69.

Ganßmann, H. and Haas, M. (1999) *Arbeitsmärkte im Vergleich. Deutschland–Japan–USA*, Marburg: Schüren.

Gautié, J. (2002) 'The impact of the labour market changes on individual life courses and trajectories: From internal to transitional labour markets', Paper presented at the international seminar 'Recomposing the stages in the life course', 5-6 June, Maison des Sciences de l'Homme, Paris.

George, V. and Wilding, P. (1999) *British society and social welfare. Towards a sustainable society*, London: Macmillan.

Gerfin, M. and Lechner, M. (2000) 'Microeconometric evaluation of active labor market measures in Switzerland', *Mimeo*, University of St Gall.

Gersbach, H. and Sheldon, G. (1996) 'Structural reforms and their implications for macroeconomic policies', *Macroeconomic Policies and Structural Reform*, OECD Proceedings, pp 131-67.

Giddens, A. (1998) *The Third Way. The renewal of social democracy*, London: Polity Press.

Giddens, A. (2000) *The Third Way and its critics*, London: Polity Press.

Gilbert, N. (1992) 'From entitlement to incentives: the changing philosophy of social protection', *International Social Security Review*, no 45, p 3.

Gilbert, N. (1995) *Welfare justice. Restoring social equity*, New Haven: Yale University Press.

Gilbert, N. (ed) (2000) *Targeting social benefits. International perspectives and trends*, New Brunswick and New York: Transaction Publishers.

Gilbert, N. and Van Voorhis, R.A. (eds) (2001) *Activating the unemployed*, New Jersey: Transaction Books.

Goodman, A., Johnson, P. and Webb, S. (1997) *Inequality in the UK*, Oxford: Oxford University Press.

Gorz, A. (1999) *Reclaiming work. Beyond the wage-based society*, London: Polity Press.

Gottschall, K. and Dingeldey, I. (2000) 'Arbeitsmarktpolitik im konservativ-korporatistischen Wohlfahrtsstaat: Auf dem Weg zu reflexiver Deregulierung?', in S. Leibfried, and U. Wagschal (eds) *Der deutsche Sozialstaat. Bilanzen–Reformen–Perspektiven*, Frankfurt and New York: Campus, pp 306-39.

Goul Andersen, J. (1984) 'Udviklingen i sociale modsætningsforhold frem mod år 2000', in J. Goul Andersen, F.K. Hansen and O. Borre *Konflikt og tilpasning. Om sociale modsætninger, indkomstulighed, demokrati. Egmont Fondens Fremtidsstudie vol 3*, Copenhagen: Aschehoug, pp 13-89.

Goul Andersen, J. (1991) 'Vælgernes vurderinger af kriseårsager', in E. Petersen (ed) *De trivsomme og arbejdsomme danskere. Krisen og den politisk-psykologiske udvikling 1982-90*, Aarhus: Department of Psychology and Aarhus University Press, pp 61-80.

Goul Andersen, J. (1993a) 'Skal ledigheden bekæmpes ved at satse på servicesektoren?', *FA Årsberetning*, Copenhagen: Finanssektorens Arbejdsgivere, pp 12-17.

Goul Andersen, J. (1993b) *Politik og samfund i forandring*, Copenhagen: Forlaget Columbus.

Goul Andersen, J. (1995) *De ledige ressourcer*, Copenhagen: Ugebrevet Mandag Morgen.

Goul Andersen, J. (1996) 'Marginalisation, citizenship and the economy: the capacities of the universalist welfare state in Denmark', in E.O. Eriksen and J. Loftager (eds) *The rationality of the welfare state*, Oslo: Scandinavian University Press, pp 155-202.

Goul Andersen, J. (1997a) 'The Scandinavian welfare model in crisis?', *Scandinavian Political Studies*, vol 20, no 1, pp 1-31.

Goul Andersen, J. (1997b) 'Beyond retrenchment: welfare policies in Denmark in the 1990s', Paper prepared for the ECPR Round Table 'The Survival of the Welfare State', Bergen, 18-21 September, Department of Economics, Politics and Public Administration, Aalborg University.

Goul Andersen, J. (1999) 'Work and citizenship: unemployment and unemployment policies in Denmark, 1980-1999', Paper presented at COST A13 Conference, Brussels, 16-18 September, and at the Research Symposium 'Social Democracy in a Post-Industrial World', Tokai University European Center, Vedbæk, 23-24 September.

Goul Andersen, J. (2000a) 'Work and citizenship: Unemployment and unemployment policies in Denmark, 1980-2000', Paper prepared for seminar in COST A13 Working Group Unemployment, Munich, 31 March-2 April, CCWS Working Paper, no 18, Aalborg: Department of Economics, Politics and Public Administration, University of Aalborg.

Goul Andersen, J. (2000b) 'Change without challenge? Welfare states, social construction of challenge and dynamics of path dependency', Paper prepared for 'What Future for Social Security? Cross-National and Multi-Disciplinary Perspectives', University of Stirling, 15-17 June.

Goul Andersen, J. (2000c) 'Welfare crisis and beyond: Danish welfare policies in the 1980s and 1990s', in S. Kuhnle (eds) *Survival of the European welfare state*, London: Routledge, pp 69-87.

Goul Andersen, J. (2001a) 'Dansk socialpolitik i internationalt perspektiv: medborgerskab og markedskonformitet', Contribution to the Social Ministries' 75th Anniversary Script, Copenhagen: Ministry of Social Affairs.

Goul Andersen, J. (2001b) *How much should the unemployed be searching and available for a job? Unemployment criteria, search theory, and the transition from unemployment to employment among long-term unemployed in Denmark*, CCWS Working Papers, Aalborg: Department of Economics, Politics and Public Administration, University of Aalborg (revised version of paper prepared for COST A13 Workshop, Ljubljana, 8-9 June).

Goul Andersen, J. (2001c) 'Citizenship, marginalisation and political participation: outline of an empirically oriented approach', Paper presented at COST A13 Conference 'Social Policy, Marginalisation and Citizenship', Aalborg University, 1-4 November.

Goul Andersen, J. (2001d) 'Work and citizenship: unemployment and unemployment policies in Denmark, 1980-2000', in J. Goul Andersen and P.H. Jensen (eds) *Changing labour markets, welfare policies and citizenship*, Bristol: The Policy Press.

Goul Andersen, J. (2002a) 'Coping with long-term unemployment: economic security, labour market integration and well-being. Results from a Danish panel study, 1994-1999', *International Journal of Social Welfare*, vol 11, no 2, pp 178-90.

Goul Andersen, J. (2002b) 'De-standardisation of the life course in the context of a Scandinavian welfare model: the case of Denmark', Paper presented at international seminar 'Recomposing the Stages in the Life Course', Maison des Sciences de l'Homme, Paris, 5-6 June.

Goul Andersen, J. (2002c) 'Velfærd uden skatter: Det danske velfærdsmirakel i 1990'erne', *Politica*, vol 34, no 1, pp 5-23.

Goul Andersen, J. and Christiansen, P. (1991) *Skatter uden velfærd. De offentlige udgifter i international belysning*, Copenhagen: Jurist- og Økonomforbundets Forlag.

Goul Andersen, J., Halvorsen, K. and Ervasti, H. (eds) (forthcoming) *Unemployment, marginalisation and citizenship in the Scandinavian welfare states.*

Goul Andersen, J., Torpe, L. and Andersen, J. (2000) 'Indledning: demokrati, magt og afmagt', in J. Goul Andersen, L. Torpe and J. Andersen (eds) *Hvad folket magter*, Copenhagen: Jurist- og Økonomforbundets Forlag, pp 1-20.

Gregg, P. and Manning, A. (1997) 'Labour market regulation and unemployment', in D. Snower and G. de la Dehesa (eds) *Unemployment policy: Government options for the labour market*, Cambridge: Cambridge University Press.

Gregg, P. and Wadsworth, J. (1998) 'Unemployment and households: causes and consequences of employment polarisation among European countries', *MISEP Policies*, no 63, Luxembourg: Employment Observatory, Office for Official Publications of the European Communities, pp 31-35.

Gregg, P. and Wadsworth, J. (1999) 'Economic inactivity', in P. Gregg and J. Wadsworth (eds) *The state of working Britain*, Manchester: Manchester University Press, pp 47-57.

Gregg, P., Hansen, K. and Wadsworth, J. (1999) 'The rise of the workless household', in P. Gregg and J. Wadsworth (eds) *The state of working Britain*, Manchester: Manchester University Press, pp 59-74.

Green-Pedersen, C., van Kersbergen, K. and Hemerijck, A. (2001) 'Neo-liberalism, the 'third way' or what? Recent social democratic welfare policies in Denmark and the Netherlands', *Journal of European Public Policy*, vol 8, no 2, pp 307-25.

Groß, M. (1999) 'Die Folgen prekärer Arbeitsverhältnisse für das Ausmaß sozialer Ungleichheit: Einkommensbenachteiligung befristeter Arbeitsverträge', in P.A. Lüttinger (ed) *Sozialstrukturanalysen mit dem Mikrozensus*, (ZUMA-Nachrichten Spezial, Band 6), Mannheim: ZUMA, pp 323-53.

Grubb, D. and Wells, W. (1993) 'Employment regulation and patterns of work in EC countries', *OECD Economic Studies*, no 21, pp 7-58.

Haataja, A. (1999) 'Unemployment, employment and social exclusion', in O. Kangas and R. Myhrman (eds) *Social policy in Tandem with the labour market in the European Union*, Helsinki: Ministry of Social Affairs and Health, pp 43-69.

Hall, P. (1993) 'Policy paradigms, social learning and the state', *Comparative Politics*, vol 25, pp 275-96.

Halleröd, B. and Heikkilä, M. (1999) 'Poverty and social exclusion in the Nordic countries', in M. Kautto, M. Heikkilä, B. Hvinden, S. Marklund and N. Ploug (eds) *Nordic social policy: Changing welfare states*, London: Routledge, pp 185-214.

Halvorsen, K. (1994) *Arbeidsløshet og arbeidsmarginalisering – levekår og mestring*, Oslo: Oslo University Press.

Halvorsen, K. (1998) 'Symbolic purpose and factual consequences of the concepts of 'self-reliance' and 'dependecy' in contemporary discourses on welfare', *Scandinavian Journal of Social Welfare*, vol 7, pp 56-64.

Halvorsen, K. (1999a) 'Employment commitment among-long-term unemployed in Norway: Is a "culture of dependency" about to develop?', *European Journal of Social Work*, vol 2, issue 2 (July), pp 177-92.

Halvorsen, K. (2000b) 'Employment commitment among the long-term unemployed in Norway: is a "culture of dependency" about to develop?', *European Journal of Social Work*, vol 2, no 2, pp 177-92.

Halvorsen, K. (2000a) 'Tilbud og etterspørsel etter arbeidskraft: betydningen av normer og incentiver i arbeidsmarkedet', *HiO Notat 2000/19*, Oslo: Oslo College, pp 1-4.

Halvorsen, K. (2000b) 'Sosial eksklusion som problem', *Tidsskrift for velferdsforskning*, vol 3, no 3, pp 157-70.

Halvorsen, K. and Johannessen, A. (2001) 'Social participation in the Nordic Countries: Included through paid work or excluded through welfare state arrangements?', Paper presented at COST A13 Workshop, Ljubljana, 8-10 June.

Hansen, H. (1999) *Elements of social security. A comparison covering Denmark, Sweden, Finland, Austria, Germany, the Netherlands, Great Britain, Canada*, Copenhagen: The Danish National Institute of Social Research.

Hansen, H., Lind, J. and Moeller, I.H. (2001) 'Aktivering som inklusion', in J. Goul Andersen and P.H. Jensen (eds) *Marginalisering, integration, velfærd*, Aalborg: Aalborg University Press, pp 181-98.

Harsløf, I. and Bach, H.B. (2001) *Kontanthjælpsmodtagernes forhold – aktivering og arbejdsudbud*, Copenhagen: The Danish National Institute of Social Research.

Hartog, J. (1999) *The Netherlands: So what's so special about the Dutch model?*, Employment and Training Papers, no 54, Geneva: Employment and Training Department, ILO.

Hauser, R. and Nolan, B. et al (2000) 'Unemployment and poverty: change over time', in D. Gallie and S. Paugam (eds) *Welfare regimes and the experience of unemployment in Europe*, Oxford: Oxford University Press, pp 25-46.

Hay, C. and Rosamond, B. (2002) 'Globalisation, European integration and the discursive construction of economic imperatives', *Journal of European Public Policy*, vol 9, no 2, pp 147-67.

Heclo, H. (1974) *Modern social policies in Britain and Sweden*, New Haven: Yale University Press.

Heclo, H. (1994) 'Ideas, interests, and institutions', in C. Dodd and C. Jillson (eds) *The dynamics of American politics*, Boulder: Westview Press.

Heikkilä, M. (1997) 'Justification for cutbacks in the area of social policy', in M. Heikkilä and H. Uusitalo (eds) *The cost of cuts. Stakes*, Saarijärvi: Gummerus Printing, pp 15-28.

Heinelt, H. and Weck, M. (1998) *Arbeitsmarktpolitik. Vom Vereinigungskonsens zur Standortdebatte*, Opladen: Leske and Budrich.

Heise, A., Mülhaupt, B., Seifert, H., Schäfer, C., Störmann, W. and Ziegler, A. (1998) 'Begutachtung des Wirtschaftsstandorts Deutschland – aus einer anderen Sicht', *WSI-Mitteilungen*, pp 393-417.

Hemerijck, A. and Visser, J. (2000) 'Change and immobility: three decades of policy adjustments in the Netherlands and Belgium', *West European Politics*, vol 23, no 2, (Special Issue 'Recasting European Welfare States'), pp 229-56.

Hemerijck, A., Manow, P. and van Kersbergen, K. (2000) 'Welfare without work? Divergent experiences of reform in Germany and the Netherlands', in S. Kuhnle (ed) *Survival of the European welfare state*, London: Routledge, pp 106-27.

Hemerijck, A., Unger, B. and Visser, J. (2000) 'How small countries negotiate change: twenty-five years of policy adjustment in Austria, the Netherlands, and Belgium', in F.W. Scharpf and V.A. Schmidt (eds) *Welfare and work in the open economy. Vol II: Diverse responses to common challenges*, Oxford: Oxford University Press, pp 175-263.

Henwood, D. (1998) 'Talking about work', in E.M. Wood, P. Mellksins and M. Yates (eds) *Rising from the ashes? Labor in the age of "global capitalism"*, New York, NY: Monthly Review Press.

Hill, M. (1994) 'Social security policy under the Conservatives', in S. Savage, R. Atkinson and L. Robins (eds) *Public policy in Britain*, Basingstoke: Macmillan, pp 241-58.

Hoff, S. and Jehoel-Gijsbers, G. (1998) *Een bestaan zonder baan*, The Hague: Social and Cultural Planning Office.

Hoffmann, E. and Walwei, U. (2000) *The change in work arrangements in Denmark and Germany: Erosion or renaissance of standards?*, Upjohn Institute.

Holcblat, N. (1998) 'La politique de l'emploi en France', in J.C. Barbier and J. Gautié (eds) *Les politiques de l'emploi en Europe et aux Etats-Unis*, Paris: PUF, pp 125-47.

Holcman, R. (1997) *Le chômage. Mécanismes économiques, conséquences sociales et humaines*, Paris: La documentation française.

Holmlund, B. (1998) 'Unemployment insurance in theory and practice', *Scandinavian Journal of Economics*, vol 100, no 1, pp 113-41.

Howard, M., Garnham, A., Fimister, G. and Veit-Wilson, J. (2001) *Poverty: The facts*, London: CPAG, 4th edition.

Husson, M. (2000) 'Pourquoi les taux de chômage diffèrent en Europe?', *Revue de l'IRES*, vol 32, pp 45-79.

Hvinden, B. (1998) 'The new activation discourse: Welfare and work in Western-Europe', Paper prepared for the 14th World Congress of Sociology, Montreal, 26 July-1 August.

Hyde, M., Dixon, J. and Joyner, M. (1999) 'Work for those who can, security for those who cannot: the United Kingdom's new social security reform agenda', *International Social Security Association*, vol 52, no 4, pp 69-86.

Ibsen, F. (1992) 'Efter Zeuthen-rapporten', *Samfundsøkonomen*, vol 6.

Ignjatovic, M., Svetlik, I. and Vehovar, V. (1992) *Employment barometer: Slovenija in Europe*, Ljubljana: Institute of Social Sciences.

IRES (2000) *Les marchés du travail en Europe*, Paris: La Découverte.

Isachsen, A.J. (2001) 'Hva gjør oljepengene med oss?', *Aftenposten*, 11 January.

Iversen, T and Wren, A. (1998) 'Equality, employment and budgetary restraint: the trilemma of the service economy', *World Politics*, vol 49, July.

Jackman, R. (1998) 'European unemployment: why is it so high and what should be done about it?', in G. Debello and J. Borland (eds), *Unemployment and the Australian labour market*, Sydney: Reserve Bank of Australia, pp 39-63.

Jackman, R., Layard, R. and Nickell, S. (1996) 'Combatting unemployment: Is flexibility enough?', Paper presented at the OECD Conference 'Interactions between Structural Reform, Macroeconomic Policies and Economic Performance', London, London School of Economics, March.

Jefferys, S. (2000) 'A "Copernician Revolution" in French industrial relations: are the times a-changing?', *British Journal of Industrial Relations*, vol 38, no 2, pp 241-60.

Jensen, P.H. (1999) *Activation of the unemployed in Denmark since the early 1990s: Welfare or workfare?*, CCWS Working Papers 1/1999, Aalborg: Department of Economics, Politics and Public Administration, Aalborg University.

Jochem, S. and Siegel, N.A. (2000) 'Wohlfahrtskapitalismen und Beschäftigungsperformanz – Das "Modell Deutschland" im Vergleich', *Zeitschrift für Sozialreform*, vol 46, pp 38-64.

Johannessen, A. (1997) *Marginalisering og ekskludering – samme eller forskjellige fenomen?*, HiO-notat no 6, Oslo: Høgskolen i Oslo.

Johansson, S. and Selén, J. (2000) 'Arbetslöshetsförsäkringen och arbetslösheten. En reanalys av IFAU's studie', *FIEF Arbetsrapportserie*, vol 162, Stockholm: FIEF.

Johansson, S. and Selén, J. (2001) 'Arbetslöshetsförsäkringen och arbetslösheten (2). Reformeffekt vid 1993 års sänkning av ersättningsgraden i arbetslöshetsförsäkringen?', *FIEF Arbetsrapportserie*, vol 170, Stockholm: FIEF.

Jonasen, V. (1998) *Dansk Socialpolitik 1708-1994: Menneske, økonomi, samfund – og socialt arbejde*, Aarhus: Den sociale højskole i Aarhus.

Jordan, B. (1998) *The politics of welfare*, London: Sage.

Juhn, C., Murphy, K. and Topel, R. (1991) *Why has the natural rate of unemployment increased over time?*, Brooking Papers on Economic Activity No 2, pp 75-142.

Jäntti, M. and Ritakallio, V.-M. (1999) 'Income poverty in Finland', in B. Gustafsson and P.J. Pedersen (eds) *Poverty and low income in the Nordic countries*, Aldershot: Ashgate, pp 63-99.

Kalisch, D.W., Aman, T. and Buchele, L.A. (1998) *Social and health policies in OECD countries: A survey of current programmes and recent developments*, Labour Market and Social Policy Occasional Papers No 33, Paris: OECD.

Karl, T.L. (1997) *The paradox of plenty*, Los Angeles: University of California Press.

Kasvio, A. (2001) 'Työvoiman saatavuus tulevaisuuden työmarkkinoilla', *Työpoliittinen aikakauskirja* (Finnish Labour Review), vol 44, no 1, pp 5-14.

Kaufmann, F.-X. (1997) *Herausforderungen des Sozialstaates*, Frankfurt-am-Main: Suhrkamp.

Kauhanen, M. (2000) *Määräaikaiset työsuhteet ja sosiaaliturvajärjestelmän kestävyys*, Sosiaali- ja terveysministeriö, Selvityksiä 9, Helsinki: STM.

Kautto, M., Heikkila, M., Hvinden, B., Marklund, S. and Ploug, N. (1999) 'The Nordic welfare states in the 1990s', in M. Kautto, M. Heikkila, B. Hvinden, S. Marklund and N. Ploug *Nordic social policy*, London: Routledge, pp 1-18.

Kautto, M. (2001) *Diversity among welfare states comparative studies on welfare state adjustment in Nordic countries*, Helsinki: Stakes.

Kildal, N. (2001) *Workfare tendencies in Scandinavian welfare policies*, SES-Papers, Geneva: ILO.

Kleppe, P. (1999) *Arbeidsliv. Arbeidslinjen og de svake gruppene i arbeidsmarkedet*, Fafo-rapport no 280, Oslo: Fafo.

Korpi, W. (2002) *Velfaerdsstat og socialt medborgerskab: Danmark i et komparativt perspektiv*, Aarhus: Magtudredningen.

Kortteinen, M. and Tuomikoski, H. (1998) *Työtön. Tutkimus pitkäaikaistyöttömien selviytymisestä*, Helsinki: Tammi.

Kosonen, P. (1998) *Pohjoismaiset mallit murroksessa*, Tampere: Vastapaino.

Kosonen, P. (1999) 'Activation, incentives and workfare', in P. Abrahamson et al (eds) *Comparing social welfare systems in Nordic Europe and France*, Copenhagen Conference, Paris: Mire-Drees.

Kosunen, V. (1997) 'The recession and changes in social security in the 1990s', in M. Heikkilä and H. Uusitalo (eds) *The cost of cuts*, Helsinki: Stakes, pp 41-68.

Krätke, M. (1985) 'Klassen im Sozialstaat', *ProKla*, vol 58, pp 89-108.

Kroft, H., Engbersen, G., Schuyt, K. and van Waarden, F. (1989) *Een tijd zonder werk: Een onderzoek naar de belevingswereld van langdurig werklozen*, Leiden: Stenfert Kroese.

Krugman, P. (1994) 'Past and prospective causes of high unemployment', in *Reducing unemployment: Current issues and policy options*, Kansas City: MI, Federal Reserve Bank of Kansas City, pp 49-80.

Krugman, P. (1996) *Pop internationalism*, Cambridge, MA: MIT Press.

Kugler, P., Müller, U. and Sheldon, G. (1989) 'Non-neutral technical change, capital, white collar and blue collar labor: some empirical results', *Economic Letters*, vol 31, pp 91-94.

Kugler, P. and Spycher, S. (1992) 'Der Einfluss des Technologiewandels auf die Struktur der Arbeitsnachfrage in der Schweiz von 1950-1988', *Swiss Journal of Economics and Statistics*, vol 128, pp 617-41.

Kuhnle, S. and Alestalo, M. (2000) 'Introduction: growth, adjustments and survival of European welfare states', in S. Kuhnle (ed) *Survival of the European welfare state*, London: Routledge, pp 3-18.

Kukar, S. (1993) *Siva ekonomija v Sloveniji* (Grey Economy in Slovenia), Ljubljana: Institute of Economic Research.

Kvist, J. (1998) 'Complexities in assessing unemployment benefits and policies', *International Social Security Review*, vol 51, pp 33-55.

Kvist, J. (2001) 'Activating welfare states. How social policies can promote employment', in J. Clasen (ed) *What future for social security? Debates and reforms in national and cross-national perspective*, The Hague: Kluwer Law International, pp 197-210.

Labour Market Trends (various years and issues), London: Office for National Statistics.

Laaksonen, H. (2000) 'Young adults in changing welfare states. Prolonged transitions and delayed entries for under-30s in Finland, Sweden and Germany in the "90s"', Arbeitspapiere no 12, Mannheimer Zentrum fur Europäische Sozialforschung.

Lalive, R., Van Ours, J. and Zweimüller, J. (2000) *The impact of active labor market programs and entitlement rules on the duration of unemployment*, Working Paper no 41, Institute for Empirical Research in Economics, University of Zurich.

Land, H. (1994) 'The demise of the male breadwinner – in practice but not in theory: a challenge for social security systems', in S. Baldwin and J. Falkingham (eds) *Social security and social change*, Hemel Hempstead: Harvester.

Langset, B., Lian, B. and Thoresen, T.O. (2000) 'Kontantstøtten - hva har skjedd med yrkesdeltakelsen?', *SSB: Økonomiske analyser* no 3/2000, pp 3-6.

Larsen, C.A. (2000) 'Employment miracles and active labour market policy – summarising the Danish effect evaluations', Paper presented at research seminar 'Unemployment, early retirement and citizenship', Aalborg, 8-10 December, CCWS Working Paper, vol 19/2000, Aalborg: Department of Economics, Politics and Public Administration.

Larsen, C.A. (2002a) 'Policy paradigms and cross-national policy (mis-) learning from the Danish employment miracle', *Journal of European Public Policy*, vol 9, no 5.

Larsen, C.A. (2002b) 'Økonomiske incitamenter, søgeadfærd og integration på arbejdsmarkedet', in J. Goul Andersen, C.A. Larsen and J.B. Jensen (eds) *Marginalisering og velfærdspolitik, Arbejdsløshed, jobchancer og trivsel*, Copenhagen: Frydenlund.

Larsen, F. and Stamhus, J. (2000) 'Active labour market policy in Denmark: crucial design features and problems of Implementation', *Institut for Økonomi, Politik og Forvaltnings skriftserie*, April.

Larsen, K.A. and Eriksen, J. (1995) *Arbeidsstyrkens fleksibilitet*, Rapport 1995/2, Oslo: Arbeidsdirektoratet.

Larsson, L. (2000) *Evaluation of Swedish youth labour market programmes*, Working Paper 2000/1, Uppsala: IFAU (Office of Labour Market Policy Evaluation).

Layard, R., Nickell, S., and Jackman, R. (1991) *Unemployment*, Oxford: Oxford University Press.

Lepsius, M.R. (1979) 'Soziale Ungleichheit und Klassenstrukturen in der Bundesrepublik Deutschland', in H.-U. Wehler (ed) *Klassen in der europäischen Sozialgeschichte*, Göttingen: Vandenhoek and Ruprecht, pp 166-209.

Levitas, R. (1996) 'The concept of social exclusion and the new Durkheimian hegemony', *Critical Social Policy*, vol 16, pp 5-20.

Lewis, J. (1992) 'Gender and the development of gender regimes', *Journal of European Social Policy*, vol 2, pp 159-73.

Lewis, J. (1997) 'Gender and welfare regimes: further thoughts', *Social Politics*, vol 4, pp 160-77.

Lilja, R. and Hämälainen, U. (2001) *Working time preferences at different phases of life*, Dublin: European Foundation for Living and Working Conditions.

Lindbeck, A. (1994) 'The welfare state and the employment problem', *American Economic Review*, vol 84, no 2, May, pp 71-75.

Lindbeck, A. and Snower, D. (1988) *The insider-outsider theory of unemployment*, Cambridge, MA: MIT Press.

Lindlar, L. and Scheremet, W. (1998) *Does Germany have the "world's highest wage costs"?*, Discussion Paper no 166, Berlin: DIW.

Lister, R. (1997) *Citizenship: Feminist perspectives*, Basingstoke: Macmillan.

Lister, R. (2002) 'Citizenship and the welfare state', in J. Goul Andersen and P.H. Jensen (eds) *Changing labour markets, welfare policies and citizenship*, Bristol: The Policy Press, pp 39-58.

Littlewood, P. and Herkommer, S. (1999) 'Identifying social exclusion: some problems of meaning', in P. Littlewood, I. Glorieux, S. Herkommer and I. Jonsson (eds) *Social exclusion in Europe: Problems and paradigms*, Aldershot: Ashgate, pp 1-22.

Ljungqvist, L. and Sargent, T.J. (1996) 'A supply-side explanation of European unemployment', *Federal Reserve Bank of Chicago Economic Review*, vol 20, no 5, pp 2-15.

Ljungkvist, L. and Sargent, T.J. (1998) 'The European unemployment dilemma', *The Journal of Political Economy*, vol 106, no 3, pp 514-50.

Lødemel, I. (2001) 'National objectives and local implementation of workfare in Norway', in I. Lødemel and H. Trickey (2001) *'An offer you can't refuse': Workfare in international perspective*, Bristol: The Policy Press, pp 133-58.

Lødemel, I. and Trickey, H. (2001) *'An offer you can't refuse': Workfare in international perspective*, Bristol: The Policy Press.

Lodovici, M.S. (2000) 'The dynamics of labour market reform in European countries', In G. Esping-Andersen and M. Regini (eds) *Why deregulate labour markets?*, Oxford: Oxford University Press, pp 30-65.

Loftager, J. (2002) 'Aktivering som (ny) velfærdspolitisk tredjevej', *Politica*, vol 34, no 3, pp 296-312.

Lompe, K. (1987) *Die Realität der Neuen Armut. Analysen der Beziehungen zwischen Arbeitslosigkeit und Armut in einer Problemregion*, Regensburg: Transfer.

Ludwig-Mayerhofer, W. (2000) 'System description of unemployment and (un)employment policies: Germany', Paper presented at seminar in COST A13 Working Group Unemployment, Brussels, 3-4 November.

Madsen, P.K. (1999a) *Denmark: Flexibility, security and labour market success*, Employment and Training Papers No 53, Geneva: Employment and Training Department, ILO.

Madsen, P.K. (1999b) *Denmark: Labour market recovery through labour market policy*, Employment and Training Paper no 53, Employment and Training Department, Geneva: ILO.

Madsen, P.K. (2002) 'The Danish model of flexicurity: a paradise – with some snakes', in H. Sarfati and G. Bonoli (eds), *Labour market and social protection reforms in international perspective: Parallel or converging tracks?*, Aldershot: Ashgate, pp 243-65.

Manow, P. and Seils, E. (2000a) 'The employment crisis of the German welfare state', *West European Politics,* vol 23, no 2, (Special Issue, 'Recasting European welfare states'), pp 137-60.

Manow, P. and Seils, E. (2000b) 'Adjusting badly: the German welfare state, structural change, and the open economy', in F.W. Scharpf and V.A. Schmidt (eds) *Welfare and work in the open economy*, Vol II, Oxford: Oxford University Press.

Marshall, T.H. (1950) *Citizenship and social class*, Cambridge: Cambridge University Press.

Martin, J.P. (2000) 'What works among active labour market policies: evidence from OECD countries' experiences', *OECD Economic Studies*, no 30, pp 79-113.

Martin, J.P. and Grubb, D. (2001) *What works and for whom: A review of OECD countries' experiences with active labour market policies*, Working Paper 2001/14, Uppsala: IFAU (Office of Labour Market Policy Evaluation).

Meads, L. (1986) *Beyond entitlements: The social obligations of citizenship*, New York, NY: The Free Press.

Mencinger, J. (1989) 'Gospodarska reforma in brezposelnost (Economic reform and unemployment)', *Gospodarska gibanja*, no 193, pp 23-56.

Millar, J. (2000) *Keeping track of welfare reform. The New Deal programmes*, York: Joseph Rowntree Foundation and York Publishing Services.

Millar, J. (2002) 'Adjusting welfare policies to stimulate job entry: the example of the United Kingdom', in H. Sarfati and G. Bonoli (eds) *Labour market and social protection reforms in international perspective*, Aldershot: Ashgate, pp 266-84.

Milner, H. (1994) *Social democracy and rational choice: The Scandinavian experience and beyond*, London: Routledge.

Ministerie van soziale Zaken en Werkgelegenheid (1995) *Unemployment benefits and social assistance in seven European countries – A comparative study*, Werkdocumenten No 10, Den Haag: Ministerie van soziale Zaken en Werkgelegenheid.

Ministry of Labour (2000) *Older workers in the labour market and outside. National programme on ageing workers*, Implementation Report 1999 by an Expert Group, Helsinki: Ministry of Labour.

Ministry of Labour et al (1998) *Status for arbejdsmarkedsreformerne*, 2005-udvalget om videreførelse af arbejdsmarkedsreformerne, Copenhagen: Finansministeriet.

MLFSA (Ministry of Labour, Family and Social Affairs) (1999) *Nacionalni program boja proti revscini in socialni izkljucenosti* (National Programme of the Fight against Poverty and Social Exclusion), Ljubljana: MLFSA.

MLFSA (1999) *Strateški cilji razvoja trga dela in zaposlovanja do 2006* (Strategic Goals of Labour Market and Employment Development up to 2006); *Nacionalni akcijski program zaposlovanja za leti 2000-2001* (National Action Employment Plan for 2000-2001), Ljubljana: MLFSA.

Moe, A. (1999) 'Aktiv arbeidsmarkedspolitikk i Norge 1989-95. Effekter av kvalifisering og arbeidstrening', *Tidsskrift for Samfunnsforskning*, vol 1, pp 3-37.

Moene, K. (1999) 'Er den nordiske samfunnsmodellen truet av globalisering?', *Søkelys på arbeidsmarkedet*, vol 16, pp 79-84

Mogensen, G.V. (2001) 'Forskningsenhedens resultater om integrationen på arbejdsmarkedet', *Nyt fra Rockwool Fondens Forskningsenhed*, June.

Mogensen, G.V. and Mathiessen, P.C. (eds) (2000) *Integrationen i Danmark omkring årtusindskiftet. Indvandrernes møde med arbejdsmarkedet og velfærdssamfundet*, Aarhus: Aarhus University Press.

Moreno, L. (2000) 'The Spanish development of southern European welfare', in S. Kuhnle (ed) *Survival of the European welfare state*, London: Routledge, pp 146-65.

Mortensen, D.T. (1977) 'Unemployment insurance and job search decisions', *Industrial and Labor Relations Review*, vol 30, pp 505-17

Murray, C. (1984) *Losing ground. American social policy 1950-1980*, New York: Basic Books.

Mustonen, A. (1998) 'Pitkäaikaistyöttömäksi valikoituminen', *Työpoliittinen tutkimus* 181, Helsinki: Työministeriö.

Nätti, J. (1993) 'Atypical employment in the Nordic countries: towards marginalisation or normalisation', in T. Boje and S. Olsson (eds) *Scandinavia in a new Europe*, Oslo: Scandinavian University Press, pp 181-99.

NEI (Nederlands Economisch Instituut) (1999) *Wordt succes bepaald door de vorm? Onderzoek naar de doorstroom van gesubsidieerde naar reguliere arbeid*, Rotterdam: NEI.

Nickell, S. (1997) 'Unemployment and labor market rigidities: Europe versus North America', *Journal of Economic Perspectives*, vol 11, no 3, pp 55-74.

Nickell, S. and Layard, R. (1999) 'Labor market institutions and economic performance', in O. Ashenfelter and D. Card (eds) *Handbook of labor economics*, vol 3c, pp 3029-84.

Nolan, B., Hauser, R. and Zoyem, J.-P. (2000) 'The changing effects of social protection on poverty', in D. Gallie and S. Paugam (eds) *Welfare regimes and the experience of unemployment in Europe*, Oxford: Oxford University Press, pp 87-106.

Norman, V.D., Roland, K. and Reve, T. (eds) (2001) *Rikdommens problem*, Oslo: ECON.

NOSOSKO (Nordisk Socialstatistisk Komite) (1999) *Social tryghed i de nordiske lande 1997*, Copenhagen: NOSOSKO.

NOU (1992) *En nasjonal strategi for økt sysselsetting i 1990-årene*, no 26, Oslo: NOU.

NOU (2000) *En strategi for sysselsetting og verdiskaping*, no 21, Oslo: NOU.

NOU (2000) *Sykefravær og uførepensjonering*, no 27, Oslo: NOU.

Nurmi, K. (1999) 'Changes in women's and men's labour market positions in the EU', in O. Kangas and R. Myhrman (eds) *Social policy in tandem with the labour market in the European Union*, Helsinki: Ministry of Social Affairs and Health, pp 97-147.

OECD (Organisation for Economic Cooperation and Development) (1993) *High and persistent unemployment: Assessment of the problem and its causes*, Working Paper, March, Paris: OECD.

OECD (1994a) *Employment outlook*, Paris: OECD.

OECD (1994b) *The OECD jobs study. Evidence and Explanations. Part I: Labour market trends and underlying forces of change; Part II: The adjustment potential of the labour market*, Paris: OECD.

OECD (1994c) *The OECD jobs study. Facts analysis strategies*, Paris: OECD

OECD (1995) *Employment outlook*, Paris: OECD.

OECD (1996a) *The OECD jobs strategy. Enhancing the effectiveness of active labour market policies*, Paris: OECD.

OECD (1996b) *Employment outlook*, Paris: OECD.

OECD (1997a) *The OECD jobs strategy. Implementing the OECD jobs strategy: Member countries' experiences*, Paris: OECD.

OECD (1997b) *The OECD jobs strategy. Making work pay. Taxation, benefit, employment and unemployment*, Paris: OECD.

OECD (1997c) *Employment outlook*, Paris: OECD.

OECD (1997d) *Economic outlook*, no 61, Paris: OECD.

OECD (1997e) *The OECD jobs strategy*, Paris: OECD.

OECD (1998a) *Employment outlook*, Paris: OECD.

OECD (1998b) *Key employment challenges faced by OECD countries*, OECD submission to the G8 Growth, Employability and Inclusion Conference, London, 21-22 February, Labour Market and Social Policy Occasional Papers no 31, Paris: OECD.

OECD (1998c) *The battle against exclusion. Vol.1: Social assistance in Australia, Finland, Sweden and the United Kingdom*, Paris: OECD.

OECD (1998d) *The battle against exclusion. Vol.2: Social assistance in Belgium, the Czech Republic, the Netherlands and Norway*, Paris: OECD.

OECD (1999a) *The OECD jobs strategy. Implementing the OECD jobs strategy: Assessing performance and policy*, Paris: OECD.

OECD (1999b) *Employment outlook*, June Paris: OECD.

OECD (1999c) *Historical statistics 1960-1997*, CD-ROM, Paris: OECD.

OECD (1999d) *Quarterly labour force statistics*, Paris: OECD.

OECD (1999e) *A caring world: The new social policy agenda*, Paris: OECD.

OECD (1999f) *Benefit systems and work incentives, 1999 edition*, Paris: OECD.

OECD (1999g) *Economic outlook*, June, Paris: OECD.

OECD (2000a) *Employment outlook*, June, Paris: OECD.

OECD (2000b) *Main economic indicators*, Standardised Unemployment Rates (www.oecd.org/media/new-numbers/index.htm).

OECD (2000c) *OECD economic surveys: Netherlands 2000*, Paris: OECD.

OECD (2001a) *Economic outlook,* no 69, Paris: OECD.

OECD (2001b) *Employment outlook*, Paris: OECD.

OECD (2001c) *Trends in international migration*, Paris: OECD.

OECD (2002a) *Employment outlook*, Paris: OECD.

OECD (2002b) *Labour force statistics 1981-2001. Part III*, Paris: OECD.

OECD (2002c) *Historical statistics 1970-2000*, Paris: OECD.

Offe, C. (1991) 'Smooth consolidation in the West German welfare state: structural change, fiscal policies, and populist politics', in F.F. Piven (ed) *Labor parties in postindustrial societies*, Cambridge: Polity Press, pp 124-46.

Offe, C. (1996) 'Full employment: asking the wrong question?', in E.O. Eriksen and J. Loftager (eds) *The rationality of the welfare state*, Oslo: Scandinavian University Press, pp 120-33.

Olesen, S.P. (1999) *Handlingsplansamtaler: Intentioner og aktører*, CARMA Arbejdstekst no 1, Aalborg: Aalborg University.

ONS (Office for National Statistics) (annual) *Labour force survey*, London: HMSO.

Opdal, K., Schøne, P. and Torp, H. (1997) *Ny jobb i sikte? Evaluering av arbeidsmarkedstiltak basert på registerdata*, Rapport 97:14, Oslo: Institute for Social Research.

Ormerud, P. (1998) 'Unemployment and social exclusion: an economic view', in M. Rhodes and Y. Mény (eds) *The future of European welfare: A new social contract?*, New York, NY: St Martins Press, pp 21-40.

Overbye, E. (1998) *Risk and welfare*, NOVA Report 5/98, Oslo: Nova.

Palier, B. (2000) '"Defrosting" the French welfare state', *West European Politics*, vol 23, no 2, pp 113-36.

Palier, B. (2002) 'The politics of Bismarckian welfare state reforms', Paper presented at the 'European welfare states: dynamics and patterns of change. Challenges, institutions and actors' conference, Sandbjerg Castle, Denmark, 2-5 May.

Parjanne, M.-L. (1998) 'Määräaikaiset työntekijät – joustava työvoimapuskuri', *Työpoliittinen aikakauskirja (Finnish Labour Review)*, vol 41, no 2, pp 3-10.

Paugam, S. (ed) (1996) *L'exclusion. L'état des savoirs*, Paris: La Découverte.

Paugam, S. (2000) *Le salarié de la précarité*, Paris: Presses Universitaires de France.

Peck, J. and Theodore, N. (2000) 'Beyond "employability"', *Cambridge Journal of Economics*, vol 24, pp 729-49.

Pekkarinen, J. (1992) 'Corporatism in the Nordic countries', in J. Pekkarinen, M. Pohjola and B. Rowthorn (eds) *Social corporatism: A superior economic system?*, Oxford: Clarendon Press, pp 298-337.

Pekkarinen, J. and Vartiainen, J. (1993) *Suomen talouspolitiikan pitkä linja*. Helsinki: WSOY.

Phelps, E. (1967) 'Money wage dynamics and labour market equilibrium', *Journal of Political Economy*, vol 75, pp 678-711.

Pierson, P. (1994) *Dismantling the welfare state*, Cambridge: Cambridge University Press.

Pierson, P. (1998) 'Irresistible forces, immovable objects: Post-industrial welfare states confront permanent austerity', *Journal of European Social Policy*, vol 5, no 4, pp 539-60.

Pierson, P. (2001) 'Coping with permanent austerity: welfare state restructuring in affluent democracies' in P. Pierson (ed) *The new politics of the welfare state*, Oxford: Oxford University Press.

Pisani-Ferry, J. (2000) *Plein emploi*, Rapport au Conseil d'analyse économique, Paris, La Documentation française.

Pixley, J. (1993) *Citizenship and employment. Investegating post-industrial options*, Cambridge: Cambridge University Press.

Plant, R. (1998) 'So you want to be a citizen', *New Statesman*, February 6.

Pohl, R. (1999) 'Wirtschaftliche Entwicklung in den neuen Bundesländern und ihre Hintergründe', in E. Wiedemann, C. Brinkmann, E. Spitznagel and U. Walwei (eds) *Die arbeitsmarkt- und beschäftigungspolitische Herausforderung in Ostdeutschland*, Nürnberg: Institut für Arbeitsmarkt- und Berufsforschung der Bundesanstalt für Arbeit (BeitrAB 223), pp 25-33.

Punakallio, M. (2001) *Työn kannattavuus työntekijän ja työnantajan näkökulmasta*, Helsinki: Palvelutyönantajat.

Quadagno, J. (1999) 'Creating the capital investment welfare state: the new American exceptionalism', Presidential Address, *American Sociological Review*, vol 64, pp 1-11.

Rahman, M., Palmer, G., Kenway, P. and Howarth, C. (2000) *Monitoring poverty and social exclusion 2000*, York: Joseph Rowntree Foundation.

Regeringen (Danish Government) (1989) *Hvidbog om Arbejdsmarkedets Strukturproblemer*, Copenhagen: Ministry of Labour.

Regeringen (1993) *Ny kurs mod bedre tider*. Copenhagen: Regeringen.

Regeringen (1999) *Strukturovervågning – International Benchmarking af Danmark*, Copenhagen: Ministry of Finance.

Reinberg, A. and Rauch, A. (1998) *Bildung und Arbeitsmarkt: Der Trend zur höheren Qualifikation ist ungebrochen*, Werkstattbericht No 15, Nürnberg: Institut für Arbeitsmarkt- und Berufsforschung.

Reissert, B. and Schmid, G. (1994) 'Unemployment compensation and active labor market policy', in G. Schmid (ed) *Labor market institutions in Europe. A socioeconomic evaluation of performance*, New York: M.E. Sharpe.

Research voor Beleid (1998) *Hoe zoeken ingeschrevenen?*, Leiden: Research voor Beleid.

Rifkin, J. (1995) *The end of work*, New York: Putnam.

Ritakallio, V.-M. (2002) 'Multidimensional poverty in the aftermath of the recession: Finland 1995 and 2000', in J. Kalela, J. Kiander, U. Kivikuru, H.A. Loikkanen and J. Simpura (eds) *Down from the heavens, up from the ashes*, Helsinki: VATT, pp 411-32.

Robinson, P. (2000) 'Active labour-market policies: a case of evidence-based policy-making?', *Oxford Review of Economic Policy*, vol 16, no 1, pp 13-26.

Roche, M. (1992) *Rethinking citizenship: Welfare, ideology and change in modern society*, Cambridge: Polity Press.

Romppanen, A. (2000) *Ikääntymisen vaikutuksista työmarkkinoilla*, Helsinki: STM

Room, G. (1995) 'Poverty and social exclusion: the new European agenda for policy and research', in G. Room (ed) *Beyond the threshold: The measurement and analysis of social exclusion*, Bristol: The Policy Press.

Rothstein, B. (1998) *Just institutions matter*, Cambridge: Cambridge University Press.

Rowthorn, R. (2000) 'Kalecki centenary lecture: the political economy of full employment in modern Britain', *Oxford Bulletin of Economics and Statistics*, vol 62, no 2, pp 139-73.

Røed, K. (2000) 'Arbeidsledighet, stabiliseringspolitikk og lønnsdannelse – er kollektiv lønnsmoderasjon en farbar vei mot lav arbeidsledighet?', *NOU 2000:21. En strategi for sysselsetting og* verdiskaping, Oslo: NOU.

Saffer, H. (1982) 'Layoffs and unemployment insurance', *Journal of Public Economics*, vol 19, pp 121-29.

Saffer, H. (1983) 'The effects of unemployment insurance on temporary and permanent layoffs', *Review of Economics and Statistics*, vol 65, pp 647-52.

Sandmo, A. (1991) 'Presidential address: economists and the welfare state', *European Economic Review*, vol 35, no 2-3, pp 213-39.

Sarfati, H. (2002) 'Labour market and social protection politics: linkages and interactions', in H. Sarfati and G. Bonoli (eds) *Labour market and social protection reforms in international perspective*, Aldershot: Ashgate, pp 11-57.

Scarpetta, S. (1996) 'Assessing the role of labour market policies and institutional settings on unemployment: a cross-country study', *OECD Economic Studies*, vol 26, no 1, pp 43-98.

SCB (Statistics Sweden) database.

SCB (various years) *Arbetskraftsundersökningen. Årsmedeltal*, Stockholm: SCB.

Scharpf, F.W. (1987) *Sozialdemokratische Krisenpolitik in Europa*, Frankfurt/New York: Campus.

Scharpf, F.W. (2000) 'Economic changes, vunerabilities, and institutional capabilities', in F.W. Scharpf and V.A. Schmidt (eds) *Welfare and work in the open economy*, Oxford: Oxford University Press, pp 125-228.

Schellekens, E. et al (1999) *SZW-Werkgeverspanel rapportage 1997-1998*, The Hague: Ministry of Social Affairs.

Schlozman, K.L. and Verba, S. (1979) *Injury to insult. Unemployment, class and political response*, Cambridge, MA: Harvard University Press.

Schmid, A., Krömmelbein, S., Klems, W. and Gaß, G. (1994) *Neue Wege der Arbeitsmarktpolitik für Langzeitarbeitslose*, Berlin: Edition Sigma.

Schmid, G. (1996) 'Process evaluation: policy formation and implementation', in G. Schmid, J. O'Reilly, and K. Schomann (eds) *International handbook of labour market policy and evaluation*, Cheltenham: Edward Elgar.

Schoenmakers, I. and Merens, A. (2000) 'Arbeids(re)integratie', in M. de Klerk (ed) *Rapportage Gehandicapten 2000*, The Hague: Social and Cultural Planning Office.

Schroeder, W. and Esser, J. (1999) 'Modell Deutschland: Von der Konzertierten Aktion zum Bündnis für Arbeit', *Aus Politik und Zeitgeschichte*, B37/99, pp 3-12.

Schwartz, H. (2000) 'The Danish "Miracle": luck, pluck or stuck?' *Comparative Political Studies*, vol 34, no 2, pp 131-55.

SCP (Social and Cultural Planning Office) (1992) *Sociaal en Cultureel Rapport 1992*, The Hague: SCP.

SCP (1996) *Sociale en Culturele Verkenningen 1996*, The Hague: SCP.

SCP (1998a) *Sociaal en Cultureel Rapport 1998*, The Hague: SCP.

SCP (1998b) *Een bestaan zonder baan*, The Hague: SCP.

SCP (1999) *Armoedemonitor 1999*, The Hague: SCP.

SCP (2000) *Sociaal en Cultureel Rapport 2000*, The Hague: SCP.

Shavit, Y. and Müller, W. (2000) 'Vocational secondary education. Where diversion and where safety net?', *European Societies*, vol 2, pp 29-50.

Sheldon, G. (1996) 'Unemployment and unemployment insurance in Switzerland', in P. Bacchetta and W. Wasserfallen (eds) *Economic policy in Switzerland*, London, pp 62-92.

Sheldon, G. (1999a) *Langzeitarbeitslosigkeit in der Schweiz: Diagnose und Therapie*, Haupt: Bern.

Sheldon, G. (1999b) 'Arbeitsmarkt, Arbeitslosenversicherung', in Kommission für Konjunkturfragen (ed) *Liberales wirtschaftspolitisches Konzept. Materialband*, Bern, pp 1-32.

Sheldon, G. (2000a) 'The impact of foreign labor on relative wages and growth in Switzerland', Labor Market and Industrial Organization Research Unit (FAI), University of Basel (www.unibas.ch/wwz/fai).

Sheldon, G. (2000b) 'Risikoabhängige Prämien bei der Arbeitslosenversicherung', Expertise prepared for the State Secretariat for Economic Affairs (Bern), Labor Market and Industrial Organization Research Unit (FAI), University of Basel, (www.unibas.ch/wwz/fai).

Sheldon, G. (2000c) *Die Effizienz der öffentlichen Arbeitsvermittlung*, 'Arbeitsmarktpolitik' series, no 3, Bern: State Secretariat for Economic Affairs.

Sheldon, G. (2001) 'Auswirkungen der Arbeitslosenversicherung auf die Arbeitslosigkeit in der Schweiz 1990 – 1999', Expertise prepared for the State Secretariat for Economic Affairs (Bern), Labor Market and Industrial Organization Research Unit (FAI), University of Basel, (www.unibas.ch/wwz/fai).

Siebert, H. (1997) 'Labour market rigidities: at the root of unemployment in Europe', *Journal of Economic Perspectives*, vol 11, no 3, pp 37-54.

Siim, B. (2000) *Gender and citizenship*, Cambridge: Cambridge University Press.

Sinfield, A. (1997) 'Blaiming the benefit: the costs of the distinction between active and passive programmes', in J. Holmer and J.C. Karlsson (eds) *Work- quo vadis?*, Aldershot: Ashgate.

Sjöberg, O. (2000) 'Unemployment and unemployment benefits in the OECD 1960-1990 – an empirical test of neo-classical economic theory', *Work, Employment, and Society*, vol 14, no 1, pp 51-76.

Skollerud, K. (1997) 'Er midlertidig ansatte og deltidsansatte marginalisert på arbeidsmarkedet?', *Søkelys på arbeidsmarkedet*, vol 14, pp 107-11.

Skånland, H. (2000) 'Arbeidsvilkår for den kollektive fornuft', *Aftenposten*, no 17.

Social Commission (1993) *Reformer. Socialkommissionens samlede forslag*, Copenhagen: Socialkommissionen.

Social Security Administration Office of Research and Statistics (1999) *Social security programs throughout the world*, Washington DC: Social Security Administration Office of Research and Statistics.

Sorrentino, C. (1993) 'International comparisons unemployment indicators', *Monthly Labor Review*, vol 116, no 3, pp 3-24.

Sorrentino, C. (1995) 'International unemployment indicators, 1983-93', *Monthly Labour Review*, vol 118, no 8, pp 31-50.

Sorrentino, C. (2000) 'International unemployment rates: how comparable are they?', *Monthly Labour Review*, vol 123, no 6, pp 3-20.

SORS (Statistical Office of the Republic of Slovenia) (1999) *Labour Force Survey data 1999, second quarter*, Ljubljana: Statistical Office of the Republic of Slovenia.

SORS (2000) *Labour Force Survey data 1993 through 1998*, Ljubljana: Statistical Office of the Republic of Slovenia.

SORS (2001a) *Statistical information, level of living, no 241*, (September), Ljubljana: Statistical Office of the Republic of Slovenia.

SORS (2001b) *Household expenditure data 1997 through 1999*, Ljubljana: Statistical Office of the Republic of Slovenia.

SORS (2001c) *Labour Force Survey data 1998 through 2000*, Ljubljana: Statistical Office of the Republic of Slovenia.

Soskice, D. (1999) 'Divergent production regimes: coordinated and uncoordinated market economies in the 1980s and 1990s', in H. Kitschelt, P. Lange, G. Marks and J.D. Stephens (eds) *Continuity and change in contemporary capitalism*, Cambridge: Cambridge University Press, pp 101-34.

SPA (Social Protection Act) (1992) 'Zakon o socialnem varstvu – 'Social Protection Act', *Official Gazette of the Republic of Slovenia*, no 54/92.

Statistics Norway (1997) *Arbeidsmarkedsstatistikk 1996-97*, Oslo: Statistics Norway

Statistics Norway (1998) *Sosialt utsyn 1998*, Oslo: Statistics Norway.

Statistics Norway (2000a) *Sosialt utsyn 2000*, Oslo: Statistics Norway.

Statistics Norway (2000b) *Labour force survey 2000*, Oslo: Statistics Norway.

St. meld. nr. 2 for 1995-96 *Revidert Nasjonalbudsjett*, (Government White Paper).

St. meld. nr. 4 for 1996-99: 7, *Langtidsprogrammet 1998-2001*, (Government White Paper).

St. meld. nr. 2 for 1998-99, *Revidert Nasjonalbudsjett*, (Government White Paper).

St. meld. nr. 50 for 1998-99, *Utjamningsmeldinga*, (Government White Paper).

St. meld. nr. 2 for 2000-2001, *Revidert Nasjonalbudsjett*, (Government White Paper).

St. meld. nr. 30 for 2000-2001, *Langtidsprogrammet 2002-2005*, (Government White Paper).

St. meld. nr. 43 for 2000-2001, *Om evaluering av kontantstøtten*, (Government White Paper).

Statistisches Bundesamt in Verbindung mit dem Wissenschaftschaftszentrum für Sozialforschung Berlin und dem Zentrum für Methoden, Umfragen und Analysen Mannheim (ed) (1999) *Datenreport 1999. Zahlen und Fakten für die Bundesrepublik Deutschland*, Bonn: Bundeszentrale für politische Bildung.

Statistisches Jahrbuch für die Bundesrepublik Deutschland (Statistical Yearbook for the Federal Republic of Germany), (Various issues).

Statistisk Tiårsoversigt, (Various issues), Copenhagen: Statistics Denmark.

Streeck, W. (1991) 'On the institutional conditions of diversified quality production', in E. Matzner and W. Streeck (eds) *The socio-economics of production and employment*, Cheltenham: Edward Elgar.

Streeck, W. (1997) 'German capitalism: does it exist? Can it survive?', in C. Crouch and W. Streeck (eds) *Political economy of modern capitalism*, London: Sage, pp 33-54.

Svallfors, S., Halvorsen, K. and Goul Andersen, J. (2001) 'Work orientatins in Scandinavia: employment commitment and organizational commitment in Danmark, Norway and Sweden, *Acta Sociologica*, vol 44, no 2, pp 139-56.

Svedberg, L. (1995) *Marginalitet*, Lund: Studentlitteratur.

Svetlik, I. (1998) *Integration of work and learning – Country report on Slovenia*, Working paper for an international project, Ljubljana: Faculty of Social Sciences.

Svetlik, I. (ed) (1992) *Social policy in Slovenia*, Aldershot: Avebury.

Svetlik, I. and Trbanc, M. (1991) *Zaposlitveni barometer 1984-1990* (Employment Barometer 1984-1990), Ljubljana: Faculty of Social Sciences.

SZW (1998) *Sociale Nota 1998*, The Hague: Ministry of Social Affairs and Employment.

SZW (1999) *Sociale Nota 1999*, The Hague: Ministry of Social Affairs and Employment.

SZW (2000a) *In goede banen: een aanpak van knelpunten op de arbeidsmarkt*, The Hague: Ministry of Social Affairs.

SZW (2000b) *Sociale Nota 2000*, The Hague: Ministry of Social Affairs and Employment.

Tema Nord (1999) *Dagpengesystemene i Norden og tilpasning på arbeidsmarkedet*, Copenhagen: Nordisk Ministerråd.

Thonstad, T. (2001) 'Mindre handel, men mer sårbarhet? Norsk utenrikshandel 1970-2000', in B.S. Tranøy and Ø. Østerud (eds) *Mot et globalisert Norge?*, Oslo Gyldendal Akademisk.

Thornton, P., Sainsbury, R. and Barnes, H. (1997) *Helping disabled people to work*, London: The Stationary Office.

Threlfall, Monica (2000) 'Comparing unemployment in the UK and European Union: A gender and working time analysis', *Policy and Politics*, vol 28, no 3, pp 309-29.

Tiainen, P. (2001) 'Työpaikkoja avautuu suurten ikäluokkien poistuessa työelämästä', *Työpoliittinen aikakauskirja* (Finnish Labour Review), vol 44, no 1, pp 25-38.

Topel, R. (1983) 'On layoffs and unemployment insurance', *American Economic Review*, vol 73, pp 541-59.

Topel, R. (1984) 'Experience rating of unemployment insurance and the incidence of unemployment', *Journal of Law and Economics*, vol 27, pp 61-90.

Topel, R. (1985) 'Unemployment and unemployment insurance', in R. Ehrenberg (ed) *Research in labor economics*, vol 7, pp 91-135.

Torfing, J. (1999) 'Workfare with welfare: some reflections on the Danish case', *Journal of European Social Policy*, vol 9, no 1, pp 5-28.

Torp, H. (1998) 'Midlertidige ansatte: Hvor arbeider de?', *Søkelys på arbeidsmarkedet*, vol 15, pp 111-18.

Torp, H. (1999) 'Dagpengesystemene i Norden', in Nordisk Ministerråd *Dagpengesystemene i Norden og tilpasning til arbeidsmarkedet*, TemaNord 1999/572, Copenhagen: Nordisk Ministerråd.

Torp, H. and Barth, E. (2001) *Actual and preferred working time*, Report 3/2001, Oslo: Institute for Social Research.

Trbanc, M. (1996) 'Social exclusion: the concept and data indicating exclusion in Slovenia', *Dru•boslovne razprave* (Social Science Review English edition), vol 12, nos 22-23, Ljubljana: Faculty of Social Sciences, pp 99-114.

Trickey, H. and Walker, R. (2001) 'Steps to compulsion within British labour market policies', in I. Lødemel and H. Trickey (eds) *'An offer you can't refuse': Workfare in international perspective*, Bristol: The Policy Press, pp 181-214.

Turok, I. and Edge, N. (1999) *The jobs gap in Britain's cities: Employment loss and labour market consequences*, Bristol/York: The Policy Press/Joseph Rowntree Foundation.

Uusitalo, H. (1997) 'Four years of recession: what happened to income distribution?', in M. Heikkilä and H. Uusitalo (eds) *The cost of cuts*, Saarijärvi: Stakes, pp 101-18.

Uusitalo, H. (2000) 'Köyhyys ja tulonjako', in M. Heikkilä and J. Karjalainen (eds) *Köyhyys ja hyvinvointivaltion murros*, Helsinki: Gaudeamus, pp 43-57.

Uusitalo, P. (1990) 'Yleinen etu, erityisintressit ja suomalainen vallankäyttö', in O. Riihinen (ed) *Suomi 2017*, Jyväskylä: Gummerus, pp 289-310.

Van Beek, K. (1994) 'We hebben liever een blanke', in H. Scholten and S. de Groot (eds) *Arbeidsmarkt en sociale zekerheid: Beleid in beweging*, Tilburg/ Amsterdam: IVA/SISWO.

Van der Giezen, A. and Jehoel-Gijsbers, G. (1999) *Zoekgedrag, bemiddeling en reintegratie van langdurig arbeidsongeschikten in 1998*, Amsterdam: LISV.

Van der Ploeg, F. (1998) 'The political economy of a consensus society', in F. den Butter et al (eds) *Jaarboek van de Koninklijke Vereniging voor de Staathuishoudkunde*, Rotterdam.

Van der Veen, R., Trommel, W. and De Vroom, B. (1999) *Institutional change of welfare states,* Twente: University of Twente.

Van der Velden, Rolf, K.W. and Wolbergs, M.H.J. (2000) *The intergration of young people in the labour market within the European Union: The role of institutional seetings*, Maastricht: Research Centre for Education and the Labour Market, Maastricht University.

Van Kersbergen, K. (1995) *Social capitalism. A study of christian democracy and the welfare state*, London: Routledge.

Van Oorschot, W. (1998a) 'From solidarity to selectivity: the reconstruction of the Dutch social security system 1980-2000', *Social Policy Review*, no 10, pp 183-202.

Van Oorschot, W. (1998b) *Dutch public opinion on social security*, Loughborough: Centre for Research in Social Policy, Loughborough University.

Van Oorschot, W. (2000) 'Work, work, work: Labour market participation in the Netherlands. A critical review of policies and outcomes', Paper presented at COST A13 Working Group Unemployment seminar, Brussels, 3-4 November, Tilburg: Department of Sociology, Tilburg University.

Van Oorschot, W. and Boos, C. (2001) 'The battle against numbers: disability policies in the Netherlands' in W. van Oorschot and B. Hvinden (eds) *Disability policies in European countries*, The Hague: Kluwer Law International, pp 53-72.

Van Oorschot, W. and Engelfriet, R. (1999) 'Work, work, work: labour market participation policies in the Netherlands 1970-2000', Paper presented at the conference 'The modernisation of social protection and employment', 15-16 April, Conference paper WS/70, Florence: European University Institute.

Van Polanen, P. et al (1999) *Werkgelegenheidseffecten van SPAK en VLW*, Rotterdam: Nederlands Economisch Instituut.

Vik-Mo, B. and Nervik, J.A. (1999) *Arbeidsplikten i Arbeidslinjen. Kommunenes iverksetting av vilkåret om arbeid for sosialhjelp*, Trondheim: NTNU.

Visser, J. (1999) 'De sociologie van het halve werk', *Mens & Maatschappij*, vol 74, no 4, pp 333-359.

Visser, J. (2002) 'The first part-time economy in the world: a model to be followed', *Journal of European Social Policy*, vol 12, no 1, pp 23-42.

Visser, J. and Hemerijck, A. (1997) *The Dutch miracle: Job growth, welfare reform and corporatism in the Netherlands*, Amsterdam: Amsterdam University Press.

Vleminckx, K. and Berghman, J. (2001) 'Social exclusion and the welfare state: an overview of conceptual issues and policy implications', in D. Mayes, J. Berghman and R. Salais (eds) *Social exclusion and European policy*, Cheltenham: Edward Elgar.

Vodopivec, M. (1996) 'The Slovenian labour market in transition: empirical analysis based on data on individuals', *IB Revija*, vol 30, nos 1-2, pp 19-30.

Voges, W., Jacobs, H. and Trickey, H. (2000) 'Uneven development – local authorities and workfare in Germany', in I. Lødemel and H. Trickey (eds) *'An offer you can't refuse': Workfare in international perspective*, Bristol: The Policy Press, pp 71-103.

Vähätalo, K. (1998) *Työttömyys ja suomalainen yhteiskunta*, Helsinki: Gaudeamus.

Wagner, G. (1999) 'Einige Bemerkungen zur Diskussion einer "Dienstleistungslücke" in (West)Deutschland', *Beihefte der Konjunkturpolitik*, vol 48, pp 77-92.

Warton, R., Walker, R. and McKay, S. (1998) *Implementing 'welfare to work' in Britain: Evidence from applied research*, Loughborough: Centre for Reseach in Social Policy, Loughborough University.

Webster, D. (2000a) 'The geographical cncentration of labour-market disadvantage', *Oxford Review of Economic Policy*, vol 16, no 1, pp 114-28.

Webster, D. (2000b) *UK employment failure: New evidence from LFS 1998*, (contribution to www.mailbase.ac.uk/lists/unemployment-research).

Webster, D. (2001) 'Disguised unemployment in Great Britain: extent and measurement', Paper presented to the Department of Applied Social Science, University of Stirling.

Webster, D. (2002) 'Unemployment: how official statistics distort analysis and policy, and why', Paper presented at Radical Statistics Annual Conference, University of Northumbria at Newcastle, 16 February.

Welfare Commission (1995) *Velstand og velfærd. Bilag 2: Marginalisering på arbejdsmarkedet*, Copenhagen: Sekretariatet for Kommissionen om fremtidens beskæftigelses- og erhvervsmuligheder.

Wiedemann, E., Brinkmann, C., Spitznagel, E. and Walwei, U. (1999) *Die arbeitsmarkt- und beschäftigungspolitische Herausforderung in Ostdeutschland* (BeitrAB 223), Nürnberg: Institut für Arbeitsmarkt- und Berufsforschung der Bundesanstalt für Arbeit.

Wingens, M. and Sackmann, R. (2000a) 'Evaluation AFG-finanzierter Weiterbildung. Arbeitslosigkeit und Qualifizierung in Ostdeutschland', *Mitteilungen aus der Arbeitsmarkt- und Berufsforschung*, vol 33, pp 39-53.

Wingens, M., Sackmann, R. and Grotheer, M. (2000b) 'Berufliche Qualifizierung für Arbeitslose. Zur Effektivität AFG-finanzierter Weiterbildung im Transformationsprozess', *Kölner Zeitschrift für Soziologie und Sozialpsychologie*, vol 52, pp 60-80.

Zwinkels, W. and Besseling, J. (1997) *Werkhervatting van de client in de WW*, The Hague: Ministry of Social Affairs.

Øverbye, E. (2000) 'Uførepensjon og sysselsetting i Norge og EU', *Trygd og* pensjon, vol 3, pp 4-5.

Websites

Bundesanstalt für Arbeit internet information service: www.arbeitsamt.de/hst/services/statistik/ detail/index.html. (An English version of most recent data is available at www.arbeitsamt.de/hst/services/statistik/english/s001e.pdf).

ESS (Employment Service of Slovenia): www.ess.gov.si.

Ministry of Labour (2000a): www.am.dk/arbejdsmarkedet/Noegletal/januar_2000.htm.

OECD (including 1997 information on social security rules and replacement rates): www.oecd.org.

OECD (2000b) *Main economic indicators*, available at www.oecd.org/media/new-numbers/index.htm (Standardised Unemployment Rates).

Index

A

B

C

F

G

H

I

J

K

L

O

P

T

U

V

W

Y